Augustine's Conversion
A Guide to the Argument
of *Confessions* I-IX

COLIN STARNES

From the time of its composition (approximately A.D. 400) to the present day St. Augustine's *Confessions* has been regarded as one of the greatest classics of Western spirituality.

Augustine's Conversion presents Augustine's argument in the first part of the *Confessions*. As a whole, the *Confessions* is composed of three confessions (hence the plural title) concerning three different aspects of Augustine's life. *Augustine's Conversion*'s main claim on the reader's attention, and what has not been shown before, is that the first part of the *Confessions* is composed of a single connected argument in addition to its more obvious historical and autobiographical character.

This guide, like all others, should be read in conjunction with the original. However, the author has also wanted to create a work accessible to the interested student, and in so doing uses direct quotations, enabling the reader to see the argument without having to flip back and forth between commentary and *Confessions*.

Colin Starnes teaches Patristics in the Classics Department at Dalhousie University in Halifax. In addition to publishing numerous articles on the transition from antiquity to the medieval period, he is the author of The New Republic: A Commentary on Book I of More's *Utopia* Showing Its Relation to Plato's *Republic (WLU Press, 1990).*

Augustine's Conversion

A Guide to the Argument of *Confessions* I-IX

Augustine's Conversion

A Guide to the Argument
of *Confessions* I-IX

COLIN STARNES

Wilfrid Laurier University Press

Canadian Cataloguing in Publication Data

Starnes, Colin.
  Augustine's conversion

Includes bibliographical references.
ISBN 0-88920-991-X

1. Augustine, Saint, Bishop of Hippo. Confessiones.
Book 1-9.   2. Conversion.   3. Christian saints –
Algeria – Hippo – Biography.   4. Hippo (Ancient city) –
Biography.   I. Title.

BR65.A62S8 1990   242   C90-095340-3

BR
65
.A62
S73
1990

Copyright © 1990
Wilfrid Laurier University Press
Waterloo, Ontario, Canada
N2L 3C5

Cover design by Leslie Macredie

Printed in Canada

Cover illustration after an illuminated initial from Plate XII of
Courcelle's *Recherches sur les Confessions de saint Augustin* (Paris:
E. de Boccard, 1968).

CONTENTS

ABBREVIATIONS

References to the *Confessions* only are normally given without any title: thus, I,i,1 = *Confessions* I,i,1. Quotations without references come from the book, chapter, and section of the *Confessions* as indicated in the heading of the commentary. In the notes the page and line numbers of Skutella's text (as reproduced in the Bibliothèque Augustinienne [=*BA*] edition of the *Confessions — Oeuvres de saint Augustin*, Paris, Desclée de Brouwer, 1962, volumes 13 and 14 with the Introduction and Notes of A. Solignac and the French translation of E. Tréhorel and G. Bouissou) are given along with the first and last words. The titles of other works and series are abbreviated as follows.

Augustine

CEF	*Contra epistulam Manichaei quam vocant Fundamenti*
CFM	*Contra Faustum Manichaeum*
CFeM	*Contra Felicem Manichaeum*
CJI	*Opus imperfectum contra secundam Juliani responsionem*
DBC	*De bono conjugali*
DBV	*De beata vita*
DCD	*De civitate Dei*
DCM	*De cura pro mortuis gerenda*
DDA	*De duabus animabus contra Manichaeos*
DDC	*De doctrina christiana*
DD7	*De diversis quaestionibus VII ad Simplicianum*
DD83	*De diversis quaestionibus LXXXIII*
DGC	*De gratia Christi et peccato originali*
DGL	*De Genesi ad litteram liber imperfectus*
DM	*De magistro*
DMM	*De moribus ecclesiae Catholicae et de moribus Manichaeorum*
DO	*De ordine*
DT	*De Trinitate*
DUC	*De utilitate credendi*
EP	*Ennarationes in Psalmos*
LDH	*Liber de haeresibus ad Quodvultdeum*
Letter	*Epistulae*
Retr	*Retractationes*
Ser	*Sermones*
Sol	*Soliliquia*
TJ	*In Joannis Evangelium tractatus*

Other Works and Series

ACW   Ancient Christian Writers Series
ALD   *A Latin Dictionary*, C. T. Lewis and C. S. Short, Oxford, Clarendon Press, 1969.
BA   Bibliothèque Augustinienne, *Oeuvres de saint Augustin*
LCC   Library of Christian Classics Series
Loeb   Loeb Classical Library Series
LXX   Septuagint
NPNF Select Library of the Nicene and Post-Nicene Fathers

Comments, in quotations, within square brackets are my own. In my translations from the *Confessions* I indicate the Scriptural references found in the *BA* edition in round brackets.

PREFACE

From the time of its composition (in about 400 A.D.) to the present day the *Confessions* has been regarded as one of the greatest classics of Western spirituality. Until well into the modern period there was no complete commentary on the work, for it remained more or less directly accessible to its readers. For some 1,400 years it spoke of and to a world which was, and which knew itself to be, explicitly Christian. With the secularization of this tradition, completed in the past century and a half, the premises of the work have become foreign. Its meaning has been called into question by the general reader and scholars alike, and thus the need of commentaries has arisen.

My aim is to present Augustine's argument in the first part of the *Confessions*. The work is composed of three confessions (hence the plural title) about three different aspects of his life.[1] Taken together, he understood these three parts as comprising everything of note that he could say of himself to God and to men. Our concern here is solely with the first confession in Books I-IX. The main claim of this book on the reader's attention, and what has not been shown before, is that the first part of the *Confessions* is composed of a single connected *argument* in addition to its more obvious historical and autobiographical character.

In the first nine books Augustine tells the reader of his life. The account begins with his birth in North Africa in 354 A.D. It ends some thirty-three years later at the time of his mother's death, shortly after his own conversion to Christianity. This part of the *Confessions* constitutes what we would call an autobiography, but we must beware of interpreting it from a purely modern point of view — that is, as if it has *only* an historical interest.[2] Augustine himself called it a "confession." Its form is an extended statement in which he recounts, or confesses, both to God and to us, certain things about his life.

Obviously there must be some principle of selection if thirty-three years of a man's life are to be condensed into nine chapters of a book. The plan Augustine had in mind, according to which he included certain events and excluded others, was to give a complete statement of both the *circumstances* and the *logic* which are necessary to provide a full explanation of the move he made from his birth in nature to his rebirth in grace — that is, to his conversion to Catholic Christianity. In writing the *Confessions*, some ten years after he had become a Christian, Augustine selected from his life just those things which seemed to him to be necessary to provide a sufficient account of the circumstances and reasons that moved him to prefer Catholic Christianity to every other position. In these nine books there are thus two sides to this principle which are continuously interrelated.[3]

On the one hand there *is* the history. Augustine is recollecting and placing before God the particular events and circumstances of his life which led him to Christianity. Nothing is included which he thinks extraneous. No incident, how-

---

ever sordid or shameful for him to confess, which played a part in bringing him to the church, is excluded. So far as the story is true, we are given a very full and detailed historical account of one man's conversion.

But this is not all: Augustine never fails to look to the *reason* why he moved from one position to the next. He does this through both the selection and (above all) the interpretation of the events he includes. In this way he also provides us with an argument in which the logic of each stage of his conversion is fully grounded in what has gone before. Insofar as he uncovers, in a connected argument, the reasons that led him to the church, his account takes on a universal significance. By discovering the reason behind his actions — in addition to those historical circumstances that were peculiar to himself alone — he exposes the general process through which every one of his contemporaries must have passed, in one way or another, who actually moved from birth in nature to a rebirth in grace.

In the *Confessions* history and logic, particular events and universal reasons, are so interwoven that, like warp and woof in a piece of whole cloth, neither is ever without the other. This union of history and reason in which their differences are distinctly preserved derives solely from Augustine's Christianity — i.e., from the belief that, in Christ, universal and particular are united, without destroying their difference — and in this sense the whole account is coloured by Augustine's final position as a Christian. Nothing in the ancient world, for which such a union was either blasphemy or foolishness, compares to this feature of the *Confessions*. Amongst moderns, who no longer take such a relation of reason and history for granted, this interweaving has caused the greatest difficulties in understanding the text in its entirety.

Other scholars have thus tended to find that Augustine left out many things which seem important and included much that is not. Such judgements depend on some assumption about his purpose and method — in terms of which one can say, "Something is missing here" or, "This is a digression." I want to state my own premises from the beginning. I began this study, over fifteen years ago, with two important assumptions. The first, which is not controversial, is that the text as we have it is substantially what Augustine wrote. I have not been troubled by any thought that the text is corrupt in any important sense, or that I was not working with Augustine's exact words in the order in which he put them down. The second is perhaps more controversial — or at least unusual — because I also assumed that he had omitted nothing which was important to his purpose, whatever that was, nor included any irrelevant digressions. This was the one firm principle to which I held throughout the whole inquiry, so that whenever I found what seemed to be a gap between one part and the next, or what looked like a nodding digression, I supposed that *I* had not understood Augustine rather than that *he* was at fault.

Some readers may perhaps suspect that, with this principle, I will have so completely subordinated myself to Augustine that nothing of critical value could possibly emerge. In one sense this is true. I certainly don't intend that there is anything here which is not in the *Confessions*. I don't claim to have found any new sources to account for this or that position, there is no new "key" to his meaning, and I make no corrections or emendations. On the other hand I do claim to present a reading of Augustine's whole text in which we can come to understand it in its own terms. If this allows us to overcome the great differences that separate us from him, so that we can see with clarity and completeness his own account of the reasons that made him prefer Christianity to the forms of antiquity, this will be no small gain.

The result is a commentary, but only in a qualified sense. I have not moved word by word, nor line by line, but only from position to position, the aim being to show how Augustine has always provided a sufficient reason for his move from one position to the next. Like all commentaries this one must be read in conjunction with the original, and for those scholars who have Augustine's text pretty much in mind this will not be a difficulty. But I also want the work to be accessible to the interested student. I have therefore tried to make it stand on its own, using a lot of direct quotation so the reader could see the argument as much as possible in Augustine's own words without having to flip back and forth between commentary and *Confessions.*

This also meant that all quotations must be in translation — but which translation? For an English audience none approach the sustained accuracy of the French version of Tréhorel and Bouissou in the *Bibliothèque Augustinienne* edition. There are a number of fine English translations but none aim to be as literal as that of the French — and for my reading this creates a problem. Where, for example, I see a single connected argument running through the nine books I think the little words are very important. Augustine begins almost every paragraph with one or another (*cum, ergo, ideo, itaque, nonne,* etc.). In my reading these are used very precisely as logical connectives joining what he is about to say with what has gone before. This sense is inevitably glossed over unless the translator aims to be strictly literal, or has seen the argument. There is no English translation which does either. Instead of picking one and making an endless series of qualifications I have thought it the lesser of two evils to provide my own. This leaves the general reader with the task of locating the text in a translation, and the specialist with locating it in Latin. For the former I have provided the book, chapter, and section references. For the latter, the footnotes give the page and line references to Skutella as reproduced on the left-hand pages of the *BA* edition, which with its introduction, notes, translation, Scriptural references, and indices is incomparably the best and most useful edition of the *Confessions.*

As my purpose is to show Augustine's argument in its own terms I have followed the order of his chapters very closely — assuming that everything necessary is contained in the text itself. For this reason I have drawn on other sources only where I believe they contribute to our understanding of the *Confessions,* because we no longer share a knowledge of the positions he took for granted — such as the character of late Roman education, Manichaeism, Scepticism, and the like. There are thousands of references that might have been collected in such a book — to other Augustinian works, to the general patristic, philosophical, and literary culture of the time, and to the enormous body of modern research that had been done on this part of the *Confessions.* I have excluded all but those that seemed indispensable.

For specialists and scholars I think that no attempt to interpret the *Confessions* as a whole can ignore the questions and results of the century of intensive study since the meaning of the work came to be seen as a problem in the late 1800s. Research on these first nine books has centred on the question of their "historicity." Are they a true historical account of Augustine's conversion or are they not? The genesis and outlines of this debate are sketched in the Appendix. It is now generally agreed that the work of scholars such as Henry, Courcelle, and O'Meara has vindicated the historical truth of Augustine's account, yet the argument of the text, as I show it here, indicates that a certain correction of the resulting position is necessary if we are to have a true interpretation of Augustine's conversion. On the whole I have confined this side of things to the Footnotes and to the Appendix, which contains my account of the nature of the debate and of reasons for the difficulties on each side.

Earlier versions of Chapters One and Seven have appeared as articles in *Augustinian Studies*, 6 (1975), and *Dionysius*, 1 (1977). The book was largely written while I was on sabbatical leave from Dalhousie University and the University of King's College. During that year, spent in France, I am thankful to have received support from the Social Sciences and Humanities Research Council of Canada and from the Government of France. More than seven years have now passed and the manuscript was completed on another sabbatical. It owes much to many in a variety of ways: to my parents and my brother who read the book and offered friendly and useful criticism; to my children for their patience; to friends who helped me find a publisher; to colleagues and students whose many contributions, at the points where I failed, are noted in the text and footnotes; to the anonymous readers of various publishing houses and the Canadian Federation for the Humanities; and especially to Sandra Woolfrey and Olive Koyama of Wilfrid Laurier University Press. But above all I have depended on R. D. Crouse who taught me first and last what Augustine was saying, on J. A. Doull who put the argument of the *Confessions* for me in its pure logical form and, lastly, on my wife Susannah who has put up with nothing and with everything. Errors, I can say with Augustine, are solely my own.

This book has been published with the help of a grant from the Canadian Federation for the Humanities, using funds provided by the Social Sciences and Humanities Research Council of Canada.

The University of King's College and
Dalhousie University, Halifax, 1989

NOTES

1 This tripartite division is indicated by Augustine at X,ii,2 and XI,ii,2 where he tells us that his confession takes on a new form and object. His first confession is therefore contained in Books I-IX, the second in Book X, and the third in Books XI-XIII. For an account of my understanding of the trinitarian structure of the whole work see "The Unity of the *Confessions*," forthcoming in *Studia Patristica* and available in Spanish translation, "La unidad de las *Confesiones*," *AVGVSTINVS*, 31 (1986). See also "The Place and Purpose of the Tenth Book of the *Confessions*," *Studia Ephermeridis "Augustinianum,"* 25 (1987), pp. 95-103, being the *Atti* of the Congresso Internazionale su s. Agostino nel XVI centenario della conversion (Rome, September, 1986). I may briefly summarize my position as follows. Each part is addressed to God and man but each is directed, in a special sense, to a particular person of the Trinity and to a particular human audience. The first is directed to God considered as creator – i.e., to God the Father, and on the human side to any reader whatsoever. The second is directed on the divine side to the Son – that is to Christ the Mediator – and on the human side to Augustine's fellow

Christians. The third is directed to the Holy Spirit and to the Christian philosopher. The whole trinitarian structure reappears again within each of these major divisions. Thus, in the first, there is a part on his relation to the Father (Books I-VII), a part on his relation to the Son (Book VIII), and a part on his relation to the Spirit (Book IX). The second confession is likewise divided (leaving aside the introduction in chapters i-v, and the conclusion in xli-xliii), chapters vi-xxvi relating to the Father, chapters xxvii-xxix to the Son, and chapters xxx-xl to the Spirit. Likewise, in the last part, Book XI relates to the Father, Book XII to the Son, and Book XIII to the Holy Spirit.

2 On the question of the autobiographical character of the first nine books of the *Confessions*, see "The Place and Purpose of the Tenth Book of the *Confessions*" (n. 2): "Although the first nine books are often called the 'autobiographical' part of the *Confessions*, the same can be said with equal justice about Book X and Books XI-XIII. In the second part he writes about the condition of his inner life in the present, and in the third, about his knowledge of the spiritual sense of Scripture. In all three he is writing about different aspects of his life and in this sense all three parts, taken as a whole, constitute his complete autobiography."

3 Augustine insists on *both* points when at the end of his life he remarks that the *Confessions* moved both his *heart* and his *mind* towards God when he wrote it and whenever he reread it — and he hopes it will do the same for us, his readers (see *Retr.*, II, vi (xxxiii), *Confessionum/scio*). That is, he hopes that the historical account can move the reader's heart towards God by its full and frank confession of how he acted in various circumstances, yet because it is a history with a meaning, guaranteed by the logic — and no mere collection of facts whose relation to one another is merely arbitrary and unique — it can also move the mind. And likewise, while the logical argument may move the mind of the reader to God by showing the universal reasons which caused him to move to the church, yet because it is a logic with a definite content and no merely abstract argument — having nothing to do with anyone in particular or with any concrete experience — it can also move the heart. He saw both sides as essential and as interrelated in this way.

Chapter One

COMMENTARY ON BOOK I

Books I-IX are Augustine's confession — both to God and to whoever reads his book — of how he became a Christian. He starts with his birth in 354 A.D. in the village of Thagaste in Roman Africa, goes on to describe each of the circumstances and reasons that finally led him to join the church, and ends soon after his baptism in Milan on Easter eve in 387.

Augustine began to write the book some ten years later, in 398.[1] By this time he had become bishop of the busy North African seaport of Hippo where he was to spend his last thirty-four years. Looking back from this vantage point it seemed to him that he could see how providence had led him to the church even though, for the entire thirty-three years before his conversion, he had either ignored, scorned, opposed, doubted or been unable to embrace Christianity.[2]

He regarded his conversion as the best thing that had ever happened to him, and he knew that he had done nothing to deserve it. The best way of expressing his thanks to God was to tell the truth about the course of his life leading up to his baptism. In this way he could publicly acknowledge his debt. By testifying to all the marvellous means by which a divine grace had guided him every step of the way in spite of himself, he could show his gratitude.[3]

Augustine wrote from the orthodox Trinitarian position in which the church worshipped one God in three persons — the Father, Son and Holy Spirit. This first confession is directed in a special sense to God the Father. It includes a part on his relation to Christ as Mediator (Book VIII), another on his relation to the church or the Holy Spirit (Book IX), as well as the long section in Books I-VII about his discovery of the true idea of God the Father — but Augustine discusses all three in terms that are peculiarly appropriate to the Father, i.e., to God considered as creator. That is, he shows how he was moved to become a Christian through the objective principles implanted in the created world. These alone are what he describes as operative in his conversion. For his human audience this means that the first confession is addressed to anyone at all. It does not presuppose that his readers are Christians (as does Book X), nor, even more exclusively, that they are Christian philosophers (as does his final confession in Books XI-XIII).[4] This first part presumes nothing more than acquaintance with the common realities of human nature, the divine law, and with the objective elements of the Christian gospel and church.[5]

* * * * *

Notes to Chapter One appear on pages 24-32.

INFANCY: I,vi,7-I,vii,12

What was to be Augustine's starting-point: his conception? his birth? his first hearing of God? There were many points that might do, but Augustine wanted his account to be complete. He begins with two extraordinary chapters on his infancy (vi and vii) as the first point at which he had reliable knowledge. He remembered nothing of this period, but he had been able to learn of it both from those who knew him then and by observing other infants.[6] Of his life in the womb, his knowledge was even more indirect, being dependent on the say-so of "ordinary girls" (I,vi,10).[7] Where, if anywhere, he had been even before conception he absolutely did not know. His birth was thus the earliest point at which he could start his account and speak from his own experience and his opening words express this limit: "What is it that I want to confess to you, O Lord, except that I do not know from what place I came into this world, into this — shall I call it a dying life or a living death? I do not know" (I,vi,7).[8]

If we think of the work as an autobiography — in the ordinary sense of an historical account of the details of a man's life — Augustine's treatment of his infancy will seem very strange indeed. He has not a word to say about anything that is peculiar to himself. Where he was born, when, who his parents were, what were their circumstances, who ruled the world and so forth are all ignored. But what else than these things, we may ask, can be of interest about an infant? The only facts he mentions are the obvious things every reader knows to be true about all babies — that he was born of two parents and that he sucked and cried. We may be tempted to move on quickly to what we can hope are more interesting parts.

But the banality of these observations, which was as plain to Augustine as it is to us, should warn us against this mistake. Why did he think it worthwhile to make these observations? Once asked, the answer is clear. He is not interested in the particulars of his situation. These trivial observations provide Augustine with precisely what he is looking for — the evidence from which he can show what his nature was from the earliest observable moment. He does this by drawing out what is presupposed and revealed in the capacity to suck and cry.

I,vi,7-10. The state of infancy

I,vi,7 — He begins from the observation that he came into an ordered world which provided him with everything he needed. From the moment he was born — requiring milk for his sustenance — his mother was there with milk to feed him. But neither his mother nor his nurses filled their own breasts. This happens according to an order that sees to it that a baby and the milk it needs come into the world together, and ensures that the one needs no more than the other has to give. We would say today that these things are arranged by nature and so does Augustine. But he goes one step further and speaks of God as the one who created and maintains the natural order. And why not, since it is clearly not the work of any human agency?[9]

There is more. This order is also a harmony in which each of its parts works together with others for their mutual benefit. The woman's breasts become full when the infant's stomach becomes empty. She wants to give up her milk when the baby wants to take it in. And so each one, simply in pursuing his or her own ends, works also for the benefit of the other. They are sustained in this wonderful harmony by the natural order which informs both alike:

> For it was a good to them [i.e., for his lactating nurses to give up their milk], the good which came to me [milk] from them, though this good was not really from them but through them: for from you, O God, are all goods and it is from my God that my entire well-being comes. (I,vi,7)[10]

Up to this point, when "I knew nothing more than to suck and to be contented with what pleased my flesh [i.e., woman's milk, when needed], or to cry at what harmed it [when hungry]" (I,vi,7),[11] the new-born infant appears simply as part of a beneficent natural order, so arranged that the baby is sustained and supported with riches at every moment, and every need is satisfied as soon as it arises.[12] The baby like any other animal adds his own note to the universal harmony merely by pursuing his particular ends which cannot be opposed to the good of the whole since they are informed by it. It is a picture of a kind of earthly paradise where everything works together in peace and concord. But this is not all that Augustine found in his infancy.

I,vi,8 — In this paragraph Augustine introduces another piece of evidence which, though faint, definitely shows that the infant is not simply contained in the natural order. From this evidence he draws a number of conclusions which are as somber as they are certain. The discussion is hard and ours, following Augustine, is no easier. Partly this is because the facts to which he can point are so slight that they can only be made out with difficulty, and partly because his radical and shocking conclusions run directly counter to modern presuppositions.

What is this new evidence? Augustine first observes that in a matter of months other ways of behaving began to appear which show that he was not simply like all other animals. He points to something his mother or his nurses had told him. They said that he soon started to laugh — at first in his sleep and then later when awake. He has no reason to doubt them because he saw that other babies did the same.[13] This is all he says on this score. The point will be lost to us unless we recognize that it was a commonplace of ancient popular wisdom that man is the only animal which laughs.[14] What Augustine implies is that since laughter proper comes only from the sense of a contradiction, then a baby who laughs must be distinguished from a simple animal without rational powers with which to see the contradiction. He does not labour the point since he cannot remember how or in what way he saw something funny as a baby, but these rational powers soon showed themselves in more harmful ways.

He observes that, as the months pass, all babies begin to have strange desires which are inexplicable simply in terms of the natural order.

> And behold, little by little I began to be conscious of where I was and I wanted to make known my desires to those people who could fill them; and I was not able because the desires were within me and the other people were without and they were not able, by any of their senses, to get into my mind. Thus I used to expostulate with my limbs and my voice making signs indicating my desires — though the few signs that I could manage and use did not truly resemble my desires. And when other people did not submit to me, either because they did

not understand, or because they knew I would be harmed if they obeyed my desires, I became angry with these big people who would not submit and with these independent people who would not be my slaves, and I sought to get my revenge against them by screaming. This, as I have discovered from the babies I have observed, is just how all infants are. Though they did not know it, these infants that I have seen have taught me that I myself was such a one more clearly than did the people who looked after me and fed me and knew that I behaved this way at first hand.[15]

Here we are in a totally different world from the first paradise. A mother ordinarily knows what her child wants by its cry and this is true so far as one looks only to the natural order. She knows that her child is crying from emptiness and hunger because her breasts are full and aching — the order establishes that her breasts become full at the same time as her baby becomes hungry. She feeds the baby and it stops crying since the needs of its flesh have been satisfied.

But Augustine observes here that babies must also have in their minds wants of another kind than those their flesh or bodies require. He cites, as evidence, that they cry at times for things beyond what they need from nature — i.e., for something which those to whom they are in a natural relation are unable to understand or, if they can, are unable to give because it would harm the baby. Such behaviour in an infant cannot be explained in terms of the regular working of the natural order. Nature does not produce creatures with a desire for what would harm themselves — unless the individual is sick. But the baby who has a temper tantrum is not sick; its crying in these cases does not come from some hidden physical illness. Nor is it exceptional. Augustine observes correctly that all babies act in this way. The evidence is slight but the conclusion is certain. The infant who behaves in this way — any infant who behaves in this way — is not simply contained in the natural order but has ends and desires which are not determined by it. The conclusion is that humans are not simply natural animals but rational animals. He has much to say in chapter vii about what this means, but first he turns to consider the adequacy of these observations as his starting-point.

I,vi,9 — Augustine began in I,vi,7 with the recognition that in confessing his life in this way he was opening himself to the laughter of men who might mock him for what he showed about himself. And perhaps God, too, would laugh at him for these things. All the same he was determined to make his confession trusting in God's mercy.[16] The very first thing he confessed was the limits of his knowledge.

> What is it that I want to confess to you, O Lord, except that I do not know from what place I came into this world, into this — shall I call it a dying life or a living death? I do not know. (I,vi,7)[17]

He has now told us what he could about his infancy, yet his ignorance is as great as before. He asks:

> [T]ell me whether my infancy succeeded some other period of my life which died before it. Was it that period which I spent in my mother's womb? For about that also I know a little bit and I have myself seen pregnant women. And what period was there before even this one, O my delight, my God? Was I anywhere? Was I anyone? Who is there to tell me the answer? I have no one. Nei-

ther my father nor my mother were able, nor could I find it out from the observation of others nor from my own memory.[18]

These questions establish Augustine's starting point and his goal. He begins with
his birth because this was the first point about which he had any reliable knowledge. And this means that his account in the *Confessions* is, and is intended to be,
historical from the beginning. Of course we do not ordinarily think of the information that a child sucks and cries as history. It is certainly general but all the same it
is undeniably historical: it can be checked, he gives his sources, it is not imaginary,
and it relates to events in time.[19]

On the other hand, although the starting point is in history, Augustine's questions make clear that this is not an absolute beginning. Birth may be the first
moment about which he had any historical knowledge, but were there not periods
before this which his science was simply not able to discern? He asks about his life
in the womb: and were there not perhaps others even before this? These answers
could not be sought in history, for here his knowledge failed.

Again he imagines God laughing at him for "inquiring after these things,"[20]
and then he dismisses these questions by determining that his task is to confess
and praise God "for what he knows."[21] All the same, from his standpoint at the
time of writing, he knew very certainly that in God,

> [T]he causes of all unstable things [i.e., the historical moments, some of which
> like his infancy he can partly recover, others of which he cannot], stand firm and
> the immutable origins of all mutable things remain fixed forever and the sempi-
> ternal reasons of all irrational and temporal things live forever.[22]

Augustine therefore has two kinds of knowledge. The one is historical and comes
from such concrete sensible evidence as he has given about his infancy. The other
is a knowledge about God as the stable principle of the changing realities of this
world. At this point it is not clear to the reader how he had this second kind of
knowledge, which is certainly not historical, but he will show us before he is done.

I,vi,10 — For the moment he stays with his starting point in history and, for those
gifts which he had as an infant, he "gives praise to [God] for my time in the
womb and my infancy."[23] And why should he not? As a baby he had being and
life and, by the end of his infancy, had begun to move towards speech in order to
make his desires known.[24] The fact that he had and could do these marvellous
things was certainly not the work of any human being — "Or will anyone say that
he was the artificer of his own creation?"[25] The implied answer is clearly, no.
Thanks then are due for these things even though we may not have a philosophical
knowledge that God is the necessary principle of them all. Better, he says, this
than, having the knowledge of God as first principle, refuse to give thanks for
what we have actually been given and do enjoy.[26]

I,vii,11-12. The sin of infancy

I,vii,11 — The second of these two chapters on infancy contains teachings that are
hard for the modern reader to grasp. What are we to make of it when he says,

Hear, O God. Woe to the sins of men! And a man says this and you have mercy on him because you made him although you did not make sin in him. Who can recall to me the sins of my infancy since [your Scriptures say], *no one is free from sin in your eyes, not even the infant whose life is only a day old on earth?* (Job 14:4-5, LXX).[27]

So far Augustine has observed good things (I,vi,7) and bad things (I,vi,8) in his infancy, and in the last chapter (I,vi,10) has attributed the good things to God. He now affirms that God is not the author of the bad things and further, on Scriptural authority, that there is sin in each of us from the day of our birth. It can easily appear that this conclusion comes solely from Scripture and has been forced on the historical account of his infancy. But this is not so. His conclusion does agree with Scripture but it is not derived from it.

The evidence is what he has already shown: the human child is a rational animal. The conclusion follows inevitably if one grasps what Augustine understands by a 'rational animal.' He repeats what he has already said, but now in the form of a question, and then gives us his answer.

Even considering the time, who can think that these things were good [i.e., innocent]: by weeping to demand what would harm the infant if it were given; to be sharply indignant with men who were free, just because they would not act as his slaves, at elders and at his parents and with many other more prudent people [i.e., than the infant] who would not comply with his every whim, trying as much as he could to harm them by thrashing about because they would not obey his orders which, were they obeyed, would only harm him? This shows that it is the weakness of infantile bodies that is innocent and lacks the power to harm, not the soul (*animus*) of babies.[28]

This conclusion is startling. We do not see anything very serious in these things. Even Augustine explicitly recognizes that mothers and nurses can deal with such tantrums, and that they disappear as the baby grows up.[29] None of this seems to warrant the conclusion that the baby is not innocent. But in making this judgement Augustine draws on the direct sense of the Latin word, *in-nocens,* which means literally, "that does no harm." He holds that he was in a harmful relation to the whole well-regulated order of nature which he had observed in the first chapter, since he tried to pervert it to suit ends that did not come from nature as such but from his rational powers. This is exactly what he means when he asks, in a rhetorical question, if he did not sin when he "cried too fiercely"[30] — as in a tantrum — for milk. Such intemperate behaviour, which is literally dis-ordered, outside of the order, does not come from the natural realm not does it serve its ends but is hostile to them.

To illustrate the point Augustine gives an example of the potentially lethal damage that a baby can intend simply in order to satisfy its own unnatural desires — i.e., desires which do not come from the natural order but from its rational powers insofar as they are independent of nature. He describes a baby who, though at the breast and receiving all the milk it needed or could suckle, nevertheless became pale with jealousy and threw bitter glances at another who was feeding from the same breasts. In such a case the jealous baby had all the milk it wanted — and yet wanted more.[31] Augustine concludes that the cause of its jealousy must be 'unnatural' — in the precise sense of 'not coming from its (bodily) nature.' In order to be jealous it must have had a sense of ownership, abstracted from its immediate bodily needs, which was sufficiently clear for it to lay claim to the other's milk. This is the work of the infant's incipient rational powers for it is these that apprehend the things of the world in this abstract and universal manner – i.e., without any particular sensation being present – in this case, without the baby having a sensation of hunger. The infant claimed as its 'own,' milk which it did not need, which would have been harmful if it had been obtained, and which, if the baby had had its way and could have denied it to the other, would have led to the rival's death.[32]

Nature's established order provides milk enough for the needs of all, and yet the infant claims all for itself though it does not need it. Augustine concludes that such things were surely faults for which he deserved to be corrected, though "since I could not understand the censure, neither custom nor reason allowed me to be reprehended."[33] Although the infant is too weak to carry out its purposes, it is evident that in its mind, in soul, in *animus*, it does aim at what would disturb the established order if it could actually get what it desires. Such a harmful relationship to the order which bore it is thus an index of its want of innocence.

It is nothing contrary to Augustine's argument that the child does not know what it is doing. Indeed, the infant's ignorance serves to demonstrate Augustine's point. Just because the baby does not explicitly know what it is doing, such actions show that it is, in its actual nature as a rational animal, in a harmful relation to the natural order.

I,vii,12 – In this final paragraph in his treatment of infancy, Augustine once again praises God for his first beginnings. He can do this in spite of the fact that he has shown that he was not innocent from the day of his birth because, as he said at the start of this chapter, God made man but did not make sin in him. He does not stop here to inquire how man (i.e., the species) got to be in this disordered relation to nature.[34] All that is necessary to his confession is to show what kind of a creature he was. But although he was not the cause of his being a rational animal in a disorder relation to nature it is clear that, whatever the cause might be, he was unable to harm the natural order itself in any fundamental sense. This is not only because the baby is weak. Even if the infant in his example had the power to get what it wanted, even if it could actually consume all the milk it claims as its own, all it would accomplish would be to eat itself to death and thus destroy the very basis from which its rational powers operate against nature's order.

By its rational powers the baby can, potentially, pervert the natural order, but in doing so it can only harm the whole in its parts – primarily in harming itself. For its rational powers depend on its animal nature at every moment in at least this sense – that it is a rational animal only so long as it is first of all an animal simply. In spite of the harm which Augustine has shown that the baby intends, he can still say to God, with respect to the natural order which gave him being and life, that "you make all things and you order all things according to your law."[35] Considered as a whole, the natural order remains undisturbed; the separation of man's rational powers cannot destroy its fundamental unity. It remains to be seen whether the natural order is the only control on man's dis-ordered reason or if this is not also governed, internally, by a rational order that is just as much "implanted at the very base of things" (I,vi,7)[36] by the creator of the world. Augustine takes up this question in the discussion of his childhood.

Because he can neither remember nor deduce anything further about his infancy he resolves to move to the next period of his life. But first he casts a backward glance to the time preceding infancy — from conception to birth — which he calls *primordia*. He treats *primordia* and *infantia* as a single period because he has no memory of either, yet he is very careful not to violate the limits of the historical inquiry through which he has established the defects of infancy. He does not pretend that he can show that its conclusions apply also to his life in the womb. There is a strong suspicion that he was a rational animal from his very conception but, since this can neither be recalled nor deduced from any observation that was available to him, he merely ends with a quotation from Scripture, which asserts as much, and a question. "But if *I was conceived in iniquity and in sin my mother nourished me in the womb* (Ps. 50:7), where, I pray to you, my God, where, O Lord, was *I your servant* (Ps. 115:16), where or when was I ever innocent?"[37] The answer to this rhetorical question is — nowhere in space and never in time.

CHILDHOOD: I,viii,13-I,xx,31

Early childhood: I,viii,13-I,xii,19

To this point Augustine has shown how he was cut off from an immediate unity with the being and life of the whole of the rest of nature at the moment of birth. He now turns to consider the second age of life, his childhood (*puertia*).[38] In infancy, the rational powers from which this division arose were only present implicitly in such examples as the baby's distempered crying. Not only does this make the infant's rationality hard to discern, but it also means that an infant is, in fact, little more than a sensitive animal. And this is what it must remain until these powers come to realize themselves.[39]

In Augustine's account, the transition occurs chiefly through the development of speech. He will show how this brought him into opposition not merely with the being and life of the universe but with the truth that also belongs to the divinely established order. In childhood he came into relation to a truth which was not of his own making — and he was to sin against it just as much as he did against the being and life of the universe present in the natural order.

On the other hand, Augustine distinguishes childhood from adolescence (*adulescentia*) — the next stage of life — because the child, who does not recognize the rational order *qua* rational order, is unable to sin knowingly and intentionally against the divine law itself. As a child he was still limited to opposing some particular authority rather than the rational order itself.

Childhood is also distinguished from infancy in that he could remember things that happened during this second stage of his life.[40] This means that the events and circumstances which he describes here are peculiar to his own life in a higher degree than were the facts about his infancy. Nevertheless, here as before, he aims to interpret them according to the universal significance which they can be shown to possess. In speaking about himself he is also speaking about all of his readers. His talent in this regard is uncanny.

I,viii,13. Speech and society

Augustine begins with a discussion about the development of speech. The reason for this connection (childhood-speech) may not be obvious to us though it was doubtless clear to his Latin readers. The word *in-fans*, strictly translated, means "one not speaking": *fans* is the present participle of the irregular verb *for* — "to say, to speak" — of which the imperfect subjunctive is *farer*. Augustine gives this etymology at the beginning of the chapter. *Non enim eram infans, qui non farer, sed iam puer loquens eram* — "For I was no longer an infant, who could not speak, but now a boy who was speaking." The distinction between infancy and childhood is that the former is, by definition, the time in which one is not yet able to speak.

Behind this etymology there are important considerations which Augustine is at pains to make clear. In the infant it may be almost impossible to distinguish, by the sound alone, between the crying that belongs to his nature as a sensitive animal and the crying that belongs to his rational nature, but in time the latter must develop into rationally informed sound, or speech.

Why is this so? In nature there is no need for speech since a mother can tell by her senses alone what her offspring require. She knows, when her baby cries, that it is hungry because *her* breasts are full, or she can see that it is crying because it has fallen. She has no need to enter its mind — the *animus* of I,vi,8 — so long as it only desires, or desires to avoid, things that the senses can grasp. But the human animal has the power to apprehend things not only by means of the five senses but also rationally — i.e., in an essential and universal manner. Such things have no place in the established order of nature nor can they be grasped by any of the senses. Until the baby learns to speak it has no adequate or accurate way of expressing these things. It therefore suffers from the frustration of desiring, or desiring to avoid, what it apprehends in this rational manner. Until it learns to speak it has only the sounds of nature at its disposal and the meaning of these is strictly limited by the natural order where its cries have only a sensible meaning: "Something is hurting me," "I am hungry," etc. Through the mediation of words it is freed from this bondage to the sensible and acquires a way of expressing its relation to the rational forms it perceives with the mind. Words, as rationally informed sound, are simply adequate signs for these essences.[41] The word "milk," for example, is a sign for what the mind grasps as the essence, the definition, of this substance by which it is distinguished from every other rational essence in the universe, everything with a different definition — and, on the other, is identified with everything that shares the same definition — mother's milk, cow's milk, goat's milk, etc. By means of these words a child is able to signify the object of its (rational) desire which must otherwise remain obscure even to itself — as no doubt it is to the infant just because it has not yet learned to speak.

At the end of the discussion on infancy Augustine had brought out the apparent lack of any internal connection between infancy and childhood. This seems to call into question the adequacy of his starting point since it would be false to start with something that is only externally and accidentally himself. He said, "I will now pass over that time: what have I still got to do with it, of which I cannot remember the slightest thing?" (I,vi,12)[42] It seems as if the relationship between these two

ages can only be found at the level of corporeal existence — inasmuch as the body
of the infant becomes the body of the child. But this lack of an internal connection
is only apparent. In the very next lines, at the beginning of the chapter on childhood, Augustine finds an internal relationship because the infant is bound to
develop the power of speech as the natural consequence of its rational powers.
Childhood is thus connected with infancy through speech which is implicit in the
rational animal from the moment of birth.

Augustine observes that a child is not really taught to speak but rather comes to
it from within as the natural development of its own powers of mind.

> It was not grown-ups who taught me to speak, as they did a little later when
> they taught me the letters of the alphabet, presenting the words in a given order
> of instruction, but I taught myself with the mind that you, my God, gave to
> me.[43]

That children learn to speak 'by nature' and without any formal instruction is
explained by the necessity that, if our rational powers are to realize themselves,
the world must actually be presented to them as a rational, and not merely as a
sensible, object. Language transforms the particulars of the sensible world into
words and thereby renders them into a universal form which is adequate to reason.

It follows that until an infant comes to speak it can be explicitly conscious of
itself only through sensation — even though a rational self-consciousness is presupposed in its unlimited and aggressive cry. From the development of speech a
breach with the immediate and particular becomes actual. In other words the child
acquires an identity outside and beyond the sensible — it comes to a rational self-
consciousness. This gives it a certain freedom from the natural world and a corresponding dominion over it since it can arrange nature to suit these rational desires.
Indeed, from this point on, even the desires of our sensitive nature are, in large
part, pursued in a rationally self-conscious manner for the rest of our lives.

As a result of the ability to speak the child is also moved decisively from the
instinctive order of animal life. As infants we are like novice members of human
society. Insofar as society is run by a rational order, the infant cannot be subjected
to it because there is no direct means of communicating that order to it. This is
why there is no sense in scolding or punishing the jealous baby who is having a
tantrum. It could not understand the rebuke. But once the child can speak it is
definitively delivered into the turbulent society of man and subjected to its government.

We can now see why Augustine ends the first chapter on his childhood, which is
mainly concerned with the development of speech, with this statement about his
new condition as one who had become subject to authority.

> Thus did I make my desires known by the exchange of signs [words] with those
> amongst whom I found myself; and thereby I entered more deeply than before
> into the storm-tossed society of human life, becoming dependent on the author-
> ity of my parents and the command of grown-up persons.[44]

Although it is true that Augustine is always speaking of his own life, he deals here
with things that are common to all of us; thus whatever he correctly deduces from
his own ability to speak will also be true for all who can do the same.

I,ix,14-15. The contradictions of human society

The child now finds itself a member of the society of man. And this, in Augustine's account, is anything but a paradise.

> O God, my God, what miseries I then experienced and what mockery I suffered. For I was told as a child that, in order to live rightly, I should obey my teachers so that I might do well in the world and so that I could excel in the arts of the tongue, using this servile means to gain the honour of men and deceitful riches. Thus I was sent to school to learn my letters though I, unfortunate child, had not the slightest idea what use they might have. But nevertheless if I was dilatory in learning I was beaten. (I,ix,14)[45]

Augustine goes on at some length about the beatings he received as a young child from the hands of his teachers. The general intent of Roman education was to subdue the will of the individual to the higher demands of the universal. Other societies, whose principle is less of an abstract universal order than was the Roman, have treated their children differently. Augustine himself contemplates a different arrangement in a later chapter where he says that, as he learned to speak his mother-tongue without violent threats and cruel punishments, "This shows sufficiently that for learning such things a free curiosity is much more effective than is frightful necessity" (I,xiv,23).[46] However, as he points out in the next line of that chapter, "God's laws" permit the free flow of curiosity to be restrained by force.[47]

What he means is this. Because we possess rational powers which are "outside" the order of nature we cannot simply be governed by nature as are other animals. This means that we are forced to create and maintain our own order where we both rule and are ruled by authority — and there are two possible sources for this authority; brute force, or reason. In the earliest stages of human history Augustine understands that mankind was governed by raw force, which can happen because we are a society of rational *animals*.[48] But mere force can never be adequate to the demands of reason, and it is our reason which creates the need for government in the first place. In the end, the only source of an authority which is adequate to the needs of a society of *rational* animals is one which is itself rational. Such was the basis of rule in the Roman Empire — expressed in its single law for all mankind.[49] And, where an external divine law is recognized as the principle of human society, the natural will of the individual must be broken to make it serviceable to that law — otherwise these (irrational) desires would be primary instead of the law. This, rather than any strictly educational purpose, is the reason why both law and tradition sanctioned punishment, and this was the wretched course into which Augustine had now come through the power of speech.[50]

He recalls that as a young child he had no idea why he should learn his letters, but from his beatings he understood that his parents and teachers expected him to do so. He very soon discovered that men prayed to God to avoid such tortures and he did the same, appealing as it were to a great, but unseen, power who might save him from being beaten for failing to do something the good of which he did not understand. But God did not always answer these prayers and he remembers that his parents would often laugh and make light of his torments. This moves Augustine to a consideration of the nature of the authorities to which he was actually subject, and he finds that they were profoundly vain and contradictory.

He shows that their position was contradictory, both inwardly and outwardly, by means of two examples. His parents often laughed at the beatings he got at school. He asks how they, who loved him, could have laughed and made light of these punishments which obviously terrified him. He is certain that it was not because they were cruel, wishing him harm, nor were they callous people who were indifferent to the pain of others because they were dull-witted and insensitive.[51] No, they laughed at his terror or misery because they pretended to love the divine law, for the sake of which he was beaten, so much that they could look on such petty bodily sufferings as nothing in comparison with that good. If this had been the truth of the situation their laughter would not have been contradictory. But Augustine asks, in a rhetorical question, if anyone can be so closely attached to God that he could really count bodily pain as nothing and so could make light of another's fear without contradicting himself. The answer implied is no — for he doubts, if his parents had been threatened with the rack or some other instrument of adult torture, that they would have feared it any less than he feared the cane of his master.[52]

Outwardly too their position was contradictory. They thought it right that he should be beaten for playing games instead of studying — and yet the whole purpose of his education, in their eyes, was to equip him to succeed at the grown-up version of the same games which is called ''business.'' This judgement of adult affairs may seem harsh but Augustine immediately cites an example of what he had in mind. He asks, rhetorically:

> Or, did the master himself who beat me do anything different since, if in any little question [of scholarship] he was beaten by a fellow-scholar, he would be more twisted by anger and envy than I was when I was beaten by a fellow-player in a game of ball? (I,ix,15)[53]

The master who beat Augustine for playing instead of studying used his learning for the same ends as Augustine sought in fleeing from his studies. His teacher's aim was to be first in his world just as Augustine's was to be first in the games he played, and for both the important thing was to come out on top regardless of the truth of the situation. Yet Augustine was beaten for doing, in his own way, the same thing his parents wanted his education to prepare him for in later life — namely, to succeed in the eyes of the world, to get ahead and become important. Would not any true judge find this contradictory?

I,x,16. The sin of early childhood

As a young child Augustine soon revolted against being forced to school for the sake of a rational good he did not understand. He avoided his studies whenever possible and sought instead a natural community free of any external reason. He found this first with his playmates in their games and sports and, a little later, in sneaking off to see the shows and spectacles of the adult world.[54] He interprets this behaviour as perfectly natural — he was certainly not the only boy to do this — and this was the whole problem.

For, even though he has just shown that the adults who sent him to school did so for foolish and contradictory reasons, Augustine nevertheless judges that he sinned against God in trying to avoid these studies. He sinned because he did so not out of obedience to some better and more rational order than his parents proposed, but simply to flee reason altogether. "For I was not disobedient because I had chosen to follow a better course, but from the love of playing" (I,x,16).[55] The effort to do this was wrong. His rational powers were as much a good as were his being and life, and he owed all three to the divine order since he did not make any of them himself. He has already pointed out that he lacked neither memory nor intelligence. To harm or prevent the proper development of these powers, by running away from school, was no more innocent than when, as an infant, he strove for things which would harm his body.

> And yet I sinned, O Lord my God, ruler and creator of all natural things, though of sins the ruler only, I sinned, O Lord my God, by going against the orders of my parents and the masters I speak of. For I could have made good use afterwards of the letters which they wanted me to learn — regardless of the [improper] purpose which they had in mind. For I was not disobedient because I had chosen to follow a better course, but from love of playing.[56]

In infancy he had sinned through his will to pervert the natural order to purposes conceived by his rational nature. In childhood the other side of this picture is filled in as he began to sin through his will to pervert the rational order to natural ends — here, by ignoring the education his rational powers required in favour of what seemed like a purely natural existence. And once again (as in I,vii,11) he prefaces this discussion about his sin with the affirmation that while God creates and rules everything he is not the author of any sin. For the moment Augustine can only assert this dogmatically — the proof will come in the seventh book.

I,x,17-18. The deferred baptism

I,x,17 — Augustine now turns to the next significant point in his life, the incident of his deferred baptism. This was the moment in which he first accepted his mother's idea of God and made the equation God = Christ. This was to remain with him through the rest of his life in the sense that, as his first and most fundamental idea on the subject, it was this notion that he had either to prove inadequate and discard or else accept.

In large part he attributed his eventual conversion to his mother. Monica was, to Augustine, both the mother of his first birth in nature and the mother of his spiritual rebirth in Christ — and she laboured far more to ensure his eternal salvation than she had at his birth. In his final eulogy he says, "she brought me forth both in the flesh that I might be born in this temporal light, and in her heart that I might be born in the light of eternity" (IX,vii,17).[57] Recall that when he spoke of his birth Monica only figured, impersonally, as one of the "parents of my flesh" (I,vi,7)[58] but now, with a wonderful logic, he first mentions her in a personal way. This is because he is not here concerned with her merely natural capacity — as a reproductive agent — but speaks about the things she did — not by nature, but as a person, by faith — that eventually helped lead him beyond nature to the church.

For her part she simply acted as a Christian mother. She had enrolled him as a catechumen "right from her womb" and saw that he was regularly signed with the cross and "seasoned" with holy salt.[59] On the other hand, Augustine's father, Patricius (who was converted only shortly before his death in 369-370, when Augustine was in his 16th year) took "next to no thought" about God (II,iii,8).[60] He left this side of things entirely up to Monica: it was a matter which he considered of no real importance.[61] None of this signified very much to Augustine until he was about seven years old and suddenly became seriously ill with a stomach disorder from which he seemed about to die. He was scared. Monica had already told him of the eternal life promised by Christ and had explained how the promise was made only to those who belonged to the church. Patricius' position had no such hope to offer, and so Augustine begged Monica, with great fervour and faith, to have him baptized. The rest of his life to his conversion can be seen as Augustine's attempt to discover whether and how this hope was justified.

1,x,18 — The illness passed before Augustine could be baptized and his mother let the matter drop. She did this in the belief that, as he was bound to sin while growing up, it was better to let the sin happen to an unreformed nature than to one which had already received the once-only forgiveness of baptism. What she particularly feared was the sexual profligacy for which Africans were notorious.[62] As it turned out her premonitions in Augustine's case were well founded — and even though the practice had no theological justification it was widespread throughout the fourth century.[63] Carried to the logical extreme it would delay baptism, and thus the Christian life, to the moment of death — whereas the truth of the matter, as Augustine points out, is that the soul's continuation in the grace of baptism depends entirely on the same Christ who offered us forgiveness in the first place.[64] Without attacking Monica for her naïveté, Augustine also brings out the contradiction, on the human side, in the custom she followed. "When the health of the body is at stake we don't say, 'Let him harm himself some more for he is not yet cured.' "[65] Yet this, he judges in retrospect, was just what happened to him as a result of her well-meaning but mistaken action. If he had been baptized as a boy and had become a member of the Christian community the church would, at the very least, have been urging him to act as such as he grew to sexual maturity. And this would have been better — whatever he made of it — than the careless silence he actually experienced where he was left to do as he pleased without having to answer to anyone.[66]

In this conclusion he also contrasts the church with the secular order. Even though he has shown that contradictions are present in all human affairs, both in the world and in the church, Augustine sees in the church an infinitely preferable order because there the fate of the soul is placed in God's hands rather than in man's. Because he understands that the church is founded and governed by God this is where he looks to find a true authority in human affairs: that is, one which is not, in principle, contradictory, in spite of the contradictions which men bring to the church. He will explain the essential reasons behind this judgement later in the work. For the moment we need only take note of his assertion that there is the possibility of such a true authority and that it is to be found in the church.

I,xii,19. Summary

In this chapter Augustine sums up his findings about the fundamentally corrupt and contradictory character of the authorities to which he was subject and about his own sins. Instead of cultivating his rational powers to the end that through them he might discover and serve God, who had made them in the first place, his parents wanted him to learn for no other reason than because, with the ability to read and number, he would be better able to get ahead in the world. For his own part he was equally vain and contradictory. It is true that he learned many things by which his rational powers were developed. But, as he would not have studied at all unless he had been forced to it, he could no more take credit for the good that came to him than could his parents. All the benefit that he got out of these studies he had therefore to attribute to God, since he neither willed it nor was it intended by his parents or teachers. And God used his own sin in seeking to avoid these studies as his punishment, since he only harmed himself every time he fled from those lessons that were the only means by which his rational powers could be developed and nurtured.

> But you, *to whom the hairs of our head are numbered* (Mt. 10:3), you took the error of those who forced me to study and turned it to my own good; and you used my own error of refusing to study for my punishment. . . . For you have so arranged things, and this is the way they actually are, that each disordered soul is to itself its own punishment.[67]

Augustine draws our attention to both sides of a coin. He points to a rational order of divine origin which, in no way disturbed by man's sin, can bring good out of corrupt intentions and which also invariably brings punishment to those who break its laws. He gives this matter a much fuller treatment in later chapters. Here he raises the point for the sake of completeness — having done the same at the end of his discussion of infancy — since this chapter marks the end of his treatment of early childhood.

Later childhood: I,xiii,20-I,xx,31

At a certain point in Augustine's childhood a change of sorts occurred: from hating his studies and seeking to flee from them he came to love them and threw himself into them completely. This happened when he was about twelve and went on to the secondary level under a teacher known as a *grammaticus* — at first in Thagaste, and then, when he was about fourteen, in the neighbouring town of Madaura.[68]

I,xiii,20,21 and 22. Secular literature

The lessons at the primary level — taught by a *primus magister*[69] — were very abstract, being essentially studies in grammar and number. Their aim, at least on the side of language, was not to teach the children to speak, which they already did, but to speak correctly without slang or barbarism. They mostly consisted of memorizing vocabulary and the abstract rules of grammar. The same was true of arithmetic where the times tables and the rules of mathematics were the order of the day. Augustine hated these first studies.He saw them as the imposition of an empty, harsh, and alien order that conflicted with his natural inclinations. But once he got to the secondary level where he started to read books and to practice the art of oratory, his attitude changed. Here he was first introduced to the study of literature — both Greek and Latin — and especially to Vergil's stories in the *Aeneid* which he loved at once. Here was rich content full of images with which he could easily sympathize — the wooden horse and its load of soldiers, Troy in flames, Dido killing herself for love, and the ghost of Creusa. All this seemed the very antithesis of the dull, dry and meaningless character of the elementary studies. " 'One and one is two, two and two are four' was truly a hateful jingle" (I,xiii,22),[70] but Vergil was another story. He threw himself into this wonderful new work with delight and strove to excel.[71]

We might be inclined to say that, having started to apply himself to his school-work, he had left behind a certain childish irresponsibility and had made a step in the right direction. The adults in his world thought so and he began to be seen as a "boy from whom one could hope for great things" (I,xvi,26).[72] But he asks whether their judgement was correct and whether he was right to love the one study and hate the other. Simply in terms of the formal content of each, the answer is a clear "No" — in spite of the fact that the stories of the poets had, by common consent, a kind of divinely inspired authority for the ancient world.[73] Augustine points out that if we had to choose between remembering every detail of the wanderings of Aeneas or knowing how to read and write, we would all pick the second unless bent on harming ourselves. His point is that the elementary studies must be the more valuable because in them the child develops, as an extension of the power of speech, the rational powers which are ours by nature.[74] Through them we are enabled to arrive at whatever end our God-given reason is capable of attaining more adequately than if we remained illiterate. Thus he concludes that he did sin in hating the primary and loving the secondary studies for such reasons.

What he says of himself, using a favourite image from Scripture, is that in this delight he was guilty of "fornicating away from you [God]" (I,xiii,21)[75] — meaning that he was guilty of using his rational powers (the ability to read and understand, etc.) for an end that was neither rational nor substantive (the fictional and, as he will soon show, contradictory content of the stories). In Augustine's idiom the expression *fornicatio abs te* always means to turn one's back on God and the rational order and to lose oneself in nature.[76] At the time he did so by ignoring what reason required of him, being simply content to use it for irrational natural delights such as he found in the literature. He panted after them, empty figments, while avoiding the very real demands of the rational order to which his reason belonged.[77] He describes his situation in this way:

> What can be more wretched than a wretch who does not grieve for his own condition, who nevertheless weeps for the death of Dido which came about through her love of Aeneas, but who does not weep over his own death which comes about from not loving you, O God. (I,xiii,21)[78]

I,xiv,23. Greek literature

This chapter looks very much like a digression, yet is not. Having just shown how he turned to literature with great delight because of its stories, he now recalls something that seems to undermine this conclusion. Rather than ignoring the matter he turns to deal with it because others may also see the same thing. The difficulty is this. If what he loved was Vergil's stories, then why did he not love the *Iliad* or the *Odyssey*? "For Homer, too, is skilled at weaving such fables and is most agreeably deceitful (*vanus*)."[79] But the problem is only seeming, and his conclusion can stand. The vanity *is* what he loved — but Homer was read in Greek. Augustine's education had been bilingual from the start but he was not good at the Greek, so Homer never lost the unsavoury character of the elementary studies.[80] Augustine always had to work it out, he could not just read it — and immediate pleasure was what he wanted.

This in turn leads him to consider why he learned Latin so easily and Greek only with great difficulty.[81] His answer[82] is that the mother tongue is learned naturally, while a foreign language, just like the formal structure of Latin itself, was only taught to him in the rational and abstract manner of schools and under the threat of punishments — and from both of these he rebelled.

I,xv,24. The good of literature

Augustine does not for a moment suggest that he should have spent his time in grammar books and dictionaries. He acknowledges that he learned to count and use numbers and that, from the literature he was set to study, he did learn many useful words in the only way in which this is really possible — i.e., through their concrete use as saying something. He recognizes that all he learned could have been put to good use in the service of God, although this was not his intention at the time. His complaint is that the content of the literature that was set before him was not only empty and imaginary but also contradictory and corrupting.

I,xvi,25-26. The contradictions in the literature

He points out that the "classics" he was given to study, as part of the normal curriculum, not only pictured the gods acting in licentious and contradictory ways but, worse, authorized men to do the same.[83] It may seem fastidious if not downright fanatical to suggest, as Augustine does, that the great works of Homer and Vergil should be banned from the schools on this account.[84] What, after all, do a few contradictions or indiscretions matter in such a glorious literature — then, as now, regarded as masterpieces? The problem was just here. Homer, Vergil and other poets were thought of as inspired. Their works, in consequence, had a kind of divine authority in the ancient world and it was in this sense that they were presented to Augustine.[85] Indeed, it was through them, as much as anything else, that children were taught about the nature of the gods and of the relation which we ought to have towards them. Yet what did he find but that Jupiter, the supreme god, who forbade adultery and licentious fornication — punishing them with his thunderbolt — himself committed adultery and fornicated as he pleased, using any force or ruse that would gain his purpose?[86] One may be tempted to ask, "So what? This is just a story." But, if the authority of such stories is granted, the question becomes — "What behaviour do they authorize?" Do they teach that we should refrain from adultery, or that we may copulate with whomever we will and are free to use any means to this end?

The answer, obviously, is both — with the result that men are left free to pick either course with the sanction of the highest god. But this reduces divine authority to a mockery since it can be invoked for either of these contradictory purposes. The comical conclusion had long been recognized and exploited, as in the example Augustine gives here from Terrence's play the *Eunuch*. Terrence introduces a dissolute young man who justifies his licentious behaviour by pointing to the example of Jupiter, saying that while he cannot imitate the righteous power of Jove's thunderbolts, he was able, and happy, to follow him in the deceitful seduction of a girl by pretending to be someone else. If such things could appear on the Roman stage — not as a shocking matter but as a joke everyone would enjoy — it is only, Augustine suggests, because everyone was complacent about such behaviour in themselves since the gods did the same. And how, he asks, should it be otherwise when generation after generation had been brought up to regard these tales as the most authoritative account of the nature of the gods? He asks:

> [W]oe to you, O river of human custom! Who can resist your current? When will you ever dry up? How long will you continue to sweep the sons of Eve into the great and terrible sea which even they who climb on the wood [of Christ's cross] are scarcely able to cross? (I,xvi,25)[87]

Augustine is at pains to make clear that it was no accident that he was taught in this way, nor was it merely a private matter — as if his parents had picked this type of education over some other option. This was the traditional education encouraged by the state itself since, in addition to the fees paid by the pupils, the law decreed the teachers should be given a salary from the public purse. It is, he says, as if the state said, " 'Here words are taught, here one acquires the eloquence which is most necessary for persuading [the people] about things and for explaining the decisions [of state]' " (I,xvi,26).[88] Numerate and literate men were necessary to the government of the world; Augustine does not deny this. Certainly the words must be learned. But, he says, the words are "like choice and costly glasses" (I,xvi,26)[89] which can be filled with a whole variety of meanings — either with the clear and lifegiving truth or with a dark and intoxicating "wine of error" (I,xvi,26).[90] And the only texts he was given — with the full approval of his parents, teachers and even the state — were ones which taught him that it was perfectly all right to cheat and deceive in order to indulge his passions.

At the time however he loved reading these things and would have hated to be forbidden to do so.[91] But even if this had not been the case, and if out of a purer spirit he had wanted to have nothing to do with them, he points out that it would have been almost impossible for a child to stand alone against the approval of the grown-up world and centuries of tradition. If he had refused to drink the intoxicating stuff he would have been beaten by his masters who were themselves drunk on it and who, moreover, had a vested interest because they derived their whole living and status as purveyors of this noxious wine.

I,xvii,27. The sin of his later childhood

But Augustine loved the work and sought to be first in it. He gives us an example of what he came to look upon as the foolish and empty things on which he once delighted to waste the powers of mind which God had given him. Under the threat of disgrace or a beating, and in hope of winning the praise of such corrupt and besotted men, he threw himself into the task of expressing, in prose, the anger of the queen of heaven at her inability to prevent Aeneas from sailing to Italy. He knew that Juno had never really spoken these words and so it was clear even then that the whole thing was simply an exercise in fancy — and yet it was fancy that represented the sister and wife of the highest god as wracked with pain and jealousy at the life of a good man. It was bad enough to have squandered his efforts on fictions instead of substantial realities — but it was doubly wrong because the fiction presented the gods as opposed to what they themselves had decreed was pious and righteous. Aeneas, after all, was sailing to Italy in obedience to the divine command.[92]

As it happened he came out at the top of his class.[93] He got a lot of praise and was highly pleased — but what was it worth? What can be the value of praise from such men for such things? All it proved was that he was adept at using words to incite the vilest emotions of jealousy and anger. Was this anything to be proud of? Everyone about him thought so — and so did he — but was it so in truth? His final answer, in this list of rhetorical questions, is that this was all just "smoke and wind."[94]

But this raises the question whether there is *any* literature that is not shot through with contradictions and does not encourage and praise the lowest passions. His answer is Scripture, which he likens here to a sheltered prop on which his soul, as a young vine, could have grown to produce a fine and good fruit rather than being left to run riot, producing nothing but mean and bitter grapes fit only for wild birds.[95] At this point he cannot show us the reasons why he thinks thus — no more than he could show before why he thinks that the church is the true community.[96] The proof will come in time but, for the moment, the suggestion has been made and he has shown us the direction in which he was moving.

I,xviii,28-29. The sin of his teachers

I,xviii,28 — Whatever possibilities there may have been for a better interpretation of this literature, they could scarcely come from such masters as he had. These men were held up as models for children to imitate, yet their only concern was to make a good impression in the eyes of men — without caring in the slightest what improper things they did or whom they unjustly hurt in the process. Augustine points, in the first case, to the master who was much applauded and admired for a fine, well-worded and witty account of his hopes, say, of seducing the mother of one of his students. Such a man thought nothing of parading his lust so long as it could be used to make him shine. But he would have been really embarrassed if, in telling some harmless thing, he had mispronounced a word or misquoted a well-known saying so that he looked like a fool to his audience. Mispronouncing a word is an innocent mistake of no consequence — but this is not true of the desire to seduce another man's wife. Daily Augustine saw examples of how his masters feared the former and thought nothing of the latter.

As he points out, we may be inclined to think such things are of no consequence because the man in his example only boasted of his lustful desires and had not actually committed adultery. This is certainly the standpoint of a worldly wisdom which, because we cannot see into one another's hearts, can only judge a person if a crime has actually been committed. But Augustine insists that this does not mean that such things are of no consequence to us or to God. We know our own intentions and so, he says, does God who sees the truth of all that goes on in us. We fool ourselves if we think we are safe merely because the world cannot haul us into court. If we break a law by actually committing adultery, we do so just as surely by an unrepented intention to do so. We would do it if we could and only external circumstances, for which we can take no credit, keep us from the deed. Thus, while the world may not be able to accuse us in such matters, each of us knows the truth in his heart. Such truths we wilfully ignore, by a kind of self-imposed blindness, in order to indulge these passions as if they were matters of no consequence. Just so, the prodigal son of the Scriptures went away from his father's house not by any outward act — by taking horse, carriage, or ship — but by his wilful determination to squander what he had from his father on pleasures that the world provided and approved though he knew that his father did not. Yet Augustine asserts that, like the father in the story of the prodigal son, God does not abandon us and is patient and full of compassion if only we repent and seek to hold on to his truth rather than the world's.

I,xviii,29 — This chapter is crucial because in it Augustine shows the logic of what is wrong with such behaviour. He says:

> Behold us with patience, O Lord my God — as you do in fact look on us — behold how the sons of men diligently observe conventions about letters and syllables which they have received from former speakers while they neglect the eternal covenants of everlasting salvation which they have received from you: so that he who holds or teaches the ancient agreements concerning sounds more greatly displeases men if, contrary to the teaching of grammar, he shall say the first syllable of "human" without aspiration [i.e., as in the slang, 'uman], than if, against your precept, he shall hate a man although he is a man.[97]

Augustine has already shown how we are freed from the immediate control of nature by our rational powers. But here we find him introducing another order to which man is subject precisely in respect of his rationality. For, against the rules of language and grammar which are clearly a human creation and convention, received from former generations, he now opposes the "eternal rules of everlasting salvation," which, he maintains, mankind has certainly received from God.

What is this divine law or order to which our reason is subject? and how is it made known to us with certainty? He continues: "And certainly the knowledge of letters is no more inwardly present than is that law which is written in conscience that one is doing to another what one would be unwilling to suffer."[98] In this teaching Augustine asserts that the same powers which give us a knowledge of letters also bring us, of necessity, to the inward recognition that we do wrong whenever we do to another what we would be unwilling to suffer ourselves.

He refers here to the law of non-contradiction which had long been recognized as the primary and most fundamental principle of human rationality. Aristotle gave the definitive formulation of this principle in his *Metaphysics* (IV,3): "the same attribute cannot at the same time belong and not belong to the same subject and in the same respect." This principle, Aristotle says, "everyone must have who understands anything that is,"[99] and Augustine refers to it as a divine law in the sense that it is not made by man, nor are we subject to it at our pleasure. This is the most fundamental condition of all human knowledge, since we do not know anything if, on the one hand, we recognize a distinction ("The book," say, "is good") and then deny it at the same time and in the same respect ("The book is bad"). In this case what do we know? — is the book good or bad? — we don't know. Likewise, we contradict ourselves if we recognize an identity between two things which we then deny at the same time and in the same respect. This is the way in which the religious and ethical form of the law of non-contradiction, which Augustine uses here, is stated in the Golden Rule — that one must not do to another what one is unwilling to suffer from him. For whatever our particular differences, we all share a common identity in our rational natures which are all subject to this law. And we cannot be ignorant of this identity. In Augustine's example, the same reason by which one man recognizes the science of language and uses it to establish his authority amongst men, *must* recognize a like reason in those to whom he is related in this way. The eloquence which comes from a grasp of the rules of grammar and speech — by which the first man wants to raise himself above others — can only have weight and authority amongst those who recognize the same science and who must therefore possess the same rational powers.

It is the purest self-contradiction for one man to hate another and seek to destroy him merely because he himself wants to raise himself above the other, when the first is a man just like the other and no god or some higher species of being. The first man would not tolerate it if the other said, "Look, I know I am a man just like you but I am going to lord it over you." He would object, "That's not fair, you have no right, you're no different than I am and you know it." Yet this is just what he is willing to do to the other man — and the world not only lets him get away with it but counts him a great man worthy of respect. Augustine gives the example of the teacher who, in a fine and witty speech, wins great praise for demolishing some other man's thesis — in which, as was his intent, he so managed to discredit the other that he ruined his career. He could easily have objected to the thesis without attacking the man — who had done nothing to harm him except that, by his mere existence, he was a potential rival — yet here he was, willing to destroy a man simply in order to gratify his desire to be first. His name is on every lip. "Isn't so and so clever!" "What a man to be reckoned with — did you hear how he destroyed professor X?" The audience applauds him though it knows his wicked intention, yet it would reject another man as inconsequential who, though free of any malevolent purpose, merely spoke incorrectly.

Augustine points out that it is perverse to give our respect to the one instead of the other, for it is completely wrong to suppose that the malicious man can harm his enemy in any essential way — although this is exactly what he does to himself. All he can do to his enemy is to harm his worldly prospects (but this can happen to any of us at any time through sickness, bad luck, or any other circumstance). Such things have nothing to do with whether we are good or bad. On the other hand we simply cannot contradict ourselves without making ourselves worse in the most inward and essential way. For our rational powers cannot contradict themselves and remain rational. Every time this happens, as when one man does to another what he himself would be unwilling to suffer, he merely shuts himself off from the truth. By the law of its own nature, human reason inevitably blinds itself in the irrational (i.e., contradictory) pursuit of its ends. How could it be otherwise? Its power is to see rational distinctions and identities, which it does — but then it blinds itself and obscures what it knows by denying, with exactly the same force, what it has just affirmed. All such activity must tend to the destruction of the same rational powers by which a man would realize these illicit desires in the first place. Thus, when Augustine speaks of God dispensing blindness by unfailing law on the unlawful desires of men, this is not to be understood as a fancied or arbitrary imposition of divine authority. It belongs rather to the very nature of things in the created order. Every disordered soul that seeks to use its rational powers in irrational and contradictory ways is, to itself, its own fitting punishment.[100] It thinks that it sees, that it knows how things are — but it does not and cannot because of what it has done to itself.

I,xix,30. Augustine's sin

This was the kind of world in which Augustine grew up. These were the people he was expected to imitate and the kind of judgements he was taught to respect. He makes it perfectly clear that he does not blame the world for the fact that he adopted these positions because, as he confesses, he *wanted* its respect. As he grew towards the end of his childhood he tried more and more to please his masters by excelling in his studies, because he began to realize that the arts of speech which they taught were the best means to power and preeminence available to him. He saw that in this world power comes ultimately through the word. He who has the eloquence to move and persuade others has power. For this reason Augustine soon learned to have a horror of faulty grammar, with never a thought, when he committed some error, not to hate and envy his fellow students who did not make such a mistake.

He contradicted himself in other more blatant ways too. He tells that he often lied to his tutor,[101] masters, and parents, deceiving them about what he was doing when he wanted to play some game or see some show they would have forbidden. He also stole from his parents' kitchen, either from greed or to barter with other boys for their toys — taking things which his parents did not want him to take and which he did not want them to know he had taken. And in the games he used to play with his fellows he often used to cheat in order to come out on top. Of course nothing made him more furious and nothing made him argue more bitterly than when he found others cheating him as he cheated them — but if he was found out he would argue or lose his temper and break up the game rather than admit the truth.

These things are regarded as childish peccadilloes. The world does not take them seriously because nothing it values is at stake — a toy, the odd piece of bread, and so on. But Augustine's conclusion, here as in infancy, is that it is wrong to regard such behaviour as innocent. From the standpoint of the truth there is no difference between contradiction in the child and in the adult. The child who cheats at a game to win some marbles does the same thing, according to the capacities of his age, as does the adult who cheats his fellow out of a vast estate. It is true that nuts, balls, and pet birds give way to money, estates, and servants but the intention is the same in both cases.

From Augustine's standpoint at the time of writing, as for any other Christian reader, it can seem that this conclusion is opposed by Christ's words in Scripture (Mt. 19:44) where he says: *"The kingdom of heaven belongs to such as these* [i.e., little children]."[102] Augustine is however able to affirm — without any uncertainty, and on the basis of the argument he has just shown — that Christ cannot be taken to mean that children are innocent but that he used little children to symbolize humility because they are small and powerless. The meaning is that the kingdom of heaven belongs to the humble, not that children are innocent.

I,xx,31. Conclusion

Augustine has now said all he thinks it necessary to say about his childhood. He has shown that he was no more innocent as a child than he was as an infant. Indeed, he had become worse — in the sense that his rational powers were not only turned against nature and the natural order but now also against reason and the rational order. Every time he cheated, stole, lied, or contradicted himself in any other way he was attempting to twist the truth of things to his own desires — to twist the rational order of the universe to suit himself alone — and this was not innocence. But the truth did not change each time he lied — he only blinded himself and cut himself off further from it. Thus neither the rational nor the natural order of the universe could be disturbed in any essential way by a creature such as he was.

Since human reason is itself limited in this way by the order God placed in creation, we can see that it is not the source of all wickedness — as if the only way to return to an innocent relation to the whole was through the destruction of our rational powers and the 'return' to a purely natural existence. Our rational nature not only comes from God but, as Augustine has shown, it is governed at every moment by a divinely established law. This means that it is both a product of a divine truth and is related to that truth as its end. By its nature reason seeks the rational. It is therefore as wrong and futile to try to flee from the demands of our rational nature as it is to pervert the natural order to suit desires which come from our rational nature. Neither beast (a purely animal nature) nor angel (a purely rational nature), Augustine teaches that we sin equally when we will to be either. And the want of innocence — understood in its fullest sense — derives neither from the fact that we are animals nor from the fact that we are rational. Rather, it comes from the disordered confusion of the universal and the particular, of reason and nature, that we are because we are both rational and animals who seek our good, on either side, in independence from God. It is Augustine's constant teaching that our independence, and the consequent confusion of the two aspects of our being, are not the work of God but of man. The doctrine of original sin is intended to explain how, from the good rational animal which God created, we fell into this condition as a species — but here Augustine's only concern has been to show that he was such a sinful creature and that he would continue to be such until the independence of each of these aspects was overcome and they were brought into perfect harmony with one another and with the divinely created orders of nature and reason.[103]

As both his animal and rational natures were created by God — in the sense that Augustine did not make himself nor was he ultimately made by any other created agency — he concludes that he owes God thanks for these things. He says that he had (*i*) being, (*ii*) life, and (*iii*) was capable of thinking — which three things he understood, at the time of writing, as created images of God's Trinitarian nature.[104] In themselves each of these was good and each automatically sought its own proper good. He had (*i*) an instinct for self-preservation, to keep himself in being; (*ii*) as a form of sentient life he spontaneously guarded the integrity of his senses; (*iii*) and even in the little thoughts with which he was concerned he intuitively sought the truth — he did not like to be wrong, his memory was strong, he was learning command of words, he enjoyed friendship, and he shrank from pain, ignorance, and sorrow.[105] He had not made any of these powers for himself and so he says that even if he had not lived beyond childhood he would still owe God thanks for these gifts which were both marvellous and good and which, of themselves, sought their own good and avoided its opposite.

But he was not good — as he did not allow each of these powers to look for its proper good in God who had made both him and them. Instead, he sought (*i*) pleasures, and (*ii*) eminence, and (*iii*) truths in the only other place to which he could turn — which is to say, in the world. But these things could not really be found there. Try as he might, the order which God had instituted in creation — both natural and rational — and by which it was governed, did not disappear each time he tried to twist it to his own purposes. Instead he only got for himself (*i*) grief, (*ii*) confusion — of the reality of his vile position with the eminence he affected, and (*iii*) error.[106] He ends the book with this prayer.

> Thanks be to you, (*i*) O my sweetness,
> and (*ii*) my honour, and (*iii*) my security;
> My God, thanks be to you for your gifts.
> But you must preserve them for me.
> For thus (*i*) you will preserve me,
> And (*ii*) the things which you have given me
> will be increased and will reach perfection,
> And (*iii*) I myself will be with you,
> For that I am is also your gift to me.[107]

NOTES

1 For the date of composition, see Solignac, *BA*, 13, pp. 45-54.

2 I intend each of these adjectives to characterize one of the five false relations to God through which Augustine moved from the time he came to rational self-consciousness in childhood until just before his conversion. These are, (*i*) the insouciance of childhood, (*ii*) the rebellion of adolescence, (*iii*) the dualism of Manichaeism, (*iv*) the doubt of scepticism, and (*v*) the final stage when he knew that Christianity not only had the true idea of God in common with the Platonists but also a true mediator, yet he remained unwilling to join the church.

3 This double sense of the words *confiteri* and *confessio* is noted by Augustine in many places and is well recognized in the literature. See the references in Solignac, *BA*, 13, pp. 9-12.

4 See Preface, n. 1 for a brief account of my understanding of these divisions. In X,iv,5-6 Augustine specifies that his second confession is directed exclusively to the "brotherly soul" (*animus . . . fraternus* — 212/13), i.e., to his fellow Christians. In XI,ii,2 he states the object of his third confession as "to meditate on your law" (*meditari/tua* — 264/16-17), where his aim is to confess his knowledge of the things he has by faith (*et/meam* — 264/17-18 — "and to confess to you both what I know and what I do not [yet] know about [your law]"). This means that the final confession is directed to Christians who wish to understand what they hold by faith — i.e., to the Christian philosopher.

5 The *Confessions* actually begins with a general preface to the whole work in I,i,1-I,v,6. As this falls outside of the account of Augustine's life I have not commented on it. Interested readers may consult the impressionistic essay of R. Guardini, *Anfang. Eine Auslegung der ersten fünf Kapitel von Augustins Bekenntnissen*, Munich, Kosel, 1950. For a more objective account of the logical structure of the preface, see the brief comments of J. A. Doull, "Augustinian Trinitarianism and Existential Theology," *Dionysius*, 3 (1979), 124-25 or G. N. Knauer, "*Peregrinatio animae*. Zur Frage nach der Einheit der augustinischen Konfessionen," *Hermes* 85 (1957), 216-48. In the French translation of the *BA* ed. this preface is set off in poetic form for the reasons explained in Bouissou's essay, "Le style des Confessions" (*BA*, 13, pp. 207-35, see esp. pp. 217-21, 233-35). I have followed this practice in my translations.

6 Augustine mentions in many places in I,vi and vii that he did not remember his infancy: see 5/20, 6/10-11, 7/13, 9/25-26, 9/30-10/1, 10/6-7. The sources of his knowledge of his infancy were either from those who knew him then or from his own observation of other infants: see I,vi,8 *Post/memini* (6/8-11), *Tales/mei* (6/20-23), I,vi,10 *Confiteor/credere* (7/12-15), I,vii,12 *Hanc/saeculo* (9/25-30).

7 See I,vi,9 *Nam/feminas* (7/40-5). The use of *muliercula* (7/15) — "mere women" — while it undoubtedly reveals the male chauvinism of the Romans generally, is intended to distinguish the anecdotal hearsay evidence of mothers — which was all that was available on the subject — from a more objective kind of evidence available to all. For a discussion of the view of women which Augustine inherited from the culture of late Roman antiquity, see E. A. Clark's well-documented article, "Adam's Only Companion: Augustine and the Early Christian Debate on Marriage," *Recherches Augustiniennes*, 31 (1986), 157-62.

8 *Quid/nescio* (5/15-18).

9 See I,vi,7 *Exceperunt/dispositas* (5/20-25), I,vi,10 *Unde/est* (7/18-23).

10 *Nam/universa* (5/28-6/3).

11 *Nam/amplius* (6/5-7).

12 See I,vi,7 *secundum/dispositas* (5/23-25) — "[God gives to infants all that they need] according to your foundation and the riches which you have laid down at the very base of things." Augustine points here to one of the regular cycles of nature such as any student of biology would easily recognize. One has only to think, for example, of the illustrations of the photosynthetic cycle in a textbook — where plants are shown taking in CO_2 and giving off O_2 while the animals breathe in O_2 and give off CO_2.

13 See I,vi,8 *Post/memini* (6/8-11).

14 This adage, in the form *homo animal cachinnabile*, is found in Apuleius (*De dogmate Platonis*, 3). Martianus Capella, a younger contemporary of Augustine's from Carthage, uses the saying as an incontrovertible and long accepted example in his discussion of dialectic in *The Marriage of Philology and Mercury*. He says (IV,398): "For just as it is a property of man to be capable of laughter, so it is a property of beings other than man not to be able to laugh." The translation is from the edition by W. H. Stahl, R. Johnson, and E. L. Bunge, *Martianus Capella and the Seven Liberal Arts*, New York, Columbia University Press, 1971-1977, Vol. 2, p. 140.

15 *Et/mei* (6/11-23).

16 See I,vi,7 *Sed/mei* (5/11-15).

17 *Quid/nescio?* (5/15-17).

18 *dic/mea* (7/2-9).

19 If we limit the meaning of 'history' to the unique and specific there is little of value for historical inquiry in the first books of the *Confessions*. Courcelle, in his *Recherches sur les Confessions de saint Augustin* (Paris: Éditions E. de Boccard, 2nd ed., 1968: this is the edition to
which I refer throughout), explicitly adopts this point of view (pp. 49, 248) which means that
he glosses over most of the content of Books I and II. Indeed, he moves very rapidly through
Augustine's Manichaean period in Books III to V: though richer in personal detail, Courcelle has not much to add to the already thorough work of Alfaric (*L'évolution intellectuelle
de saint Augustine, 1, Du Manicheisme au Neoplatonisme*, Paris, Nourry, 1918), and others.
Courcelle's discussion really only gets under way on the period in which Augustine was in
Milan for here he has discovered new texts — other than the *Dialogues* — which, he claims,
enable us to verify the account of the *Confessions*. While there can be no quarrel with his
aim or method, about which he is explicit (see pp. 12, 247), it does mean that well over half
of the first nine books is largely ignored because it contains little that is specific to
Augustine — and this is especially true of the first two books where Augustine sets the problem to which Christianity was to be the final solution. What I want to bring to the reader's
attention is the fact that the paucity of historical information peculiar to Augustine does not
mean that their content is any the less historical or verifiable for being general. In the early
books (especially I and II) one can say that Augustine's *intention* is precisely to shun the
particular historical fact for the general one. But these general points, and the conclusions he
draws from them, are no less historical than the later parts of the text where he discusses
events that are unique to himself — and they must be taken into account if we are to understand what Augustine is attempting in the *Confessions*.

20 *An/quaerentem* (7/9)

21 *teque/tibi?* (7/10-11).

22 *rerum/rationes* (6/28-7/1).

23 *laudem/mea* (7/12-13).

24 See I,vi,10 *Eram/quaerebam* (7/15-18).

25 *An/artifex?* (7/18-19). One of the greatest difficulties for the modern reader is Augustine's
pervasive use of the rhetorical question, where he gives his final answer to the point under
consideration in the form of a question which "assumes that only one answer is possible and
that if the hearer is compelled to make it mentally himself it will impress him more than the
speaker's statement" — Fowler, *Modern English Usage*, Oxford, Clarendon Press, 1937:
"Technical Terms, Rhetorical Question." If this is not appreciated and these questions are
taken at face value the work will seem much more open and indefinite than it is. Examples of
Augustine's use of this device can be found on almost every page, often mixed in with genuine questions. This is a feature of the *Confessions* which the reader must bear constantly in
mind. I will signal those places where I think it deserves special notice.

26 See I,vi,10 *Quid/te* (8/6-9).

27 *Exaudi/terram?* (8/10-15).

28 *An/infantium* (8/25-9/4).

29 See I,vii,11 *Expiare/remediis* (9/7-8) where mothers and nurses are able to get rid of tantrums. Augustine says he does not know how they do it but, in principle, it must be by divert-
ing the infant's attention from universal ends to some sensible object. See also *ibid., sed/sunt*
(9/12-13) where Augustine recognizes that such tantrums pass as the infant grows into
childhood — presumably (?) because once it can speak it no longer suffers the frustration of
wanting something which it is unable to express.

30 Trans. W. Watts (*Loeb*). Although strongly Jacobean in tone, this is still, in many respects,
the best English translation of the *Confessions*. The important word in Augustine's rhetorical
question about how he sinned as an infant is *inhiabam. An quia uberibus inhiabam plorans?*
(8/17-18) — "Or was it because I cried too fiercely after the breast?" While the French
translation of *inhio* (= "to stand open, gape") as "la bouche ouverte" (*BA*, Vol. 13, p. 291)

is literally correct, Watts' "too fiercely" conveys the meaning better — i.e., of a disordered, intemperate, un-natural desire.

31 We easily recognize this kind of jealousy in children, but Augustine specifies that he is speaking here of an infant: *nondum loquebatur* (9/5) — "he was not yet speaking." In I,viii,13 Augustine makes it clear that the power of speech is what distinguishes childhood from infancy. Augustine specifies that the jealous baby already had, or could have had for the mere sucking, all the milk it needed when he says that it was "at the source of the milk [i.e., at the breast] which was flowing copiously and abundantly" (*in/abundante* 9/8-9).

32 *opis/pati* (9/9-11).

33 *sed/sinebat* (8/21-23).

34 This question would involve the doctrine of original sin which intends to explain how the species got to be this way — without blaming it on God or, in the dualistic alternative, on a separate principle of evil. Augustine can ignore this question here because his only purpose is to explain what kind of a creature he was — not how the species got to be this way. He treats the question of original sin in many works, but see esp. *DD7*, I,2, *DCD*, XIII and XIV, and the anti-Pelagian works generally. Augustine maintains that reason is created by God; the disordered use of reason is a consequence of human action and the condition of all since Adam. See also below, n. 103.

35 *formas/omnia* (9/24-25).

36 *usque/dispositas* (5/24-25).

37 *Quod/fui?* (10/1-5).

38 In the *Confessions* Augustine follows the general Latin division of the ages or periods of life which he distinguishes as follows: (*i*) *primordia*, for his life in the womb until (*ii*) *infantia*, from birth until (*iii*) *puertia*, from the acquisition of speech until (*iv*) *adolescentia*, from puberty to (*v*) *iuventus*, the youthful maturity of his early thirties. These are the five ages through which he moves in the *Confessions*. The other two generally recognized periods are *seniores*, from the fortieth or forty-fifth year to *senectus*. See *ALD*, art., *aetas*. See also Solignac's references to studies of the different ages (*BA*, Vol. 13, p. 295, n. 1).

39 Already in the two chapters on infancy Augustine recognized that, as the infant does not have an explicitly rational self-consciousness — because it cannot speak — it cannot be regarded as rationally responsible for its actions. This means that an infant is incapable of self-consciously committing a sin and so neither reason nor custom allow it to be reprehended or punished. See I,vii,11 *sed/sinebat* (8/21-23). In *DGC* (II,42) Augustine uses this formula: "infants, although incapable of sinning, are yet not born without the contagion of sin" (trans. *NPNF*).

40 See I,viii,13 *Et/hoc* (10/12). Compare the oblivion of infancy mentioned in I,vi and vii — texts noted above, n. 6.

41 Augustine's most complete discussion of words as signs is found in *DDC*.

42 *Sed/recolo?* (10/5-7).

43 *Non/meus* (10/13-16).

44 *Sic/hominum* (11/4-8). The *procellosam societatem* — "storm-tossed society" — in this passage belongs to an image Augustine uses often of human society as a tempestuous and bitter sea (i.e., salty vs sweet, or drinkable, water). Compare XIII,xvii,20 and the very explicit passage from *EP* (LXIV,9) cited by P. de Labriolle in his useful edition of the *Confessions*, Paris, Collection Guillaume Budé, "Les Belles Lettres," Vol. 2, p. 380, n. 1, and quoted in *BA*, Vol. 14, p. 461, n. 1. In I,xvi,25 he speaks of it as a "great and terrible sea" (*mare/formidulosum* — 19/1), fed by the "river of human custom" (*flumen/humani* — 19/7), which is also the "Tartarean river" of I,xvi,26 (*flumen tartareum* — 19/23), i.e., bounding the lowest part of the underworld, see Vergil, *Aeneid* VI, 577. The violent, tortured course of this raging "gulf" (*gurges* — 25/22) is described in a masterpiece of Augustinian pungency in II,ii,2. On Augustine's use of this image see H. Rondet, "Le symbolisme de la mer chez saint Augustin," *Augustinus Magister*, Vol. 2, pp. 691-701 and the additions made by F. Chatillon, "Références et remarques complémentaires sur le symbolisme de la mer chez saint Augustin," *Revue du moyen âge latin*, 10 (1954), 218-19.

45 *Deus/vapulabam* (11/9-16).

46 *Hinc/necessitatem* (18/14-16).

47 See I,xvi,26 *Sed/deus* (18/16-17) — "But the waves of the former [free curiosity in learning] are restrained by the latter [fear-inspired necessity], thanks to your laws, O God." The *fluxum* ("waves") in this passage belong to the image of the turbulent, chaotic waters of human society: see above, n. 44.

48 See, for example, Augustine's account of the empire of the Assyrians which he understood to be the first and greatest in the world. It was based on pure force (*DCD*, IV,6). Likewise Augustine understood that the rule of the world's first kings from Cain to Lamech, mentioned in Genesis 4:1-6:13, was based on ferocious force. It was this that led God to be sorry that he made man because "the earth is filled with violence through them" (Gen. 6:13), and so he brought about the destruction, through the Flood, of all except the family of Lamech's righteous son Noah and the beasts — whose ferocity was innocent because they are not rational animals.

49 For Vergil's 'classic' statement of Rome's divine calling, see Jupiter's speech to Venus, *Aeneid* I, 257-96, his words about Rome's task, IV, 231 ("to bring the whole world under the rule of the [divine] laws"), and Anchises' speech to Aeneas in the underworld, VI, 847-53.

50 See I,ix,14 *Laudabatur/Adam* (11/17-20). See I,xiv,23 *Sed/te* (18/16-20) where Augustine points out that such punishments are legal in the sense that they are permitted by divine law as a necessary and acceptable restraint on human corruption.

51 His parents wished him no harm: see I,ix,14 *qui/volebant* (12/1). They were not callous: see I,ix,15 *facit/stoliditas* (12/5).

52 See I,ix,15 *Non/deprecabamur* (12/12-13).

53 *Aut/superabar?* (12/25-29). Compare I,xi,16 and I,xix,30.

54 See *amans/maiorum* (13/8-11). I understand there are three things here — childhood games in which there were winners and losers (*certamines*), stage productions (*falsae fabellae*), and circus games (*spectacula*).

55 *Non/ludendi* (13/6-8).

56 *Et/ludendi* (13/1-8).

57 *me/nascerer* (193/21-22). Compare I,xi,17 *Audieram/te* (13/19-23) and *Et/tua* (14/2-4); V,ix,16 *Non/pepererat* (90/2-5).

58 *a/meae* (5/14).

59 *signabar/meae* (13/19-23). "These acts [being signed with the cross and touched with blessed salt] refer to what we would call today 'preliminary rites of baptism'; done to an infant at the moment of birth, they sufficed to signify that such a one was counted as a 'catechumen'." (Solignac, *BA*, Vol. 13, p. 303, n. 1.) See also his remarks and references on this subject (*ibid.*, p. 114), where he notes that these "gestures were, it seems, often repeated according to the usage of the African church." This is indicated in the text above by Augustine's use of the imperfect tense — *signabar, condiebar*.

60 *de/cogitabat* (29/25-26). See the following references to Patricius: II,iii,6 — a new catechumen — (*nam/erat* 28/12-13) in Augustine's sixteenth year: III,iv,7 where Augustine speaks of his nineteenth year (i.e., 13 November 372-13 November 373) and says that his father had died two years before (*cum/biennium* 41/10-11) — Solignac dates Patricius' death in 370 (*BA*, Vol. 13, p. 201) — and IX,ix,22 where Augustine states that Monica brought Patricius to the church in the very last days of his life (*Denique/toleraverat* 198/15-17). For a review of what is known about Monica's life see M. M. O'Ferrall, "Monica, the Mother of Augustine. A Reconsideration," *Recherches Augustiniennes*, 10 (1975), 23-43.

61 See *Ita/serviebat* (14/10-17). For Patricius' lack of concern about such things see II,iii,5, "meanwhile this same father did not trouble himself about how I was growing up in your sight" (*cum/tibi*, 27/26-27) and II,iii,8, "about you he took almost no thought" (*de/cogitabat* (29/25-26).

62 See for example the text from Salvian (*De gubernatione Dei* VII,16) quoted by Solignac (*BA*, Vol. 13, p. 117, n. 1). Whatever Salvian says, all Africans were not as unchaste as Augustine. His friend Alypius, for example, had only one (?) "hurried and furtive"

(VI,xii,22 *raptim et furtim* – 119/24-25) sexual experience in his adolescence and, when years later he decided to try it again, he did so not out of lust but curiosity (see *ibid.*, *coeperat/curiositas* 120/1-2). P. Brown (*Augustine of Hippo: A Biography*, Berkeley and Los Angeles, University of California Press, 1967, p. 172) notes that the Africans "tended to think a boy was innocent until he reached puberty as if [quoting *DGL*, X,xiii,23] 'the only sins you could commit were those in which you used your genitals.' "

63 The emperor Constantine, for example, had only been baptized on his deathbed (Eusebius, *Vita Constantini* IV, 61-62). Ambrose, born in Trier in 339, of a Christian family, was baptized, priested and made bishop all on the same day (1 or 7 December, 373) when he was 34 (see Solignac, *BA*, Vol. 14, p. 529). H. Leitzmann, *History of the Early Church*, Vol. 4: *The Era of the Church Fathers* (trans. B. L. Woolf, Cleveland and New York, Meridian Books, rev. ed., 1953), referring to the many notices collected in E. Diehl's *Inscriptiones Latinae Christianae Veteres*, says, "Numberless are the inscriptions telling of the administration of baptism immediately before death took place, at all ages from the first to the fortieth year.... Throughout the early centuries, adult baptism was the rule: children were not usually baptized unless they fell ill" (p. 100).

64 See I,xi,18 *Quanto/eam* (14/25-28). See the same teaching in IX,xiii,34-36. Although Augustine criticizes Monica's decision to delay his baptism he is clear it came from a true, if misguided, piety. See II,iii,6 where he says that her reaction to the news that he had reached puberty was a "*pious* consternation and trembling" (*pia/tremore* 28/14) for the sins she feared he would now commit by fornicating, and this "in spite of the fact that I was not yet baptized" (*et/fideli* 28/14-15). In other words she did not regard baptism as a magical device which made it indifferent what one did before it was 'used.' Something of the seriousness attached to maintaining post-baptismal purity can be gathered from what Augustine says in the last chapter of Book IX (xiii,34). He has just praised Monica's character and listed the good works she did throughout her life, yet he concludes that, as he cannot presume to say that from the time she was baptized no word against God's commandments ever left her lips, he must end by calling on God's grace. He does this because he takes it for granted (on the authority of Mt. 5:22) that the standard to which Christ holds his followers is that if after baptism they so much as say to another, "You fool," they will be answerable for it in the fires of hell.

65 *in/est* (14/23-25).

66 See *Melius/videbat* (14/28-15/2): the "waves of temptation" *fluctus ... temptationum* 14/28-29) mentioned here belong to the image of the turbulent, chaotic waters of this world – see above, n. 44. Augustine uses the same image at the start of Book II (ii,2-4) where he describes the onset of puberty. See II,iii,6-8 for the freedom Augustine actually experienced at the time – when no more pressure was brought on him to control his lust than Monica's admonitions which he brushed aside and she did not repeat.

67 *Tu/poenam ... Iussisti/animus* (15/13-16 ... 19/20).

68 See II,iii,5 *mihi/peregrinari* (27/10-12). Solignac tentatively dates this in the autumn of 367 (*BA*, Vol. 13, p. 201). His brief essay, "L'éducation à l'époque d'Augustin," (*ibid.*, pp. 659-61) gives a convenient summary of the question as it relates to Augustine. The standard works in the field are H.-I. Marrou's *L'histoire de l'éducation dans l'Antiquité*, Paris, Éditions du Seuil, 1948 (trans. G. Lamb, *A History of Education in Antiquity*, London, Sheed & Ward, 1956), and his *Saint Augustin et la fin de la culture antique. Retractatio*, Paris, E. de Boccard, 1949.

69 I,xiii,20 *non/vocantur* (15/24-25). Solignac lists other titles for these first teachers (*BA*, Vol. 13, p. 659) and makes the following distinctions: the first level was taught by a *primus magister* (from roughly 7 to 11), the second by a *grammaticus* (from 11 to 13) and then by a *rhetor* (from 14 to 16). Augustine's higher (what we would call tertiary) education began in his seventeenth year in Carthage (III,i,1) in the fall of 370 (*BA*, Vol. 13, p. 202). The teacher at this level was also known as a *rhetor*. This was the post Augustine himself was to occupy, first at Carthage (VI,vii,11 *ego/uterer* 109/10-11), then at Rome (*ut/rhetoricam* 94/24), and finally at Milan (V,xiii,23 *ut/provideretur* 95/16-17).

70 *Iam/erat* (17/19-21).
71 See the applause Augustine speaks of winning in I,xiii,21 (*sonabat/euge* (16/13-14). See also I,xvi,26 *libenter/appellabar* (20/23-24) and I,xvii,27 *Quid/meis?* (21/11-12).
72 *bona spei puer (appellabar)* (20/24).
73 It is this belief that lies behind Augustine's remarks in I,xiii,22 that his teachers had "no rea-son to complain against me" (*non/me* 17/5) — i.e., on the grounds of the divinely inspired authority of the works they taught — when he derides the value of the stories. He says, with heavy sarcasm, that the curtains hung "over the doors of literature schools" (*liminibus/ scholarum* 16/27-28) are not so much to veil from profanation the "honour of a [divinely inspired] mystery" (*honorem secreti* — 16/28-17/1) but to hide the error of the poets. This objection against the poet's teachings about the gods had a long tradition going back to Plato's *Republic*, see esp. II, 377a-II, 392c.
74 See I,xiii,22 *melior/prior* (16/24-25). The *prorsus* in this passage means "without doubt, cer-tainly."
75 *fornicabar abs te (Ps. 72:27)* (16/12-13).
76 See I,xiii,21 *Amicitia/te* (16/14-15). Cf. IV,ii,3 and V,xii,22.
77 As Augustine had remarked in I,xii,21, this is a kind of "madness" (*dementia*): see *et/didici* (16/19-22). On the demands of the rational order, see my commentary on I,xviii,28-29.
78 *Quid/deus* (16/7-10).
79 *Nam/est* (17/25-26).
80 See I,xiii,20 where he says he was taught Greek as a *puerulus*, (15/22) = as a "*little* boy." Marrou (1949), pp. 27-28, notes that Greek was probably presented to students even before they started the study of Latin — which itself was less a study of the living tongue than of a literary language fixed in the ancient classics. This practice was a legacy from the time when, for a Roman, the only culture was Greek and Greek was the only language of culture. See also Marrou (1956), pp. 255-67.
81 On the much debated question of when or whether Augustine really mastered Greek, see Solignac's note and references in *BA*, Vol. 13, p. 662. See also Marrou (1949), pp. 27-46. Brown (1967), p. 36, restating Marrou, says "[Augustine] will become the only Latin philos-opher in antiquity to be virtually ignorant of Greek." This "virtually" should be given the sense of Marrou's conclusions (1949), p. 637, that, by the end of his life, Augustine could compare, verify, and correct a Greek text with a Latin translation, could occasionally trans-late a short and easy Greek passage on his own, was fairly at home in the Greek Scriptures, got most of his working knowledge of Greek philosophy from Latin translations and knew the Greek Fathers only very little and late in life.
82 See my commentary on I,viii,13.
83 See I,xvi,25 *Nonne/tonitru* (19/10-14). See Marrou (1949), pp. 17-28, for a review of the content, method and aims of Augustine's education at the level of the *grammaticus*: on the Latin side it centred on Vergil, Terrence, and Cicero, and on the Greek, on Homer.
84 See I,xv,24 *Didici/ambularent* (19/4-6) and I,xvii,27 *Ut/angelis* (21/10-18).
85 See above, n. 83.
86 The reference is to Jupiter as portrayed in Terrence's *Eunuch*. I accept, with Solignac (*BA*, Vol. 13, p. 317, n. 1), the suggestion of L. Herrmann ("Remarque philologiques: *Confes-sions*, I,16,25: VIII,2,3: X,6,9 et 10," *Augustinus Magister*, 1, pp. 136-37), that the *te* of *nonne ego in te legi* (I,xvi,25 — 19/10-11) refers not to the "river of human custom" but to Terrence. It amounts to saying "Have I not read in Terrence."
87 *vae/conscenderint?* (19/7-10). See Solignac's note on Augustine's use of "wood" to signify a "ship" which is also the cross of Christ (*BA*, Vol. 13, p. 316, n. 1). On this image of the sea, see above, n. 44. On faith in Christ as the ship by which we can safely be ferried over the turbulent waters of this world to the heavenly city on another plane of existence, see the particularly clear passage from *DT* (IV,15) quoted below, Chapter Seven, n. 69.
88 *hinc/necessaria* (19/27-29). As opposed to the translators of the *BA* edition (Vol. 13, p. 319) who render the *sententiisque explicandis* of this passage in a psychological sense as "developper ses pensées," I think the context — i.e., the state's interest in education —

demands the more specific sense of *sententia* as "an official determination, a decision, sentence, judgement, vote" (*ALD*, art., *sententia*).

89 *quasi/pretiosa* (20/17-18).

90 *vinum erroris* (20/18-19). The notion of worldly goods, success, etc., as an inebriating liquor leading to drunken irrational behaviour is one of Augustine's favourite images in the *Confessions*. See, in the same chapter and section, *quod/licebat* (20/19-21).

91 See I,xiii,21 *et/dolerem* (16/19-20).

92 Vergil, *Aeneid*, I, 2. This is the meaning of *fato profugus* in the first sentence of the epic, i.e., "sent forth by divine command."

93 I take this to be the meaning of *Quid/meis?* (I,xvii,27-21/11-12) — "What was it to me to have my recital acclaimed ahead of those of many of my fellow students of the same age?" By the time Augustine was 19, in Carthage, he was still at the top of his class in the school of rhetoric: see III,iii,6 *Et/rhetoris* (40/10-11). See also the "prize" he won (IV,iii,5 *corona agonistica* — 56/27), presumably in "the contest for theatrical poetry" of IV,ii,3 (*theatri carminis certamen* — 55/17), when he was in his early twenties.

94 See I,xvii,27 *fumus et ventus?* (21/13).

95 See I,xvii,27 *Itane/angelis* (21/13-18). The "flying creatures" (*volatiles*, 21/17) are wild birds and, by metonymy, fallen angels.

96 See the commentary on I,xi,18.

97 *Vide/homo* (22/11-19).

98 *Et/pati* (22/23-25). The very popular Penguin edition of the *Confessions* (trans. R. S. Pine-Coffin), which has gone through 23 reprints between the time it first appeared in 1961 and 1986, inexplicably omits this crucial sentence.

99 Aristotle, *Metaphysics* 1005b (trans. W. D. Ross, 2nd ed., Oxford, Clarendon Press, 1928).

100 As Augustine had already said in I,xii,19 *Iussisti/animus* (15/19-20).

101 This "tutor" (*paedagogus* — I,xix,30 — 23/16) is not another level of instructor, but "a slave who took the children to school and had charge of them at home" (*ALD*, art., *paedagogus*). That his parents could afford one is an indication of their financial solvency at the time.

102 *talium/caelorum* (24/6).

103 Augustine's position both early and late in his career is that, as created, man was good — there is nothing wrong with nature as such, nor with reason, nor, in principle, with their union in man. Nevertheless he also holds that our fallen nature cannot *not* sin and that this is the condition of all since Adam. The inevitability of sin in this state — i.e., in our nature as fallen rational animals — comes from the actual independence of reason from nature and nature from reason, such that the one opposes the other in ways like those he has shown in himself. Augustine teaches that there are only two states in which this discord is not present: either in the moment before all division and discourse which was the unconscious perfection of Adam in the original Paradise where he was "able not to sin," or in human nature restored in Christ — beyond division because it self-consciously and knowingly wills that divine union of nature and reason, human and divine as revealed in Christ. The stability of this rational will in a state of spiritual grace (i.e., as a gift from the Holy Spirit) is "not able to sin." This, as he will show in the ninth book, is the condition of the saints in the heavenly Paradise. Augustine discusses these points in Books XI-XIII; see also the references given above, n. 34.

104 See *Eram ... vivebam ... veritate delectabar* (24/10-15). On my understanding of the general trinitarian structure of the *Confessions* see the Preface, n. 1. In his discussion of infancy, Augustine — with exquisite precision — had listed only being and life as the things for which he should thank God concerning that period of his life, although he also says that towards the end of his infancy he was moving towards a relation to the truth even though he had not actually come to it yet because he could not speak. See I,vi,10 *eram/quaerebam* (7/15-18) — "For even then I was and I lived and, already at the end of my infancy, was seeking for signs [words] by which I could make known my feelings to others" — compare I,vii,12 *Tu/istis* (9/16-20). The reason, which we can now understand, is that the infant had not yet actually realized his relation to the truth. Here in I,xx,31, at the end of the discussion of his

childhood, he thanks God not only for the being and life which he had, but also for the truth to which he was now actually related through the rational self-consciousness he acquired as a result of having learned to speak.

105 *Falli/ignorantiam* (24/15-17).
106 See *Hoc/errores* (24/22-25).
107 *Gratias/mihi* (24/25-29).

Chapter Two

COMMENTARY ON BOOK II

ADOLESCENCE: II,i,1-V,xiv,25

Early adolescence (II,i,1-III,iii,6)[1]

Augustine begins the second book with the next period of his life after the onset of puberty in his sixteenth year and the move from childhood to adolescence.[2] What was new that both his animal and rational natures came to maturity as each grasped its universal end. After a brief introduction (II,i,1) the book is divided into two parts, each concerned to show the effects of this development. Chapters ii and iii deal with his efforts to pervert the order of nature to suit his own desires, and chapters iv to ix deal with his attempt to pervert the rational order of the universe to the same end.

II,i,1. Introduction

Here Augustine presents the whole content of the book in a very abbreviated form. He says, "I mean to recall my filthy deeds / and the fleshly corruptions of my soul, / not because I love them / but so that I may love you, my God."[3] He makes this qualification because what he is about to confess is both pornographic and shameful and it may seem as if he is bragging — otherwise why mention these things if he really was not proud of them? He answers that he must do so because they are essential to the purpose of showing how God brought him to the church. The reader is invited to consider them in this light.[4] He goes on to explain the two ways in which he got into this state.

> For I burnt at that time, in my adolescence,
> To be sated with things from the lower parts of creation [i.e., this world],
> and I both dared [i] to let myself grow wild like a vine run to wood (*silvescere*)
> by means of various shady loves
> and my beauty withered
> and, [ii] I let myself decompose (*computescere*) before your eyes
> all the while being pleasing to myself
> and desiring to please in the eyes of men.[5]

Throughout this book Augustine characterizes the problem in this period of his life as his effort to avoid God and subvert the demands of his law. He did this not simply by fleeing human authorities and seeking to lose himself in the immediacy of his natural existence — as he had done as a child — but by maintaining that his immediate desires, where natural or rational, were *the* good. Both are ways of

---

"fornicating away from God"[6] — examined here in the fully developed form that became possible in adolescence as his animal and rational natures reached their mature powers. The philosophical expression of his fault is that he turned "from you [God], the one, and squandered [himself] in the many."[7]

The same point is driven home again and again in the words of the introduction: "dispersion," "to cut up," "from one . . . to the many"[8] and, above all, in the words he uses to describe his sin against the sensitive and rational orders — for the first, *silvescere*, "to run wild," and for the second, *computescere*, "to decompose."[9] The first evokes a young grapevine which cannot produce its proper fruit because it is uncultivated; the second employs the image of a unity in the process of decaying into elements other than itself. The implication of each is clear. With the lack of proper discipline and culture his sexuality turned from its true end; and his reason, seeking goals not in the universal and the unitary, allowed itself to disintegrate in subservience to many worldly powers.[10]

II,ii,2-II,iii,8. His sin against the natural order: adolescent sex

II,ii,2-4 — In the ability to reproduce, man's animal nature comes to the one activity where every animal works directly for a universal end. This is because the objective end of sex is the reproduction of the species. In the order of nature — "as your law prescribes, O Lord" (II,ii,3)[11] — man reproduces by sexual generation and thus, for Augustine, the procreation of children is the natural end of sexual activity and the sole purpose in accord with established order of things as constituted by God (i.e., in accord with divine law).[12]

In animals sexual desire can only be innocent. It is governed by instinct and, since it is informed by the order of the whole, cannot be opposed to that order. In a rational animal sex can be turned to other purposes. Men are not restrained by nature's times or seasons nor limited to fulfilling its purposes. We are the only animals who can turn our sexuality from natural to un-natural ends and these latter, and they alone, are all that he sought. "And what was it that delighted me except to love and be loved?" (II,ii,2).[13] Augustine makes it clear that he was only looking for the "pleasure" (*libido*) associated with the act rather than for the procreation of children.[14]

In II,ii,2 Augustine likens his new-found sexual desires to a "mist" or "fog"[15] rising up from the raging gulf beneath him. In his image these vapours, though insubstantial nothings in themselves, were, all the same, enough to blind him so that he did not stay on the "luminous road of friendship."[16] Instead he confused real friendship, spoken of as a "union of soul with soul,"[17] with the mere union of bodies.[18] Once he had gone beyond these bounds and confused the two[19] he found himself lost in waters made filthy with impurity, boiling and crashing over rocks, and pulled in a hundred directions by the currents of the vile torrent[20] — which is the "river of human custom," the "hellish river," mentioned already in I,xvi.[21]

Although in one sense man's sexual powers are free of the natural order, Augustine fully understood that this kind of thing was all too "natural." From this point of view he asks (II,ii,3) what could have tempered these tempestuous desires, which he speaks of as a "hardship," a "thorn" in the flesh, and a "wave" that swept him away.[22]

His answer is threefold. Perfect relief would be divine, taking the form of a quieting of all sexual desire which was not in accord with the rational will to beget children. Such he suggests was the condition of man in paradise.[23] Augustine was far from this state. It is clear that he was much troubled throughout the period covered in the *Confessions*, both before and after his conversion, by powerful sexual drives.[24] Failing divine quieting, unregulated sexual desires must be brought under the control of the rational will, either by allowing them no other outlet than in a legal marriage entered into for the sake of begetting children,[25] or else by total chastity. The difference between marriage and chastity was to become very important in Augustine's conversion. Here he simply distinguishes between them as between a good and a better solution on the Pauline grounds — which he quotes — that while marriage is divinely sanctioned, it inevitably involves one with worldly concerns and thus tempers rather than resolves the distinction between nature and reason.[26] That chastity and virginity provided a more complete (i.e., a higher or better) resolution of this division is merely asserted here. The full explanation of this position will be discovered in the eighth and ninth books.

He finishes the chapter (II,ii,4) by noting that at the time, although he had no thought at all of trying to restrict his new-found desires and gave himself wholly to satisfying them,[27] he did not escape divine punishment. "But having abandoned you I boiled over, wretch that I was, following an impetuous ardour away from my proper course [i.e., the "luminous path of friendship" of II,ii,2] and I broke all your laws though I did not escape your scourges — and who, amongst mortals, can?"[28] Augustine may seem dogmatic when he speaks of a divine law forbidding lust, and of his inevitable punishment for ignoring it, but a moment's reflection shows that he is simply stating the fact that the same rational powers by which man is freed from instinctive sexuality aspire, by their nature, after the universal. And yet instead of searching for God and looking for the rational order of the universe, he allowed his reason to be seduced from its proper end and bound to the continual pursuit of sensual pleasure in the many loves in which he sought gratification. To do so inevitably brings disaster: reason's end is not in the particular. To put itself in the service of such ends is therefore a bondage from which it can derive no lasting satisfaction. This is just what he intends when he goes on to say to God that:

> you were always there being merciful with your rigours, sprinkling with bitterness and discontent all my unlawful pleasures so that I might thus seek a joy that is without offence and, there where this can be found, not to find anything but you, O Lord, but you *who turn our pain into a teaching and strike to heal* (Ps. 93:20) and slay us lest we perish apart from you.[29]

This teaching may be hard but the logic behind it is undeniably clear.

II,iii,5-8. The failure of Augustine's parents

In this chapter Augustine explains why he was allowed to behave in this way, what help might have been offered, and why it was not.

Because of financial difficulties, Patricius, who had sent Augustine to the neighbouring town of Madaura to continue his secondary studies, was forced to bring him back to Thagaste in his sixteenth year (369-370). During this year Augustine lived at home while his father tried to get together the money to send him on to Carthage.

The idle year made it easy for him to lose himself in his sexual appetites, yet he points to a far more serious cause when he says, "and to hold me more closely to the centre of Babylon [i.e., the city of lust], the invisible enemy pinned me down and seduced me because I was easy to seduce" (II,iii,8).[30] In speaking of the hold that lust had over him, Augustine has it in mind that until such time as a person comes to recognize the universal *qua* universal, it is inevitable, when the opportunity presents itself and the appetites are strong, that his rational powers should seek their goal in this way. Just because they do not yet have their own proper object they are easily seduced to serving the ever-present desires of the senses unless they are restrained by some sufficient authority.

But if this is the reason why Augustine reckons he could not have been chaste, he nevertheless argues that he could, and should, have been restrained by the authority of his parents — if not to chastity then at least to the restrictions of marriage.[31] Even if *he* did not know why he should not be lustful, those who did, or should have known, ought not to have left him without restriction. It is true that Monica had advised him not to fornicate and above all not to commit adultery.[32] The latter is more grievous because in addition to breaking the divine law against lust — which the Roman state did not recognize[33] — it also explicitly contravenes the divine law against adultery which the state did recognize. But Monica did not insist on the point and gave in to her husband's desire that Augustine be free to continue his education without the encumbrance of a "she-clog" (II,iii,8).[34] Augustine for his part could scarcely be moved by her admonition since he knew nothing of, and cared nothing for, the grave and divine reasons which ultimately stood behind this advice. He says:

> These seemed to me to be womanish advices which it would have been shameful to accept. But they were yours indeed though I knew it not, for I thought that she only had spoken and that you had said nothing, through whom in fact you were not silent but did speak to me, and in whom you were despised by me. (II,iii,7)[35]

Furthermore, for reasons he shows us in his discussion of the theft of pears, he was not about to obey any authority if he could possibly avoid it while, from the side of his parents,

> the reins were let go as far as I was concerned and I was left free to play beyond every measure of due and proper severity, which led to an utter licentiousness of various passions, and in all these there was a thick mist blocking me, my God, from the clearness of your truth and my *iniquity came out, oozing, as it were, from pampered fatty flesh* (Ps. 72:7). (II,iii,8)[36]

In asking himself why his parents allowed him to run free he provides a candid thumbnail sketch of each. If he seems unduly harsh on his father who, as he freely allows, did far more for his education than did other fathers who could better afford it,[37] the answer lies in what we have already seen. The problem is just that Patricius' chief concern was that his son get the very best education so that he could get along in the world and become an important man.[38] This was a laudable aim in the eyes of the world and the world "extolled [him] with praises" (II,iii,5).[39] But Augustine's question is whether the world is the proper standpoint from which to make such judgements. In the first book Augustine had shown us what this education amounted to in truth. He now adds the complaint that, for the sake of this education, his father took no care to restrict the licentiousness of his adolescence within the bounds of marriage — even while rejoicing in the prospect of grandchildren — just so that nothing would prevent him from getting on in the world.[40] If his judgement is harsh, the reason is plain.

Yet the nobility of Augustine's spirit is nowhere better shown than in his treatment of his mother. For while it is clear that, at the time of writing, he thought as little of his father's efforts in his upbringing as he thought a lot of Monica's, he does not disguise the fact that she was to some extent involved in the same spirit as her husband. As he says, though Monica had escaped from the centre of Babylon, she was going rather slowly in fleeing from its suburbs.[41] She did this not from her husband's disinterest in his spiritual welfare[42] but from a naïve and credulous belief that the education Patricius desired for Augustine was some great thing that would be a help in leading him to God.[43] Since she accepted that his studies would be jeopardized by a wife she did not push him to marry. And since, apart from marriage, she thought there was no hope of restraining or preventing his sexual activity,[44] she left him free to do as he pleased and stopped nagging him with the admonitions she had given before he came to puberty.[45]

II,iv,9-II,ix,17. The sin against the rational order: the theft of pears

In the famous discussion of the theft of pears Augustine turns to the harm he attempted against the rational order of things. The incident itself was insignificant. One night he and some friends, on their way home through a neighbour's orchard, stole some pears. They were immensely pleased with themselves because they did not get caught, and having had their sport, threw the fruit to some pigs. Augustine's interest lies wholly on the side of what was involved in doing such an act. Here he finds the most serious consequences which brought him to the "very bottom of the deep" (II,v,9)[46] — to the lowest point in his life as measured by his distance from God.

It is difficult for us to appreciate Augustine's remorse. We are probably inclined to regard this kind of thing as a natural part of growing up, to be dismissed with an indulgent "boys will be boys." This view was expressed by Oliver Wendell Holmes when he wrote to Harold Laski, "Rum thing to see a man making a mountain out of robbing a pear tree in his teens."[47] From this standpoint one can only look at Augustine's lengthy treatment of the incident as the pious, or neurotic, hyperbole of the great saint making much ado over nothing. This would be especially true of his implication that in this act he was even worse than the savage

Catiline, the arch-villain of the Roman Republic.[48] But this merely reveals our own prejudices about Augustine's character.

Augustine certainly agrees that the incident is natural enough. It is, in part, for this reason that he includes it in his *Confessions*. But although this theft was peculiar to Augustine and his few companions, he discusses it at length to discover the universal conditions and consequences of such a deed. So far as these conclusions are true they will apply to any who have ever done a similar thing.

II,iv,9. Theft and the law of non-contradiction

The background against which Augustine treats this theft is what his first chapters have already shown us: an inadequate apprehension of the truth. The undue pampering of the desires of the flesh produced a kind of swelling fatness that blocked his sight by puffing up his cheeks.[49]

Yet however inadequate his vision may have been and however obscured by his sin, Augustine immediately proposes that there is a divine law which forbids and punishes theft and of which it is *impossible* for man to be ignorant.

> Without doubt, O Lord, you law punishes theft, and *the law is so written on men's hearts* (Rom. 2:15) that not even iniquity itself can blot it out. For what thief can suffer a thief with equanimity? Not even a rich thief when the other is driven to steal by want.[50]

When Augustine affirms that there is a divine law which is written on our hearts, he intends a law already present in man before it is given by, or known from, *any* external source whether human or divine. His objection against himself is not that he broke the Scriptural command that man must not steal, nor that he broke the Roman law forbidding theft, nor even that he disobeyed his parents' injunctions in this matter. What he condemns is that he broke a divine law present in man internally, as a part of his very nature, before it ever appears in the form of an external authority. He refers to something which he claims is a principle of man's very identity as a rational being. It is a law because it is a rational principle which applies to all. It is divine because it is an inescapable part of the constituted order of things which man himself did not make.

What is this law? As Augustine puts it, the law is shown in the fact that no thief can suffer a theft with equanimity, which is a way of saying that in all his finite rational activities man is subject to the law of non-contradiction. The divine law which forbids theft is simply the law of non-contradiction applied to property.

Unlike animals, man can steal because he places the things in the world in a rational relationship to himself. He appropriates them and makes them his own not merely by an immediate and particular possession — consuming them, sitting on them, etc. — but also in a remote and universal manner. Simply by virtue of his rational will towards them he makes things his own. He does this even if, for the moment, he may not actually have them in hand. But as by his rational powers man is potentially related to everything in the world and not just to those things immediately present to his senses, he can potentially lay claim to own the world in all its parts. Where two or more people are concerned, the same power is found in each; thus there arises the necessity of establishing a rational order to govern the relation of the individuals in a community to the things in the world. Brute force can always intervene to establish possession, but only that order which is both rational and universal (i.e., law) will, in the end, provide an adequate solution to conflicts which arise in the first place from man's rational powers. Reason's claim to an object may be decided by irrational force but it can never be satisfied in this way.

Of course the particular content of property law — how ownership is established, what may be owned, who may own, and so on — differs from society to society. What is constant is that in human society ownership is established by law. So much is this the case that, as Augustine notes, these laws govern even the necessities of man's sensitive nature. It is as much a theft if a man breaks the law when he is compelled by hunger as it is if he does so out of a mere desire for luxury. Thus Augustine says, "What thief can suffer another thief with equanimity? Not even a rich one when the other is driven to steal by want."

But where ownership is established by law theft becomes possible, since ownership is rationally determined and is not simply a matter of consumption or immediate possession. In his example the victim's soul (his *animus*) cannot remain indifferent, unmoved, or unseeing (*aequus*). Because he knows what is his as defined by law, he must also know that in such a case he has suffered a theft — even if the thief was driven to steal by want. Regardless of whether he cares, his soul cannot avoid recognizing that someone stole from him. In this sense no one can suffer a theft with equanimity — that is, without it registering as a theft instead of something which is ethically indifferent. Here instinct has been transformed into ethical activity. Animals cannot steal just because they "know" no other form of ownership than immediate possession. But, having once recognized the rational ordering of things — "the pears belong to my neighbour" — the thief goes on, in one and the same breath, to deny that order to suit his own particular interest — "the pears are mine." This is the purest self-contradiction which, in relation to property, is the universal form of theft.

In Book I Augustine had already shown that the law of non-contradiction is a divine law (i.e., not made by man), and one to which all men are subject inwardly in their nature as rational creatures. This is reason's law, written on our hearts so that iniquity itself cannot blot it out. It can only disappear from man through the concomitant destruction of his rational nature. It is the fundamental presupposition of all finite rational activity. And this, applied to property relations amongst rational animals, is the law Augustine confesses he broke in stealing the pears.

Although it is true that he escaped the punishment that Roman or Christian law, or even his parents, would have imposed on him, it is certain that he did not escape divine punishment. For, as he says, the divine law inexorably punishes theft. He has already shown that it is the most fundamental principle of man's rational nature that, in the contradictory pursuit of our own particular desires, we destroy the same rational powers by which we would realize these desires. It is certain that reason cannot contradict itself and remain rational. In just this sense no theft goes unpunished and every theft remains inescapably subject to the divine law.[51] The exact form of his punishment Augustine explains in the sequel (III,i,1-III,iii,6).

Although this is what is involved in any theft, in any legal community, any time or any place, we still do not know why Augustine regards his theft so seriously.

Certainly this was not the first he had ever done, for he told us in Book I that he used to steal from his parents' table and larder (I,xix,30). It is not then simply because he stole that he discusses the incident but because there was something unique about this particular theft which is what he wants to bring to light. His answer occupies the rest of the book. Here he tells us that in his theft "[his] evil deed had, as a cause, nothing other than [the desire to do] evil itself."[52] This is the strange and terrible thing of which he accuses himself.

II,v,10-II,vi,14. Evil for evil's sake

Augustine insists over and again that he was not compelled to steal by any necessity of his sensitive nature such as hunger or poverty.[53] Not that hunger or poverty would justify his theft or render it innocent, since he has shown that the law is broken even if we steal in order to live. But, had he needed the pears for food, this would have constituted a sufficient reason for his action such as he wants to discover. This was not the case, so he must look elsewhere.

The appetites of man embrace not merely bodily necessities but also the entire spectrum of goods which his rational nature is able to conceive. In II,vi,10 Augustine gives us a list of such goods, which he divides in two parts. In the "better and upper" part are "God, your truth and your law."[54] In the lowest part are (*i*) not bodies as such but their beauty which attracts each of the five senses, (*ii*) honour, power, and command in this world, and (*iii*) life itself because of its own grace, its harmonious relationship to other lower goods, and friendship.[55] These are the rational goods which a person can desire and for their sake also one might commit a crime.[56]

Indeed, as Augustine notes (in II,v,11), when an inquiry is made into the cause of a crime the only reason that is normally believed is the apparent possibility of obtaining some of these positive goods which are either sensible or rational — or else through fear of their loss.[57] But neither was the reason for which Augustine stole the pears. He certainly didn't want them for food since he scarcely bothered to taste them[58] and had better at home.[59] Nor did he want them for any of the rational qualities he has listed, since he flung them away to some pigs almost as soon as they had been stolen.[60]

Because he did not steal for any positive good that he saw in the pears, he concludes that what he loved must have been the crime itself.[61] Here his inquiry moves inward and he asks what it was that he loved, or could love, in the very act of stealing. "What was it that I, a wretch, loved in you, O my theft, O crime of darkness which was mine in that sixteenth year of my life?" (II,vi,12).[62]

Since his theft was not directed toward obtaining any positive end, neither could it have the beauty or substantial reality of any of the positive orders of creation from the highest to the lowest.

> And now, O Lord my God, I ask what I saw to be good in my theft, and behold, there is no beauty in it. I deny that it has, [i] a beauty like that which there is in equity and prudence nor, [ii] like that which there is in the mind of man and in memory and the senses and vegetative life nor, [iii] is it beautiful as the stars are beautiful and suited to their places, and as the earth and sea, full of progeny which without cease replace the dying with the new-born nor, [iv] does it even

have the sort of shadowy and defective beauty that is found in deceiving vices. (II,vi,12)[63]

Here Augustine has given a summary of the main divisions of the *created* goods of the universe. At the top he places (*i*) equity and prudence (n.b., *not* wisdom — *sapientia* — which is divine), followed (*ii*) by the mind of man, memory, the senses and life, (*iii*) heavenly and earthly bodies and finally, (*iv*) the small and shadowy good that belongs even to man's vices.

In none of these first three classes of goods could Augustine find the reason or cause for his theft. And yet, if it was devoid of all substantial good or positive content, how was it even possible to speak about it — since one cannot speak of a nothing? "For you were not beautiful since you were a theft. But in truth are you anything so that I can reason the case with you?" (II,vi,12).[64] There was only one alternative. Augustine turns (in II,vi,13) to consider the "shadowy and defective beauty" that belongs to human vices: the lowest form of good in the summary of created goods which he has just given. His catalogue of human vices shows that even these activities have in them some kind of beauty and good, inasmuch as they are all imitations of a real good which men apprehend in their true form outside of themselves: thus pride imitates true superiority (found absolutely in God), ambition seeks real honours and glory (present only in God), etc.[65] From this he concludes:

> Just so does the soul *fornicate* when it turns *away from you* (Ps. 72:27) and seeks apart from you those things which it cannot find pure and clear except when it returns to you. All thus perversely imitate you even when they turn away from you and raise themselves up against you. By the very fact that they imitate you they show that you are the creator of all nature and thus that there is nowhere where they can go to be in any way away from you. (II,vi,14)[66]

But if all vice *must* be the imitation of some positive good perceived, Augustine asks again, "What therefore did I love in that theft and in what way did I try by it, perversely and corruptly, to imitate my Lord?" (II,vi,14).[67]

The answer is extraordinary. Augustine does not find the cause of his theft in any of those vices which he has presented. It is, as it were, off the scale but at the same time it is the ground of the possibility of committing any of them. It has at once less reality or beauty in it than grief, the last and least of the faults he has enumerated, since he says that his theft did not even have the shadowy species of good that is found in *any* of the vices that he lists — and yet for the same reason it was also in some way worse than the first of them, pride:[68] as he has said, by it he was brought "to the very bottom of the deep" (II,iv,9).[69] But if the good that he sought in the very act of stealing is none of those listed, what then was it? Augustine gives his final answer, as he so often does, in a rhetorical question.

> Did I enjoy going against your law even if only in appearance — since I did not have the power to actually break it — so that, though bound under the law in truth, I might have a pretend liberty, getting a shadowy likeness of omnipotence, by doing unpunished what was forbidden? (II,vi,14)[70]

This is the cause or reason why he stole and it is, as he says, "a foul, abominable thing" (II,x,18).[71] His desire was not to imitate God in respect to any of his particular attributes, but in respect to his essential characteristic as God: his freedom and omnipotence. This Augustine sought to achieve by doing unpunished what, according to the laws of the rational universe, it is not permitted to do — i.e., to steal. His thought went like this. "Everyone knows there is a divine law which forbids theft, so if I can steal and get away with it this will show that I am not subject to God or to any divine law. And if I am not subject to any law which defines what is good, then the good will simply be what I say it is. Hence I will be free and omnipotent. I can do what I want and what I want is the good." It is no wonder that he ends these two chapters with words of total abhorrence. "O rottenness, O monstrosity of life and depth of death!" (II,vi,14).[72]

II,vii,15. These sins are not unique

The seriousness which Augustine attaches to this theft now seems fully justified and it is Oliver Wendell Holmes' remark that appears to be wide of the mark. This is true even of the implication that in it he was worse than Catiline. In Sallust's history, Catiline, an impoverished patrician who in 63 B.C. had attempted to set fire to Rome and stir up a rebellion through Italy just so that he could get office and pay off his debts, was said to be "by preference cruel and evil without reason."[73] As such he would appear to be like Augustine, and by Augustine's day Catiline's name had become a byword for ferocious, pointless cruelty. Nevertheless Augustine has noted (in II,v,11) that, whatever was commonly said of him, Sallust clearly states that his savage cruelty did have a reason, "lest through disuse his hand or heart become useless."[74] In this his evil was clearly less than Augustine's who had no end in mind but evil itself.

He has shown us how in this theft he had, for the first time, consciously and actually moved into an absolute opposition to the rational order of the universe. The potential to do so existed from the moment of his birth, but it was only at this point that the potency became actual through his effort to substitute his subjectivity for the rational order of the universe. Indeed it was just by this act, because done for no natural end, that Augustine came to his 'spiritual' maturity — if by this we understand the actual appearance of a free rational subject (or person) with an identity *explicitly* beyond the needs and limits of the natural.

Augustine is very precise when he identifies this as the sin of adolescence rather than childhood. Like his sensitive nature which came to maturity through reaching its universal end in the ability to reproduce, so his rational nature also came to maturity when it arrived at its universal end through recognizing the universal *qua* universal. This is exactly what he must have done to be capable of attempting to avoid his subjection to God and the divine law. What he sought to oppose through his theft was not this or that human authority, in the manner of children, but the rational laws of the universe, clearly recognized and brazenly rejected. Having done this he became capable of all the 'adult' vices listed in the catalogue of II,vi,13. These sins are a perverted imitation of the good and they presuppose that a person actually recognizes the good *qua* good. They differ from the sin of a child who only knows the good on the authority of others. Thus he asks, in another rhetorical question, "what evil was I not able to do, who had loved sin for its own sake?"[75] This is why he says that this sin brought him to "the very bottom of the deep'' (II,iv,9).[76] In principle this is the furthest one can go in opposition to the rational order of the universe and its maker.

Although this theft was peculiar to Augustine and his few companions, it is clear that the implications of such an act will be the same for all those who have ever done a similar thing and sought to put their subjectivity in place of the rational order of creation. Of course Augustine recognized that some of his readers might not have gone as far as he did either in the want of chastity or in the want of innocence. But such people do not fall outside the scope of his argument. He asks specifically, as if in anticipation of the reader's objection that such things do not concern him:

> What man is there who, on considering his own weakness, dares to attribute either his chastity or his innocence to his own powers so that he should love you the less as if he has less need of your mercy . . . ? . . . rather indeed let him love you the more because he sees that the same one by whom I was freed from such great weaknesses in respect of my sins is also the one through whom he sees that he is spared involvement in such great weaknesses in respect of [his] sin.[77]

The point is clear. The person who has not succumbed to these wrongs cannot ascribe either his chastity or his innocence to his own virtue, because in this case he would be chaste or innocent merely because he had not realized the potential of his nature to be otherwise. A child who has not reached puberty is actually chaste — but he is not chaste in the same sense as an adult who can actually be otherwise. Neither can he rightly be said to be free from adult crimes who has not yet affirmed the rational individuality or personality which makes them possible. Indeed, the chastity and innocence which Augustine shows that he lacked as an adolescent can only be had by losing those which he first possessed as a child. And that first innocence once lost, can no more be regained than can an adolescent return to childhood. Having once willed and consciously realized his absolute opposition to the universe, he cannot return directly to the earlier, immediate and unconscious innocence except by an act of his own — he must now will to return. But to return to his starting point he would have to will an innocence which was innocent just because it was not willed. There is no going back.

II,viii,16-II,ix,17. The exceedingly unfriendly friendship

Of course the effort to assert his freedom was futile. His rational powers could not escape from the law of non-contradiction. The freedom which he gained could only be illusory since every theft and, more broadly speaking, every kind of self-contradictory behaviour inexorably entails its own punishment.[78] Augustine asks, in a bitter pun, what fruit he had from these deeds — pointing chiefly to the theft but also to his fornications, since both have the same formal character as efforts to pervert the divine order to the desires of the individual. The difference is that in his fornications he was not intentionally and self-consciously opposing the natural order itself, although this was actually the result, whereas in relation to the rational order he had not other purpose. He asks:

> *What fruit* did I, wretched man, ever have *from these things* (Rom. 6:21), the
> recollection of which makes me now blush for shame, and chiefly in that theft
> in which I loved the theft itself, nothing else . . . ? (II,viii,16)[79]

At first sight this question is puzzling since he has already shown that he loved
nothing but the theft itself, in which his purpose was to arrogate to himself the
freedom and omnipotence of God. But then why does he raise this question? To
understand we must bear in mind that Augustine is striving to discover an adequate reason for his theft. The problem is that the desire for the omnipotence of
God, considered by itself, is inadequate as an explanation of this act. In order for
him to actually be free of the divine law it is not enough that, alone, he merely will
it to be so. It is also necessary that there be some objective recognition that this
was the case — that he had achieved an independence. But this is precisely what
the universe would not give him; since Augustine could not force it to do so, his
theft cannot be understood, in any direct sense, as achieving this end. For who
recognized his liberty except himself? The effort to pervert the universal order in
this way is, objectively speaking, impossible and so the question remains as to
why he did it.

This is why he asks what, objectively, he got out of it. In searching for an
answer he was driven to recollect another element which he had so far overlooked.
He recalled with certainty that by himself alone he would never have done it.
Indeed, as he will show, by himself alone he could never have done it since such
an act, done for this purpose, is quite impossible unless there are at least two
people of the same mind. ''And yet alone I would never have done it — this, as I
recall, was the state of my soul at the time — alone I absolutely would not have
done it'' (II,viii,16).[80]

The reason is the following. The universe will not recognize the freedom and
omnipotence which Augustine desired to establish for himself. But in order to be
established objectively it must in some way be recognized by someone other than
Augustine — unless he was to retreat into idiocy. But by whom? If he had tried to
flaunt the deed in front of his parents, or the farmer he had robbed, they certainly
would not have let him go unpunished.[81] He could only get the recognition he
desired from others who desired and got the same thing from him in return. The
reality escapes man, the illusion he can have. ''Behold, here is a servant fleeing
from his Lord and getting a shadow'' (II,vi,14)[82] — i.e., the illusory, insubstantial
imitation of the real freedom of a master. But then, as Augustine concludes, it was
not precisely for nothing that he stole but for the love of those with whom he stole.
From them he acquired, in their regard, not the substance of freedom and omnipotence, but its illusion.

> Therefore what I loved in this business was the company of those with whom I
> did it. I did not therefore love nothing but the theft — or rather, I loved nothing
> other [than nothing] because the company I loved was itself a nothing.
> (II,viii,16)[83]

This ''friendship'' of like-minded companions is the meagre fruit he got from
this deed. It is also the very condition of the possibility that such an act could be
the means of realizing the desires to be free of God's law. Without these others he
neither could, not would, have stolen for this purpose and his desire for an abso-

lute independence would therefore have remained an unrealized potency of his nature.

In fact Augustine could only gain the omnipotence he desired in a horribly false and perverted sense through the creation of a tiny sodality, whose members gave one another the illusion of absolute freedom which the universe denied them in reality. They got the illusion through their complicity in such wanton and destructive acts as the gratuitous theft of pears; by doing unpunished what they knew to be punishable, each one satisfied the other that he had the omnipotence all desired. Such a company, such a gang, was, as Augustine says, a very unfriendly kind of friendship.[84] It was a tiny society which catered exclusively to mutual sin, coming together for no other purpose than to give its members falsely what none could have in truth. Because this is the only way in which the desire for absolute freedom can be recognized and satisfied objectively, no one can resist the importunities of any other member of the gang when he says, "Let's go and do this or that." Aiming for omnipotence Augustine achieved only impotence. Here are his last words from this chapter on the nature of the gang and his relation to it.

> O exceedingly unfriendly friendship, inscrutable seducer of the mind. Out of the game and a jest came the avid desire to harm and the eagerness to hurt another without any thought to my own advantage, without any expectation of revenge, but simply because someone says, "Let's go, let's go do it," and one is ashamed not to be shameless. (II,ix,17)[85]

Only thus, by a slavish pandering to one another's illicit desires, is the shadowy likeness of God's true freedom and omnipotence established and maintained. Elsewhere Augustine argues that the same logic operated between Adam and Eve.[86] At the start of this book he had already noticed the same unfriendly friendship and the same slavish adherence to the whims of a gang in relation to the fornications of his adolescence. By boasting among such "friends" about his sexual prowess he had tried to established the illusion of his freedom from the sensitive order of nature which he could not have in truth. There too the price of illusion was a bondage to the beastly.

> I, to avoid being called a sissy, made myself worse than I really was, and when there was nothing I had actually done to make me equal to the really depraved, I pretended to have done what I had not done, lest I would seem to be worse because I was more innocent and lest I be taken to be more vile because I was [actually] more chaste. (II,iii,7)[87]

II,x,18. Conclusion

It is no wonder that Augustine concludes by recoiling in horror and disgust from what he has discovered to be the sins which he did in his adolescence. "It is a filthy business. I don't want to think about it, / I don't want to look at it."[88] His final word is that at this time he had made himself into a "place of want," "a wasteland" — a *regio egestatis*. He has shown that in his adolescence he willed nothing less than the negation of the being, life and truth of the universe as a whole. Through his fornications and through the theft of pears he had tried to pervert the natural and rational orders themselves, considered *qua* orders, to his own private desires. And in both, but in the latter especially and self-consciously, he set himself in absolute opposition to the universe and to the designs of its maker. Against the full richness of creation he preferred the narrow and empty desires of his own soul in its isolation from all the rest. And he could maintain this only by negating every positive good. The form of his negations — his actual fornications, bragging about what he had not actually done with a girl, the waste of a few pears — are very small things from a worldly point of view but inwardly and in truth they brought him as far from the truth as it is possible to go. "I turned away from you my God and *I erred* (Ps. 118:176), / I went very far from the path of your stability in my adolescence / and I became to myself a wasteland."[89]

In these words Augustine brings this book to a close with perfect symmetry. He began with the affirmation that in this period his fault consisted in turning from God, the one, and wasting himself in the many. We now see that he not only perverted his natural powers from their proper end through unrestricted fornication but also his rational powers through the attempted perversion of the rational order of the universe to his subjective desires. Having sought to avoid God's law he only managed to bring on himself what was indeed a divine punishment — subservience to an irrational and endless sexual desire cut off from its natural purpose, and subjection to the ever changing and irrational demands of the gang. This will be his starting point in Book III.

NOTES

1 The reason for this division between early and late adolescence is explained at the start of Chapter 3 under the heading, "Augustine's method."

2 For references to the new period see II,i,1 (adolescence) *in adulescentia* (25/10), II,ii,2 (puberty) *pubertatis* (25/18), II,ii,4 (his sixteenth year) *anno/meae* (27/2), II,iii,6 (all the above) *Sed/adulescentia* (28/1-6).

3 *Recordari/meus* (25/2-4). In this passage I understand that "My filthy deeds" refer to his literal fornications, and the "fleshly corruptions of my soul" to the theft of pears: (i) and (ii) respectively in the text of the quotation at n. 5.

4 See *Amore/evanui* (25/4-9).

5 *Exarsi/hominum* (25/9-13). The *silvescere* — lit., "of the grapevine, to grow or run wild, to run to wood" (*ALD*) — recalls the image Augustine has already used in I,xvii,27 where he spoke of his soul as a *palmes* (21/16) — "a young branch or shoot of a vine, a vine sprout" (*ALD*).

6 See the discussion of this phrase in the commentary on I,xiii,21. Augustine frequently uses the word 'fornication' in this second book as the epitome of the sin of adolescence. In II,ii,2 and II,iii,7 it is applied to his literal fornications and in II,vi,4, to his spiritual fornication. In the latter text he gives an explanation of this usage, *Ita/te* (33/28-30) — this passage is translated at n. 66.

7 *dum/evanui* (25/8-9).

8 *et/evanui* (25/7-10).

9 See above, n. 5.

10 See II,iii,5 where Augustine uses the image of his soul or heart as a field lacking cultivation: *dummodo/mei* (27/28-30). This is closely related to the image of his soul as a young vine, see above, n. 5.

11 *sicut/domine* (26/6-7).

12 Augustine speaks of this divine law against lust — i.e., sex with the end of pleasure rather than procreation — several other times in this chapter. See II,ii,3 *excessi/tua* (26/23), II,ii,4 *omnes/meas* (26/26), *inlicitae/tuas?* (27/4-5).

13 *Et/amari?* (25/14-15).

14 See the *libido* of II,ii,2 (25/20), II,ii,4 (27/4), II,iii,6 (28/4), and II,iii,7 (29/4).

15 See *nebula* (25/17) and *caligo* (25/20).

16 *luminosus limes amicitiae* (25/16). See the note in de Labriolle's edition of the *Confessions* on the *dealbatiores vias* of VII,vi,8 (133/25-26) — the "whitened roads" — i.e., those repaired with lime caulking (quoted in *BA*, Vol. 13, pp. 598-99). The sense of "luminous, bright" here is that he did not stay on the well-kept (i.e., bright) main road of true friendship but left this highway for dark, shady and tortuous ways.

17 *ab animo usque ad animum* (25/15-16). In this Augustine agrees with the classical tradition that friendship was a union of souls and a friend a second self. Augustine speaks this way in IV,vi,11 where he quotes Horace, *Odes*, I,3,8 (62/7-8). For other references to this tradition see E. A. Clark, *Jerome, Chrysostom, and Friends: Essays and Translations*, Studies in Women and Religion, Vol. 2, New York and Toronto, Edwin Mellen Press, 1979, pp. 41-44.

18 In III,ii,1, speaking of the same period, Augustine says that what he sought was the "touch of sensible [bodies]" — *contactu sensibilium* (37/6-7). He makes the same point in other words in II,ii,2.

19 See *Sed/flagitiorum* (25/15-22).

20 See *atque/flagitiorum* (25/22).

21 See Chapter One, n. 44.

22 See *fine/nostrae* (26/5-8). Here Augustine uses both his images of human affairs — as uncultivated growth, and as turbulent waters.

23 See II,ii,3 *potens/seclusarum?* (26/8-9). Augustine's teaching on the true form of human sexuality as it was in Eden, and on the nature and reason of its present condition in fallen man, may be found in a very clear form in *DCD*, XIV, 10-28 and *DGC*, II, 39-43.

24 Of the time before his conversion, Augustine mentions over and again that he supposed he could never live without a woman. See for example VI,xi,20 and VI,xv,25. After his conversion, in which he resolved to live a life of chastity (VIII,xii,30), and did so from that moment on (X,xxxi,47), his sexual drives still continued to trouble him — see X,xxx,41-43 where he speaks of the problems that still plagued him at the time of writing the tenth book, around 400, when he would have been in his mid forties. For a discussion of these matters see Starnes, "The Place and Purpose."

25 See II,ii,3 *ut/contenta* (26/3-6). In the *Confessions* Augustine insists that, so far as human sexuality is concerned, the only rational (i.e., divine) purpose of marriage is a union for the sake of having children. See for example the formula he uses in IV,ii,2 *foederatum esset generandi gratia* (55/13-14). But see also Clark, "Adam's Only Companion," who shows convincingly that alongside this view Augustine also developed a notion of the end of marriage as companionship — valid even if sexual union was neither realized nor intended, as in the case of Joseph and Mary. Clark argues that this social side of Augustine's consideration of marriage was overshadowed by its sexual and reproductive purpose due to the continued requirements of his polemic against the Manichees first, then against Pelagians. For a less modern understanding of this companionate marriage see below, n. 86.

26 See II,ii,3 *Aut/tuos* (26/11-21). On the importance of this distinction between marriage and chastity, see VIII,i,2 where Augustine rejects the possibility of becoming a married Christian (i.e., a Christian who can still have sexual relations with a woman), because he refused to join the church unless he could do so totally (i.e., as a celibate).

27 See *cum/libidinis* (27/2-4).

28 *Sed/mortalium?* (26/22-24).

29 *tu/te* (26/24-30).

30 *Et/eram* (29/13-15).

31 See II,ii,3 *Quis/seclusarum?* (26/1-9) and II,ii,4 *Non/dictione* (27/5-8).

32 See II,iii,7 *Volebat/uxorem* (28/21-24) and II,iii,8 *monuit me pudicitiam* (29/18).

33 See II,iii,4 "the insane search for pleasure which is allowed by human infamy" — *vesania/humanum* (27/3-4).

34 The phrase "she-clog" for *compes uxoria* (29/13) — lit. "with the shackle of a wife" — is from the Watts translation (*Loeb*).

35 *Qui/me* (28/24-29).

36 *relaxabantur/mea* (29/30-30/3). This image of his condition as a sickness is the fifth of the great images we have so far come across which Augustine uses through the first part of the *Confessions* — it goes along with the image of his sin as fornication, of his soul as an uncultivated field or vine, and of human society as troubled waters or composed of drunken madmen.

37 See II,iii,5 *Quis/esset?* (27/21-25).

38 See II,ii,4 *Non/dictione* (27/5-8), II,iii,5 *cum/mei* (27/26-30), and II,iii,8 *sed/inania* (29/24-26).

39 *extollebat laudibus* (27/21-22).

40 See II,iii,5 *cum/mei* (27/26-30), II,iii,6 *excesserunt/suae* (28/3-11), and II,iii,8 *sed/meorum* (29/24-30). By way of mitigating this judgement Augustine adds that his father was, at the time, still only a catechumen and a new one at that (II,iii,6 *nam/erat* — 28/12-13). He was thus still involved in his natural and worldly interests, much as Augustine was after he had come to think of himself as a catechumen when he left the Manichees. For a less Augustinian view of the efforts Patricius made on his son's behalf, see Brown, *Augustine*, pp. 21, 26, 31, 37. He makes the point (p. 21) that "A classical education was one of the only passports to success for such men." With such an education Augustine could aspire, as he did, to rise above the lot of the common man and join the bureaucracy of the empire (see VI,xi,19 "or I could be given a presidency" — *vel praesidatus dari potest* — 118/10; on the office of *praesidatus*, governor of the lowest of the three classes of provinces, see *BA*, Vol. 13, p. 560, n. 1).

41 See II,iii,8 *Non/meae* (29/15-17).

42 See II,iii,6 *Itaque/faciem* (28/13-16).

43 See II,iii,8 *illa/doctrinae* (29/26-29).

44 See II,iii,8 *si/poterat* (29/21).

45 See II,iii,8 *ita/meorum* (29/18-30). This passage means that Monica gave up her admonitions when she heard from Patricius that Augustine had reached puberty — which he knew from having seen him in the baths: it should be read in conjunction with II,iii,6 *Quin/adulescentia* (28/4-6).

46 *in imo abyssi* (30/21).

47 Quoted in Brown, *Augustine*, p. 172, n. 5.

48 See II,v,11 for Augustine's reference to Catiline, and n. 73 below. Commentators who do not find any internal logic for Augustine's lengthy treatment of his theft are bound to look for an external reason. Courcelle, for example (*Recherches*, pp. 51-52), cites a similar story about Macarius the Egyptian, noted by Vischer, of Macarius' great grief over a minor theft. He concludes that Augustine's account is simply "romaine" — an exaggerated statement in conformity with an ancient literary tradition that made much ado over nothing. The parallel is striking but the problem with this external juxtaposition of texts is that it prejudges the issue. Macarius explains Augustine's comparison of himself and Catiline, in Courcelle's sense, *only* if one assumes that such a theft is, and can only be, a mere peccadillo. As we will see, the whole purpose of Augustine's lengthy treatment is to demonstrate that the opposite was the case.

49 See II,iii,8 *et/mea* (29/32-30/2) and n. 36 above. Augustine took the image from Ps. 72:7.

50 *Furtum/inopia* (30/4-7). The Scriptural references of the *BA* edition, which are wonderfully complete, fail to note the locus of this important text — *lex scripta in cordibus hominum* — "the law written on men's hearts" — in Rom. 2:15 (*qui ostendunt opis) legis scripta in cordibus (suis)*.

51 Augustine has already stated and discussed this principle in I, xviii, 29. On the inevitability of punishment see the formula of I,xii,19 *Iussisti/animus* (15/19-20). Solignac (*BA*, Vol. 13, pp. 663-64), without identifying this with the law of non-contradiction, notes that Augustine's teaching about this inner law echoes Cicero and Stoic sources. This is probably true but too much should not be made of the point. As the quotation he gives makes clear, the Stoics

identified their principle with the "reason and spirit of the sage" while Augustine's point, like Aristotle's, is that this law is present in everyone in the act of understanding anything at all, and not just in the wise man.

52 *malitiae/malitia* (30/23-24).

53 See II,iv,9 *Et/appetebam* (30/7-11), II,vi,12 *pulchra/erat* (32/14-19), and II,viii,16 *Sed/erat* (35/20-21).

54 *meliora/tua* (31/13-14).

55 See *Etenim/animis* (30/29-31/11). I understand that the three categories of lower goods correspond, as created images, of the three categories of higher, uncreated goods. The punctuation of Skutella's text makes friendship a fourth item in the lower category but I take the *quoque* (31/9) as subjoining what follows to the former sentence. Solignac (*BA*, Vol. 13, p. 664) also recognizes a tripartite division of the goods in this chapter but his discussion is not tied closely to this text.

56 See II,v,10 *Propter/tue* (31/11-15).

57 See II,v,11 *Cum/amittendi* (31/18-21).

58 See II,iv,9 *etiamsi/comedimus* (30/18-19), and II,vi,12 *Nam/erat* (32/18-19).

59 See II,iv,9 *quod/melius* (30/10), and II,vi,12 *Erat/copia* (32/15).

60 See II,iv,9 *et/porcis* (30/17-18).

61 See II,iv,9 *nec/peccato* (30/11-12), and II,vi,12 *illa/erat* (32/15-19).

62 *Quid/meae?* (32/7-9).

63 *Et/fallentibus* (32/19-27).

64 *Non/te?* (32/9-10).

65 This list of vices does not seem to come directly from any of the obvious pagan sources such as Aristotle's *Ethics*, nor from any list in Scripture (but see Gal. 5:19-21 and Augustine's use of it in *DCD*, XIV,2), nor from any other Christian source I am aware of. His list includes the following fifteen items in this order: (*i*) *superbia* (pride, which imitates superiority), (*ii*) *ambitio* (ambition, going about for honour and glory), (*iii*) *saevitia* (ferociousness, the desire to be feared), (*iv*) *blanditia lascivientium* (the caresses of the lascivious, who want to be loved), (*v*) *curiositas* (curiosity, which wants to be seen to be eager to know), (*vi*) *ignorantia* (ignorance, which covers itself with the name of simplicity, (*vii*) *stultitia* (folly, covering itself under the name of innocence), (*viii*) *ignavia* (sloth, which desires quiet), (*ix*) *luxuria* (luxury, desiring to be seen as fullness and abundance), (*x*) *effusio* (extravagance, which is the shadow of liberality), (*xi*) *avaritia* (avarice, which wants to possess all), (*xii*) *invidentia* (envy, seeking excellence), (*xiii*) *ira* (anger, seeking revenge), (*xiv*) *timor* (fear of sudden and unseen threats to the things it loves, wanting safety), (*xv*) *tristitia* (grief bemoaning the loss of things it desired, wanting nothing to be taken from itself). Without working out the complicated relations between the items in this list, two points at least can be made. First, I understand that the list is intended to be inclusive of all human vices. This appears in the fact that the first and last terms (i.e., *superbia* and *tristitia*) are opposite poles. On Scriptural authority Augustine accepted and taught that "*pride is the beginning of all sin* (Ecclus. 10:13)" (*DCD*, XII,6) and, in this list, grief is the negative opposite of pride. Where pride positively claims for itself God's loftiness and is, one might say, the closest imitation of God, grief stands at the opposite pole, bemoaning the loss of all goods and is in this sense the most unlike God from whom nothing can be taken. Secondly, I suggest that Augustine treats these fifteen vices as falling into three groups of five each, with each group containing vices that are, in a special sense, perverted imitations of the Father, Son, and Holy Spirit respectively. The only clear oppositions within the list (and thus its clear divisions), are those between the fifth and sixth terms (curiosity/ignorance), and the tenth and eleventh (extravagance/avarice).

66 *Ita/recedatur* (33/28-34/2).

67 *Quid/sum?* (34/2-4).

68 See II,vi,12 *non/fallentibus* (32/26-27).

69 *in imo abyssi* (30/21).

70 *An/similitudine?* (34/4-7).

71 *Foeda est* (36/15).

72 *O/profunditas!* (34/9): compare this *putredo* with the *computrescere* of II,i,1. See the similar revulsion in the final chapter, II,x,18.

73 Sallust, *Bellum Catilinae* 16, quoted by Augustine in II,v,11 — *gratuito/erat* (31/29-30). On Catiline see H. H. Scullard's succinct account (*From the Gracchi to Nero: A History of Rome from 133 B.C. to A.D. 68*, London and New York, Methuen, 1958, pp. 105-10). Sallust deals only with one episode in the story. Of the many possible Romans whose names might have become synonymous with doing harm for harm's sake, Catiline owes his notoriety to Cicero's sententious accounts of how he foiled the conspiracy. Although Catiline doubtless deserved to be regarded as a "man without reason and excessively cruel" (*vaecordi et nimis crudeli homine* — 31/28-29) in his own right, it seems to me likely that by Augustine's day, the characterization had been assimilated to Vergil's poetic representation of the type — in the ferocious Mezentius, "scorner of the gods," (*Aeneid* VII, 648) who went so far in his mindless savagery as to tie together the living and the dead as a form of torture (*Aeneid* VIII, 481-88).

74 Sallust, *Bellum Catilinae* 16 quoted by Augustine in II,v,11 — *ne/animus* (31/30 — 32/1).

75 *quid/amavi?* (34/18-19).

76 *in imo abyssi* (30/21).

77 *Quis/tua* (34/21-25), *immo/inplicari* (34/30-35/3). The translators of the *BA* edition (Vol. 13, p. 355) call this chapter (II,vii,15) a "digression." It is not so once we see that it was necessary if Augustine's argument was to include those who could say that they had never fornicated like him nor stolen for such a purpose. I understand that by "his chastity or his innocence," he refers to both aspects of the sin of adolescence which he discusses in this book: see below, n. 79.

78 See I,xii,19 *Iussisti/animus* (15/19-20).

79 *Quem/aliud* (35/4-6). I take it that the plural *his* (35/5) — "these things" — refers both to the want of chastity and the lack of innocence exemplified by the theft of pears — i.e., the two things in the text quoted above, n. 77.

80 *Et/fecissem* (35/7-9). In the same chapter Augustine distinguishes between a theft done for these reasons, which is impossible without companions, and one done for the sake of some positive good, which can be done alone — *quia/meae?* (35/16-20). See also II,ix,17 *At/solus* (36/4-5).

81 See II,ix,17 *vehementer nolebant* (35/28) — "the owners were furious" (trans. Pine-Coffin, Penguin).

82 *Ecce/umbram* (34/7-8). Without insisting that the parallelism was intended, it is worth noting that the theft of pears stands in the same relation to Augustine's life as does the theft of the fruit of the tree of knowledge of good and evil in relation to the life of the human race according to the cosmogony of Genesis (2:3f.). Augustine's story represents the moment in which the individual goes into conscious opposition to God: the Genesis story, the moment in which the human race does so. The difference is that whereas Augustine realized a potency of his nature, the myth of the fall aims to explain how we came to have such a nature.

83 *Ergo/est* (35/9-12).

84 In II,ix,17 Augustine mentions — almost in passing — that he and his friends got a great laugh out of the incident in imagining the anger of the owners. With marvellous rigour he pauses to ask if perhaps this laughter was not, after all, a positive good which he sought in the theft. This would overthrow what he has just concluded — but all the same he asks if he joined with the others because we have ordinarily to be with friends to enjoy a laugh. He was able to reject this explanation when he recalled that, while we will sometimes laugh alone, he is certain he would not have done the theft alone. In other words the explanation he has given can stand.

85 *O/inpudentem* (36/9-12).

86 I am thinking here of the argument Augustine presents in *DCD* (XIV,11) where, following the Genesis account of the fall, and 1 Tim. 2:14 ("And Adam was not deceived, but the woman was deceived and became a transgressor"), he concludes that Eve only was deceived by the serpent. To the question as to why Adam went along with her, he answers, "he however was unwilling to be separated from his only companion." In the light of what he has said in the

Confessions — about the impossibility of opposing God's order unless one can at least get the illusion of freedom from another human being — I think Augustine probably had this thought in mind in giving his answer in the *City of God*. Adam's choice was between joining Eve's 'gang' where each of them would agree that the other was "like [the] gods" (Gen. 3:5) or, by staying with God, losing her to madness. The choice is the same as Augustine's when one of his friends said "Let's take some of so and so's pears — he'll be furious." This gives a somewhat more somber view of what Clark calls Augustine's "social view of marriage" (as opposed to seeing it simply in its sexual and reproductive function) and about which she says, "Had he developed its implication unswervingly ... [he] would have arrived at a notion of marital friendship unique for his time and place" (Clark, "Adam's Only Companion," p. 139). I do not think Augustine was anywhere near to leaving his time and place.

87 *Ego/castior* (29/6-10).

88 *Foeda/videre* (36/15-16).

89 *Defluxi/egestatis* (36/21-23). Because this *regio egestatis* parallels the expression of certain Neo-Platonic texts it (and the related *regio dissimilitudinis* of VII,x,16) are often cited as evidence of Augustine's dependence on Plotinus or Porphyry. It fits equally well however with the Scriptural image of the "land of want" — mentioned already in I,xviii,28 *"in regione illa ... coepit egere* (Lk. 15:14, Vulgate)" — in which the Prodigal Son found himself, having wasted his patrimony. Solignac (*BA*, Vol. 13, pp. 664-65) gives possible Neo-Platonic sources for the phrase: see also his discussion and references pp. 662-63, 682-93. On the other hand, L.C. Ferrari ("Symbols of Sinfulness in Book II of Augustine's *Confessions*," *Augustinian Studies*, 2 [1971], 93-104), treats of the phrase solely in terms of Biblical imagery with no mention of Neo-Platonic texts: see also, by the same author, "The Theme of the Prodigal Son in Augustine's *Confessions*" (*Recherches Augustiniennes*, 12 [1977], 105-18). It seems best to say that, at the time of writing, Augustine knew he was using words which would strike a chord in those who knew the Scriptures and in those who knew Neo-Platonic texts. There is no reason to prefer one over the other.

Chapter Three
COMMENTARY ON BOOK III

Early adolescence *(continued)*

Augustine's method: principle and practice

The first three chapters of Book III give a short account of Augustine's life between the theft of pears and the next stage, which began in his nineteenth year through a chance reading of Cicero's *Hortensius.*

What should we make of this curious division of books? If the reading of *Hortensius* was the start of a new period, why didn't he begin Book III with this episode and either omit the material in the first three chapters or else put them back at the end of Book II? In this way he would have had infancy and childhood in Book I, his early adolescence collected in Book II and, in Book II, nothing except what belonged directly to the next period.

Augustine does not explain why he divided things in this way but I think this is what he had in mind. The division between Book II and the first three chapters of Book III — both dealing with the same period of his life — is between a theoretical statement of the nature of his position and an account of the practical difficulties that resulted from it. These are what eventually forced him on to the next stage where he became a Manichee.

From principle to practice, and from practice to a new principle, is a pattern we will see over and again in the first nine books. The alteration and constant interplay of logical position and concrete history is just what gives the argument of the *Confessions* its unique character. We can see this in some detail if we turn to the text which is before us in III,i,1-III,iii,6.

Brief as they are, these chapters provide an account of the life which resulted from his determination to ignore the demands of the law. If he had moved directly from the theft of pears to the account of the next stage in his life we would have had no explanation of how he got from one position to the other. A bridge was needed if the account was not to be an abstract statement of various possible relations to God, rather than a history capable of ''exciting the heart.''

And, from the history of these difficulties — when related to the inadequacy of the position from which they arose — he shows how he was forced, by day-to-day events, to move to the more adequate theoretical position represented in Manichaeism. This aspect of the work prevents it from being merely a sensational account of particular incidents and makes it capable, as he also intended, of ''exciting the mind.''[1]

Notes to Chapter Three appear on pages 76-87.

III,i,1-III,iii,6. Life beyond the law

The general sense of these chapters is to show the kind of life Augustine led as a result of preferring his own desires to the demands of the rational order of the universe. Everything in these years was controlled by his determination to be free of any good which was not of his own choosing. In the argument of the second book we saw that Augustine acquired the illusion he could determine good and evil by denying any standard other than his will. This is a very different thing from when he, as a child, disobeyed this or that authority to suit his likes and dislikes. As a child he did not maintain that his natural inclinations were themselves rational. Recall what he had said of his childish disobediences: "I was not disobedient because I chose a better course, but *from a love of playing*" (I,x,16 — italics mine).[2] The case was very different after the theft of pears where his whole position depended on the ability to pretend that his desires were rational. His "play" was no longer opposed to reason but had now to be immediately identified with it.

III,i,1. The community of unfriendly friends

Augustine first describes the community in which he lived. "I came to Carthage / and everywhere about me / crackled the fires of abominable loves."[3] In these years his companions, his friends, his loves, were everything. "To love and to be loved was my heart's desire / and the more so if I could also enjoy the body of my lover."[4]

This does not look very different from the beginning of Book II: "And what was it that delighted me except to love and be loved?" (II,ii,2).[5] Here he says, "I was not yet in love, yet I loved to be in love"[6] and again, "I was looking for something to love / loving to love."[7] The difference seems slight but a great deal hangs on it. In the second book there is simply lust — the immediate pleasure a young man finds in the satisfaction of his sexual appetites. But this immediacy has been lost when he says, "Not yet in love, I loved to be in love." This is not passion but the need for passion. What does this mean and why was it so?

The answer is clear if we think of the position he was trying to maintain. His insistence that he was free of the law of non-contradiction had removed him from any community which recognized this principle. But this meant that he had effectively cut himself off not only from the state but also from (real) friends and even from his family. His only home was with the gang. And here he had, as it were, to create his position. He was a member only insofar as he could make those in the gang love him since, apart from their regard, he had no status. This is the source of his need to be loved. It had nothing to do with sexual passion as such, or at least only in a secondary sense as he has observed. The main thing was to belong — though it was good if he could also enjoy some girl's body.

If we look at this from the other side we see the same thing. He could claim that he was free of the divine law — and not think of himself as a criminal who merely broke the law while acknowledging its claims — only by insisting that his immediate desires were inherently rational. What he naturally liked and disliked was also what was, from the point of view of reason, good and evil. But having equated the good with his immediate natural pleasure he now found that the good must wait on desire. And so he was driven to hate himself for the paucity of his desires since these alone were what he could regard as good. "I was not yet in love yet I loved to be in love / and, with an inner want, I hated myself for having little want."[8] Eventually he found what he wanted. "I fell in love by which I desired to be taken"[9] — which is to say, into carnal love, the "touch of bodies."[10] But he was looking for the good in the sensual love of bodies without noticing that "if they did not have a soul they would not be loved at all."[11] The point is blunt. If the good is to be found in the touch of bodies, then a dead body without soul is as lovable as one that has a soul. This was not at all Augustine's situation. He needed his lover not merely as a body but as a rational soul who would tell him that he was wonderful and give him a place in the gang. Here we are brought back to the community of the unfriendly friendship — the only place in which such a "free" individual can exist.

As we know from the argument of the second book, the whole possibility of maintaining that one's natural likes and dislikes are rational, are goods and evils, is given through the mediation of another. In this case his lover who, just by complying with his desires, enabled him to maintain the illusion that he was *elegans et urbanus* — "out of the ordinary and special"[12] — meaning that the good, the right, and the beautiful were just what he said they were. But just because it was only through these others that he could preserve the illusion, he became absolutely dependent on his "friends." And the girl who assured him one minute that he was wonderful and sophisticated, going along with his every whim and agreeing with his every word, could just as easily turn against him in the next and he had no defence. He had taken a road sown with "traps"[13] since he had bound himself to accept her judgement without question as the price for her accepting his on similar terms. But the harmony experienced in the mutual enjoyment of particular goods could just as easily become strife and pain if his girl found anything attractive in another or if she expressed any opinion contrary to his own. Whenever this happened he had no recourse to an objective measure since this was the one thing his position ruled out from the beginning. If the lack of a lover was bad, having one turned out to be equally horrible.

> I fell in love
> by which I desired to be taken.
> *My God, my mercy,* (Ps. 58:18)
> with what a lot of bitterness did you in your goodness
> sprinkle that sweetness.
> Because, when I got to be loved
> and came secretly to the consummation which binds,
> and gladly let myself be bound in toilsome knots,
> the result was that I was lashed
> with the burning iron rods of jealousy and suspicions
> and fears and angers and quarrels.[14]

The logic of his position made such things inevitable.

III,ii,2-4. The theatre of illusion

Augustine now turns to the theatrical productions which took hold of his soul. These take us deeper into the life he then lived and, at the same time, show how he began to be freed from it. The facts of the case are stated in the opening sentence. "I was seduced by theatrical spectacles full of images of my own misery and fuel which fed my fires" (III,ii,2).[15]

In the previous chapter Augustine had shown the miseries to which he had bound himself in the world of the gang. The jealousies, suspicions, fears, angers, and quarrels which belonged to the position were certainly no delight when he actually suffered them — yet he tells that he loved to go to the theatre to be moved to sorrow by the same things represented on the stage.

> [the spectator] loves the authors of these fictions the more he is moved to sorrow. And if the agonies of men — either real men long since dead, or else imaginary characters — are so lamely treated that the spectator does not grieve, he gets up and leaves the theatre disgusted and grumbling. If however he is moved to a feeling of grief he remains intent and is delighted. (III,ii,2)[16]

To this Augustine asks, why? Why on earth did he want to be moved to sorrow by the representation of miseries which he hated in his own life? The answer lies in the necessary connection between mercy and misery when one looks to immediate sensations and emotions.

> Certainly all men desire to be joyful. But though no one likes to be miserable, one does like to be merciful and, because this cannot be without [prior] grief, is it not for this sole reason that sorrows are loved? (III,ii,3)[17]

Here is another of Augustine's questions which is really an answer. The point is simple. Where the emotions and natural pleasures are taken as the good, there pain and pleasure are, in the nature of things, mixed in with one another. Just as there is no pleasure in eating without the pain of a prior hunger, so there is no possibility of being compassionate without a prior cause for grief. Whoever, therefore, wants to enjoy the feeling of sympathy must first go looking for sorrow in order to have the pleasure of compassion in the end. And if he wants complete control, if he does not want to be subject to anything external, he will not wait on some actual calamity — where he would suffer a real grief — but will go to the theatre which panders to these desires. Its purpose is to "invite the spectator to sorrow" (III,ii,2)[18] and its griefs are safe because they have not happened to him but he has willed them.

This is the reverse of the coin he showed in the first chapter, where he began by looking for pleasure only to end up with pain. Here he went seeking a kind of pain in order to end up with pleasure and this too came from "that same stream of [unfriendly] friendship" (III,ii,3).[19] He means that shows of this sort cater to those who have chosen illusion over reality — and the one is as truly merciful as the other is truly friendly.

As opposed to a real or objective friendship which "prefers in the first place that there be no cause for grief" (III,ii,3),[20] and where one is called upon to give real help rather than merely being invited to sorrow, this whole business is entirely subjective. The rational distinctions of good and evil cannot be brought to bear where nothing is fixed and definite — where, as Augustine puts it, he rejoiced at one minute with the stage lovers when they got one another, was saddened in the next when they lost each other, and delighted in both his sadness and gladness alike.[21] Such theatre and such theatre-goers are in a world beyond reason.

All the same, the theatre was a relief from the actual miseries of his relationships, since here he was only a spectator. On the one hand he was sympathetically one with the characters on the stage but at the same time he had been sufficiently chastened by the reality of his loves to prefer to experience them in the attenuated form of a theatre-goer.

> [F]rom thence came the love of sorrows. Not for such as could wound me deeply — for I did not want to have to actually endure anything like the things I loved to watch — but for sorrows made up and listened to which were of a sort as to graze me superficially. (III,ii,4)[22]

This division between the enjoyment which he took in the irrational world of natural emotions and pleasures, as portrayed on the stage, and his revulsion from the same thing in his real life, led Augustine to the final step in repudiating the position he had adopted in the theft of pears.

III,iii,5-6. The worship of demons — divine and human

In these two paragraphs Augustine shows the very bottom he reached in this position and at the same time the things that made it impossible to remain in it. He discusses both in terms of the service of demons.

III,iii,5. Divine demons — In the Roman world the cults of the nature deities such as (the male) Dionysus, or the Great Mother, were the focus of the worship of natural immediacy — i.e., treating the natural as divine. In this paragraph Augustine tells how, by the logic of his position, he ended up doing service to such powers.

> In what iniquities did I flow away and with what a sacrilegious curiosity did I attend [the rites of demons] that, having abandoned you, it led me to the very bottom of falseness and the fallacious service of demons to whom I sacrificed my evil deeds.[23]

In the *City of God* Augustine describes his attendance at such services in Carthage in honour of the Heavenly Virgin (i.e., the Syrian Astarte = the Carthaginian titulary deity, Caelestis, assimilated by Augustine's day to Cybele, the Great Mother, of Mt. Berecynthia, the centre of her worship in Phrygia).[24]

> When I was a young man I used to go to sacrilegious shows and entertainments. I watched the antics of madmen; I listened to singing boys; I thoroughly enjoyed the most degrading spectacles put on in honour of gods and goddesses — in honour of the Heavenly Virgin, and of Berecynthia, mother of all. On the yearly festival of Berecynthia's purification the lowest kind of actors sang, in front of her litter, songs unfit for the ears of even one of those mountebanks, to say nothing of any decent citizen, or of a senator; while as for the Mother of the Gods — ! For there is something in the natural respect that we have towards our parents that the extreme of infamy cannot wholly destroy; and certainly those very mountebanks would be ashamed to give a rehearsal performance in their homes, before their mothers, of those disgusting verbal and acted

obscenities. Yet they performed them in the presence of the Mother of the Gods, before an immense audience of spectators of both sexes. (*DCD*, II,4)[25]

And further on,

> We had a good view of her image standing in front of her temple; there were crowds converging from all directions, everyone taking the best position he could find, and we watched the acted shows with the greatest interest. We divided our gaze between the processions of harlots on the one side, and the virgin goddess on the other. I saw prayerful worship offered to her, and indecent performances acted before her. I saw no sense of shame in the mimes, no trace of modesty in any actress — all the duly prescribed obscenities were punctiliously performed. It was well known what would please the maiden goddess; and the exhibitions would enable the matron to leave the temple for home enriched by her experiences.... There is an evil spirit which drives men's minds to wickedness by a secret compulsion, which goads men on to commit adultery and finds satisfaction when they do so; it is this same evil spirit which rejoices in such rites as these. (*DCD*, II,26)[26]

Such crude rites were normal in the late empire[27] and in the *Confessions* Augustine mentions, as an instance of his own involvement in such things, the fact that he "even dared, during the celebration of your [God's] service within the walls of your church, to desire and to do a thing worthy of procuring the fruit of death."[28] He does not say exactly what he did but we will not be very far wrong if we imagine some gross sexual act.[29] Here was another version of the theft of pears, but this time he thumbed his nose at God in his very house. The church forbade the worship of natural immediacy so Augustine had sex (?) within the walls of a church, during divine service, and thereby "proved" that God was impotent because he neither prevented nor punished the debauchery. His comment here is the same as his comment on the theft of pears: loving his own ways and not God's he merely loved "the false liberty of a runaway slave."[30]

Centuries before Augustine's time — in the late Republic and early Empire — the worship of natural immediacy in the cult of such like deities was still, officially, a "subordinate and disreputable aspect of Roman religion."[31] It was the refuge of those who sought to preserve the natural against the imposition of an apparently alien reason. This is what Vergil thought of the blind fury raised by Allecto.[32] In the *Aeneid* this naturalism is understood as opposed to the divine reason and is crushed by it in the fatal course of events leading to the general defeat of Turnus and the Latins at the hands of Aeneas. By the dying days of the Empire, in Augustine's time, the inadequacy of the abstract rational order imposed by the earlier view was keenly felt on every side. The formerly disreputable and inferior aspects of Roman religion had become increasingly respectable and prominent as all kinds of people sought to preserve and enjoy the natural against any subordination imposed by the abstract rationality of the divine word, or *fatum*.[33]

The whole course of Augustine's education shows how little the fourth century understood this divine reason which had moved Rome in former days — as for example with Aeneas. The result was that the *Aeneid* itself was taught for purely formal reasons or else with an eye to the grossest sentimentality.[34] Augustine, along with most of the rest of his world, could not be moved to sacrifice nature for the sake of Rome's divine mission. Yet we have also seen that, from the beginning of his adolescence, he did not merely want to revel in the natural as opposed to reason, but was looking to find reason in nature. By this logic he came to the worship of demons (i.e., divine powers in nature) where he discovered, in the religion of natural immediacy, only a pure senseless indecency with nothing rational about it.

III,iii,6. Human demons: the "Overturners" — Augustine ends the discussion of his early adolescence where it began — with the unfriendly friendship of a gang like the one with whom he stole the pears. The difference is that where he joined the first, he kept his distance from the second. This gang was a group of older students, fellows with Augustine in the rhetoric school in Carthage. Calling themselves the "Overturners,"[35] "they used wantonly to harass the shyness of new students whom they assailed for no cause but their own amusement and from this they fed their malevolent pleasures."[36] From a worldly point of view none of this was serious. Its modern equivalent would be the hazing of freshmen. Augustine allows that he admired these students but he makes it clear that he would have nothing to do with them *qua* gang.

> *[Y]ou know* (Ps. 68:6) I was much quieter, Lord, and altogether removed from all overturnings which the Overturners used to do — such was the cruel and diabolical name taken as a sign of urbanity — amongst whom I used to live, shamelessly shameful that I was not as they were. I was with them and their friendship I used formerly to delight in, whose deeds however I always abhorred, that is, their overturnings.[37]

He admired them because they still appeared to be the only free men who denied that anything beyond their own will was of any importance[38] — while the rest of humanity, bound by the limits of the law, were hopelessly servile. But Augustine found he could not join them, and the reason is clear. His aim, since the theft of pears, had been to adopt a position which was total, complete, and beyond any division of nature and reason. He had it all in himself, nothing else counted. As a result he had sought to find reason in his immediate nature. But he had discovered that this led to an endless succession of pain and pleasure in which both reason and nature were lost. Reason was lost because there was nothing for it to get hold of where there were no firm and abiding distinctions, and the religion of the position, the worship of demons, was resolutely irrational. Nature too was lost since particular goods were only sought — as the pears before and the new students here — not for whatever positive value they might have in themselves, but merely to be destroyed and negated in order to maintain a free and empty subjectivity — the "wasteland" of the last chapter of Book II. This was the only way of maintaining that nothing beyond his own will was of any value.

Chastened by his experience of the miseries and emptiness of this position Augustine found he could no longer run with the pack even though, for want of a truer attitude, he still looked for his friends amongst such companions. Here was the ultimate irony: he had adopted the position to get beyond any division only to end in the hopelessly divided position of admiring, for their actions, those whose actions he disapproved and refused to imitate. Neither rational nor natural, the position was simply diabolical. His final word on the Overturners is also his final word on this stage of his life in which he took himself as far away from God as it is humanly possible to go.[39]

> There is nothing which is more like the conduct of demons than in this behaviour [of the Overturners — i.e., its wantonness, its pure arbitrariness]. What indeed could be truer than the name of Overturners by which they were called? Clearly they themselves are overturned first and turned about by deceiving spirits secretly seducing and deriding them in the very fact that they themselves love to mock and deceive others.[40]

This was the bottom. But although he had turned from God, God had not abandoned him: "And your mercy continued to hover far above me" (III,iii,5).[41] The instability of his position — in the simultaneous attraction and repulsion of the Overturners — led to its being easily overthrown once he discovered a totality more complete than his own will and comprehensive of it.

Later adolescence (III,iv,7-V,xiv,25)[42]

III,iv,7-8. The *Hortensius* and the discovery of Wisdom

In his nineteenth year, as part of the ordinary course of studies, Augustine was set Cicero's (now lost) work called *Hortensius*.[43] It was included in the curriculum because of Cicero's exemplary eloquence — "whose tongue almost all men admire — though they don't pay so much attention to what he teaches" (III,iv,7).[44] From it Augustine drew a far different lesson.

> In truth this book changed my disposition and to you yourself, O Lord, it moved my prayers, and my wishes and desires it made quite other [i.e., than for natural ends]. Suddenly all groundless hope became worthless to me and I ardently desired the immortality of Wisdom, and this with an extraordinary passion of the heart. And I had begun to arise in order that I might return to you. (III,iv,7)[45]

This was not a result Augustine expected. He was fully taken up in the study of rhetoric simply to become famous and powerful in the world.[46] But the exhortation to divine Wisdom (*sapientia*) — as the stable whole in which all finite things were contained — was precisely the thing for which he had unwittingly been searching. Here was the only other totality, aside from his individual will, and this one included his will and all that was other than it.

In a way Augustine had simply returned to the moment before he stole the pears. At that time he recognized, in the divine law forbidding theft, a rational, universal, and objective good. While then he turned away, thinking to replace it with his own definition of the good, he now discovered that he was left in a position that was determinedly irrational and quite unable to include anything other than itself. Insofar as he desired a good that was adequate to his reason, and a way to comprehend whatever in nature was set against his will, he was forced to look beyond nature and outside his subjectivity. This is what the *Hortensius* taught him — and its effect was revolutionary.[47] The divine truth which he formerly spurned now appeared as Wisdom and infinitely attractive, in comparison with all earthly goods that had proven partial, incomplete, and constantly changing into their opposites. He had become a philosopher or, in other words, a lover of Wisdom.[48] *Hortensius* urged him to search for this above all other things. He responded at once.

> How then did I burn, my God, how did I burn to fly away from earthly things to you ... [and] this alone delighted me in that exhortation, that I should not [follow] this or that sect [of philosophy], but Wisdom itself, whatever it might be. (III,iv,8)[49]

It is not that Augustine had given up what he was seeking in the theft of pears — a position beyond finite limits — but that he had been "turned about" (III,iv,7)[50] in such a way that he no longer sought this in himself. From henceforth he would look for a comprehensive principle outside himself and all the rest of nature. He had begun his return from the depths on the journey which was eventually to lead him to God.[51] Over and again Augustine indicates that he regarded his reading of the *Hortensius* as the first significant turning point in his life and the one in which he was directed towards God.[52]

But much as he desired and loved this divine Wisdom rather than any other thing, he could and did fall away from the good he desired. The cause and sense of this fall is what he now turns to explain. The chief problem was that while the love of Wisdom was the beginning of the return to God, it was merely the first moment in that movement. For the Wisdom he desired was present at this point only in the most abstract and indefinite form. It was simply known as other than nature and natural goods, and so far Augustine had no idea what it might be in itself.

This is why, even as he describes how he burned with a desire for God, he adds that he did not know, concretely, what God required of him. "How did I burn, my God, how did I burn to fly away from earthly things to you — *though I did not know what you would do with me!*" (III,iv,8 — italics mine).[53] In hindsight Augustine could spell out with great precision the task that lay ahead of him from the moment of reading the *Hortensius*.

> [T]his alone delighted me in that exhortation, that I should not love this or that sect, but Wisdom itself, whatever it was: that I should love it (*diligo*), and seek it (*quaereo*), and follow it (*adsequor*), and hold it (*teneo*), and embrace it (*amplexor*) strongly. (III,iv,8)[54]

These five verbs are chosen with great care to indicate those moments which, taken together, constitute the beginning (*diligo*), the middle (*adsequor*), and the end (*amplexor*) of the movement to Wisdom, as well as the connecting terms which join them together (*quaereo* and *teneo*). We can get a sense of the distance he had yet to go by comparing the first and last terms. *Diligo* has the sense of loving something for its value to the lover, while *amplexor* means loving or honouring a thing for its intrinsic value rather than for its value to the one who loves.[55] In the first what is loved serves the lover. In the second the lover serves what is loved. The remainder of the first nine books show how Augustine moved through each of these steps.

Enflamed with a desire for Wisdom itself (God), but possessing it merely as an abstract idea, Augustine's immediate task was to seek out its concrete content (*quaereo*). The problem was to know where to look. One thing checked the ardour which the *Hortensius* had kindled in him. It made no mention of the name of Christ which, he says, he had imbibed with his mother's milk in infancy and held

in his heart in such a way that nothing from which it was lacking was able to capti-
vate him entirely.[56] This statement seems strange when we consider that he had
evinced no interest in baptism since his brush with death a dozen years before
(I,xi,17-18), was ashamed of his mother's Christian admonitions (II,iii,7), and had
gone out of his way to show his complete disrespect for the church (III,iii,5).

There is nothing untoward here. All he says is that, because, in growing up, he
took his idea of God from Monica,[57] the name of Christ was the one he primarily
associated with the idea of divine Wisdom — rather than Jupiter or whomever.[58] In
searching for its objective content he was therefore bound, first of all, to satisfy
himself whether or not this association was adequate. It was not that he had any
brief one way or the other but he started his search from some definite point and
this happened to be it. And from Monica he had also the expectation that Wisdom
was both beyond the world as divine and in the world as a way or *via* to itself.

III,v,9. Scripture rejected

"Therefore I decided to apply my mind to the Holy Scriptures to see what sort of
teachings they contained."[59] This was Augustine's first serious look at the New
Testament and the effort resulted in complete failure.[60] He found no Wisdom but
only a mass of crude stories and myths. He explains this in two ways — first, by
reporting how he saw them at the time, which was "unworthy of comparison with
the dignity of Tully's [Cicero's] texts."[61] He has already shown the central importance of eloquence in his world and for many years he had avidly pursued it as a
key to success. From this point of view the lack of sophistication in the Bible and
its want of eloquence, when measured against the traditions with whom he was
acquainted, immediately disqualified it from serious consideration. Here were no
sublime teachings about Wisdom but only a mass of silly stories about unimportant people that Augustine scorned at once. He wanted a Wisdom which would
impress the worldly-wise. The Scriptures contained nothing of the sort.

More fundamentally he maintains that he was unable to see Wisdom in the
Scriptures because he was too puffed up with pride. "And behold, I discovered a
thing which is not disclosed to the proud nor laid bare to children."[62] The point is
remarkable. If, on the one hand, the content of Scripture is really Wisdom, then
this will be concealed from all who are, intellectually, children — i.e., who have
not yet begun to search for Wisdom, as he had not until he read the *Hortensius*. At
every mention of God those who are children in this sense will only be able to
understand a powerful, but invisible, father like the view he held as a child
(I,ix,14). But this is not what the Scriptures really teach and in this way its meaning is "not laid bare to children."

On the other hand, because the New Testament reveals a union of God and man
in Christ, when taken literally it appears to speak only of nature and the natural.[63]
That there is anything more in the Gospels than crude stories of insignificant
people and events depends wholly on belief — the more so since they are introduced by contradictory genealogies of Christ. But Augustine wanted nothing to do
with belief, for this would mean he would be subject to another's authority: "I
disdained to be a little one and with swollen pride I saw myself as a great man."[64]
What he wanted was science — a sure knowledge of God possessed in his own

right. As a result the real content of the Scriptures (the *mysterium*) remained an impenetrable darkness from which he was cut off by his determination to come at once to a true knowledge of God.[65] The aim sounds laudable but it was just the reverse. For he confesses that he desired this knowledge only to serve his own private purposes — which is to say, to make himself a great man in the world. As long as the proud man insists that God must be just what he imagines, he makes himself unable to see whatever truth the Scriptures do contain and by this logic their meaning is "not disclosed to the proud."

III,vi,10-11. The fall into Manichaeism

III,vi,10 — This is the start of the long treatment of Augustine's nine-year attachment to the Manichees. He did not set out to become acquainted with their teachings as he had done with the Scriptures but simply stumbled across them. This is reflected in the words he uses to describe this encounter — "to fall into," "to blunder upon," "to rush into."[66] In another sense, however, Augustine saw an inexorable necessity governing this apparent accident, indicated by the fact that he begins this chapter — as the one before — with the logical connective, "therefore." Falling in with the Manichees was somehow a consequence of his failure to find the truth in the Catholic Scriptures just as his turning to Scripture was a consequence of his early upbringing. He begins the discussion of his Manichaean period in this way.

> Therefore I fell in with deranged and proud men who were exceedingly carnal and also exceedingly loquacious, in whose mouths were the snares of the devil — a sticky glue made up of a mixture of the syllables of your name [i.e., the name of God the Father], and the name of the Lord Jesus Christ, and the name of the Paraclete, that is, our comforter, the Holy Spirit.[67]

He was attracted to the Manichees because he had failed to find any teaching about Wisdom in the Bible and because he was too proud to accept any account that required him to believe it on the authority of another — as would be necessary if he were to accept the Scriptures he had just examined. Of course the church did not maintain that the Bible was ultimately contradictory nor that Christians never moved beyond faith. But it did insist that its members had to believe, must rely on its authority, and be obedient to its precepts, on the strength of a mere promise that by humble and childlike service now they would in the end come to see the truth face to face. But if the evident grossness and contradictions of Scripture had to be tolerated now, the truth could not be known immediately. And what could not be known at once would not serve the ends Augustine had in mind. So long as this was his position he was bound to reject the belief which the Catholic revelation demanded and look instead for some more evidently rational doctrine.

At this point his attention was drawn to the Manichees who not only claimed that they knew what the truth was — "And they used to say over and again: 'Truth, truth,' and spoke much of it to me"[68] — but who did so with a ceaseless invocation of the names of Christ, God (the Father), and the Holy Spirit. They claimed to represent the true and purified form of Christianity and thus seemed to possess the very thing for which he was looking.[69]

From the start of his account Augustine accuses the Manichees of "speaking lies, not only about you [God] who are truly the truth, but also about the elements of this world [i.e., nature] which is your creature."[70] He calls them "exceedingly carnal" men who had no notion of spiritual substance and who supposed that the only realities were corporeal. In brief, they affirmed the existence of two eternally opposed corporeal substances, one good, the other evil, which they understood as light and darkness — i.e., the light and dark which are seen with the eyes of the flesh. They identified God with this light and especially with the great celestial lights, "the sun and the moon [which] they offered up [to Augustine] as God."[71] Visible darkness was the Devil's. Ruled respectively by the Prince of Light and the Prince of Darkness, the two kingdoms were infinite in every direction except where they touched one another along a common frontier. Through the machinations of the Prince of Darkness, who wished to expand his empire into the Kingdom of Light, the neat separation of light and dark was locally destroyed as he gained a foothold in a "corner" of the realm of Light.[72] From this kingdom he took particles captive. The natural universe which we see about us was made by this evil mingling of the two contraries of light and dark, good and evil. All nature is composed of tiny pieces of these two contraries from which, by their mixture in varying degrees, men and all other things are made. Nature is thus a battleground of the two cosmic forces in which evil tries to overcome the good, and the good, evil. The Manichees taught that in the end the forces of light would prevail in the sense that the dark would once more, and this time forever, be shut up in the Kingdom of Evil and cut off by a new and impenetrable frontier from the Kingdom of Good. For man, who is composed of both good and evil, the task was to separate himself from the evil which was entangled in his nature and to get himself on the right side of the frontier before it was closed forever.

Although they were materialists, the light, the sun and moon etc. of which they spoke, were not in fact the actual visible light or the visible celestial bodies but what Augustine calls *phantasmata splendida* — "resplendent fantasies." They were fantastic images, "grander and infinite," — i.e., in comparison to what our eyes actually see — which were derived from the visible yet, having no definite relation to it, had no reality except in the imagination:[73] "they were corporeal fantasies, false bodies, than which the true bodies, which we see with the eyes of the flesh, are more certain."[74]

Augustine's treatment is clearly unsympathetic and it can appear to be highly dogmatic. He does not argue here that the contents of the Manichean teachings are fantasies — he only asserts it. This has led to the criticism that he misrepresents their position. François Decret, in *L'Afrique manichéene*, argues that the Manichees understood these images of the sun and moon not literally but as myths. They conveyed a truth perceived by a *gnosis* or spiritual knowledge rather than in the categories of classical philosophical thought.[75] He claims that while Augustine knew this[76] he chose to ignore it in order to discredit the position more effectively[77] — and because it was an approach to the truth which was uncongenial to his spirit.[78] As a result he never locked horns with the real gnosticism of the Manichaean doctrines, here or in any of his writings, so his arguments give only illusory victories rather than a rebuttal of their true position.[79]

There is no doubt that Manichaeism was a gnosticism and that Augustine knew it as such.[80] Unlike the Catholics — who offered a revealed way to God which, on their own account, must start from belief — Manichaeism asserted that God had revealed a spiritual knowledge of all truth to the founder of the sect, Mani, and this gnosis was what they offered to their adherents who could therefore start immediately from the truth rather than from belief.[81] Against Decret, David Smith asks what it would mean for Augustine to acknowledge the gnostic character of their doctrines. The answer, presumably, is that their meaning would have to be understood by an illumination beyond the normal categories of thought. But if Augustine did not share the illumination which had been granted to Mani, how was he to argue with those who claimed to have it? Smith suggests two possibilities.[82] On the one hand Augustine could explain his own categories of thought (i.e., the sensible and the intelligible) and then argue from them — as he does in many of his anti-Manichaean treatises.

> If the Manichees wish to argue they must either accept Augustine's categories or propose others which Augustine can then argue from. If they do not wish to argue then they can assert their personal *gnosis* but it will go unsupported and undefended, though ultimately unrefuted. One cannot go further than this in arguing discursively against a position that claims to have an illumination beyond reason that the opponent does not have.

The alternative, which Augustine uses in the *Confessions* where he is not so much arguing against the Manichees as explaining why he fell in with them, is "to set the[ir] position against the background of a larger picture of life so that ... Manicheism will be adequately accounted for, without a direct refutation of its gnostic claims." Augustine's contention that the Manichaean teachings are *phantasmata* is in fact placed in such a larger picture when he locates the objects of Manichaean belief (the sun, moon, and the other parts of their teaching) on a vast scale of all possible objects of knowledge, where they form the lowest step at a fivefold remove from the highest and best. He says:

> How far are you [O God] from [i] those fantasies of mine, fantasies of bodies, which have no certain existence whatsoever [i.e., other than as fantasies]. More certain than they are [ii] the images of bodies [i.e., pictures, statues, etc.], and more certain than these are [iii] the bodies themselves which however are not you. And nor are you [iv] the soul which is the life of bodies — and which is therefore better, as the life of bodies is more certain [i.e., stable, indissoluble] than bodies — but you are [v] the life of the soul, the life of lives, living in yourself, and you do not change, O life of my soul.[83]

This is a scale of being, truth, and life where the degree of certainty or unchangeableness is the criterion for the degree of each of these attributes. "Certain" is the key word. Each of these stages is said to be "more certain" — i.e., more fixed, definite, and unchangeable — than the one below it.[84] At the bottom are the "fantasies of bodies" which refer to no existing sense object and are potentially the most changeable of things without actually being nothing.[85] At the top is God, conceived as Being and Truth, "*in whom is no change nor shadow of motion* (James 1:17)"[86] and, as the Life of lives, "living in yourself [i.e., not receiving life from some other source], and you do not change."[87]

Augustine takes this scale to include the major divisions of all the possible (and actual) forms of being, truth, and life. It is one he expects will be agreed to by the generality of his readers — even if they did not recognize its affinity with the Platonic line[88] — for common sense will acknowledge that a fig is less changeable than a picture of a fig, which could be as big as a horse or a house. And who would deny that what is intended to be a picture of a real fig is less changeable than what we may fancy from a fig which can be taken as a child of its mother (the tree), or as containing god, or the devil, or whatever?[89]

Augustine declares that, on this scale, the Manichees only served him, in their "many and huge volumes,"[90] "empty figments,"[91] and "glorious appearances"[92] — which he took to be real, true, and nourishing but which were in fact at the furthest possible remove from the changeless. The mind that seeks the changeless cannot be fed or satisfied by what it takes to be so if it is not really so — any more than we can really be sustained by the food we eat in dreams.[93] "On such empty things I used to feed and was never fed."[94] A Manichee would testify to the contrary but this does not mean that we are faced with an arbitrary choice between the two. It is true that Augustine has not refuted their position but he has fully stated the grounds of his criticism and if any reader should wish to defend the Manichees Augustine has provided a context in which the discussion can take place. Unless the Manichee is merely willing to reiterate his position he must refute Augustine's contention that there is such a scale of being, truth, and life and that the Manichaean doctrines occupy the lowest place on it.

III,iii,11 — Objectively there is no difference between a poetic fancy — like Ovid's tale of Medea flying through the air in her chariot of winged serpents — and the things of which the Manichees spoke.[95] Both are *phantasmata* — fanciful imaginings pieced together from real bodies but corresponding to nothing that actually exists. For Augustine however the great difference was that he never thought Medea really flew through the air, yet he believed that the Manichees' things did actually exist.[96]

The question is how he could have made this mistake — and not just for a short time but for almost nine years. He answers that it was because "I sought for you [God] not according to the understanding of the mind, by which you wished me to be distinguished from the beasts, but according to the senses of the flesh."[97] In other words he accuses himself of turning from the real demands of philosophy and against his own reason because he let it be seduced by the gorgeous appearance and easy availability of the Manichees' teachings, which he likens to a harlot offering him immediate gratification of his desires.

> I fell on that bold woman, devoid of sense who, in Solomon's allegory, sits on a chair at her door and says: *"Eat willingly secret bread and drink stolen waters."* (Pr. 9:17) And she seduced me because she found me pointed outwards, living in the eyes of the flesh and chewing over such things as I had taken in through them.[98]

A passage from *On the Two Souls* explains this "seduction." Augustine gives two reasons for becoming a Manichee. One was their friendliness. The other was his seemingly invincible ability to win arguments with naïve Catholics who attempted to defend their faith against the Manichees.[99] He was eventually to learn to his shame that these arguments — which convinced him; by which he won many friends to the sect; and which allowed him to seem wise by crushing the position of simple Catholics — were all beside the point.[100] They had nothing to do with the real Catholic position, but at the time he could not see this because he was "seduced" by the Manichees' sophistic ability to manipulate appearances.

III,vii,12-14

III,vii,12 — Augustine had no inkling of the existence of spiritual substance: he simply did not recognize any reality other than what had a body. As he puts it, "I did not know of that other [spiritual, intelligible reality] which truly is"[101] — i.e., in comparison to bodies which, because changeable, come into existence and pass out of it. It was not that he lacked intelligence or was unacquainted with the most universal concepts (God, law, etc.) but that he had not yet distinguished the intelligible from the sensible as its form (i.e., the Platonic ideas). As a result he was bound to look for intelligibles such as truth, good, and evil as if they were immediately present in the sensible. If we ask why he refused so much as to look for intelligible being, the answer is the same as before. He was searching for the concrete content of truth and he wanted it immediately. But this meant that it would have to have a nature which he could immediately recognize. And to this point, void of any philosophical culture or the patience and piety to accept truth on the authority of another, the only real things he knew were sensible bodies.[102]

As a consequence he was soon persuaded that the Manichees' objections to Catholicism were correct. They insisted on certain glaring contradictions in the Catholic Scriptures — which are certainly there but which are resolved by the notion of spiritual substance. He lists the three that were the most important in convincing him.

> I was moved rather quickly to hold the ideas of my stupid deceivers when they asked me [i] whence comes evil, and [ii] whether God was limited to a bodily form and if he had hair and nails, and [iii] whether it was right to count amongst the righteous those men who had many wives at the same time and who killed men and sacrificed animals.[103]

Augustine was persuaded to join the Manichees by these *questions* because they appeared to be informed by a knowledge which, it seemed, must know the content of Wisdom, since it was able to show so surely and convincingly why the Catholics could not possible have it. He was searching for a rational, objective, and universal Wisdom. The Catholics said this was the content of their Scriptures. The Manichees asked in reply how this could possibly be when they taught that God forbade animal sacrifices, homicide, and polygamy, yet was said to regard the patriarchs, who did these very things, as righteous men. And who but a credulous fool could accept that God was infinite and at the same time limited to the shape of a human body, however big, as Scripture teaches where it says that God made man in his image? Above all, how could the Catholics account for the origin of evil in a universe which, according to Genesis, was created solely by a good and omnipotent God?[104]

Of course these were only reasons why Augustine should not have become a Catholic. What actually drew him to the Manichees was not at first the rigmarole of their own doctrines but their argumentative ability and the apparent rationality of their methods.[105] He states this clearly in a passage from *On the Usefulness of Believing*, written (391-92, shortly after he had become a priest) in order to dissuade Honoratus, one of the many friends he had lured to the sect, from the errors to which he had once persuaded him.

> As you know Honoratus, we fell in with such men for no other cause than that they claimed they would lead their hearers to God and free them from all errors by pure and simple reason rather than by any terrifying authority. What else indeed constrained me for about nine years — rejecting the religion which my parents had commended to me since I was a young child [i.e., Catholicism] — to follow and diligently listen to those men: what else except their claim that we [i.e., Catholics] are frightened by superstition and enjoined to a faith before reason while they press no one to faith unless the truth had first been discussed and freed from obscurity. (*DUC*, I,2)[106]

Augustine could take the Manichees to have a science because they took him behind the changing world of appearances to the contrary principles of good and evil which they distinguished absolutely. In this the law of non-contradiction was assumed. On the basis of such rational distinctions the Manichees objected that it was credulous to believe the Scriptures contained the Wisdom of God when one part of the Bible contradicted another.

In this section (12) Augustine merely states the Catholic answers to the first two of the three seeming contradictions — i.e., about the origin of evil and whether God had a bodily form.[107] An argued defence of the Catholic position depends on the recognition of the divine as an incorruptible spiritual substance. At the time he had no inkling of such a reality, and so the full refutation of these charges is delayed until Book VII when he has brought his readers to see how he came to recognize this principle.[108] Until he had done this his defence of Catholicism — on these two points — could only be dogmatic. This was not true of the third Manichaean objection, that the patriarchs of the Old Testament were immoral. For this reason he spends the rest of this chapter and the two following explaining why, even given his lights at the time, he ought not to have found fault with the Catholics on this score.

III,vii,13-14 — The Manichees asserted that since God had prohibited polygamy, homicide, and the sacrifice of living animals, it followed that the patriarchs, who did such things, were immoral — and thus the Catholic reverence for their authority was contradictory.[109]

Augustine argues that such contradictions do not provide an adequate ground for rejecting the Catholic position because, in itself, the principle of non-contradiction does not give a knowledge of the whole in which it can happen that a good thing at one time or place becomes an evil thing at another. Such transformations occur every day, and everyone, including the Manichees, acknowledged that justice was not compromised because what is permitted at one time or place is not permitted at another.

Augustine presents a series of three examples that show, in an increasingly inward fashion, how there can be a single justice in a whole where the parts are treated differently. On the first level he discusses both space (where the fit of each piece of a suit of armour is appropriate to only one part of the body), and time (where a law may stipulate that an activity that is appropriate at one time of the day is inappropriate at another — without contradicting itself). On the second level he presents the case of a household, understood as an organic whole, where the well-being of each part depends on differences of function so that a stable-boy, covered with manure, ought not to handle the cups from which all drink nor, for the health of all, should one relieve oneself in front of the table although it is permitted to do so behind the stable. His third example is the poetic art where the good and beauty of the whole poem is present in an even more inward form since the justice, or right placement of the different feet, cannot be brought about externally (as would be possible in the previous example if, for example, everyone washed their own cup before drinking so it made no difference who handled them). He concludes, "these things beat on my eyes from every direction but I did not see them" (III,vii,14).[110]

The Manichees refused to see these things because they wanted to retain the ability to criticize others on the basis of the law of non-contradiction and their own imaginary definition of the good. They found fault with the patriarchs — for behaving in a different way than what, admittedly, all agreed was just by contemporary standards — without considering the demands of a total rational explanation which must go behind the law of non-contradiction to consider the whole in which these differences were contained. As a result neither they, nor Augustine, had any notion of the real justice to which the fathers adhered and which, he suggests, more perfectly than even the poetic art, contains within itself the law which determines that different things should be done at different times and places — and yet remains one law.

> And blind to these things I found fault with the pious fathers not only because they acted in their own times as God ordered and inspired them, but also because they acted as God revealed they should in a way which prefigured the future. (III,vii,14)[111]

There are two points here which Augustine discusses in each of the following chapters.

III,viii,15-16. Justice, injustice, and the whole

III,viii,15 — As justice requires different things at different times and places, Augustine now answers the question of how one can know what is just at a given time or place. He gives the Biblical answer that justice is to love God with heart, soul, and mind, and to love one's neighbour as oneself.[112] These two parts of justice correspond to the divisions of this chapter into the discussion of *flagitia*, or corrupt acts, in section 15, and *facinora*, or crimes, in section 16.[113] The first correspond to sins against God because "That society which ought to be between us and God is violated when that same nature, of which he is the author, is polluted by the perversity of lust."[114] Crimes are unjust acts against our neighbour.

Augustine distinguishes three kinds of *flagitia*: sins against nature, against custom, and against the direct commandment of God. Taken together they constitute the totality of wholes from which we may turn to seek our own private advantage. At the bottom are the sins against nature — his example is homosexuality — where the purposes of the natural order, seen here in the sexual function, are perverted. The result is that at this most fundamental level our fellowship with God is broken by turning our nature from the end for which he designed it to one of our own making. Such things "ought everywhere and always to be detested and punished,"[115] being in no way dependent on time or place.

The next whole is human custom in which time and place are included, making it at once less universal (as the examples from the previous chapter illustrate) and more comprehensive because it includes the various possible forms of a rational ordering of things. Here the rule is that "Every part that does not agree with its whole is indeed corrupt."[116] A man who lives in a society whose laws insist on monogamy may not, without fault, take many wives on the grounds that polygamy is permitted in other societies. Nature's end in the reproduction of the species is met equally well by either system — but each is just that, a system, an ordered rational whole, whose justice must be sought in its own terms.[117]

Finally, at once the narrowest and the most absolute whole, is a direct order from God — such as any one of the ten commandments. These are more restrictive than custom in the sense that God can order something to be done which was never done before (as, for example, the command to observe the Sabbath), or something discontinued which had "always" been done (making images of God). At the same time their basis is more absolute than human custom where there are many possible — and thus mutually exclusive — legal systems. God's commands, informed by the reason which governs the whole universe, cannot be opposed by the logic of any greater whole since none other exists. These commands must be obeyed unconditionally.

III,viii,16 — Augustine understands the ten commandments as divided into two groups, "the three and the seven, the psalter of ten chords, your decalogue."[118] The first three define our relation to God and thus correspond to the three *flagitia* described in the previous section. The seven define the crimes (*facinora*) by which we depart from justice in relations with our fellows. The aim of all crimes is to harm our neighbour either by word or deed, both of which, Augustine says, may be done for one of five reasons: revenge, covetousness, avoidance of injury, envy, or pleasure in another's evil. This list is parallel to the fivefold scale of being, truth, and life presented earlier (III,vi,10). Each of these motives corresponds to one of the levels on that scale. In revenge what is sought is one's own definition of justice — as if we were in God's position. In covetousness we seek for ourselves what the rational soul recognizes as another's. In the fear of injury we seek to avoid something material and sensible as if this were more important than what the justice of the situation requires. In envy we are not threatened by the other in our material well-being, since his position has no actual bearing on our happiness — but only in the image of our desired equality or superiority with him. And finally, in taking pleasure at another's harm (Augustine gives the examples of those who delight in gladiatorial games, mockers, and scoffers), it is not the positive aspects of the other's position which move us, as in envy, but purely negative moments which correspond to no reality except in the mind of the one who fantasizes that he is exalted as others are harmed.[119] This is intended as a comprehensive list of the reasons for which men will commit crimes because it covers all the possible levels of being, truth, and life to which we may aspire in seeking to harm one another.

Augustine now turns inward to the person who is unjust. He posits three aspects of the soul — as being, knowing, and loving (the created images of the persons of the Trinity) — which either singly or in combination are the sources of injustice. "These are the heads of injustice which spring from the desire of ruling, and of knowing, and of feeling — either from one, or from two, or from all together."[120] In our relations with God these three desires correspond to each of the three vices.[121] In our relations with one another the seven possible combinations represent every possible source of the (seven) crimes forbidden in the second half of the decalogue.

In a very brief compass Augustine has given us a complete account of justice — what it is, as well as the sources and ends of all the possible forms of declension from it. All are a matter of preferring a private (false) whole to the totality that is actually there — when "through a private pride a false whole is loved in a part."[122] This provides us with the context in which we can understand his criticism of the Manichaean objections to the morality of the patriarchs and the reason why he was guilty in condemning the patriarchs in spite of the fact that, at the time, he did not know true justice.[123] He has shown that the Manichaean objections did not come from some other idea of justice than the one which he has set before us: their own standard shows its dependence on true justice by imitating its wholeness. The standards by which the Manichees judged were unjust and disordered, being rooted in a false and arbitrary whole — contemporary practice in their criticism of the Old Testament and, on the positive side, in their own fantasies.[124] Yet as they *had* to claim their position was a whole — *the* whole — they could not avoid paying the price which true justice (or the true whole) imposed on them.

> But you avenge this, what men bring about in themselves, because even as they sin against you, they act impiously in their own souls and their iniquity gives the lie to itself.[125]

Augustine concludes the chapter by listing the various consequences which result from wilfully maintaining that some part is the whole — and he does so in relation to the three heads of iniquity mentioned above.[126]

III,ix,17. Justice, injustice, and the future

Augustine concludes his discussion of justice by considering certain problems that have not been answered in what he has already said.[127] He gives us three situations in which, because of the limitations of human knowledge, a person may be judged to be unjust who is not so in reality. All have to do with the Manichees' refusal to consider the role of the future in arriving at a true judgement — which they could not do without compromising their claim to a total gnosis.

First are the lapses of those who are nevertheless primarily just. Here we may think of David's lust for Bathsheba and his iniquitous treatment of her righteous husband (2 Sam. 11-12). The Manichees took this as cause for condemning David altogether but Augustine says that while the injustice was to be condemned, David could justly be praised as long as there was hope of his doing better and repenting.[128]

The second case concerns the impossibility of our seeing within one another's hearts. An act which may have all the appearance of a vice or crime may not really be so, either because its evil result was a consequence of an unforeseen circumstance or because no sin was intended. Augustine gives examples.[129]

Finally, at the head of this list, is the situation where a man seems to commit a manifest crime — we may think of Abraham's willingness to kill Isaac (Gen. 22) — and yet he has not acted unjustly because he did so in obedience to a direct divine command. At the time the reasons for this order were not clear but the ultimate justice of the act is eventually revealed, either as appropriate to its own time or as a prophecy and sign for the future.[130]

III,x,18. The science fiction of the Manichees

Not knowing these things I used to mock those holy servants and prophets of yours [i.e., Catholics].[131] And what did I gain when I laughed at them except that you laughed at me who was gradually and little by little led to believe that a fig wept when it was plucked and that its mother, the tree, shed milky tears. From which fig, moreover, if it was eaten by some [Manichaean] saint ... [and] mixed in his stomach, he would then burp up angels, or rather, particles of God, by his groaning in prayer and belching — which particles of the highest and true God would remain bound in that fruit unless they were freed by the teeth and stomach of the elect saint.[132]

To understand this passage we need to know that at the top of the Manichaean hierarchy were the "saints" or, as they were also called, the "Elect," who were supposed, in this digestive manner, to be able to liberate the bits of the divine substance from their entanglement in evil matter. These liberated bits would in turn help the lower grade of Manichees, the "Auditors," who had assisted the Elect by picking the fruit which their own sanctity precluded them from doing.[133]

Although these doctrines, and the other parts of the Manichaean teachings, were to seem ridiculous to Augustine later in life, we must take note of what was truer in the Manichees' position than in his earlier stance — for this was what attracted him at the time. He no longer sought to think of the finite as independent of God. Augustine had discovered that if the finite was held to have no relation to a stable self-identical principle it became a nullity for thought, a nonentity in its independence, where nothing was anything since all things were in a constant flux in which every distinction was destroyed as soon as it was made. The Manichaean position was quite different, for it saw the finite as composed of contraries. They had divided nature into principal parts: the one (light) and the many (dark). Though the actual finite was evil, and the multiplicity and diversity of nature was the work of an evil principle, this was not all that it was. In the entrapped particles of light which were present in all nature, it was also understood to have an inner relation to the stable and self-identical.[134] On this basis they had come to a position where, at least in theory, a science or knowledge of nature becomes possible. Nature was not simply an irrational flow of infinitely different moments but these had a relation to an abiding unity which underlay them and which therefore provided the possibility of knowledge or science. Manichaeism thus presented itself not only as a religion leading to personal salvation (i.e., the disentanglement of one's light, or truth, from matter), but also as a complete science of nature. Henri-Christian Puech describes this feature:

> [the Manichaean] gnosis is at the same time theology and cosmology. It develops a universal science of things divine, celestial, terrestrial, and infernal where everything — transcendent realities as well as physical phenomena and historical events — finds its place and its explanation.[135]

This total knowledge which the Manichees promised was what Augustine wanted. But this was not to be, for although he, and they, had come to the beginning of a real science — i.e., knowledge arrived at through the distinction of contraries — this was as far as they went. All the rest of their teaching was pure fiction.[136]

Failing knowledge of a spiritual reality in which the oppositions of nature were united and contained, the Manichees could only offer an irrational and fantastic account of nature and its principle. The knowledge which they promised their hearers turned out to be empty. It required belief for its acceptance. Indeed it demanded an unconditional, total, and irrational assent to their doctrines. As Augustine puts it (in the passage, quoted above, from the *Usefulness of Believing*), the Manichees proposed an economy of salvation which was the reverse of that proposed by the Catholic church. The Catholics moved from faith to understanding. The Manichees started from a seeming knowledge only to end up in credulous belief. In the *Confessions* he insists over and again that the Manichees did not accept the doctrines because they saw their reason, but because they were "ordered to believe."[137] Longing to be fed with the truth, he was instead filled with fictions which failed to satisfy him.

> [T]hinking these [fantasies] were you, I ate them, though not eagerly because you did not have the taste in my mouth of how you really are, for you were not there in those inane fantasies — nor was I nourished by them but rather exhausted. (III,vi,10)[138]

In spite of this Augustine was to remain with the Manichees for nine years — from his nineteenth to his twenty-eighth year[139] — yet during all this time, he never sought to advance himself beyond the lowest rank of the Manichaean hierarchy, that of "Auditor." Auditors were only expected to follow a watered-down version of the conduct required of the Elect. In *On the Usefulness of Believing*, still speaking to Honoratus, he says:

> But in hindsight, what reason held me back so that I did not altogether join them and so that I stayed in that rank which they call "Auditors" without renouncing the hopes and affairs of this world [as required of the Elect]? What, except that I saw they were more skilful and copious in disproving others than they were in standing firm and certain at proving their own [positions]? (I,2)[140]

Augustine would remain satisfied as long as he could continue in the belief that their own teachings contained great things which they would soon reveal to him. As he says, "I did not give myself to them wholly but I did think that they hid under these covers something great which they would soon reveal to me" (*DBV*, I,4).[141] This was not the Catholic position of faith seeking understanding. Here Augustine's belief — which he had not yet recognized as such — was not understood as a function of his immediate inability to grasp Wisdom, nor was it moved by a humble desire to serve the truth. It was only a function of the Manichees' temporary unwillingness to reveal the true meaning of their doctrines. Augustine put up with this because he was convinced that they had what he wanted — a knowledge of the truth which would serve his worldly aims and which he would get as soon as they took him fully into their confidence. The sequel will show that what he took to be their unwillingness to reveal the truth was, in reality, an inability to do so.

He has much more to say about his Manichaean period in the next two books. For the moment we will conclude with his own precise summary of this stage of his life — "going away from the truth, I seemed to myself to be going towards it" (III,vii,12).[142] The practical consequences of this error form the content of the next book.

III,xi,19-III,xii,21. Monica and Manichaeism

In these final chapters Augustine includes two episodes which mark both his distance from the Catholic faith and what he later understood as the first steps by which he was eventually to be brought to it. He sees both as providential.

> And you put forth your hand from on high and from this profound blindness *you rescued my soul* (Ps. 85:13), when my mother, your faithful one, wept for me, before you, more abundant tears than mothers are wont to shed over the dead body [of a child]. For she saw that I was dead by the faith and spirit that she had from you, and you answered her prayers, O Lord. (III,xi,19)[143]

Both of these "answers" can seem curious to modern ears. They become less so if we follow Augustine's explanation of their sense.

III,xi,19-20. Monica and the dream — The first was his mother's "dream" (III,xi,19) or "vision" (III,xi,20).[144] In it Monica saw herself standing on a wooden rule bewailing the loss of her son to the Manichees. At this point she was comforted by a glorious young man who told her that if she looked again she would see that "where she was, there he was too" (III,xi,19)[145] and, looking again, she saw Augustine beside her on the rule.

The assurance which Monica took from this *dream* was the very thing her son despised in the Catholics — their credulous belief — as opposed to the certain knowledge he demanded and thought he was getting from the Manichees. And yet, as he was to discover from this incident, Monica's belief did not entail any uncertainty as to its precise content. When he presumed to interpret it that she should not despair of being where he was, she immediately grasped the decisive difference in his words — which he himself had not really understood — and corrected him. " 'No,' she said, 'it was not said to me, where he is there you are too, but where you are there he also is' " (III,xi,19).[146] Augustine tells us that he was more deeply moved by this reply than by the dream itself.[147] This is not surprising. He knew he had gotten it wrong but what was surprising was that Monica, who was supposed to be a credulous fool, had gotten it right and was shown to have an absolute certainty that could neither be shaken nor confused by his false, but close, interpretation. He would have been right if he had suspected that he could not do as much for the content of the Manichees' doctrines.

As a result of this dream, and simply by her faith in its promise, Monica allowed him to continue living with her even though, because of his arrogance, she had "begun to be unwilling" (III,xi,19) to have him in her house.[148] She showed herself capable of a love that Augustine was willing enough to enjoy — since he continued to live with her — but was unwilling to reciprocate. His whole delight lay in mocking the Catholics whose errors he thought were so clearly manifest — even while benefitting from a hope that most certainly had its roots in the belief he scorned. On Monica's side the dream prevented her from giving up on Augustine at a time when it seemed this was the only thing she could do — and it sustained her love and care for him to the day of his conversion in which it proved to be an essential element.[149]

III,xii,21. Monica and the oracle — In the second episode, Monica told him of her meeting with a Catholic bishop. She had begged this man to show her son the errors of the Manichaean position and the truth of Catholicism. He refused, saying that Augustine was so puffed up with his "victories" in refuting Catholics that he would be incapable of appreciating his errors. He tried to console Monica with the assurance that once August came to study the Manichees' own doctrines he would become convinced of their falsity — as, at an earlier stage, he had himself.

This bishop recognized that Augustine was both unwilling to believe and ignorant of the notion of spiritual reality necessary to any intellectual discussion of the Catholic position. He therefore "prudently, wisely" refused Monica's request.[150] Monica did not understand any of this and persisted in her entreaties. Finally the bishop, seeing he was getting nowhere, dismissed her somewhat tartly saying that it was "not possible for the son of such tears to be lost."[151] He had in mind that the falsity of the Manichees' doctrines would make them untenable to anyone who was prevented from a complacent satisfaction with his errors by the care of a mother like Monica. Ignorant of this reason, Monica nevertheless took these words of the bishop as an "oracle" from God,[152] that it would be so, and was satisfied.

Monica did not understand the reasons why the bishop had refused to help her son. But her unshakeable belief in such signs and visions clearly enabled her to work for his salvation.[153] She did so by humbly serving the truth in the only way in which she could — through her continuing care and prayers — and despite the vile way in which he used her. For nine years she waited patiently and worked in this quiet way with no visible reward for her trouble. Her road was not easy. From a human reckoning it was foolish to spend so much effort, and for so long, and with so little result, on such a slight assurance that it would all be worthwhile in the end. Yet Augustine acknowledges that his conversion was in large part brought about by her care. Although her prayers were apparently ineffectual, as he simply scorned her entreaties, we can see that they were, all the same, the very thing that prevented him from remaining in any of his false positions.[154] Because of Monica he could find no rest unless he either escaped from her, disproved the Catholic position, or else was moved to accept it. She refused to allow the first to happen; he found it impossible to do the second, and in the end therefore he was to come to stand beside his mother "on that rule of faith on which you had shown me to her so many years before" (VIII,xii,30).[155]

NOTES

1 *Retr.*, II,vi (xxxiii) *(confessionum mearum) excitant humanum intellectum et affectum*. Written towards the end of his life, the *Retractations* is a review and correction of Augustine's main works. It contains 93 titles. Augustine also speaks of the purpose of the first nine books of the *Confessions* in X,iii,3-4.

2 *Non/ludendi* (13/6-8).

3 *Veni/amorum* (36/25-26). When Augustine says "I came to Carthage" he means, from Thagaste, after his idle sixteenth year. Chapters ii-iii summarize the essentials of his life in the two-year period between his seventeenth year when he first went to 'university' in Carthage and his nineteenth year when he read the *Hortensius*.

4 *Amare/fruerer* (37/8-9).

5 *Et/amari?* (25/14-15).

6 *Nondum/amabam* (36/26-27).

7 *Quaerebam/amare* (36/28-29).

8 *Nondum/indigentem* (36/26-28). A more complicated explanation of this sentence and part of the next — which was the object of a workshop by the translator, commentator, and directors of the Bibliothèque Augustinienne, working from G. Wijdeveld, "Sur quelques passages des Confessions de saint Augustin," *Vigiliae Christianae*, 10 (1956), 229-35 — is found in *BA*, Vol. 13, pp. 665-67.

9 *Rui/capi* (37/13-14).

10 *contactu sensibilium* (37/6-7).

11 *Sed/amarentur* (37/7-8).

12 *elegans et urbanus* (37/12) could just as well be translated "elegant and urbane." Both words carry a strong sense of a city-type refinement and sophistication and Augustine means them only in a bad sense. Compare the oppositions in the phrase *urbanus et rusticanus* — "elegant and inelegant" — in V,vi,10 (84/4), where it is applied to pottery vessels. One should think of the difference between rough, but adequate, peasant pottery, and fine tableware that, for all its elegance, does not hold food any better. *Urbanus* is again used in this way — for an arbitrary and false good created by human vanity — in III,iii,6 in connection with the *eversores*.

13 *muscipulis* (36/29-37/1, from *mus-capio* = mouse-trap) derives from Wisdom 14:11 or Ps. 90:3. See *EP*, XC,4 where Augustine says, "The devil and his angels spread their snares, as hunters do: and those who walk in Christ walk afar from those snares: for he dares not spread his net in Christ: he sets it on the verge of the way, not in the way. Let then thy way be Christ and thou shalt not fall into the snares of the devil" (trans. *NPNF*). Compare VII,xxi,27, *Et/supplicium* (151/27-152/6) where Augustine uses a similar image.

14 *Rui/rixarum* (37/13-19).

15 *Rapiebant/mei* (37/20-21).

16 *auctori/gaudens* (38/1-6). On tragedy and the performance of tragedy in late Roman antiquity, see the article of this title by H. Kelly, *Traditio*, 35 (1979), 21-44. Kelly concludes that we have no evidence that a full-length traditional tragedy was ever staged in its entirety in the Empire but that such plays might have been written in the hopes that they would be modified for use as *tragoedia cantata* — recited, with the actions indicated by gestures — or as *tragoedia saltata*, i.e., pantomime. See also below, n. 21.

17 *Certe/dolores?* (38/7-10).

18 *ad dolendum invitatur* (38/1). Solignac is not wrong when he draws a parallel between the purpose of this theatre and that of its modern counterparts in the cinema, TV, and pulp romances — *BA*, Vol. 13, p. 171.

19 *(et hoc) de illa vena amicitia (est)* (38/10-11).

20 *mallet/doloret* (39/1).

21 See *sed/tamen* (38/20-24). Courcelle (*Recherches*, pp. 52-56) citing texts from the *City of God* (quoted below, n. 25, 26), identifies the *spectacula theatrica* of III,ii,2-4, with the (sexual) mimicry of the festivals of the great nature deities such as Attis and Cybele whose rites portrayed them as happy lovers, then separated. While it is true that Augustine draws a very close connection between the public festivals of the gods and what was *daily* staged in song and dance in the theatres (see *DCD*, V,5-7, VII,26), there is no reason to limit the spectacles about which he speaks in III,ii,2-4 to the *yearly* performances of the former. See also below, n. 24.

22 *inde/raderer* (39/16-19). Augustine confesses that he went looking for the sorrows of the stage in just the same way, and for the same basic reason, as he went looking for love: see III,ii,4 *At/dolorem* (39/10-11), and compare III,i,1 *Nondum/amare* (36/26-29).

23 *In/mala* (39/24-27). When Augustine says this brought him "to the lowest depths of falseness" — *ad ima infida* (39/26) — he means it literally. This is, logically, the furthest one can go from God — i.e., to the worship of his opposite.

24 For this identification see Bardy's references, *BA*, Vol. 33, pp. 783-84: see also Courcelle, *Recherches*, p. 53. On the date of the festival, see H. Bettenson's note (6, p. 51) in the Penguin edition of the *City of God* (Harmondsworth, 1972): "The yearly festival of her purification was originally on 4 April, the anniversary of her arrival at Rome (cf. [*DCD*] Book I, 30) when her image was ceremonially bathed in the Almo where it joins the Tiber near Rome (Ovid, *Fast[i]*, 4, 337-55). Under the Empire this *lavatio* was on 27 March, part of the ceremonies of the vernal equinox."

25 *City of God* (trans. Bettenson, Penguin), pp. 51-52.

26 Ibid., pp. 83-84.

27 Sexual pantomimes were a feature of the oriental cults which had spread through every part of the Empire and "were the vital centre of the last generation of paganism in the West" (S. Dill, *Roman Society in the Last Century of the Western Empire*, 2nd ed., repr., New York, Meridian, 1958, p. 77; see pp. 74-112 for the tenor of these cults). Apuleius, in *The Golden Ass* (17), gives a vivid description of a licentious pantomime of the Judgement of Paris before a vast audience in an amphitheatre. Dill (p. 139) notes that as late as 460, Apollinaris Sidonius "describes, as still flourishing at Narbonne, that degraded pantomime, in which the foulest tales of the old mythology were represented in speaking gesture." Augustine is clear that it was not necessary to wait for the festivals to come around to have contact with these things since the eunuch priests of the Great Mother were to be seen daily in the streets and squares of Carthage, "with their pomaded hair and powdered [i.e., whitened] faces, gliding along with womanish languor, and demanding from the shopkeepers the means of their depraved existence" (*City of God*, VII,26, trans. Bettenson, Penguin, p. 286). On the nature of pagan religion in the fourth century see de Labriolle, *La réaction païenne. Étude sur la polémique antichrétienne du premier siècle au sixième siècle*, Paris, L'Artisan du Livre, 1934: M. D. Madden, *The Pagan Divinities and their Worship as depicted in the Works of Saint Augustine exclusive of the City of God*, Washington, Catholic University of America, 1930. Madden's work is best used as A. Mandouze suggests (p. 192, n. 30) in his own thoughtful article on the subject, "Saint Augustin et la religion romaine," *Recherches Augustiniennes*, 1 (1958), 187-223.

28 *Ausus/mortis* (39/28-40/1).

29 *negotium* (39/30) ordinarily means "business," "matter," "thing" but "As trans. of τὸ πρᾶγμα [is a] euphemism for sensual sins," see *ALD*, art. *negotium* where the only examples are from the Bible. This is the sense here. Courcelle (*Recherches*, p. 56) sees this as an (undefined) "rendez-vous d'amour." Brown (*Augustine*, p. 41) says that Augustine went to church not from contempt but from loyalty — "A stranger from the provinces, he would, of

course, go to church to find a girl-friend.'' Brown does not say how Augustine could have thought this to be worthy of procuring the fruit of death. The text he quotes from *CEF*, VIII,9 is slender ground on which to stake a claim for Augustine's innocent loyalty to the church.

30 *fugitivam libertatem* (40/6). Compare II,vi,14 *ut/imitarer* (34/5-6).

31 J. A. Doull, ''Augustinian Trinitarianism,'' p. 126, n. 13. I am indebted to Doull's comments on the general sense of Augustine's demon worship and for the illustrations from Vergil. Throughout the book I have had this brief but extraordinary account of the logic of the *Confessions* very much in mind.

32 See Vergil, *Aeneid* VII, 286f. Doull, ''Augustinian Trinitarianism,'' p. 126, n. 13, cites Livy in the same sense (*Ab urbe condita*, XXXIX,8f) and the *Senatus Consultum de Bacchanalibus*.

33 E.g., Salvian's *De Gubernatione Dei* which graphically describes the decadent Roman civilization (of southern Gaul) in the 430s. On Salvian and Augustine, see the thoughtful article of this title by O'Donnell (*Augustinian Studies*, 14 [1983], 25-34). O'Donnell argues cogently against the common view that Salvian should be seen as a semi-Pelagian and thus as opposed to Augustine.

The murals of the Villa of the Mysteries at Pompeii depict a (private) initiation into the cult of Dionysus in the late Republic at a time before these sexual rites had become open and public.

34 See I,xvii,27 where Augustine was set the task of appreciating Dido's rage rather than Aeneas' righteousness. Brown (*Augustine*, p. 23) remarks rightly that this is a ''very African [i.e., naturalistic] interlude in the life of the upright founder of Rome; and it is an African poet who will rectify the omissions of Vergil by writing the love letters of the deserted queen.'' He might well have gone further and said that this kind of thing represents a complete reversal of Vergil, where the truth and the centre of attention is not on Dido's position, but on that of Aeneas.

35 *eversores* (40/14). The modern version of this name would be something like the ''Destroyers.''

36 *proterve/suas* (40/19-21).

37 *longe/eversionibus* (40/12-19). See also V,viii,14 where Augustine remarks on the unruly behaviour of the students in Carthage. He complains that as a teacher he had to put up with behaviour which, as a student, he had spurned — *Ergo/alienos* (87/17-19).

38 This is the sense of *urbanitas* here (40/15) and in the phrase from III,i,1 — *elegans et urbanus* (37/12).

39 See above, n. 23.

40 *Nihil/fallere?* (40/21-26).

41 *Et/tua* (39/23-24).

42 Augustine divides the treatment of his adolescence into an earlier and a later period just as he had done with his childhood. The difference is that in his early adolescence he hated God and sought to turn from him, while in the later part he loved God and sought to find him.

43 The text of the *Hortensius* is no longer extant though certain fragments remain — see M. Ruch, *L'Hortensius de Cicéron: histoire et reconstitution*, Paris, Les Belles Lettres, 1958. Solignac provides a brief review of this material in *BA*, Vol. 13, pp. 667-68: see also his remarks pp. 85-87. H. Hagendahl, *Augustine and the Latin Classics* (Studia Graeca et Latina Gothoburgensia, 21-22, Göteborg, 1958), Vol. 1, pp. 79-94, has collected Augustine's references to the *Hortensius* and discusses them in Vol. 2, pp. 486-97. Augustine introduces *Hortensius* in III,iv,7 in this way, ''and in the ordinary course of studies I came across the book of a certain Cicero'' (*et/Ciceronis*, 40/29-41/1). There are many suggestions why Augustine uses the ''astonishing'' (Solignac, *BA*, Vol. 13, p. 667) *cuiusdam Ciceronis* (''a certain Cicero''): he lists those of Testard, Courcelle, and O'Meara, then adds his own. Since Cicero was well known, most assume that the expression is intended to be deprecatory and the difficulty is to explain how it jibes with the favourable dictum which Augustine adds at once — ''whose tongue almost all admire'' (*cuius/mirantur*). O. Tescari on the other hand (''Nota augustiniana [Conf. III,iv,7],'' *Convivium* 5 [1933], 414-21), thinks it means that

when Augustine read the *Hortensius* it was the first time he had come across Cicero's name. Courcelle (*Recherches*, p. 57), rightly, finds this implausible.

The problem dissolves if we are not obliged to assume that Augustine thought Cicero's name would be well known *to his intended audience* — and there is no reason to suppose that he did. I suggest that the reason he uses the *cuiusdam* is that he wrote for an audience that was, for the most part, ignorant of who Cicero was or what "almost all" those who had had a higher education (i.e., in the school of a *rhetor*), thought of him — and thus the explanation, *cuius linguam* etc. In *DBV* (I,4), dedicated to the philosopher Manlius Theodorus, Augustine recounts the same incident without using the *cuiusdam* since Theodorus would certainly have known who Cicero was: he simply says, "I read that book of Cicero's which is called *Hortensius.*" In the *City of God* (VII,x) Augustine says it was altogether possible that those brought up in a Christian household, whose education had been confined to the church's literature, would be quite unfamiliar with the writings of the philosophers or *even with the name of Plato* (and *mutatis mutandis*, with the name of Cicero as well). The same would also hold true for many non-Christians who were unlettered or had never advanced in their education beyond the mere ability to read (see for example the children of the fathers he mentions in II,iii,5).

M. Testard, *Saint Augustin et Cicéron* (Paris, Études Augustiniennes, 1958) is the standard work on the relations of these two authors: see Vol. 1, pp. 11-19 where he lists a number of explanations of the *cuiusdam Ciceronis* prior to his own day.

44 *cuius/ita* (41/1-2). The opposition here between *lingua* and *pectus* is doubtless that suggested by Testard (Vol. 1, p. 18) who, following Cicero, sees in it the distinction between rhetoric and philosophy. That Augustine had in mind a distinction between form and content is confirmed in the last sentence of the same section — *Non/persuaserat* (41/8-14). See also Courcelle (*Recherches*, pp. 59-60) who argues that the distinction was not so much an either/or as a both/and.

45 *Ille/redirem* (41/4-8).

46 See III,iv,7 *Inter/humanae* (40/27-29).

47 In later life Augustine was to recommend the *Hortensius* to his own students so that it might work in them the same effect that it had in him. In the case of Licentius and Trygetius, his hopes were fulfilled: see *CA*, I,i,4.

48 Augustine draws the etymology explicitly. See III,iv,8 *Amor autem sapientiae nomen graecum habet philosophiam* (41/11-12) — "However [what we in Latin call] the love of Wisdom (*amor sapientiae*) is, in Greek, called philosophy (*philo-sophia*)."

49 *Quomodo/te* (41/9-10) . . . *hoc/sapientiam* (42/1-3). This demand for a true knowledge of God is the sense of the text, which Augustine quotes from St. Paul (Col. 2:8f.), warning against any philosophy which is merely drawn from human sources and from the elements of this world rather than from God himself — by which Paul means Christ. *Hortensius* contained a similar warning though without the name of Christ. On the identification of Christ as the Wisdom of God, see below, n. 58.

50 *mutavit* (41/4, 5). Augustine's former position (the theft of pears) was a "turning away" from God — see II,i,1 *aversus* (25/9), and II,x,18 *defluxi* (36/21).

51 See III,iv,7 *et/redirem* (41/8).

52 See VI,xi,18, VII,i,1, VIII,vii,17, and *DBV*, I,1,4.

53 *Quomodo/mecum!* (41/9-11).

54 *hoc/fortiter* (42/1-5).

55 Lactantius, the Christian apologist (*c.* 240-*c.* 320), had written of Christ as the Wisdom of God in very similar language in his *Divine Institutions* (III,30). "Here, here is that for which all philosophers have sought [*quaerere*] throughout their life, but never once been able to track down [*investigare*], to embrace [*comprehendere*], to hold firm [*tenuere*]."

56 See III,iv,8 *et/rapiebat* (42/6-13). Augustine restates this in V,xiv,25. When Augustine says that he had drunk in the name of Christ with his mother's milk, he is referring to the sacrament of catechumens which he had received at birth (see I,xi,17). His point is that, for as long as he could remember, he had known that he was considered a catechumen in the Cath-

olic church by his parents – (the plural, *a parentibus*, in V,xiv,25 [98/3] and in the passage from *DUC*, I,2, quoted below, n. 106, implies that Patricius as well as Monica thought of him as a catechumen).

57 See above, Chapter One, at I,xi,17. From a worldly point of view it is accidental that Monica was a Christian so that Augustine grew up associating the name of Christ with the Wisdom of God. From the Christian standpoint from which he writes, Augustine can regard this acci-dent as the work of divine providence, as he does in III,iv,8 where he speaks of it as being "according to your mercy" – *secundum misericordiam tuam* (42/8-9). Behind this lies the thought of Romans 10:13-14, already announced in the first chapter of the *Confessions*, con-cerning the necessity of a human agent, or preacher (in this case Monica), in the Christian economy of salvation. Because it has to do with unique events in time and space – the life of Jesus – which reason cannot discover by any abstract consideration of things, Christianity depends on a chain of men and women to transmit these facts to each succeeding generation.

58 See Brown (*Augustine*, pp. 41-42): "The Christ of the popular imagination was not a suffer-ing Saviour. There are no crucifixes in the fourth century. He was rather 'the Great Word of God, the Wisdom of God' (Augustine, *Sermo*, 279, 7). On the sarcophagi of the age He is always shown as a Teacher, teaching his Wisdom to a coterie of budding philosophers." Of course Christians were not merely "budding philosophers" as this could be taken to say (see above, n. 57), but it does show why Augustine would have looked to Christ and his Scrip-tures to discover the content of Wisdom. For a more thorough and balanced view of this identification see Madec's article, "Christus, scientia et sapientia nostra. Le principe de cohérence de la doctrine augustinienne," *Recherches Augustiniennes*, 10 (1975), 77-85.

59 *Itaque/essent* (42/14-15).

60 I assume that when Augustine first read the Scriptures he turned to the New Testament because he was looking for Christ. It seems likely that he started with the Gospels (intro-duced by the contradictory genealogies to which the Manichees took exception) and did not get much further because, in III,iv,8, he says that at the time he read *Hortensius*, "the [words] of the apostle [Paul] were not yet known to me" – *nondum/erant* (41/31-42/1).

61 *indigna/conpararem* (42/21-22).

62 *Et/pueris* (42/15-16).

63 It was only much later, in Milan, that Augustine learned from Ambrose to see behind the lit-eral sense of Scripture: see V,xiv,24.

64 *ego/videbar* (42/25-26). In III,v,9 Augustine sets the task of negating the first (natural and corrupt) maturity by becoming a "little one" again (*parvulus*) or a "child" (*puer*). We do this by accepting, in faith, the promises of Christ and the teaching of the church so that we may grow again into our true (i.e., spiritual) maturity. This is how Augustine interpreted the words of Mt. 19:14 in I,xix,30. This is the sense of his unwillingness to be a little one in the text quoted above. This is the sense in which he speaks of Monica as having laboured twice to bring him to birth – first in the flesh and a second time according to the spirit: see I,xi,17, II,xi,19, V,ix,17, IX,vii,17. This same image is in Augustine's mind when he makes the oft repeated call for the proud natural man to come down from the heights to become humble and small, etc.: see IV,xii,18-19, V,iii,3-6, VI,xviii,24, VII,xx,26, VII,xxi,27.

    Augustine uses this image of a second childhood when he speaks of the teaching of the church as the food (sometimes bread, but especially milk) by which such a little one is suck-led and nourished into spiritual maturity. Thus, for example, Augustine speaks of himself *qua* Christian, as a baby "sucking your milk" (*sugens lac tuum*, IV,i,1 – 54/23), or again, he speaks of the (incarnate) Christ as Wisdom in the form of milk (VII,xviii,24). So too, in *DUC*, I, 2, the church is spoken of as the breast or teat to which Augustine, starved and exhausted for substantial food, finally and avidly returned.

    In a variation of this image Augustine also speaks of one who has come to seek Wisdom as a soul or bird whose wings have sprouted – see the *revolare* of III,iv,8 – 41/10). But only if it is nourished with the proper spiritual food, starting with the milk of faith, can it gain the strength to fly (to come to the true knowledge of God) rather than fall (into a false knowl-edge) when it leaves the nest. This image and its related extensions (see below, n. 66, 138) occur frequently in the *Confessions* (see esp. IV,xvi,31). It is given a particularly clear expression in a passage from *Sermo* LI,iv,5 (quoted in Courcelle, *Recherches*, pp. 61-62).

65 See *sed/mysteriis* (42/16-18).

66 III,vi,10 *incido* (42/27), III,vi,11 *offendi* (45/11), V,vii,13 *inrueram* (86/9). Augustine uses the same *incido* on other occasions when he describes how he became a Manichee: see *DBV*, I,4, and *DUC* I,2. Courcelle (*Recherches*, p. 153, n. 1) notices that Augustine uses the same words to describe his discovery of the books of the Platonists. In Augustine's usage these words convey the sense of an apparent accident which is governed by a higher, unseen, necessity: see the *inrueo* of I,xx,31 — 24/24.

In all likelihood Augustine drew this *incido* and its synonyms from Proverbs 7:23. There, the foolish harlot whom Augustine directly equates with the Manichees (see III,vi,11) is said to attract men who fall into her trap "as a bird rushes into a snare" *velut . . . avis festinet ad laqueum*, Vulgate). In combining this *incido* with the image of the soul as a young bird (see above, n. 64), Augustine imagines the Manichee's teachings as a "bird-snare" (*laqueus*, III,iv,10 — 42/28). He speaks of Faustus as a "snare of the devil" (*laqueus diaboli*, V,iii,3-78/10), and again as a "deadly snare" (*laqueus mortis*, V,vii,13 — 86/10). The word for "snare" (*laqueus*) is interchangeable with *viscum* (III,vi,10 — 42/29), meaning a sticky glue (made from mistletoe = *viscum*), smeared on branches and used for trapping birds. An account of the practice, again applied to the Manichees, is found in *DUC*, I, 2.

67 *Itaque/sancti* (42/27-43/2).

68 *Et/mihi* (43/4-5).

69 O'Meara (*The Young Augustine: The Growth of Augustine's Mind up to His Conversion*, London, Longmans, Green & Co., 1954; Chapter Four) gives an especially lucid account of the convoluted Manichaean doctrines and the points of contact they shared with Catholic Christianity according to which they regarded themselves as the true, enlightened, and purified Christians. See also Solignac, *BA*, Vol. 13, p. 668 and pp. 674-76. In *CFM* (XX,2), Faustus gives his creed: "We [Manichees] worship one deity under the threefold appellation of the Almighty God the Father, and his son Christ, and the Holy Spirit" (trans. *NPNF*). Faustus claimed to have fulfilled the beatitudes of Christ (*CFM*, V,1) and the Manichees in general thought of themselves as those who more perfectly followed Christ than did the Catholics — whom they called *semichristianae* (*CFM*, I, 3). It was because Manichaeism regarded itself as the true Christianity that Augustine could speak of it as a heresy (see V,x,19) rather than a completely unrelated religion such as the cult of Jupiter or any of the other pagan deities. In *LDH*, XLIV, 5 Augustine speaks of the Manichee "church" (*ecclesia*). Faustus regarded himself as a "bishop" — see V,iii,3 *quidam manichaeorum episcopus* (78/9). The same view of the Manichees is again put forward in *DUC*, IX,21, where also (VIII,19) heretics are defined by their pretension to be Catholics. P. Brown, "The Diffusion of Manichaeism in the Roman Empire," *Journal of Religious Studies*, 59 (1969) — repr. in his *Religion and Society in the Age of Saint Augustine* (New York, Harper and Row, 1972), pp. 99-118 — gives an account of the Christian pretensions of Manichaeism from its inception.

70 *falsa/tua* (43/6-8).

71 *inferebatur/luna* (43/15). For the Manichees, the sun and moon were seen as vehicles which transported the liberated particles of God (light) from this world back to God — and were themselves identified with God. See F. Decret, *L'Afrique manichéene (IVe-Ve siècles). Étude historique et doctrinale*, Paris, Études Augustiniennes, 1978, Vol. 1, p. 309. In *CFM*, XX,1-4, Augustine discusses the Manichean identification of God the Father with the highest or principal light, the "light inaccessible" of 1 Tim. 6:16, and God the Son with the sun (in his power) and the moon (in his wisdom), and the Holy Spirit with the circle of the atmosphere.

72 Solignac (*BA*, Vol. 13, p. 674) comments on the Manichaean doctrine of the "corner" (*cuneus*). See *CFM*, XX,22 — XXVII,29 for an explicit statement of the Manichaean understanding of the spatial relation of good and evil.

73 See *BA*, Vol. 13, p. 381 for the Manichaean reference in the phrase *phantasmata splendida* (43/21-22). J. Gibb and W. Montgomery in their edition of the *Confessions* (Cambridge

Patristic Texts, Cambridge, 1908, p. 62) provide the following note about the distinction between *phantasma(ta)* and *phantasia*. *"Phantasma(ta)*: In *de Mus.* VI,xi,32 Augustine explains 'phantasma' as the visual image formed by arbitrarily combining and working up sense impressions in contrast with the simple memory-image 'phantasia'; e.g., his mental image of his father was a 'phantasia,' that of his grandfather, whom he had never seen, a 'phantasmata.' Augustine seems to have been the first Latin writer to use the word in a philosophical sense (= ghost, Pliny, *Ep.* VII,27,1)": compare also *CFM*, XX,7. Augustine therefore means that the simple mental images (*phantasiae*) of the sun and moon were worked into something *grandiora et infinita* (44/7) by an arbitrary imagination. In IV,xv,26 he says that such things as the objects of Manichaean belief were "devised by mine own vain conceit, fancying out of a body" *sed/corpore* (73/3-4) — trans. Watts (*Loeb*).

74 *illa/carneo* (44/2-4).
75 See Decret, *L'Afrique manichéene*, Vol. 1, pp. 321-22. Much of my discussion of chs. vi-viii is drawn from D. Smith's unpublished thesis on Augustine's Criticism of Manichaeism in Confessions III,vi-viii (Dalhousie University), which discusses the internal logical of this section of the text.
76 Decret, *L'Afrique manichéene*, Vol. 1, p. 265.
77 Ibid., pp. 313, 281.
78 Ibid., p. 278.
79 Ibid., p. 282. For a list of Augustine's anti-Manichaean writings see E. Portalié, *A Guide to the Thought of Saint Augustine*, trans. R. Bastian, Chicago, Henry Regnery Co., 1960, pp. 47-50.
80 Decret, *L'Afrique manichéene*, Vol. 1, pp. 259-89. The opinion is shared by the other great scholars of Manichaeism. See the works cited below, n. 81.
81 Solignac gives a brief account of the sources of our knowledge of the Manichees in *BA*, Vol. 13, pp. 118-19, and a brief biography of the founder, Mani, pp. 119-21. The most complete work on Mani and the Manichees is still that of H-C. Puech, *Le Manichéisme. Son Fondateur. Sa Doctrine* (Paris, Civilisations du Sud, Annales du Musée Guimet, 56, 1949). Alfaric's *L'évolution* is very useful for the author's wide knowledge of Manichaeism in its relation to Augustine. So also are the more recent studies by Decret, *Aspects du manichéisme dans l'Afrique romaine. Les controverses de Fortunatus, Faustus et Felix avec saint Augustin* (Paris, Études Augustiniennes, 1970), and his *L'Afrique manichéene* (above, n. 71). English readers may consult G. Widengren, *Mani and Manichaeism* (New York, Holt, Rinehart and Winston, 1963). See also J. P. Maher, "Saint Augustine and Manichean Cosmogony" (*Augustinian Studies*, 10 (1979), 91-104) for a brief account of the remarkable discovery in Egypt in the 1930s of a cache of Manichaean texts, including two by Mani himself (*Kephalaia* and *Epistles*) and a strong defence of the accuracy of Augustine's portrayal of their teachings in his anti-Manichaean writings — as against the views of Isadore du Beausobre (*Histoire critique de Manichée et du manichéisme*, 2 vols., Amsterdam, 1734, 1739) and Alfaric.
    On Mani's claim that he was inspired by the Holy Spirit (= God), see V,v,8 *non/conatus est* (81/28-82/2), *ut/niteretur* (82/8-9), V,v,9 *In/arbitrarentur* (82/21-24): see also the references in *BA*, Vol. 13, p. 476, n. 1. See Decret (*Aspects*, pp. 293-94, 301), on the distinction between the Holy Spirit and the Paraclete (= Mani) in Manichaean thought.
82 Smith, "Augustine's Criticism."
83 *Quanto/meae* (44/13-20).
84 The *BA* ed. translates this *certior* as "more real." This is not quite accurate enough to convey Augustine's sense. Augustine uses the same word three times a few sentences before.
85 These *phantasmata* are the most changeable objects of knowledge, but beneath them Augustine distinguishes pure potency itself — what he calls formless matter — as the substance from which all created beings are made and which, deprived of all form, is almost nothing but is not altogether deprived of all existence: see XII,v,5-XII,ix,9.
86 *in/obumbratio* (43/19-20).
87 *vivens/mutaris* (44/19-20).

88 There is clearly an affinity between this scale and the terms on the Platonic line (*Republic*, VI, 509d-511e). Smith, "Augustine's Criticism" sees Augustine's criticism of the Manichees as Platonic — but one should be cautious because the terms do not correspond exactly.

89 See III,x,18 where Augustine came to accept such things from the Manichees.

90 ... *libris multis et ingentibus* (43/13-14). Brown, "Manichaeism in the Roman Empire," in *Religion and Society*, p. 112, describes the impressive place the Manichees gave their seven great works which they used to lay out on a high throne. Du Beausobre (*Histoire critique*, Vol. 1, p. 426 and Vol. 2, pp. 399f.) alleges that Augustine could not have known the content of these books which were only for the Elect who were forbidden to confide it to the Auditors — but, like so much else with the Manichees, this rule was chiefly observed in the breach. The content was not secret — the Catholic bishop from whom Monica sought help had read, and even copied, most of the books when he was a Manichaean Auditor (see III,xii,21 *omnes/eorum* (53/20-21) and Augustine himself, from an early date, knew enough of Mani's writings on astronomy to be able to compare them with those of ancient natural science — see V,iii,6, and V,vii,13 where he says explicitly that he had studied Mani's writings — *Refracto/litteras* (85/26-27). The 'secrets' of the Manichees were not so much in the texts themselves, which were accessible, as in their meaning which was not — or at least not without the guidance of the Elect. Augustine was greatly impressed by these huge volumes and calls them the "plates" (*fercula* — III,vi,10 — 43/14) on which they served him their fantasies. It is unlikely that, at first, he looked very far into their content. It seems rather that he was impressed by them as being impressive — much as a college student today might have books that he doesn't read but which are reputed to be deep and difficult — in order to appear knowledgeable.

91 *figmenta inania* (43/26).

92 *phantasmata splendida* (43/21-22).

93 See *Et/sunt* (43/24-44/8).

94 *Qualibus/pascebar* (44/8-9).

95 For the story of Medea flying see Ovid, *Metamorphoses*, VII, 215-21. Kelly, "Tragedy," p. 27, understands this as a *tragoedia cantata*, called *Medea volans*, which Augustine had in his repertoire — *cantabam*, "I used to recite" (45/3) — and could perform in competitions such as the one he mentioned in IV,ii,3. The parallel example of Manichaean *phantasmata* which Augustine gives here — "the five dens of darkness" — refer to the concentric regions of the Land of Darkness which the Manichees distinguished as darkness itself, waters, winds, fire, and smoke. Each had its own inhabitants with the Prince of Darkness in the smoke and gloom at the centre. See *CEF*, XV,19, XXVII,31 and *LDH*, XLVI.

96 *volantem/credidi* (45/2-4).

97 *te/quaererem* (45/8-10). This *quaero* was the immediate task — the second of the five verbs — as set out in III,iv,8.

98 *Offendi/vorassem* (45/11-17). The Biblical quotation is "a popular proverb applied to adultery" (*Bible*, Revised Standard Version, annotated ed., H. G. May and B. M. Metzger, New York, Oxford University Press, 1962, Pr. 9:17). Compare with the other texts in Proverbs on Wisdom and her adulterous imitation, Folly — see 5:1-23, 7:1-27, 8:1-36. In this chapter Augustine echoes Proverbs' insistence that such things kill those who believe them — *et occidunt credentem* (44/27-45/1) — by starving the soul of its true intellectual nourishment. In Augustine's imagery the soul commits fornication when it turns from God and seeks him in his works: see I,xiii,21. In the text of Proverbs (9:14-18) from which Augustine quotes, the harlot to whom he likens the Manichees, is explicitly contrasted with Lady Wisdom.

99 See *DDA*, IX.

100 A list of Augustine's Manichaean friends is found in Courcelle (*Recherches*, pp. 68-70): see also the Addenda, p. 262. Alypius became a Manichee by Augustine's influence (see VI,vii,12): so did the young friend of IV,iv,7. For the same about Romanianus, see *CA*, I,i,3; for Honoratus, see *DUC*, I, 2. On Augustine's delight in defeating the arguments of naive Catholics, see III,x,18, III,xii,21, and VI,i,1. On his shame at discovering the falsity of the Manichaean teachings, see VI,iii,4, and VI,iv,5.

101 *Nesciebam/est* (45/18). See also IV,ii,3, IV,xv,24, IV,xvi,29-31, V,x,9, V,xi,21, V,xiv,25, VI,iii,4, VI,iv,6, and VII,i,1-2.

102 From *Hortensius* Augustine had recognized Wisdom as a rational, universal, and objective truth. It was there in everything and was not the creation of any particular person or group as he had formerly attempted to maintain. But if this meant that he could no longer confuse it with his own desires, he moved forward only one step at a time and the next step was far from the position in which intelligible or spiritual reality becomes visible. See Doull, "Augustinian Trinitarianism," p. 131: "It testifies to Augustine's profound philosophical spirit that he moved no farther than the argument required him from his previous position."

103 *quasi/animalibus* (45/18-24). In *DDA*, I,1 Augustine says that his fall into Manichaeism was accomplished in the space of a "few days" (*deibus paucis*) so I have translated the *quasi acutule* (45/18-19) — lit., "as if somewhat sharply" — as "rather quickly." In V,x,19-20 Augustine again speaks of the difficulties which he found in Catholic doctrine and adds to the earlier list his inability to give his assent to the Incarnation. "And I feared therefore to believe [that Christ] was born in the flesh lest I would be compelled to believe that [he] was polluted by the flesh" (*Metuebam/inquinatum* 93/30-94/2). See *CFM*, XXII for a list of what the Manichees found inconsistent in the morality of the Old Testament fathers. Though not mentioned in the *Confessions*, the Manichees also pointed to the contradictory genealogies of Christ as given in Matthew and Luke. Faustus reverts to this point over and again: see *CFM*, II, VII, XXIII, XXVIII.

  Courcelle (*Recherches*, pp. 61-63) suggests — on the basis of a text in *Sermo* LI (*Sermon I,6* in *NPNF*) — that the contradictory genealogies were what chiefly prevented Augustine from finding the truth in Scriptures (in III,iv,9) and thus what he initially found compelling about the Manichaean objections to Catholicism. This may be true but it should not be understood as overturning what Augustine says in III,v,9 about why he did not find Wisdom in the Scriptures, nor what he says in III,vii,12 about the things that drew him to the Manichees — where he does not list the contradictory genealogies. In *Sermo* LI he says that these latter "troubled" (*perturbaruent*) him when he looked at the Bible but this is given as an indication of his pride — and thus accords with what he says in III,v,9 — in that he did not look for the Catholic interpretation but supposed that the obvious discrepancies had no explanation. On the other hand, where he does not list these matters in III,vii,12 as amongst the main questions that drew him to the Manichees, it seems unwarranted to suppose that they played this role. At the time they could have troubled him without being among the chief reasons he joined the sect. His answer to these objections is found in *Sermo* LI and in the texts from *CFM* cited above.

104 Central, of course, to Augustine's being moved by these objections was the literal and direct sense in which he accepted the Catholic claim that the Scriptures were inspired by God. On the particularly strict interpretation of this position in African Christianity, see Brown's comments (*Augustine*, pp. 42-43).

105 In III,x,18 Augustine says that he only accepted the positive content of the Manichee's teachings "little by little" — *paulatim* (III,x,18 — 51/1). This need not contradict his assertion that he decided to become a Manichee in a matter of a few days (see above, n. 103).

106 Courcelle (*Recherches*, p. 40, n. 3) lists other references to Augustine's objections to what seemed to him at the time to be an unacceptably authoritative spirit in Catholicism. Other friends became Manichees for other reasons — Alypius for example was drawn by their *practice* — their seemingly holy way of living: see VI,vii,12.

107 See *quia/ignorabam* (45/25-46/6). On the corporeal substance of evil see the text from *DMM*, VIII,11, mentioned by Courcelle (*Recherches*, p. 65), who says that when Augustine "reported to the Manichaean bishop charged with his instruction, the thesis of a Catholic according to which evil is not a substance, the other replied by an irresistible argument well suited to strike the young man: 'I would like to put a scorpion in his hand and see if he does not withdraw it; if he withdraws it he will be convinced that evil is a substance by the fact, not by my arguments.' "

108 Augustine repeats over and over that he had no idea of spiritual substance. See the texts quoted above, n. 102, and 107.

109 Solignac, (BA, Vol. 13, pp. 668-70) gives a list of the Scriptural references for these allegedly immoral acts of the Patriarchs. Augustine has a lengthy discussion of these points in CFM XXII.

110 feriebant/videbam (47/17-18).

111 Et/praenuntiantes (47/28-31).

112 See III,viii,15 Numquid/ipsum? (47/32-48/3).

113 In DDC, III,x,16 Augustine defines the distinction. "What an unconquered lust does to corrupt its own soul and body is called a corrupt act [flagitium], but what it does to harm another is called a crime [facinus]." I am especially indebited to Smith ("Augustine's Criticism"), in my discussion of this chapter.

114 Violatur/polluitur (48/8-10).

115 ubique/sunt (48/4).

116 Turpis/congruens (48/14-15).

117 See CFM XXII, 47 where Augustine writes of the polygamy of the patriarchs, "When it was custom it was not a crime, now however it is a crime because it is not custom."

118 tria/tuum (48/11-12). See also Sermo IX on Augustine's treatment of the decalogue.

119 See Item/quorumlibet (48/29-49/8).

120 Haec/omnibus (48/8-11). See O. du Roy, L'intelligence de la foi en la Trinité selon saint Augustine. Genèse de sa théologie trinitaire jusqu'en 391 (Paris, Études Augustiniennes, 1966), pp. 343-57, where he documents Augustine's use of this text (from 1 John 2:16), and discusses its significance as a trinitarian image.

121 Smith, "Augustine's Criticism."

122 privata/falsum (49/28).

123 See III,vii,13 Et/interiorem (46/7), III,x,18 Haec ego nesciens (50/30).

124 Augustine mentions some of the fantasies of the Manichaean views on justice — such as the sin in picking a fig or the capital crime (in their view) of feeding it to a non-Manichee — in III,x,18. See also below, n. 133.

125 Sed/sibi (48/15-17).

126 See sed/bonum (49/15-50/5).

127 This chapter answers the second half of the final sentence of III,vii,14 — i.e., rerum/praenuntiantes (47/30-31).

128 See Sed/segetis (50/6-9).

129 See Et/temporis (50/9-29).

130 See Cum/praenuntianda (50/20-29). See BA, Vol. 13, p. 396, n. 1, where Solignac makes the point that, however unusual the divine command, it is not to be followed merely because ordered by God but because it is ultimately possible to discover a justification either as appropriate to the times or as prefiguring things which, as God knows, will come about in the future. In other words, Augustine insists that such orders must be ultimately comprehensible to men — otherwise there would be no difference between the Catholic position and that of the Manichees.

131 servos et prophetas (59/30-31) — these two reflect the twofold character of the previous discussion in ch. vii and ch. ix — as announced in the final sentence of III,vii,14.

132 Haec/sanctus (50/30-51/3) misceret/solverentur (51/5-9). BA, Vol. 13, p. 397, gives a brief explanation and references for the business of the fig-tree weeping.

133 Augustine never moved beyond the lower rank of the Manichaean hierarchy, that of "Auditor." A brief account of this hierarchy is found in BA, Vol. 13, pp. 398-99. On the help that these freed gods would give to the Auditors who had assisted in their liberation by picking the fruit and bringing it to the Elect, see IV,i,1 — cum/liberaremur (54/12-15). The Elect themselves were not allowed to sully themselves by the "sin" (scelus, III,x,18 — 51/5) of picking any fruit because this ripped and hurt the particles of god which were said to be especially concentrated in trees and their fruits. The hurt was the cause of the milky tears shed by the tree whenever a fruit was picked: see above, n. 132. O'Meara (The Young Augus-

tine, p. 76) explain: "[Auditors] have one serious and inescapable obligation – never to be the direct instrument of giving food to anyone not of their faith. To do so is to deliver the divine substance in the food into the hands of devils": his account of the dietary practices of the sect is clear and simple (pp. 76-78).

134 See Doull, "Augustinian Trinitarianism," p. 131. "As an image of Being, light expresses an identity which remains in its diffusion."

135 Puech, *Manichéisme*, p. 72. In the very first mention of the Manichees, in III,vi,10, Augustine already noted that they claimed to know the truth not only about God but also about the elements of this world: see the text translated above at n. 70.

136 See Doull, "Augustinian Trinitarianism," p. 131, n. 22. "His [Augustine's] treatises against the Manichees insist on the same conclusion as he reaches in the *Confessions*: that the content of the Manichaean writings is not controlled by their principles, and is such a fanciful concatenation as the vastly popular genre of science fiction at the present time."

137 See IV,iv,9 *phantasmata/iubebatur* (60/12), V,iii,6 *credere iubebar* (80/26-27), and VI,v,7 *credenda imperari* (105/10).

138 *te/magis* (43/24-27). As the object of Augustine's quest, this oft-repeated image of Wisdom as the food of the soul – see above, n. 64, VII,x,16 *cibus/me* (141/9-12), VII, xvii, 23 *Tunc/possem* (147/17-22) – is not simply a figure of speech. The Latin for Wisdom – *sapientia* – has its root in the verb *sapere* with the primary meaning of "to taste, to have the savour of," and the derivative sense of having good taste or discernment: see *ALD*, art., *sapio*.

139 See III,xi,20 *Nam/sum* (50/25-28), and IV,i,1 *Per/duodetricensimum* (54/1-2).

140 A brief account of the differences between the Elect and the Auditors may be found in O'Meara, *The Young Augustine*, pp. 77-79.

141 The word *involucrum*, "cover," refers to the huge books of the Manichees. See above, n. 90.

142 *recedens/videbar* (45/25).

143 *Et/domine* (51/15-20).

144 *somnium* (51/23), *visum* (52/13). An extensive treatment of the role of dreams in the life and works of Augustine is found in M. Dulaey, *Le rêve dans la vie et pensée de saint Augustin* (Paris, Études Augustiniennes, 1973): Monica's dream of the wooden ruler is discussed pp. 158-65.

145 *ubi/me* (52/6).

146 *"Non/ille"* (52/15-16).

147 See III,xi,20 *Confiteor/somnio* (52/17-23).

148 I do not think that the passage from *CA*, II,ii,3 should be taken in the sense Courcelle gives – that Augustine actually moved in with Romanianus for a time (*Recherches*, p. 68) – nor that the text from the *Confessions* (III,xi,19 "she had begun to be unwilling" – *nolle coeperat* – 51/25) means that Monica had actually sent him away from her house. In the text from *CA*, II,ii,3, Augustine says only that Romanianus gave him the *communicatione domus tuae* – i.e., "the disposition of [his] house." This does not mean that Augustine *moved in* with Romanianus any more than does the phrase a few lines above, that earlier Romanianus had offered Augustine hospitality at his "house and table" – *et domo et sumptu*.

149 See IX,viii,17 *Sed/nascerer* (193/19-22). To appreciate the bishop's prudence we have only to read one of Augustine's later disputes with the Manichees (like *CFM*) to realize the endless difficulties in arguing the interpretation of Scripture with someone whose categories of interpretation are derived from fantasy and are therefore infinitely changeable.

150 *prudenter sane* (53/12).

151 *fieri/pereat* (53/27-28).

152 *responsum* (53/3). See also *Quod/sonuisset* (53/28-30).

153 Monica seems often to have had such "visions and answers" to her questions (*visiones et responsiones*, V,ix,17-90/24). In III,xii,21 and V,ix,27, Augustine says that he has mentioned some and omitted others. The first of these texts is not usually interpreted in this sense. It reads, *Et dedisti alterum responsum interim, quod recolo. Nam et multa praetero*

propter quod propero ad eaque me magis urgent confiteri tibi, et multa non memini (53/3-6). Some (i.e., the *BA* translation and Courcelle, see below) read the *multa* of the second sentence in a general sense, giving a translation like this: "And meanwhile you gave another response which I remember. For I both pass over *many things* because I hasten to those which urge me more to confess to you, and also I do not remember *many things*." I do not think these words should be understood in this general sense. They refer to the *responsum* of the first sentence and speak of the *many* answers/oracles God gave to Monica in her life — some of which he remembered and mentions, some of which he remembered and does not mention, and some of which he had simply forgotten (Watts translates in this sense, *Loeb*, p. 141). This reading is confirmed in the next sentence — "And you gave another [i.e., response]" (*Dedisti ergo alterum* 53/6). I think it is forced to maintain that he was not talking about the same thing in all three sentences. The thought is repeated in V,ix,17 — *Absit/conmemoravi* (90/23-25).

Courcelle (*Recherches*, p. 23), makes much of the text from III,xii,21 taken in the general sense — as indicating, along with other passages, a vast scheme for the completion of the *Confessions* which Augustine was only partially able to complete and from which he was diverted by the biography of Books I-IX. His point loses its basis if this text should be understood as I suggest — and in any event his translation goes beyond what Augustine says. It is twisted to give the sense he wants: for *Et dedisti ...*, he gives, "You gave *me ...*," which makes the oracle directed to Augustine rather than Monica! As I see it, the sense is that there were many signs which God gave to Monica — some of which Augustine had even forgotten — but, amazing as they were, he says he will not discuss them here except insofar as they relate directly to his aim of showing how he was moved to Christianity. Courcelle (*Les Confessions de saint Augustin dans la tradition littéraire, antecédents et postérité*, Paris, Études Augustiniennes, 1963, pp. 127-36) has collected a number of ancient references to the prevalence of such visions in Roman Africa — to which should be added his (controversial) discussion of "voices" in the *Confessions* (*Recherches*, pp. 291-310). He wants Augustine's Christianity to have nothing to do with such irrational things — but there is no need to regard them in this light. Monica, after all, was not moved by these "signs" to any irrational behaviour but only to the most difficult, patient, and pious labour on her son's behalf. Against Courcelle's contention that Augustine's discussion of Monica's dream was merely an "allegory" (*Les Confessions*, p. 132), see O'Ferrall, "Monica, the Mother of Augustine," pp. 30-35, where she argues cogently for a realistic interpretation. Of the visions Augustine does include in the *Confessions*, another is mentioned in VI,i,1, where Monica comforted the frightened sailors in a storm at sea on the basis of a vision: *quia/eras* (98/18). In VI,xiii,23 Augustine himself asked Monica to ask God for a vision about his proposed marriage and tells us that she claimed to be able to distinguish between the visions which came from God and mere dreams although neither she nor he knew how to explain this. In the same chapter he also says that "she was accustomed" to receive such minor revelations (*qua solebat*, 120/30). In V,ix,17 and VI,xiii,23 these visions are called God's "promises" — see *promissionibus* (91/2) for the first and, for the second, *promissa tua* (120/23). Augustine himself sometimes recognized certain things said by men as "heavenly oracles," just as Monica did to the reply of the bishop. He speaks thus of an answer Ambrose once gave him in *Letter* LIV,ii,3 (to Januarius) — *tamquam eam caelesti oraculo acceperim*, "I received it as if from a heavenly oracle." The same applies to the famous scene in the garden in Milan where he interpreted the *Tolle, lege*, as a divine command: see VIII,xii,29 and my discussion of the same in Chapter Eight.

154 See IX,viii,17 *Sed/nascerer* (193/10-22). See also V,vii,13 and V,x,16. Monica continued to be "present" to Augustine even after her death, as he tells in *DCM*, 16 where he says that "no night" went by without his dreaming of Monica — *me ipsum pia mater nulla nocte deserceret*.

155 *in/revelaveras* (179/14-15).

Chapter Four
COMMENTARY ON BOOK IV

This book covers the nine years during which Augustine thought of himself as a Manichee.[1] In it he shows how ''errors and false opinions contaminate life'' (IV,xv,25),[2] just as, in the first three chapters of Book III, he explained the kind of life he led as a result of his earlier effort to be free of the inner divine law. The next book explains how he was liberated from the Manichees.

IV,i,1. Introduction

This chapter introduces the content of the book which turns on the distinction between what the Manichees proposed in theory and what actually resulted from their position. Augustine first discusses the problem with respect to the things that he did ''privately'' (where he shows how Manichaean activities influenced his worldly position — in IV,ii,2-3), and then in relation to the things which he did ''openly'' (where he shows how his various worldly activities were influenced by his Manichaean position — in IV,iii,4-IV,xvi,31).[3] Speaking of himself and his Manichee friends during these years he says:

> [W]e were both seduced and seducing, both deceived and deceiving in all our various aims and desires: this was so both in those things which we did openly through those studies which are called liberal, and in private in the things we did under the false name of religion. [We were] proud in relation to the first, superstitious in relation to the second, and everywhere vain: on the one hand running after the emptiness of popular glory in the applause of the theatre, and in poetic competitions, and in contests for straw crowns, and in the trumpery of spectacles, and in intemperate passions; on the other hand we aspired to cleanse ourselves from these defiling things by carrying to those men who were called elect and holy, food from which they would make, in the workshop of their guts, angels and god through whom we would be freed.[4]

The first question to ask is why Augustine was in any way involved in worldly aims and ambitions. He has told us that from the moment of reading the *Hortensius* he preferred the search for Wisdom to anything the world could offer, and yet here he found himself very much embroiled in worldly ambitions. If the Manichees knew the truth, why did he not set himself to follow it to the exclusion of every other activity? The answer is that the form in which he thought he had found the truth made it impossible to do it.[5]

This defect of the Manichees' position ultimately derives from the notion that good and evil are separated corporeal substances and that the soul of man is likewise divided into two souls: a good soul from God and an evil one from the Prince

---

Notes to Chapter Four appear on pages 106-12.

of Darkness. The Manichee seeks to be liberated from his evil soul by "doing the truth" (i.e., all the various aspects of Manichaean morality and practice).[6] This is the sense of the distinction between those things done openly and in public which, from a Manichaean perspective, belong to the promptings of his evil soul ("those defiling things"), and the things done in the name of the Manichaean religion, which belonged to the activities of his good soul and were supposed to liberate him from evil. However, since these good activities took the form of negating the works of his evil soul, the latter were perpetually presupposed as the very condition of "doing the truth," and he found that while he could not accept the workings of his evil soul neither could he escape from them. In this book Augustine examines the miserable consequences of this contradiction as they appeared in his life.

I. Things done "privately"

IV,ii,2-3. The three seals of Manichaean practice

This chapter explains Augustine's involvement in the Manichaean cult. The Manichees proposed to free man from his evil soul by the application of their doctrine of the three "seals." These were, first, the *seal of the mouth*, which forbade apostasy from the sect, lying, perjury, oaths, and blasphemy, in all of which the evil soul works against the truth. This seal also included the many peculiar dietary practices of the sect. Second, the *seal of the bosom* aimed at preventing the propagation of evil through the reproduction of the species which the Manichees understood to cause a further quantity of light (God) to become imprisoned in the domain of darkness (i.e., matter). Total chastity was the ideal required of the Elect. For Auditors, sex was allowed providing every effort was made to avoid a pregnancy. Marriage, contracted for the sake of getting children, was instituted by the devil and was to be avoided at all costs. Finally, the *seal of the hand* aimed at preventing any harm to the particles of divinity which were already entrapped in matter. Homicide was forbidden and the killing of animals and plants, or, in general, any disturbance of nature, since almost all things in the world contained some portion of the substance of God. For the Elect this was carried to great lengths. Amongst other things it was interpreted as meaning that they should never use that most Roman of institutions, the bath — because on entering the water it was torn apart, with inevitable harm to the entrapped particles of God. For the same reason they must handle objects as little as possible and abstain from all manual labour.[7]

Augustine begins his account of the events of these years with a reference to this doctrine of the three seals, although I think this has not been recognized before. He notes that he was deeply involved in various worldly activities of which he distinguishes three main kinds: (*i*) the love of power — which he acquired by the practice and sale of rhetoric, (*ii*) the love of love — which he satisfied with his mistress; and (*iii*) the love of glory — which he sought by entering into poetic competitions. At the same time he also tells us of the steps he took, as a believing Manichaean Auditor, to purify himself from these (evil) attachments to the world.

For the Auditors, the seal of the mouth was relaxed inasmuch as they were permitted to eat normally and drink wine. The seal of the hand was altered to allow them to be farmers or even butchers and to take part in public life and aspire to its honours. And the total chastity of the bosom was relaxed to allow them to marry if they must and to fornicate if they could not do otherwise — though neither of these must ever be done with the intention of getting children. If we follow Augustine we will see how he applied each of these seals.

1) The purging of worldly power. He tells us that on the one hand he sought worldly wealth (or power) from his teaching. "I taught in those years the art of rhetoric and I sold the art of speaking which is used to conquer others, being myself conquered by greed" (IV,ii,2).[8] On the other hand, in accordance with the doctrine, he applied the seal of the mouth to his teaching. This is shown in the fact, which he specifically mentions, that he never did so with the intention — which he might otherwise have done — that what he taught should be used in a totally unprincipled fashion, to slay the innocent, but only that it might be used to free the guilty. To this end he also desired only likeminded students.[9]

2) The purging of worldly love. Likewise, while he desired and enjoyed the pleasures of sex, he also thought to purify himself from them by adhering to the restrictions of the seal of the bosom. In his case this meant that he gave up the many loves of his earlier days and remained faithful (for the next fourteen years), to one woman in accordance with a religious "vow" (i.e., to the Manichaean seal of the bosom), trying consciously (and we may add, successfully) to avoid making her pregnant[10] and refusing to enter into a lawful marriage for the purpose of begetting children.[11] The woman in question was his unnamed mistress and the mother of his son, Adeodatus, who had been born just before he became a Manichee.[12]

3) The purging of worldly glory. Finally he recalls an instance in which he sought after worldly glory by entering a contest for theatrical poetry. Here also he remained faithful to Manichaean doctrine, this time to the seal of the hand. He tells us that he rejected the advances of a soothsayer who promised him victory, preferring to lose the competition rather than win it at the cost of the death of an animal such as the soothsayer would have sacrificed on his behalf in contravention of the Manichees' prohibition of animal slaughter.[13]

Augustine allows that by following such precepts he may actually have done some good, considered from the standpoint of the truth. But from his side, since he neither knew the truth nor believed in it, he judges that in all these actions he erred in spite of any good he may unwittingly have done. "But this evil deed [the soothsayer's sacrifice] I did not repudiate out of the purity of morals which you, O God of my heart (Ps. 72:26) [required of me]" (IV,ii,3).[14] He did not yet know that the Manichees were wrong — that such things were fictions having nothing to do with what the truth actually required of men — but his error, for which he was solely responsible, was to suppose that he knew they were right when in fact he did not.

> Does not the soul which sighs longingly after such fictions *fornicate away from you* (Ps. 72:27), and believe in mirages and *feed the winds* (Pr. 10:4)? But although I was unwilling to have a sacrifice done to demons on my behalf, nevertheless I sacrificed myself to them in that superstition. For what else does

it mean to *feed the winds*, except to feed those demons — which is to say, by
erring, to become for them an object of their pleasure and derision? (IV,ii,3)[15]

II. Things done "openly"

In the preceding chapter Augustine has shown the things that he did "privately,"
in the name of the Manichaean religion, and how they caused him to modify his
worldly activities. In the remainder of the book he speaks of the things he did
"openly," in his worldly pursuits, and how they were affected by his Manichaean
beliefs. He devotes fourteen chapters to the latter side of the question and only one
to the former, which is an indication that the external rites and practices of Manichaeism were far less important for him during these years than the practical consequences which he suffered in his worldly life as a result of the logic he had
adopted. He treats of these difficulties in relation to the same three areas which he
discussed in chapter ii. That is, in relation to the pursuit of (*i*) worldly power
(IV,iii,4-6 in the business of astrology); (*ii*) of worldly love (IV,iv,7-IV,xii,19 in
the matter of the death of his young friend); (*iii*) of worldly glory (IV,xiii,20-
IV,xvi,31 in the *De pulchro et apto* and his other liberal studies).

IV,iii,4-6. The pursuit of worldly power: astrology

Augustine had rejected the advances of a soothsayer because of his attachment to
the Manichees but nothing in their position prevented him from seeking out the
services of astrologers to guide him to a successful outcome of his worldly activities.[16]

> Therefore I did not at all refuse to consult those cheats who are called
> astrologers — and this I did on the grounds that they used no sacrifice and
> directed no prayers to any spirit for their divinations [which would have broken
> the seal of the hand and of the mouth]. (IV,iii,4)[17]

Astrology itself did not form any part of the "canonical" doctrine of Manichaeism, but the line between it and their proper teachings was not clearly
drawn.[18] What Augustine saw as attractive in astrology was its claim to possess a
complete science of human behaviour which complemented the certainty about
God and nature that the Manichees professed to possess. By their knowledge of
how the stars were supposed to govern human action, the astrologers claimed to
know the most minute happenings on earth. This certain knowledge of the particular was what drew Augustine. It is illustrated by an incident in *Against the Academics* where his student, Licentius, recalls how, one day in Carthage, Augustine
had sent him to the famous astrologer, Albicerius, to discover the whereabouts of a
lost spoon.

> [Albicerius] replied with the greatest speed and with absolute right, not only
> what was sought but also the name of the one to whom it belonged and where it
> lay. (I,vi,17)

In the light of such successes Augustine tried to acquire the skill himself
through the study of their books and as late as a decade later he himself was reading horoscopes for others.[19] When he first became interested in astrology he did

not lack friends who tried to dissuade him from this business: both the kindly pro-consul Vindicianus and his young friend Nebridius.[20] But it was not until years later, after he had come to recognize the necessity of the divine incorruptibility, that he was able to appreciate the arguments which they put forward.[21]

He wanted a total knowledge of the particular: a knowledge like God's which knows how the world is governed, "even to the falling leaves of the trees" (VII,vi,8).[22] Against the argument of Vindicianus, Augustine objected that if the astrologers had any success (which they obviously did), how could he know whether this came from their art or simply by chance?

> I had as yet found no irrefutable argument such as I sought, by which I could know without ambiguity whether the things that they truly said in their predic-tions happened by luck or lot rather than by the art of observing the stars, as they claimed. (IV,iii,6)[23]

Augustine connects his inability to recognize the truth of what Vindicianus said — that the astrologer's successes were pure chance or an intuitive guess — with his (Manichaean) conceit about the nature of evil. This is the sense of the opening paragraph of IV,iii,4 and its Scriptural quotations to the effect that both before and after baptism sin is solely our responsibility. At the time Augustine would have none of this, and by his willingness to attribute evil to a divine princi-ple he thought he could be left without sin.

> [W]hen men say, "The inevitable cause of sin comes to you from heaven" and "Venus did this, or Saturn, or Mars," the result is clearly that man is without guilt — flesh and blood and proud rotting thing that he is — while the creator and orderer of the stars and heaven is guilty. (IV,iii,4)[24]

Two things are required for astrology to seem credible and they are the same two that are involved in the credibility of Manichaeism.[25] The first is the assump-tion that the truth is to be found in the sensible — interpreted in astrology as the assertion that man's rational will is subject to the same kind of necessity as that which governs natural bodies, as the laws of physics govern the actions of stones and water, etc. Secondly, there must be a presumption that the opposition between good and evil, as these appear to us, is also reflected in the principles of the uni-verse. Thus God is either thought to suffer evil (as follows from the Manichees' position), or else to be its ultimate cause (as implied by the astrologers). In either case evil is not our responsibility. Taken together these two opinions make it pos-sible to suppose that there could be a science which could tell the course and events of a man's life, for good or ill, with at least the same certainty as that of the astronomers who successfully predicted other natural phenomena such as sol-stices, equinoxes and eclipses (see V,iii,4-6).

To a man as Augustine then was, willing to believe these things, any success which an astrologer might have could therefore be regarded as coming from a true knowledge, and any failure could be attributed to "the imperfection of the art" (VII,vi,9).[26] To such a one there is no possibility of a certain knowledge to the contrary because he refuses to allow the things that make nonsense of the whole profession: namely, that evil is not a substance and that God is neither the cause of evil nor suffers it but that its source lies in man himself.

In *Against the Academics*, Augustine refutes the pretended science of astrologers, soothsayers and augurs by noting that the term ''science'' properly belongs to a knowledge about which one cannot possibly be mistaken.

> I do not call ''science'' that knowledge in which he who is proficient in it is ever mistaken. For there to be science, not only must a thing be understood but it must be understood in such a way that neither can one ever be wrong nor can it ever be overturned by any objection whatsoever. (I,vii,19)

Augustine could scarcely refute the astrologer's claim to have a science since he was still far from this idea of what a true science was. In Book VII he will show how an understanding of the divine incorruptibility is a *sine qua non* of any certain knowledge — and how, on its basis, astrology can be seen to be a fraud. Lacking this, he says that he was moved simply by their apparent successes or, in his words, by their ''authority'' (IV,iii,6).[27] We will leave the refutation of astrology to the argument of the seventh book. For the moment it is enough if we know why he became interested in astrology, and why he could not see that it was only guesswork or coincidence and thus wasted his efforts chasing after fictions which he confused with science.

IV,iv,7-IV,xii,19. The pursuit of worldly love: the death of a friend

In this long discussion Augustine turns to the difficulties he suffered in the love of his friends. He shows how these were a direct consequence of the inadequacy of the Manichaean position. The last three chapters of this section (IV,x,15-IV,xii,19) move beyond this experience to suggest the form of a true love which is free from these inadequacies.

IV,iv,7-9 — The account begins with the friendship which he formed at the time, in Thagaste, with a youth of similar age with whom he had grown up as a child.[28] The acquaintance blossomed to friendship when Augustine persuaded this unnamed person to become a Manichee from a weakly held Catholicism. Together they shared and enjoyed everything in a friendship which was ''ripened by the heat of like studies'' (IV,iv,7)[29] so that Augustine's ''soul could not be without him'' (IV,iv,7).[30] A year of this delight, the greatest he had yet experienced, had scarcely gone by when the friend fell ill and, soon after, died.[31] Augustine's heart was overcome with a terrible grief and he found that he not only missed his friend but that everything else which had formerly been delightful was now empty.

> [W]hatever I looked at seemed like death to me. My hometown was a torment to me and my paternal home an astonishing unhappiness and whatever I had done with him had turned into a great torture without him. (IV,iv,9)[32]

Augustine knew his Manichaean God ought to have been a solace but he was not. He wanted to understand why he suffered so much but he could find no answer.

> I myself became to myself a great question and I asked my soul why it was sad and why it troubled me greatly and it did not know what to answer to my question. And if I said, ''Place your hope in God'' it quite properly did not obey because that most dear man whom it had lost was both truer and better than the

fantasy in which it was ordered to hope [i.e., by his Manichaean beliefs]. (IV,iv,9)[33]

His God was no help — but he did find comfort and pleasure in tears and in his sorrow itself. "Only weeping was sweet for me and *it took the place of my friend* in the delights of my soul" (IV,iv,9 — emphasis mine).[34]

IV,v,10 — Augustine asks how this could be — how his tears and sorrow could actually become a source of delight. He observes that when we pray to God and sob out our sorrows to him, there is a pleasure to be found in the hope that he will hear and respond. But his tears were not sweet for this reason because, as he tells us, he had no hope that his friend would come to life again nor did he ask for this. Another cause of pleasure in sorrow comes from a "full-gorgedness of what we before enjoyed,"[35] by which he means that any pleasure, indulged to excess, can become a pain. So long as this is the case there is pleasure even in rejecting what is otherwise a source of pleasure.

IV,vi,11 — This however was not what happened to Augustine at the time and he turns from this general consideration to his own case. "But why do I speak of these things? For now is not the time to ask [such abstract questions] but to confess [my own situation] to you."[36] He was not "full-gorged" with his friend but only miserable because he "had lost his joy" (IV,v,10).[37] He describes his situation in this way.

> Thus I was very wretched but that same miserable life I accounted more dear than my friend himself. For however much I wanted to change my life I was more unwilling to lose it than I was to lose him: indeed, I do not know if I would have been willing to lose my life if that were the price of enjoying him again.[38]

In writing the *Confessions*, Augustine saw this to be a very strange state of affairs. He recognize that this position was the "exact opposite"[39] of the classic relationship of friends, such as Orestes and Pylades, who were said to have wanted to die together since it was worse than dying for either to live on without the other. At this point Augustine had two questions. Why did he want to suffer? And why did he suffer? He finds the answer to both in his Manichaean beliefs.

Why did he want his suffering? The Manichees certainly intended to stabilize and preserve the individual against the irrational plurality of evil for they did not promise to save the *light* but the *man*.[40] Accordingly, Augustine tried to place his hope in God — in the idea that his dead friend was now with God having been liberated from his entrapment in matter — only to find that this was no comfort.[41] He experienced this failure because the Manichees did not understand God as the principle of the actual sensible concrete — which is rather a mixture of Good and Evil, caused by the devil, and which ought not to be. The result was that the "liberation" they promised had logically to result in the dissolution of the actual individual into the contraries from which he was composed. But the sensible concrete, in the form of his friend, was what Augustine had actually loved. It was with him that he had enjoyed talking, etc., and not with the light. When he died, Augustine, who believed what the Manichees said, could not think that his friend was still somehow "there" in God. In theory they intended to preserve the individual: in practice they destroyed him — for the individual could only be "saved" by being dissolved into the contraries which were all that he really was.

There was no possibility of holding together his experienced intuition of the concreteness of his friend with the Manichaean concept of God. But if the object of Augustine's love had been obliterated from the universe, his love itself was not. What expression could it have? Certainly not by delighting in the things that had been delightful because shared, since this was no longer possible. The only alternative was to seek to keep his love alive by mourning and grieving over all that had formerly been wonderful when they had enjoyed it together — and this was everything. In other words, he preferred to hold on to his misery and grief, and thus keep alive the intuition of the concreteness of his friend, rather than join him in a death which he could only understand as the dissolution of all concreteness. This is why his situation was unlike that of Orestes and Pylades. Given his Manichaean principles this was the only form in which he could preserve his love, and it is also the reason why he could only find solace in tears and misery. He ends the chapter with these words.

> He spoke well who said of his friend: *Thou half my soul* (Horace *Carm.*, I,3,8). For I felt my soul and his soul to have been one soul in two bodies and so life was a horror to me because I was unwilling to live by halves. And on this account also, perhaps, I did not wish to die, lest he should altogether die whom I had loved so much.[42]

In the *Retractions* (II,vi) Augustine finds in this last sentence the only substantive correction he wants to make in the whole of the *Confessions*. It is, he says, less of a "serious confession" than a "light statement." This is correct for, as it stands, proffered as an explanation about why he feared to die even though his life was a misery, it is "inept" even though its force is blunted by the "perhaps." His fear of death did not arise from the fact that he had any hope of keeping his friend alive but rather because his love of his friend could only find expression through his continuing grief. Keeping his love was what required Augustine to stay alive and in misery — not keeping his friend.

IV,vii,12 — Augustine now turns to show what caused the terrible grief which spread over every aspect of his life. My soul, he says,

> ... could find no rest
> in [*i*] pleasant groves,
> nor [*ii*] in plays and songs,
> nor [*iii*] in pleasing scented places,
> nor [*iv*] in sumptuous banquets,
> nor [*v*] in the pleasure of the bedroom and bed,
> nor, finally, [*vi*] in books and poetry.
> All things were offensive to it
> — even [*vii*] the light itself.
> And everything that was not what he was,
> was offensive, except lamentation and tears.[43]

The difficulty here is simply the other side of the Manichaean position. In the previous chapter, Augustine has shown how the Manichaean idea of God, as light, could not be reconciled with the concrete substantiality of his friend. He now shows how their idea of God, as immediately present in the sensible world, could not be reconciled with the actual instability and insubstantiality of nature. The Manichees understood all good at the level of the senses and this was how Augustine had loved his friend. The catalogue of those things which were no longer a joy without him moves through each of the senses from (*i*) vision (*amoenus* – in the phrase, "*pleasant* groves" – is used "in general of objects affecting the sense of sight only"),[44] to (*ii*) hearing, to (*iii*) smell, to (*iv*) taste, and finally to (*v*) touch. Augustine completes the list by adding (*vi*) intellectual pleasures, of which he gives the example of reading and poetry, and (*vii*) God himself (i.e., light) – both of which were understood as sensible on the Manichaean view.

In accordance with Manichaean doctrine, he had supposed the absolute good was in the sensible and he thought he had found it in this friendship of shared pleasures. But when the absolute good is mistakenly sought in those things whose nature is to rise, run their course, and perish, then we are bound to suffer the loss not only of the individual when it perishes, but also of the good itself. "O madness," he says, "which does not know how to love men humanly!"[45] – i.e., loving one who must die as if he would never die. This is just what he had done, supposing their mutual pleasure was all the good, but now the insubstantiality of nature, experienced in the death of his friend, led inevitably to the repudiation of all other goods, including even the light itself: i.e., the Manichaean God. If death had done this to his friend and taken his joy and good from him, what was safe from its touch?[46] If he tried to look to God as a stable abiding good he found only "a void,"[47] since the good he had taken to be God was just what had vanished with his friend. Here too he was left with tears and weeping as the only possible way of holding on to the good that had vanished.

His position was intolerable: "I had become to myself a place of misery / where I could neither stay nor from which I was able to escape."[48] Thinking to get away from Thagaste, where he and his friend had enjoyed so much, he fled to Carthage – probably in the fall of 376 – "But where," he asks, "could my heart go to flee from itself?"[49]

IV,viii,13 – Something had to give. Logically it had either to be his Manichaean beliefs or the love of his friend. In fact it was the latter. "But that fable did not die in me even if one of my friends died."[50] Little by little Augustine gave up the tears by which he kept alive the love of his dead friend and found pleasure again in his old delights with other Manichaean friends in Carthage.

> Yes, that which most pieced me together and restored me was the consolation of other friends with whom I loved those things that I loved instead of you [God], and this came from that huge fable and long lie.[51]

Augustine found that if he was true to the love of his dead friend he would have to be false to his other friends – and if true to the living, then false to the dead. There were no alternatives, given his beliefs at the time. This chapter explains how he retained his Manichaeism and abandoned his love for the dead friend.

If he came out of the episode on the side of the living it was partly because this side was liveable in a way that the other, which required his perpetual misery, was not. And because his sense of the concreteness of his friend was just that but no more – and could not be understood on the basis of his Manichaean beliefs – he more easily gave up this indefinite intuition, which had faded with the passage of time, than his abiding presumption of knowledge. In short, he found it better to forget his friend and remain a Manichee than he did to hold on to his love and live in perpetual misery or admit that the Manichees' views were inadequate to account for either the concreteness or the insubstantiality of his friend — both of which he had experienced without being able to understand either. He would fly in the face of experience rather than admit that neither he nor the Manichees knew the truth.

Augustine says that the essential element in turning him from the love of his dead friend to the love of the living was the simple passage of time which "causes strange things to happen in the soul."[52] He means that the demands of that (old) friendship became less tolerable day by day in the face of the opposing and ever-present claims of his other friends — and of his own presumption of knowledge. The same temporal externality which, in the death of his friend, had precipitated the crisis was also what restored him in the end. It could not be otherwise for, while he had been attracted to the Manichees by their claim to have a gnosis which would teach him how he was the equal of God[53] and which promised to show him how to live happily above the natural flux of pleasure and pain, saying so did not make it so. As their principles could give no rational account of this flux he was bound to remain subject to it, experienced simply as an alien externality — first in the pain he suffered on the death of his friend, and later in the new pleasures he discovered on giving up his old love for the new. In this way he remained subject to his experiences and they in time carried him back into the daily life of the sect.

IV,ix,14 — Finally, Augustine points out that the strength in the demands of his new friends (as against the contrary claims of the old) lay in their expression of good-will and regard in which he delighted and which he could not ignore or fail to reciprocate without contradicting himself.[54] "This is the source of that grief if someone dies, and of the darkness of sorrows, and [why] the heart steeped in bit-terness is turned from sweetness, and [why] the life of the dying becomes a death for the living."[55] This is his final answer about the cause of his grief. This is what he had loved in the dead friend. So when in Carthage the same thing was offered again by new friends he had no reason to refuse. It was not the dead friend who demanded his grief but Augustine himself — if he was to be true to his love of the dead man. But there was no longer any point in being true to his love of the dead, which left him in misery, when the same delights for which he had loved the man in the first place were now offered again by his new friends.

It is thus with a perfect logic that Augustine omits the names of any of these Manichaean friends. So far as he knew them only in a Manichaean relationship they were interchangeable in this way. He loved them only as they were compat-ible with his own desires. Even in the case of his dead friend, he had no relation to his actual concrete *persona*. Augustine made this point in the first chapter (IV,iv,8) where he described his own self-seeking reaction to his friend's deathbed baptism. When he began to mock the unconscious baptism his friend clearly thought other-wise,[56] but Augustine wanted nothing to do with this. He was only interested in his friend insofar as he served to confirm and support his own views. This was the basis of the friendship in the first place, for Augustine had started to love him because he had brought him to the Manichees.[57] Augustine refused to allow any place for the reality of his friend's person as against the Manichees' doctrines — even though, after his baptism, the friend had been willing to do this for Augustine.[58]

IV,x,15-IV,xii,19. What is the true love of worldly things?

In these three chapters Augustine considers the question of how we can properly love the goods of this world in contrast to the false love which was all that was possible on Manichaean principles.

IV,x,15 — He argues that if the absolute good is located immediately in the sensible, then the misery which he suffered on the death of his friend was inevitable. Whatever things the senses can be aware of, however beautiful, are in fact but passing parts of a whole and as parts they ought not to be loved wholly. If we attach ourselves to them, as he had done to his friend, "loving what is bound to die as if it were never to die" (IV,viii,13),[59] we are bound to be torn in pieces, since the senses can neither stay their passing nor follow where the passing part has gone. He prays, "let not my soul be stuck to them with the glue of love through the senses of the body."[60]

> For they go whither they go that they may not be and they rip the soul from its most pestilent desires since it wants to be one with them and it wants to stay with the things it loves. But in these things there is nowhere to stay since they do not remain: they flee and who can follow them with the senses of the flesh? In fact who can stop them from fleeing even when they are present?[61]

He concludes that the things grasped by the senses are only parts, so we err if we hold to any of them as if it were the whole good. This is just what the Manichees taught when they identified God with the sensible. But if the part is not to be loved absolutely, what then? Augustine gives his answer in a poetic prayer in the next two chapters. This argument, while highly compressed and dependent on positions which he only proves in later books (VII and VIII), deserves close attention as an anticipation of the direction in which he is moving. In the first (ch. xi) he gives the true answer of Platonism, in the second (ch. xii) the necessary correction of Platonism by Christianity.

IV,xi,16-17 — The Platonic answer is that it is not the part that is to be loved absolutely, but the whole in which all the parts are contained — i.e., not nature but God. This position is not grasped by the senses of the flesh which are limited to apprehending particulars. Rather, urges Augustine, let the flesh follow the mind which, when it looks to its proper object (the universal), *wants* the parts to come and go so that, as in a sentence, it may get the whole meaning which is not in any word or syllable alone. As it is with a sentence, so with sensible goods generally. The parts fly but the whole, which is held in God and grasped by the mind, abides forever. We should therefore love the creature only as it is in God, for there alone created things "do not drag you down to the place they descend to / but they stand with you and remain / with the ever standing and remaining God" (IV,xi,16).[62] Again he says:

Behold these [sensible] things pass
that others may take their places
and that this lower world may have all its parts.
"But do I ever depart anywhere?"
says the Word of God.
There fix your dwelling,
....
and you will not lose anything. (IV,xi,16)[63]

Augustine is far from proving here that the reasons (the Platonic forms) of all temporal things stand forever in God as he will do in the discussion of the vision of the Truth, in Book VII. But for the moment the certain conclusion of this chapter is that *if* all things stand in God, then here alone we are not deceived by the love of worldly things — for we love them not as they are in the world, partial and passing, but as they are collected in God where they remain forever.

IV,xii,18-19 — One might suppose that Augustine has now settled the form in which worldly goods are properly loved. But this is not his last word. In section 18 he brings to light a problem in this answer and in 19 he presents its final resolution. Human reason speaks the truth when it says: "Worldly goods must not be loved as they are in themselves, passing and corruptible, but as they are in God, eternal and abiding." Augustine recognized this as the highest truth of human understanding, yet he says to the one who knows only this: "Where are you going in these trackless wastes? Where are you going?" (IV,xii,18).[64] "Seek what you seek," he says, "but it is not there where you are looking for it" (IV,xii,18).[65] The problem is this. Augustine was looking for the true love of worldly goods. But if it is not to be found in the soul's attachment to sensible things which perish, neither can it immediately be found in the soul's attachment to the eternal reasons of worldly things since in this case, while they abide, the person who loves them is bound to die. Here eternal things are loved by a mortal man as if he (the lover) were not to die. "But," asks Augustine, "how can this be a happy life where there is not life?" (IV,xii,18).[66] To those who know only that the world is properly loved as it is in its unchangeable principle he says: "You seek the blessed life in a *land of death* (Is. 9:2): it is not in that place" (IV,xii,18).[67]

So far it looks as if the love of worldly goods as they are in the world (passing) is incompatible with the love of worldly goods as they are in God (abiding) — while man, who must chose the one or the other, can in neither case find the rest and happiness he seeks. Even if he loves the world as it is in the Word of God, he himself perishes. In the last section (19) Augustine overcomes this division and brings the two sides together in terms of the Incarnation.

Here nature (the sensible and corporeal generally) and reason (the intelligible and universal) are brought together in terms of a divine mediation. The Word of God in whom the eternal reasons of all worldly things are contained also appears as part of the sensible, corporeal world.

Augustine points to Christ in answer to the question he has just asked about how we can have a happy life, even when we love things as they are in God, if we ourselves do not enjoy eternal life.

For the source of our life descended into this world.
and took away our death.
He killed it out of the abundance of his life.
And he thundered,
calling us to return from the land of death
to him in that secret place from whence he came to us,
at first, in that virgin's womb
where to him was married
the human creature, mortal flesh
so that it might not always be mortal:
and thence, *like a bridegroom leaving his bridal chamber,*
he sprang forth like a giant ready to run his course (Ps. 18:6).
And he wasted no time
but he ran, calling to us
by his words, deeds, death,
life, his descent, his ascension,
calling us to return to him. (IV,xii,19)[68]

So much is contained in this which Augustine has not yet explained that we can only make a few observations at this point. The proof comes later. By the eternal life of which Augustine speaks here, he clearly intends not a disembodied existence but the life of the resurrection body. The Christian position is that the Eternal Word of God was married to our mortal flesh so that our flesh might lose its mortality and be carried up to God. Quoting the New Testament (1 Tim. 1:15), Augustine says here *"he [Christ] was in this world / and he came into this world to make sinful man healthy"* (IV,xii,19).[69] The reference is to the overcoming of man's sin and the mortality which we suffer as a consequence of it: it is not a reference to overcoming the body as such.

Furthermore, and this is a hard teaching for the natural man to accept, this eternal life is nothing that we can have by our own efforts. It is not a blessed and disembodied existence achieved by the human soul which has worked its way up to the true knowledge of God. Those who aim at this are people like the Platonists whom Augustine will later criticize in Book VII on this account. Though they have come to a true and certain knowledge of God by the exercise of their own intelligence, Augustine claims that their wisdom turns to folly if they imagine they can have a happy or blessed life apart from the mediation of Christ. These are the ones whom he calls here to descend.

Now that the [source] of life has come down to you
do you not want to rise up and to live?
But how can you rise up
since you are already up there
and have put your *head in heaven* (Ps. 72:9)?
Descend in order that you can ascend to God.
For you fell when you ascended against him. (IV,xii,19)[70]

Augustine's final conclusion is that worldly goods cannot properly be loved as they are simply in themselves, nor as they are simply in God (i.e., in the Eternal Word), but only as they are in Christ, the Incarnate Word. Augustine will show us exactly what this means in Book IX but at the time he knew none of this. "These things I did not then know and I was loving beautiful things of a lower order and I was wandering about in the deep'' (IV,xiii,20).[71] We will leave the matter here for the time being.[72]

IV,xiii,20-IV,xvi,31. The pursuit of worldly glory: the study of Wisdom in the liberal arts

These last four chapters show Augustine in pursuit of worldly glory by means of his learning. The first three explain the form this took, some four or five years after the death of his friend, in his first book, *On the Beautiful and the Suitable*.[73] In the last, he reviews the course of his wider studies throughout the period.

IV,xiii,20-IV,xv,27. On the Beautiful and the Suitable—After a brief description of the work in chapter xiii, Augustine devotes a long chapter (xiv) to the fact that he dedicated this book to the famous Roman orator, Hiereus, whom he knew only by his brilliant reputation. "What was it," he asks, "which moved me, O Lord my God, to dedicate those books to Hiereus, the orator of Rome?" (IV,xiv,21).[74] The answer is clear. It was because Hiereus had a brilliant reputation as a man "most knowledgable in the things pertaining to the study of Wisdom" (IV,xiv,21).[75] If he took favourable note of it, Augustine's own eminence would be assured.

Augustine did think he had got hold of a piece of the truth but, as he shows in his discussion of the dedication, what he really wanted was not the truth but the approval of the world. In Augustine's eyes Hiereus stood at the apex of worldly honour and glory. He was "A man praised and loved even when he was not about" (IV,xiv,21).[76] This was the stuff Augustine wanted: a world-wide reputation — though not for anything frivolous or unworthy in the Manichaean scheme of things. "I certainly did not want to be praised or loved as a stage-actor . . . I would have preferred obscurity than to be famous for such reasons" (IV,xiv,22).[77] He wanted the praise of the world in that which he counted the most valuable — i.e., the knowledge of Wisdom. How was he sure that this was what he wanted rather than Wisdom itself? Because if Hiereus had not been praised by those who spoke of him, though his knowledge remained the same, Augustine was certain that he would never have dedicated the book to him: "I admired him more for the respect of those who praised him than for the things themselves for which they praised him" (IV,xiv,23).[78] Thinking Wisdom was his object, Augustine was actually moved by the world.[79] This confusion was inevitable for a Manichee.

Augustine introduces the description of what he could recall of the work (which he had lost by the time he wrote the *Confessions* and which has never been found since)[80] with these words.

> These things I did not then know and I was loving beautiful things of a lower order and I was wandering about in the deep and I used to ask my friends: "Do we love anything unless it is beautiful? But what, after all, is beautiful? And what is beauty? What is it that draws and attracts us to the things we love?" (IV,xiii,20)[81]

In other words he relates the content of the book to his ignorance of what he has just said about the true love of worldly things. In place of that truth he arrived at the position of *On the Beautiful and the Suitable* in which he attempted to work out for himself an application of the Manichaean position. The point is important because it shows that if the Manichees did not actually teach him the full content of the truth, as they had promised, this did not deter him because he was satisfied that he could, in part at least, find it out from such principles as he had from them (i.e., the dualism and the corporeal nature of good and evil). He says of the book that in it "I strove towards you [God]" (IV,xv,26),[82] which means that he thought of it as a contribution to the study of Wisdom. He was pleased with his work: "and though there was no one except me to praise the book, I admired it" (IV,xiv,23).[83]

From a Manichaean perspective the good soul was attracted by what was good and beautiful while the evil soul moved to the opposite. The problem for Augustine was that this was not his experience. His questions show that he recognized that even when he loved something the Manichees considered evil — say the body of his concubine — he was not attracted to it because it was ugly. From this he concluded that, "Unless there was a comeliness and beauty in them [the objects he loved, whether good or evil in the Manichaean view] they would in no way attract us to them" (IV,xiii,20).[84] His difficulty was to find an explanation of how those things which the Manichees considered evil could be in any way attractive. The answer which burst from his heart "like water from a spring" (IV,xiii,20)[85] was to observe a distinction between two kinds of attractiveness found in corporeal bodies. On the one hand there was real beauty, properly said of any totality which was so in itself, and on the other hand there was the suitable, a secondary attractiveness which arose from the proper "fit" of separate things, like the relation of the leg, not beautiful in itself, to the body where it belonged. This latter kind of beauty explained the attractiveness of those things which the Manichees considered evil and ugly in themselves. From this notion, duly illustrated, he "turned to the nature of the soul" (IV,xv,24).[86]

The relation between these two topics is straightforward. The distinction between the beautiful and the (merely) suitable called for a corresponding distinction in the soul: one side to appreciate the beautiful, the other to be attracted by the suitable. This is the fiction that Augustine composed for himself and he defined these principles in his own precision of the general Manichaean theory, thinking he was writing something of universal significance.

> And since what I liked in virtue was peace and what I hated in vice was discord, in the one I saw unity and in the other a kind of division. In that unity there seemed to me to be the rational mind and the nature of truth and the highest good, and in that division, wretched I imagined I don't know what substance of irrational life and the nature of the greatest evil, which I thought was not only a substance but was also altogether a life, which however was not from you, my God, *from whom are all things* (1 Cor. 8:6). And the first I called the "monad" which I pictured as a mind without any sex, and the second the "dyad," thinking here of anger in evil deeds, lust in shameful acts — without knowing what I was saying. (IV,xv,24)[87]

Augustine thought that his mind was actually a "piece" of the monad: "I thought that you, Lord God, the truth, were an immense and bright body and that I was a piece of that body" (IV,xvi,31).[88] Taking the monad as the principle of

goodness and virtue and identifying it with his rational mind — which he understood to be in conflict with the irrational dyad which he located in his flesh —
Augustine emerged from this argument in the arrogant and foolish position that
his evidently changeable mind was identical with the supposedly changeless truth.

> But I strove towards you and I was thrust away from you so that I might taste
> death since *you resist the proud* (Mt. 16:28). And what greater pride than to
> assert as I did in a terrible madness that I was by nature what you are? For
> whereas I was mutable — and this was manifest to me inasmuch as I desired to
> be wise, that out of a worse I might become better — nevertheless I preferred to
> suppose that you were mutable rather than to think that I was not what you are.
> (IV,xv,26)[89]

How could he have been satisfied with this contradictory conclusion and have
taken it to be rational? Augustine answers in two ways. First, on the side of knowledge: "I did not yet know nor had learned that evil is not a substance nor that our
mind was not the highest and unchangeable good" (IV,xv,24).[90] Secondly, on the
side of will, he finds that he could rest with such a notion because he insisted on
finding the rational truth in corporeal images and so was content to live in a
fictional world where sensible things were imaginatively transformed into rational
entities such as unity and division. As he says, he was: "wandering about in those
things which have no existence either in you [God] nor in me nor in the body nor
were they created for me by your truth but they were fashioned by my own vanity
out of a body" (IV,xv,25).[91]

In method, form, and content, *On the Beautiful and the Suitable* was a thoroughly Manichaean production and its errors the errors of corporeal dualism. In
the next books Augustine explains how he discovered the foolishness of this position. Here, his last word, which sums up the failure of his knowledge and will, is
that he had not yet been humbled.

> [T]he voices of my errors drew me outside of myself and by the weight of my
> pride I fell down to the lowest pit. For you did not yet allow *me to hear joy and
> gladness nor did my bones rejoice* for they had not yet been *humbled* (Ps.
> 50:10). (IV,xv,27)[92]

This humbling would take the form of discovering that if the principle were
mutable — if his changeable soul were a piece of the highest good — then there
could be no knowledge of nature or God since nothing would be fixed and stable.
At the time he was content to assume that he had come upon the truth and that the
Catholics who opposed his positions were simply ignorant. He reports that he
delighted to confound them, as he thought, by asking: "Since God [on their view]
made the soul, why does it err? but, as he goes on, "I did not want to be asked [in
reply], 'Why, [if what you say is true] does God err?' "(IV,xv,26).[93] Here things
are simply at loggerheads. For the time being he was content with a presumption
of knowledge that did not have to answer objections with anything other than the
repetition of his own position. In the next book he shows how all this changed
when he attempted to reconcile Mani's explanations of certain natural phenomena
with those which he had picked up from the natural sciences.

IV,xvi,28-31. The liberal arts — Augustine now puts in place the final piece to
complete the account of his Manichaean period. He does this by mentioning the

other (non-Manichaean) studies which occupied him during these nine years. These played an important role in his eventual liberation from the sect. Starting with Aristotle's *Categories*, which he read when he was about twenty, he avidly studied everything in the liberal arts on which he could lay his hands.[94] Such studies were certainly not required of any Manichee but neither were they forbidden. It seems that Augustine was driven to them by his desire to know. He turned to them because he was not satisfied that he was getting an adequate explanation of all things from the Manichees — and yet he was not moved to leave the sect on this account because he was sure he could distinguish whatever truth they might contain by their accord with the principles which he had from the Manichees.[95] This was what he sought and took from the *Categories* which attracted him as a "great and divine work" (IV,xvi,28),[96] reputedly as deep as it was difficult. He had no trouble in understanding it, yet, under the influence of his Manichaean notions, he mistakenly thought to apply Aristotle's ten categories directly to God where Aristotle applied them to natural beings. Because of this he derived nothing which profited him in his search for Wisdom.[97]

Presuming to a total knowledge he rejoiced in the particular sciences and mentions specifically that he read works on rhetoric, logic, geometry, music, and arithmetic — and from which he gained quite a reputation for learning.[98] He acknowledges that he found much that was true from these books, yet dismisses his whole effort in these years because it was animated by the same spirit that informed *On the Beautiful and the Suitable*. That is, he interpreted all he read only as he could relate it to Manichaean positions and did not bother to look any further. Gifted by nature (by God), Augustine complains against himself that he did not use these gifts to look for their giver but was content, like the Prodigal Son, to go to a far country, "in order to squander them [i.e., his rational powers — from God, his heavenly father] on the pleasures of a harlot [i.e., the seductive whore who, in Proverbs, pretends to give men the same thing as Lady Wisdom]" (IV,xvi,30).[99] He was convinced he was coming to Wisdom but actually he was going away from it.[100]

Augustine recognizes that he could take no credit for having learned those things that were true in these books: "What good was in them," he asks, "even if I learned all kinds of true things, since I neither looked for nor discovered the source of truth itself?"

> I rejoiced in them but I did not know the source of whatever was true and certain in them. For I had my back to the light and my face towards the things which were illuminated: thus my face itself [i.e., my mind] which saw the things that were illuminated, was not itself lit up. (IV,xvi,30)[101]

With no criterion to distinguish true from false, other than the subjective fantasies of the Manichees, he may have learned to believe some things that were true — but truth held in this fashion is held so accidentally that the one who has it doesn't even know he has it and is unable to distinguish it from false things which he also believes to be true. His knowledge did not even have the limited certainty of the Catholics' faith — who at least knew *that* they believed. Augustine insists on this contrast by comparing his presumed knowledge to the humble faith of the Catholics whom he despised.

What good did my natural talents do me, able as they were to grasp these teachings easily and to unravel those most knotty volumes without the help of any human teachers, since I erred disgracefully in the teaching of piety from a sacrilegious foulness? Or what did their far slower understanding do to hinder your little ones since they did not stray away from you, that instead they might grow their feathers in the security of the nest of your church, and that they might nourish the wings of love with the food of a health-giving faith? (IV,xvi,31)[102]

In one thing however Augustine did truly profit from these studies. By taking in and understanding what ancient science had to say about nature, he took in an explanation which, ultimately, he could not reconcile with the Manichees' teachings on the same subject. Here at least was one point where he could not simply dismiss what differed from the Manichees as mere ignorance, since he had actually understood what these natural scientists said. His inability to reconcile the two positions rankled. His presumption of a total knowledge would force him to attempt to choose between the two accounts. This is why he says, from the beginning of the section concerned with his studies, that although ''I erred with a swelling pride and was carried about by *every wind* (Eph. 4:14), yet I was governed by you [God] in an exceedingly mysterious manner'' (IV,xiv,23).[103] Taken to its logical conclusion his pride in his presumed knowledge was the very thing that would lead him to the truth in the end. How this happened is the content of Book V.

Augustine began this book by saying that during the nine years he was a convinced Manichee he and his friends were ''seduced and seducing, deceived and deceiving'' in all their activities.[104] He has not proven that the Manichees' doctrines were wrong or that in following them he was actually going away from the truth, but he has shown how the actual misery and futility of all his actions in these years were a direct consequence of his adherence to their position. It can seem strange that he should have put up with this unhappy state of affairs for such a long time — but he could do so just as long as he could convince himself that he knew the truth. After reading the *Hortensius* he had desired Wisdom above all else and this had not changed one iota in nine years — he would put up with anything as long as he was not forced to acknowledge that he did not know the truth. So far, nothing had brought him to this point, but everything would change with the coming of Faustus.

NOTES

1 See *Per/duodetricensimum* (54/2-4). Courcelle (*Recherches*, p. 78) finds Augustine's dating of his Manichaean period incorrect. He notes that while Augustine repeatedly affirms that he was a Manichee for nine years (from his 19th to his 28th year), his nineteenth year went from November 373-74 and yet he was still a Manichee ten years later at the end of the school year 383-84 when he was in Rome. Why did Augustine not tell the truth? — because he was embarrassed at having been a Manichee. ''He tends therefore to reduce as much as possible the length of time during which he was a disciple of Mani while he reproaches himself for having been such for a long time, for too long a time.''

There *is* an apparent discrepancy, but Courcelle's interpretation is wrong. The nine years are the period from Augustine's 19th to his 28th year when he was a *convinced* Manichee. In III,xi,20 he refers to this as the time when he was totally unable to escape from the position. ''For almost nine years followed during which time I tumbled about in that deep pit of slime and the darkness of error, and every time I tried to get out of it I only slid back more deeply" — *Nam/volutatus sum* (52/25-28). These nine years form the content of Book IV. In Book V, Augustine deals with events in his 29th year when he began to break with the Manichees — and thus, in spite of the fact that he was still nominally a Manichee, both in Rome and at the start of his stay in Milan (in the fall of 384), he did not count himself as such in the same sense as in the nine-year period. Solignac comes to a similar conclusion against Courcelle (*BA*, Vol. 13, p. 131, n. 1), though his reasons differ.

2 *errores/contaminant* (72/7-8).

3 "Openly" — *palam* (54/5): "privately" — *occulte* (54/6). This *occulte* (lit. "in conceal-ment," "in secret," "privately") has been taken to refer to the fact that in Augustine's time the Manichees were under varying degrees of legal restraint and so had to hide themselves: see for example Gibb (*Confessions*, p. 78). Courcelle (*Recherches*, p. 71, n. 5) lists the laws in question and understands the phrase of V,x,19 — *plures enim eos Roman occultat* (92/17-18) — in the same sense: "the Manichees at Rome hid themselves at the time of Augustine." This is another of Courcelle's curious mistranslations (see also above, Chapter Three, n. 153), for this text does not say that "the Manichees of Rome hid themselves," but that "Rome concealed many Manichees." While the official prescription certainly affected the conduct of some of the leaders of the sect (see *Recherches*, pp. 74-75), nothing in any of Augustine's works suggests that it was determinative for him in any way — as if he ever had to hide the fact that he was a Manichee. If anything the contrary was the case. Even while he was in Rome he got the important position of rhetor in Milan through the help of his (known) Manichaean friends (V,xiii,23), as Courcelle himself argues (*Recherches*, pp. 78-87). I take the opposition *palam/occulte* to mean "publicly/privately." In V,xi,21 Augustine uses a similar opposition (*palam/secretius* — 94/14-15) in the same sense. The sequel shows that what Augustine discusses under this head (*occulte*) are just those cult things he did in the name of the Manichaean religion (see IV,ii,2-3).

4 *Seducebamur/liberaremur* (54/4-15).

5 Courcelle (*Recherches*, p. 73, n. 5) says: "one has to admit that at this time Augustine rather lost from sight the lessons of the *Hortensius*." Against Courcelle, the argument has shown that Augustine became involved in worldly ends not because he had forgotten or lost sight of the teaching of the *Hortensius*, but rather from his presumption that the Manichees actually had what the *Hortensius* had urged him to seek. On the Manichaean inability to do the good, see Brown (*Augustine*, pp. 51-52), where he says, "The price which the Manichees had seemed to pay for this total disowning of the bad, was to render the good singularly passive and ineffective."

6 There is a good account of Manichaean practice in O'Meara (*The Young Augustine*, pp. 69-79) who also brings out the great importance which the Manichees gave to "doing the truth." For them, "The test is to do what Christ commands us to do; it is not merely to believe, but to act" (p. 75). This was also the basis of the distinction between the Elect and the Auditors who very name was derived from Rom. 2:13 where St. Paul says, "It is not the hearers of the law who are righteous before God, but the doers of the law who will be justified." Faustus, as one of the Elect, claimed to have fulfilled the demands of Christ in the Sermon on the Mount (see *CFM*, V,1).

7 An explanation of these parts of the Manichees' doctrine is found in *DMM* (esp. X,19-XVIII,66). Alfaric gives a description of these positions in *L'évolution*, Vol. 1, pp. 126-43; see also p. 297-309. See also the text from O'Meara (above, n. 6).

8 *Docebam/vendebam* (54/28-29). Augustine specifically equates rhetorical ability with worldly power — *victoriosam loquacitatem*.

9 See IV,ii,2 *Malebam/nocentis* (55/1-4). On the contraceptive practices of Augustine's day, "rhythm" or *coitus interruptus*, see Clark, "Adam's Only Companion," p. 147, n. 56-59.

10 I take this to be the sense of *contra votum* (55/15) in IV,ii,2 — i.e., "against the [religious] vow [to the seal of the bosom]." Courcelle (*Recherches*, p. 71, n. 2) understands it in the same sense.

11 See IV,ii,2 *In/diligi* (55/8-16).

12 Adeodatus was born in the late spring of 372 and Augustine did not become a Manichee till

his 19th year – i.e., after November 13, 372 (see Solignac, *BA*, Vol. 13, p. 202). This means that Augustine knew his concubine by the fall of 371. There is no reason to doubt his word that he was faithful to her – at least from the time he became a Manichee. The attachment lasted until he sent her back to Africa from Milan sometime around the start of 386. E. Schmitt, *Le Mariage chrétien dans l'oeuvre de saint Augustin. Une théologie baptismale de la vie conjugale*, Paris, Études Augustiniennes,1983, p. 26, calculates Augustine's relationship with his concubine lasted 15 years.

13 See IV,ii,3 *Recolo/videbatur* (55/17-25).

14 *Sed/mei* (55/25-26). For a discussion of the difficult phrase *ex tua castitate*, see Madec, " 'Ex tua castitate' (*Confessions* IV,ii,3), 'Adulescens . . . valde castus' (ibid., IV,iii,6)," *Revue des études augustiniennes*, 7 (1961), 245-47.

15 *Talibus/derisui?* (55/26-56/4). Note that here (and in IV,i,1, quoted above n. 4; and in IV,iv,7 – 58/26-27), Augustine turns this *superstitio* against the Manichees who accused the Catholics of just this fault – see *DUC*, I,2 (quoted above, Chapter Three, at n. 106).

16 In *DD83*, q. 45 Augustine distinguishes between a strict scientific sense of the word *mathematici* which referred to those who were legitimate astronomers – and a vulgar use, which it had acquired by his day, referring to astrologers. As well as *mathematici*, astrologers were also called *genethliaci* – "of or belonging to one's natal hour" – because they drew their horoscopes from the time of a man's birth: see IV,iii,5 *libris genethliacorum* (57/6-7) – "the books of the astrologers."

17 *Ideoque/diregerentur* (56/5-8).

18 Alfaric (*L'évolution*, Vol. l, p. 221, n. 5), notes that, "According to Epiphanus (*Haer.*, LXVI,13), Mani had written a book *On Astrology*," though he never claims that there is anything other than a close connection between the teaching of the Manichees and astrology; see *ibid.*, 1, pp. 234, 253, n. 1. Brown (*Augustine*, p. 58), citing Manichaean texts in H. J. Polotsky's *Manichäische Homilen*, claims that "The Manichees had condemned astrology; it was amateurish dabbling compared with the 'objective' Wisdom of their own books." In a sense this is true since none of the seven great books of the Manichees was on astrology but, by Augustine's day, Mani's astronomical writings had become confused with astrology so that it had become a kind of sister science. O'Meara (*The Young Augustine*, p. 95) has the essence of this spirit when he writes: "Augustine put great faith in these astrologers as indeed did all devout Manichees – for did not the sun and the moon and the stars have an important part in their teaching, and did not Mani himself encourage them to have recourse to astrology?" – see also p. 64. Beausobre *(Histoire critique*, Vol. 2, pp. 428-49), arguing from *CFM* (II,5), supposes that the Manichees rejected astrology but, as Alfaric remarks (*L'évolution*, Vol. 1, p. 221, n. 5), "The case in point concerns the Son of God who cannot be subject to aerial demons, not the children of Adam who come from them. Furthermore Augustine replies to the Doctor of Milevus [Faustus] that the Manichaeans placed the divine substance spread out here below 'not only in dependence on the stars but also in dependence on all earthly things' (Contra Faust., II,5)."

19 On Augustine's study of their books see IV,iii,5 *ex/deditum* (57/6-7). Augustine casts horoscopes for others, see VII,vi,8 *Is/videretur* (132/20-24).

20 Vindicianus is not mentioned by name in IV,iii,5 but Augustine identifies him in VII,vi,8. A brief sketch of this distinguished physician is found in Brown (*Augustine*), p. 67: see also p. 68 on Nebridius. Solignac (*BA*, Vol. 13, p. 416, n. 1) thinks Vindicianus shows a "Neo-Platonic mentality" in his objections to astrology. He gives a short account of Plotinus' views but it is not necessary to identify Vindicianus with Neo-Platonism. Augustine himself came to appreciate what Vindicianus said, and to share his views on the falsity of astrology, some time *before* his discovered the books of the Platonists and thus independent of any knowledge of Plotinus' teachings – if this is what these books contained: see VII,vi,8-10. If he could discover the reasons why astrology was not a science, without any knowledge of Neo-Platonism, the same could have been true for Vindicianus.

21 See IV,iii,6 *Et/deliniasti* (58/3-5). Compare VII,vi,8-10.

22 *usque/folia?* (132/6).

23 *nullum/dici* (58/10-13).
24 *cum/ordinator* (56/16-20). In V,x,18 Augustine states that he delighted in the Manichaean position because it removed sin from man's responsibility.
25 This is why Augustine begins the chapter by saying that he "therefore" consulted the astrologers — *Ideoque* (56/5).
26 *artis/inperitia* (134/18).
27 *auctoritas* (58/9).
28 Augustine had returned to Thagaste as a *grammaticus*, from Carthage, probably in the fall of 374, in his 20th year: see Solignac, *BA*, Vol. 13, p. 202 and below, n. 49.
29 *cocta/studiorum* (58/24). The studies Augustine and his friend enjoyed together were Manichaean, as Augustine specifies in the next sentence.
30 *et/illo* (58/28-59/1). From the start of the discussion Augustine insists that the difficulties of this friendship came from the fact that it was based on the false premises of Manichaeism, as opposed to the true form of friendship which is known as a gift of the Holy Spirit: see IV,iv,7 *Sed/nobis* (58/19-23). The logic of true friendship, and an example of it, is given in Augustine's account of his, converted, relation to Monica in IX,x,23-IX,xiii,37.
31 See IV,iv,7 *cum/meae* (59/4-6).
32 *quidquid/verterat* (59/30-60/3).
33 *Factus/iubebatur* (60/6-12).
34 *Solus/mei* (60/12-14). See also IV,vii,12 *praeter/requies* (62/25-26).
35 *prae/fruebamur* (61/7-8): trans. Watts (*Loeb*).
36 *Quid/tibi* (61/9-10).
37 *amiseram/meum* (61/6).
38 *Ita/illo* (61/15-19).
39 *nimis huic contrarius* (61/22).
40 See Doull, "Augustinian Trinitarianism," pp. 132-33.
41 See IV,iv,9 *Et/iubebatur* (60/9-12).
42 *Bene/amaveram* (62/7-12).
43 *Non/lacrimas* (62/19-25). Augustine's examples relate clearly enough to each of the five senses except for the first, about sight, which I explain in the text and, possibly, the fifth. Augustine always treats sex as an example of the sense of touch because we could be deprived of all the other four and still be capable of it. In X,xxx,41-42, where he discusses the temptations of the sense of touch, he does so in relation to his sexuality.
44 *ALD*, art. *amoenus*.
45 *O/humaniter!* (62/13-14).
46 See IV,vii,12 *O/patientem!* (62/14-15). Augustine made the same point in the previous chapter, IV,vi,11 *Miser/eas* (61/10-13), see also *Credo/potuit* (61/24-28).
47 *inane* (63/6).
48 *ego/recedere* (63/7-8).
49 *Quo/fugerem?* (63/9). For the date, see Solignac (*BA*, Vol. 13, p. 202). Augustine mentions this move to Carthage in *CA*, II,ii,3 where he thanks Romanianus, his wealthy patron from Thagaste, for his assistance. He describes himself as *magister* to Romanianus' children. The ancient biography by Augustine's friend Possidius (*Vita Augustini*, I,i,2 — ed. M. Pellegrino, *Vita di S. Agostino*, Alba, Edizioni Paoline, 1955), says: "For he first taught grammar (*prius grammaticam*) in his home town and later rhetoric (*postea rhetoricam docuit*) in Carthage, the capital of Africa."
50 *Sed/moreretur* (63/27-64/2).
51 *Maxime/mendacium* (63/23-26).
52 *faciunt [i.e., tempora]/opera* (63/14).
53 See IV,xv,26 *Quid/es?* (72/20-22). See also IV,xvi,31 where Augustine says that he thought he was a "piece" (*frustum*) of God — *Sed/corpore?* (75/22-24) — i.e., composed of particles of the light.
54 See IV,ix,14 *Hoc/benivolentiae* (64/14-18).
55 *Hinc/viventium* (64/18-21).

56 See IV,iv,8 *At/desinerem* (59/21-23).
57 See IV,iv,7 *Sed/mater* (58/23-27), and IV,iv,8 *me/fiebat* (59/12-14).
58 This is shown in the fact that the young friend, in his reply to Augustine's jest about the stupidity of Catholic baptism, allowed that they could still be friends (IV,iv,8 – *si amicus esse
   vellem* 59/22-23 – "if I wanted to be his friend") even though he was now, in fact and in
   spirit, a Catholic. Augustine's only interest, on the other hand, was to talk him out of it, thus
   keeping him for himself: see IV,iv,8 *Ego/vellem* (59/24-26).
59 *diligendo/moriturum?* (63/22-23).
60 *non/corporis* (65/17-18).
61 *Eunt/sunt?* (65/18-23).
62 *non/deum* (66/16-18).
63 *ecce/tuam* (66/8-11) . . . *et/aliquid* (66/13-14).
64 *Quo/itis?* (67/16-17). In Augustine's idiom the Platonists stand for those who have a true
   understanding of God as he can be known by human reason: see VII,ix,13f; *DCD*, VIII, 9-10.
65 *Quaerite/quaeritis* (67/22-23).
66 *Quomodo/vita?* (67/24-25).
67 *Beatum/illic* (67/23-24). The *regio mortis* of this text is one with the *regio egestatis* (36/23)
   of II,x,18 and the *regio dissimilitudinis* (141/8) of VII,x,16 – all of which are opposed to the
   regio ubertatis indeficientis (199/29-200/1) – the heavenly Jerusalem – of IX,x,24.
68 *Et/eum* (67/26-68/5).
69 *in/facere* (68/10-11).
70 *Numquid/deum* (68/14-18).
71 *Haec/profundum* (68/22-23).
72 Much of the modern commentary on the *Confessions* has turned about the discovery of its
   Neo-Platonic "sources" and has sought to interpret it in terms of this affiliation. The latest
   of these works is O'Connell's *Saint Augustine's Confessions: The Odyssey of Soul*, Cambridge, Mass., Harvard University Press, 1969, in which he interprets the book as an elaborate and marvellously orchestrated work on the Plotinian theme of the fall of the soul into
   body and its disembodied return to God. My understanding of these chapters is quite at odds
   with O'Connell's views (*Odyssey*, p. 57) because he takes no account of Augustine's
   thoroughgoing insistence on the Incarnation. In general I maintain that the heart and soul of
   the *Confessions* is Augustine's teaching about the Incarnation while O'Connell tends to dismiss this entirely. He says (p. 24), "at the time of the *Confessions*, those pressures [i.e.,
   Christianity's stress on the Incarnation and the related doctrine of the resurrection of the
   body] have only begun to make themselves felt, and can for our purposes [i.e., the explanation of the meaning of the *Confessions*] largely be discounted." My reservations about the
   Neo-Platonizing interpretation – whether of O'Connell, O'Meara, or Courcelle – are found
   mainly in the commentary on Books VII and VIII.
73 On the date, see IV,xv,27 *Et/scripsi* (73/11-12) where he says, "And I was about twenty-six
   or twenty-seven when I wrote those books" (i.e., the "two or three" books of the *De pulchro et apto* – *[libros . . . puto] duos aut tres* – IV,xiii,20 – 69/10). The translation of the
   title is difficult. In English it is given as *Beauty and Proportion* (Pine-Coffin), *On the Fair
   and Fit* (E. B. Pusey), *On the Beautiful and the Fitting* (Watts). The French translators of the
   BA edition sidestep the problem by using the Latin title only but Solignac, without actually
   naming it, gives *beau* and *convenable* (Vol. 13, p. 671) for the two terms in the title which, I
   think, correctly convey their sense.
74 *Quid/libros?* (69/13-15).
75 *scientissimus/pertinentium* (69/21-22).
76 *Laudatur/absens* (69/22-23). For Augustine's thought that he would have benefitted if
   Hiereus had taken note of the book, see IV,xiv,23 *Et/tuae* (71/1-4).
77 *Non/histriones* (70/1-2) . . . *eligens/esse* (70/3-5).
78 *illum/laudabatur?* (70/21-22).
79 See IV,xiv,23 *At/vento* (70/17-19).
80 See IV,xiii,20 *Et/modo* (69/9-12). Solignac (*BA*, Vol. 13, pp. 670-73), gives the best account

of what little is known about the *De pulchro et apto*. He suggests Neo-Platonic and Neo-Pythagorean sources. For the latter especially see his important article, "Doxographies et manuels dans la formation philosophique de saint Augustin," *Recherches Augustiniennes*, 1 (1958), esp. 129-37. In suggesting Pythagorean influences Solignac does not deny the "intrusion of Manichaean conceptions" yet finds that "the inspiration of this passage [IV,xv,24 – about the monad and dyad] is Pythagorean" (p. 129, n. 44). In the case of the early *De pulchro et apto* it seems to me that Solignac's evidence will only allow us to make this statement if the emphasis is reversed – i.e., that while there may have been Pythagorean influences in the background it was primarily a Manichean production. Although Solignac has not seen it, Augustine does tell us the source of the basic idea of the book (the distinction between the beautiful and the suitable) which, he says, "gushed forth in my soul *from the bottom of my heart*" – *scaturriuit/meo* – IV,xiii,20 – 69/8-9, emphasis mine). It does not seem right to take this as if he harboured there Neo-Pythagorean positions, about which he has not said a single word, when the main content of the book can be fully explained in terms of his Manichaean notions – including the idea of the monad and dyad: see Alfaric, *L'évolution*, Vol. 1, p. 224, n.2 and T. Katô, "Melodia interior: sur le traité *De pulchro et apto*" (*Revue des études augustiniennes*, 12 [1966], 229-40). D. Smith ("Augustine's Criticism") points out that the essential features of the monad and dyad have to do with their character as *abstracted feelings*. In IV,xv,24 Augustine lumps all his "good" feelings in the monad – peace, unity, reason, truth, sexless love, good – and his "bad" feelings in the dyad – division, discord, irrationality, anger, lust, evil. This is a Manichaean distinction with its primary basis in sensation rather than a Pythagorean distinction concerned with the rational properties of numbers.

81 *Haec/amamus?* (68/22-69/1).
82 *ego conabar ad te* (72/19).
83 *et/mirabar* (71/7). Presumably this means not only that he never heard from Hierus but that even the friends with whom he discussed these questions (IV,xii,20) did not praise the book.
84 *Nisi/moverent* (69/2-3). Solignac (*BA*, Vol. 13, p. 671) notes the connection between *decus* and *aptum*, and between *species* and *pulchrum*. Augustine explicitly connects the first pair in IV,xiii,20 and IV,xv,24.
85 *scaturriuit* (69/8).
86 *converti/naturam* (71/13-14).
87 *Et/loquerer* (71/20-72/1).
88 *putanti/corpore?* (75/22-24).
89 *Sed/es* (72/19-26).
90 *non/bonum* (72/1-3).
91 *ambulabam/corpore* (73/1-4).
92 *vocibus/erant* (73/17-21).
93 *"Cur/deus?"* (73/6-7).
94 In IV,xvi,28 Augustine says he was "about" (*ferme* – 73/22) twenty when he read the *Categories* – i.e., soon after he became a Manichee. I understand this as showing that almost as soon as he joined the sect he began to feel a difficulty in getting the knowledge of all things which the Manichees had promised him.
95 See for example the want of a much more elementary education in the traditional liberal disciplines in the famous and supposedly learned Manichaean 'bishop,' Faustus – in V,vi,11. In *DDA* (IX,11) Augustine says "after I had become a 'Hearer' (among the Manichees) whatever I picked up by my own wits or by reading, I willingly ascribed to the effects of their teaching" (trans. Brown, *Augustine*, p. 48).
96 The terms in which Augustine describes the reputation of the *Categories* (*magnum et divinum* – 73/27-28) make it clear that it was regarded as a very difficult work which brought a considerable reputation for learning to whoever professed to understand it. Augustine may have read the Latin translation of Marius Victorinus, but see P. Hadot's *Marius Victorinus. Recherches sur sa vie et ses oeuvres*, Paris, Études Augustiniennes, 1971, pp. 187-88 for a resumé of opinion on this question. Solignac (*BA*, Vol. 13, pp. 87-93) gives a

fine brief account of the works Augustine probably read in these years — for the most part digests and doxographies (resumés of the opinions of former thinkers) like the *Novem disciplinarum libri* of Varro, or Cicero's doxographies and historical resumés: for a fuller account see his "Doxographies et manuels chez s. Augustin." See also O'Donnell's "Augustine's Classical Readings," (*Recherches Augustiniennes*, 15 [1980], 144-75), on this general topic. This article is useful because it goes beyond Hagendahl (*Augustine and the Latin Classics*) in its informed conjectures about the date and manner of Augustine's appropriation of these works.

97 See IV,xvi,29. Augustine lists the ten Aristotelian categories in the preceding section: substance, quality, quantity, relation, place, time, position, state, activity, passivity.

98 See IV,xvi,30 *Quidquid/intellexi* (75/5-8). On the reputation he acquired from his mastery of these studies, see IV,xvi,30 *Non/sequeretur* (75/17-21).

99 *ut/cupiditates* (75/16). The reference to the Prodigal Son in IV,xvi,30 is combined with the idea of fornicating away from God in company with the harlot who imitates Wisdom. See above, Chapter Two, n. 89, on the important image of the Prodigal Son which Augustine uses over and again in the *Confessions*: on fornicating away from God, see Chapter Two, n. 6: on the Manichees as a harlot imitating Wisdom, see Chapter Three, n. 66.

100 See III,vii,12 *recedens/videbar* (45/25).

101 *gaudebam/inluminabatur* (75/1-5). See also the same image in IV,xv,25.

102 *Quid/nutrirent?* (75/28-76/7). On the image of the Christian soul as a little bird in the nest of the church, see above, Chapter Three, n. 64.

103 *errabam/te* (70/18-20).

104 IV,i,1 *seducebamur/fallentes* (54/4-5).

Chapter Five
COMMENTARY ON BOOK V

V,i,1-V,ii,2. Introduction

This book is about events which took place in Augustine's 29th year.[1] As it begins he was still wholly committed to the Manichees. It will end with his decision to abandon the sect altogether.[2] Augustine sees his deliverance from the error of the Manichees as the work of divine providence. He makes this point from the first chapter by praising God for his justice and mercy.

> Accept the sacrifice of my confessions
> from the hand of my tongue
> which you formed and aroused
> to confess *your name* (Ps. 53:8).
> And heal all my bones
> so that they will say,
> *Lord who is like unto you* (Ps. 6:13, 43:10).
> For a man does not teach you what is going on in himself
> when he confesses to you,
> since a closed heart does not prevent your seeing inside it,
> nor does the hardness of a man's heart keep out your hand.
> You open it when you will
> to show your mercy or your justice
> and *there is no one who can escape your heat* (Ps. 18:7).
> (V,i,1)[3]

The poem stresses the divine providence because Augustine marvels that while he was actually going away from the truth, God's rule over him was in no way lessened. He asks, "And what harm have they done to you [i.e., impious men like himself] / or how have they disturbed your knowledge which, / from eternal heaven to the latest and least things, / is whole and entire?" (V,ii,2).[4] Even for such a man the providential government is always present — either in the miseries which inevitably accompany a false notion of the truth, or in the positive things which mercifully move him towards a better one.

In Book IV he showed the miseries he suffered as a direct result of his Manichaean conceit. Here he shows how the same order that punished his errors mercifully turned him around and put him on the path to the truth. He prays that the same will happen to others in the same plight. "Let them be converted therefore and may they seek you, / because even though they have deserted their creator, / you are not like them and you have not deserted your creature" (V,ii,2).[5]

Notes to Chapter Five appear on pages 135-43.

We must also note Augustine's stress on the role which nature played in his liberation.

> The whole of your creation
> neither ceases nor is silent in your praises . . .
> so that our soul might rise up to you from its lassitude,
> leaning for support on those things which you have made
> and from them, passing over to you
> who made them so wonderfully. (V,i,1)[6]

The content of this book is the logic of the two stages (I and II, below) by which Augustine came to ''discover'' nature and was thereby freed from the Manichees. Everywhere the events which brought him to this conclusion are interpreted as an evidence of God's mercy. And why not − since he made neither the natural order nor the mind with which he grasped it?

I. V,iii,3-V,vii,13. Natural science: the first step in Augustine's break with the Manichees

V,iii,3-6. Ancient natural science

During the nine years he thought of himself as a Manichee, Augustine had read and understood, on his own, ''many of the philosophers'' (V,iii,3).[7] He does not tell us which books he read but from the context it is plain that he is speaking of works which belong to that division of ancient philosophy concerned with the natural world (the *saeculum*)[8] − and amongst these he paid particular attention to the works on astronomy.

Why did Augustine turn to these things which were neither required by the Manichees nor by his position as a *rhetor*? The answer is that Manichaeism presented itself as a universal science where everything found its place and explanation. Mani had written copiously on astronomical matters such as the explanation of solstices and equinoxes and the prediction of eclipses, but Augustine was not able to understand what Mani said.[9] This is not surprising. The Manichaean account explained the movements of the heavens as consequences of the actions of fantastic beings. Eclipses, for example, were understood as the First Man (not Adam, but a fabulous divinity), placed in the moon, veiling his face from time to time in horror as he regarded the miserable state of the particles of light trapped in earthly matter.[10] The fourteen-day lunar cycles were explained as the progressive filling of the moon − understood as a ship − with particles of light liberated from earth. These were then unloaded into the sun which in turn took them to the habitations of light. The waxing and waning of the moon were therefore understood as variations in its substance rather than as a function of its rotation.[11] The sun itself was said to shine through a triangular window in heaven, in spite of its visible roundness.[12] The earth was a flat disc supported by the World-holder on the shoulders of Atlas[13] in such a way as to preclude the Ptolemaic revolution of the heavenly spheres about the earth − on which the accurate calculations of the ancient astronomers were predicated.[14] The list can be extended considerably.[15]

Most Manichees did not bother with this aspect of Mani's teachings: at any rate none in Carthage were able to explain them to Augustine. Most were content to hold, in a vague sort of way, what they were expected to believe about such things as were not directly of religious interest. Augustine was not — but only because he wanted all the knowledge which the Manichees claimed to possess.

Since Mani's teachings about the motion of the heavenly bodies were obscure, Augustine had turned to find out what others had said. In the tradition of ancient natural philosophy he found an account which he was able to understand perfectly.[16] This was because what these philosophers said accorded with two essential criteria: the evidence of his senses and the principles of number.

> There however [in the books of the Manichees] I was ordered to believe [all] but what I found there did not agree with those explanations [of the books of the secular scientists] established by numbers and by my own eyes: in fact it was quite contrary [i.e., the light of the sun was said to be triangular in form in spite of the fact that it appeared round]. (V,iii,6)[17]

At this point Augustine had two accounts: one which he could understand and one which he could not. But here we must be careful — for while we might suppose that he would at once adopt the one and abandon the other he did not do this. Most of this chapter is devoted to a discussion of the limits of the knowledge of nature. Augustine does this to dispel any notion that might occur to his readers that because the account of the philosophers "worked," it was therefore true. Granted, he says, it is a wonderful thing to be able to predict the year, month, day, hour, and degree of an eclipse years in advance, so that everything comes to pass as foretold, "And those who don't know this science wonder and are astonished, while those who do know it triumph and are extolled" (V,iii,4).[18] Yet, however much the rules of prediction were comprehensible, because of their conformity with the principles of mathematics, and however successful, because the senses confirmed the truth of the predictions, Augustine nevertheless insists that such explanations are only probable. At best they can only provide a likely account of the matter. In fact all he will say of the comparison between the philosopher's explanations, which were clear, and those of the Manichees, which were not, is that "the former seemed to me to be more probable than what the latter said" (V,iii,3).[19] Later he says that even if the Manichees had been able to provide an account which was as acceptable as that of the philosophers (i.e., as comprehensible and successful), he would still have been "uncertain" (V,v,9)[20] as to which was absolutely right and would have selected between them on other grounds. In such a case he would have chosen Mani's account because of his "authority," because "he believed him to be a holy man" (V,v,9) — i.e., one who had the truth from above — from God — while the scientists only had it from below — from nature.[21]

There can be no absolute certainty about such things because the connection between the rational mathematical calculations of any natural science and the events which it describes is only found at the level of the senses — in the fact that things are actually seen to happen as they are predicted to occur. The calculations themselves do not establish any necessity that things must happen according to prediction. The rational mathematical "rules" (V,iii,4)[22] of astronomy do not compel the heavenly bodies to behave in one way or another. They depend on experience for their verification and Augustine calls all such knowledge a *peritia* (V,iii,3).[23] This Latin word, which lies at the root of the English "ex-perience," means precisely a practical knowledge gained from, and dependent on, experience. But the certainty of any knowledge that depends on experience can only be a greater or lesser degree of probability. Tomorrow's fact could always introduce a new element which would overthrow calculations that have worked for centuries. No skill or art which is tied in this way to the senses (and so to the particular) can ever rise to such a universal grasp of its objects as is required for an absolutely certain "scientific" knowledge.[24] What is merely probable can never be used to determine whether any position is logically (i.e., rationally and universally) true.

However, even while the astronomical theories of the secular scientists were at best a likely account, Augustine also maintains that, in comparison to the Manichee's teachings, they were true and those of the Manichees false.[25] This is because the former did at least conform to the evidence of the senses and the reasons of number while the latter, though claiming to offer a rational account of the sensible, were not bound by reason or the senses.

But even if the theories of the natural scientists were true in comparison with the "fiction" (V,iii,3)[26] of the Manichees — which claimed to be science — Augustine nevertheless takes this occasion to criticize the ancient natural philosophers for the kind of knowledge that they did possess. The argument here is similar to the one which he has already presented in chapters x-xii of Book IV. Here again he introduces, by anticipation, the Christian position to which he was moving.

Augustine's criticism of the secular scientists is that their knowledge (*peritia*), in itself, does not and cannot reveal the truth (i.e., Wisdom): "*they are able to make a judgement about nature* while *the Lord of the world they do not find* at all (Wis. 13:9)" (V,iii,3).[27] The skill to predict natural events causes wonder in those who do not know the art, and the men who have it come to image themselves as great and wise even though they have no knowledge of the truth itself (God). Their skill is only concerned with the world. Thus he says, "going away from you out of a wicked pride and lacking your light they see far in advance a future eclipse of the sun while they fail to see their own present eclipse" (V,iii,4)[28] — i.e., the darkness and lack of knowledge about their soul's relation to its principle. Nevertheless, in writing the *Confessions*,[29] Augustine recognized that even the limited knowledge of nature, such as the scientists did possess, could also lead to a certain knowledge of God.[30] This happens if, rather than merely resting with *peritia*, an inquiry is made into the conditions necessary for such explanations to achieve the degree of accuracy which they do have. Augustine maintains that for the most part those who have risen so far as "*to be able to scrutinize nature* (Wis. 13:9)" (V,iii,3)[31] do not move beyond this to the knowledge of God. But they could. Following St. Paul's text in Romans, he insists that it is in principle possible to come to the true knowledge of God through the study of nature. This is what he says of the philosophers.

> And they have said many true things concerning the creature but the truth, the creator of creation, they do not piously seek and therefore they do not find him or, if they do find him, knowing *God they do not honour him as God* or give *thanks* but they become vain *in their thinking* and say that *they are wise, attributing to themselves what is yours and through this they come, in the most perverse blindness, to attribute to you what is theirs, which is to say that they attri-*

bute their lies to you who are the truth and they change the glory of the incor-
ruptible God into the likeness of the image of corruptible man or of birds or of
quadrupeds or of serpents and they change *your truth into a lie* and they seek
and serve *the creature rather than the creator* (Rom. 1:21-25) (V,iii,5)[32]

What Augustine says here is that either the scientist knows something true
about nature but nothing of the truth or, if he has in fact come to a true knowledge
of God through the study of nature, then his knowledge is somehow transmuted
into folly. The logic of this transformation is fully explained in Book VII so we
will not pursue the matter further here — except to note that Augustine insists that
such a transformation is inevitable apart from Christ. The philosophers may have a
true knowledge of God,

> But they do not know the way [Christ], your Word, through whom you created
> all the things which they number and count and themselves who do the count-
> ing, and the senses by which they discern what they count, and the mind with
> which they count. (V,iii,5)[33]

The scientists, it seems, can come to a true knowledge of God, but if they do not
also know that Christ is the way to God they apparently have no way to avoid having their wisdom turn into folly. Once again (comp. IV,xii,19) this is presented as
a question of the proud coming down from the heights to which they have raised
themselves[34] so that, humbled, they may find the way to the God they know —
through Christ who is both the Eternal Word or Wisdom of God and also the temporal way to that Wisdom.

> They do not know this way, your Word, by which they may come down from
> themselves to him [i.e., the Incarnate Word] and through him ascend to him [the
> Eternal Word]. They do not know this way and they think themselves to be
> placed on high with the stars and to shine. But behold, they stumble on the
> ground and *their foolish heart is darkened* (Rom. 1:21). (V,iii,5)[35]

By this point the content of Augustine's teaching is coming clear even if the
reasons are not. The true knowledge of God which the natural man can obtain is
not the same thing as Christianity. The difference, on which everything depends,
has to do with the way — the Incarnation of the Eternal Word in Christ. In time
Augustine will explain this: for now we will follow him to the next chapter.

V,iv,7. Science and piety

Augustine contrasts the scientist's knowledge of nature with the piety of the
"faithful man" (Pr. 17:6, LXX)[36] in the church. He does this lest any Christian
reader should think he or she lacks something essential to happiness because they
do not know what the scientists know about nature and do not have a scientific
knowledge of God. Augustine points out that they can still hold on to the truth in a
way which is infinitely better than either class of scientists. "Surely that man is
unhappy who knows all these things but does not know you, and blessed is he who
knows you even if he does not know these things?"[37] The point is simple. What is
the value of a knowledge of the world which leaves the knower stuck in nature,
subject to its limitations, and with no way to a happy life? Even the philosophers
who have come to a true knowledge of God, unless they also know the way to

him, are not able to "hold on"[38] to the God they know when they refuse to honour God or give him the thanks which are his due. In both cases this science is a secular and worldly knowledge which brings worldly rewards – power and glory in the eyes of men – but what are these worth in the end?

If we recall Augustine's account of what lay ahead of him, from the time he first knew God after reading the *Hortensius*, the answer is clear. His task was to "love, seek, follow, hold, and strongly embrace Wisdom itself" (III,iv,8).[39] The philosophers who have come to the knowledge of God have completed the second task: they have sought and found God. But this is worthless if they cannot take the next step. In Book VII, Augustine distinguishes "between those seeing where they must go but not seeing how, and the way leading to the blessed homeland which is not only to be seen from afar, but also lived in" (VII,xx,26).[40] Against this incomplete movement Augustine proposes that in what really counts, in coming to the happy life in our true and proper home, anyone, however unlearned, holds more closely to the truth by belief in Christ and the church than do the scientists and philosophers for all their knowledge.[41]

V,v,8-9. Piety and science

If such a knowledge of nature and its cause has nothing essential to do with our relation to God, neither need religion have anything to do with this science. Turning the matter around from the previous chapter Augustine now asks:

> But who asked this fellow Mani to write also on these subjects [natural science] since even without this knowledge one can learn piety? For you have said to man: *Behold, piety is wisdom* (Job 28:28, LXX), of which Mani could be quite ignorant even if he knew these other things perfectly [i.e., natural science]. But since he did not know these things yet had the extreme impudence to teach them, this shows beyond any doubt that he could not have known anything about piety. (V,v,8)[42]

Mani claimed – and for nine years Augustine had believed – that he spoke in all his writings with the full voice and authority of the Holy Spirit (= God).[43] He made this claim not only about what he said on the more difficult and "obscure" (V,v,8)[44] questions about our relation to God but also on the simpler matters of natural science. But since, as it will turn out, Mani dared to teach not only what he did not know, but what was actually false about nature,[45] and put this stuff out as the words of a divine person, it followed that he had neither understanding in matters of piety nor piety in matters of understanding. A man can be in the proper relation to God without having a scientific knowledge of nature or God. He cannot be in this relationship where the knowledge of nature – whether true or not – is confused with the essence of piety. This is precisely what Mani did by claiming that his false teachings about nature were the very words of God.

> In that one however who had the audacity to make himself the doctor, author, guide and leader of those whom he persuaded to believe these things – so that those who followed him thought that they were not following a mere man but your Holy Spirit – how is it possible to avoid the conclusion that if anywhere

[in his teachings] he were convicted of falsity, such a great nonsense ought to be detested and thrown away [in its entirety]? (V,v,9)[46]

The inevitable logic of this argument was not however what caused Augustine to leave the sect. Had this been the case his break would have been swift and clean — i.e., if Mani were proven wrong in what he said of nature, it would therefore follow that he was no spokesman for God in any part of his teaching. In fact Augustine's liberation from the Manichees was much more protracted and complicated. The reason, as he tells us, was that he had "not yet clearly found out" (V,v,9)[47] that Mani's teachings about nature were false.

It will be well at this point to summarize his position in chapters iii to v. On the one hand Mani's books contained teachings about nature which Augustine knew he did not understand. On the other hand he had a perfectly comprehensible account of the same matters from the natural scientists. Why not leave things here? Why not take his science from the scientists and his religion from Mani? The answer is that since Mani made no distinction between the inspiration of the one and the other, what was at stake for Augustine was the credibility of his whole system. This is why he felt obliged to try and compare the two accounts of nature. "And since I had read numerous works of the philosophers and had committed them to memory where I kept them, I compared certain of these ideas with the long fables of the Manichees" (V,iii,3).[48] If Mani was to deserve the status of a divinely inspired teacher, which Augustine had given him,[49] his explanation of the movement of the heavenly bodies to be at least as probable or adequate as that of the secular scientists — who did not claim to be inspired by God.

At first the matter did not press. In fact it did not press as long as Augustine could cherish the reasonable expectation that some day, somewhere, somebody could explain the teachings and show him that there was just as good an account there as in the books of the natural scientists. As long as he could believe this he could afford to wait. He was not interested in the questions of astronomy *per se*.[50] In the meanwhile Mani and his system — in which Augustine wanted to believe — remained inviolate.

As it happened this "meanwhile" lasted for almost nine years. We know this because he says that while none of his friends in Carthage could solve these problems, all promised him Faustus, the "Manichaean bishop" of Rome (V,iii,3)[51] who, so they said, could easily answer all such questions and any other more difficult ones he might have.[52] "For almost all of those nine years when, with a soul gone astray, I was an Auditor, I waited for the coming of that Faustus with an ever-increasing desire" (V,vi,10).[53] If Augustine waited for Faustus for "almost" nine years it was only to resolve these difficulties. But at first nothing pressed: perhaps he would meet some other Manichee who could explain these points. As time went by he more and more realized that there was no one in Carthage who could do so. All his acquaintances either knew their own inability but promised him Faustus, or, as did many, "trying to teach me about these things, end up saying nothing" (V,vii,12).[54] There was still no problem — as long as he could look to getting the explanation some day. But the need to meet this man evidently grew as one after another of the Manichees of his acquaintance proved incapable of answering his queries. By his 29th year everything had come to depend on Faustus.

V,vi,10-V,vii,13. Faustus

Augustine begins these two chapters by recalling a point he had made in V,iii,3, where he noted that he had already learned to distinguish between truth and eloquence by the time Faustus came to Carthage.[55] In his efforts to compare Mani's astronomy with that of the philosophers, questions had arisen which could not be answered by mere rhetoric. This was because the latter account did not depend on its eloquence but on the principles of number and the evidence of the senses – and none of the Manichees were able to speak to this standard. Faustus was promised as a man who not only knew what Mani taught but was also "especially learned in the liberal disciplines" (V,iii,3).[56] He was the perfect one to resolve Augustine's problem of comparing both sides. Things did not work out this way and Augustine notes drily that Faustus was obviously recommended to him by men who had not yet learned the difference between eloquence and truth.[57]

Faustus came at last to Carthage in 382 – probably some time in the summer or early autumn.[58] The man was charming, eloquent, and even modest in his own way, but Augustine was sorely disappointed.[59] He soon discovered – what Faustus did not try to conceal[60] – that he had little learning in the liberal disciplines and only a passing acquaintance with a few of the better composed Latin texts of the Manichees which, as I take it, excluded those on astronomy.[61] He could neither give a comprehensible account of Mani's astronomy nor compare it with the account of the natural scientists.[62]

As the celebrated Faustus had failed Augustine, and he despaired of finding any other who might be able to answer his questions, he began to lose interest in the sect. This is how he stood:

> [A]fter it had become sufficiently clear to me that Faustus was unskilled in those arts in which I had thought him to excel, I began to despair that he could open or dissolve for me those problems which so vexed me. (V,vii,12)[63]
> ... Thus that zeal crumbled which I had brought to the books of Mani and I despaired even more of the rest of their doctors since the renowned Faustus appeared thus [incapable] of resolving the many things which troubled me. (V,vii,13)[64]
> ... [A]ll the effort which I had raised to make progress in that sect fell from me in the moment that I knew that man: not that I went so far as to break with the Manichees completely but it was as if, not finding any course better than the one into which I had once somehow stumbled, I resolved to content myself with it for the time being until by chance another course should show itself to me which was better. (V,vii,13)[65]

Augustine was now in a very curious and unstable position. He was not with the Manichees but neither had he left them. How are we to understand this? It is clear that he did not lose interest as the result of an argument such as the one he presented in chapter v – that if Mani's astronomy were proven wrong the rest must be wrong too. He had not learned anything from Faustus which proved the falsity of Mani's teachings on astronomy and so, in a sense, he was still in the same position that he had been in for the preceding nine years. What then led him to abandon the interest which had kept him so deeply involved for such a long time? The difference was that Faustus was his last reasonable hope that anyone could explain this part of Mani's teachings. And where he had failed Augustine found that he could no longer be certain that Mani had the truth because he no longer knew how to find out what Mani was saying on these questions.

In coming to this recognition, Faustus, who had attracted so many others to the sect and was for them a *"snare of death* (Ps. 17:6 and 21:6)''[66] turned out, in Augustine's case, to be a means of liberation. Once again he saw this as an evidence of God's providential care for him.

> For your hands, my God, in the mystery of your providence, did not desert my soul . . . and you made things turn out by *wonderful means* (Jl. 2:26). You made this happen my God. For, *the steps of man are directed by the Lord* and *you will his ways* (Ps. 36:23). For how else is salvation procured except by your hand which remakes what you have made? (V,vii,13)[67]

Mani of course might still be correct in what he said about astronomy – but Augustine could no longer think that he knew this. And yet, because the rest of Mani's teaching still seemed comprehensible and true, he resolved to stay with the sect in spite of his disenchantment. But (and this is an important qualification) he thought he would only do so until he saw some better or more certain course. Faustus' failure had not broken his faith but it had certainly cracked it, and this was expressed in his new-found willingness to think that there might be a better way. At the time he had no idea where such a better way might lie, since the Manichees' objections to Catholicism still seemed insuperable. Nevertheless, in acknowledging that a part of Mani's teachings were hopelessly obscure to him, the promise of a total knowledge had been compromised. The rest might still seem credible as the most likely account of our relation to good and evil – but it was no more than that. He could no longer think that he knew that Mani knew the truth, when he knew that he had no hope of understanding a part of it which Mani had insisted was integral with the rest. If he could not know a part then he could not know the whole, and so for the first time he had come to see that his relation to Mani's teachings had never been anything other than belief.

His interest in the Manichees was now purely religious. He no longer had any thought that they could give him the complete knowledge they had promised. In deciding to stay with them he did so in the hope that by following their ritual his soul would be placed in a right relation to God. At this point Augustine's liberation was only partially complete. The rest of the book shows how he was finally able to break away from them altogether.

II. V,viii,14-V,xiv,25. Augustine's scepticism and the final breach with the Manichees

V,viii,14-15. The move to Rome

At this point Augustine was persuaded by his friends to move to Rome. Here he shows how, even in matters like this which seem quite arbitrary, it is possible to see the secret workings of divine providence by which we are led to the truth.

> You therefore dealt with me so that I should be persuaded to go to Rome and prefer to teach there what I had been teaching in Carthage. And I will not omit to confess to you what persuaded me to do so, because even in these things your

deepest secrets and your ever present mercy towards us deserves to be considered and proclaimed. (V,viii,14)[68]

In considering the reasons for this move Augustine distinguishes, on the one
hand, the attraction of greater riches and honour which Rome promised and, on
the other hand — which he counted far more important — his loathing of the unruly
behaviour of the students in Carthage.[69] These reasons are worldly enough but
they can be seen as providential in two senses. First, with regard to the future, he
points out that although he did not know it at the time, Rome would lead to Milan,
Milan to Ambrose, and Ambrose to his conversion and baptism. This is what he
means when he says, "You knew, O God for what reason I went away from
Carthage and went to Rome but you did not make it known either to me or to my
mother" (V,viii,15).[70]

Considered in itself, his decision can also be seen as providential if it can be
understood as a consequence of his being led by the truth to abandon a worse position for a better one. This is just what happened. Much as his immediate reason for
leaving had nothing to do with the truth, since his chief aim was to avoid the
unruly students at Carthage who continually disturbed his peace — behaving like
the "Overturners" of his own student days — he was unknowingly moved by
these worldly reasons at just this point because of his new relation to the truth. We
may well ask why this had now become a sufficient reason for him to seek a new
position, since the poor behaviour of the pupils in Carthage was something he had
put up with for years. The answer is that he could be indifferent to worldly conditions as long as he was sure he was on the way to the truth. Once he no longer
regarded this as certain these conditions became important and he was moved to
find a better worldly position. This is the first indication of a new and truer estima-
tion of the world for although he had no thought of God in deciding to go to
Rome — and he criticizes himself on this account (in V,viii,14) — he was all the
same moved towards him by the discovery of the uncertainty of the Manichees'
teachings. In this sense divine providence was present behind the scene, working
through the nature of things, and moving him quietly but inexorably in its direction.

Not only does Augustine criticize the purely worldly concerns which were the
explicit reasons in his decision to leave, but he also criticizes Monica's too eager
desire to stay with him. She hoped to do this either by keeping him in Africa or by
going with him to Rome. Unknown to her, providence was working to refuse what
was improper in her desire so that what was true in it might come to pass.

Although she prayed daily for the salvation of his soul, expressing at once her
desire that Augustine be led to the truth and her dependence on the truth to lead
him to itself, at the same time she contradicted herself in refusing to be parted
from him. Augustine says that this side of her desire had nothing to do with the
salvation of his soul but sprang from another source.

He attributes Monica's sin — in her too strong desire to be with her son[71] — to
the "legacy of Eve" (V,viii,15).[72] There is a precise logic in what he says. He
refers to that consequence of the fall which women in particular are bound to suffer, according to the Genesis account (3:16f.), as a consequence of their being
rational animals and the mothers of rational animals. He points to the curse that
women suffer when they are considered in their natural distinction — i.e., as moth-

ers. This is different from the curse which pertains to mankind in general (i.e., death),[73] or to men who must also labour — but in a different sense than women.[74] Augustine interprets this legacy of Eve as the ''fleshly desire'' (V,viii,15)[75] of a mother to keep her children with her. Although *desiderium* is, in general, any longing or ardent desire, it is more properly the longing for something once possessed and this is just what he had in mind.[76] On this view a mother suffers not only at the moment of birth but also throughout her whole life. What was once an integral part of her ''fleshly'' nature must separate itself from her flesh not only in birth but also throughout the rest of her life as well. Children must tear themselves ever further from their natural beginnings, in their mothers, in order to come to their proper end — which is spiritual and cannot be found in their mothers or anywhere else in nature. As he says, a mother ''must seek in pain what she brought forth in pain'' (V,viii,15).[77] At this point his mother did just this: she simply tried to hold on to the flesh.[78]

But Monica was not only moved by this natural attraction for her son. She also, and more ardently, desired his spiritual rebirth.[79] He tricked her and sailed away without her knowing. She suffered greatly on account of the natural desires which she had momentarily preferred, but she soon again sought his spiritual good in the only way in which she could — by her continued prayers and tears.[80] She was eventually to see her principal desire realized and herself united to her son in a far higher and more complete sense than anything which could be realized in nature. This union, of which their joint vision of God described in Book IX is the first fruit, had its beginning in the very voyage that first took him away from her.

> But you, taking great care of her and granting the principal point of her desire, did not pay attention to what she then sought so that you might instead bring about in me what she had always sought. (V,viii,15)[81]

V,ix,16-17. The Roman sickness, false Christology, refused baptism

On arriving in Rome Augustine was struck down by a serious illness that almost killed him. He mentions this to note that although he was on the point of death he did not desire to be baptized. ''In that very great danger I did not indeed desire your baptism and I was better as a child when I had earnestly begged it of my mother's piety as I have already recorded and confessed'' (V,ix,16).[82] The purpose of this remark is both to continue his thoughts on providence and to show the state of his soul at the time.

To the first point he says: ''I do not therefore see how Monica could have been cured had my death in this state pierced through the very essence of her love'' (V,ix,17).[83] Had he died then, she believed he would have gone ''*to hell* (Job 7:9)'' (V,ix,16)[84] and ''*into the fire* (Mt. 25:41)'' (V,ix,16).[85] All her prayers and tears on his behalf would then have been for naught and, worse, ''those visions and answers'' (V,ix,17)[86] which God had granted her would simply have been deceptive. Would God have treated Monica in this way? The answer, from the Christian position where God does not scorn the humble, is ''By no means, O Lord'' (V,ix,17).[87] We have not yet been shown why the Christian has this confidence but Augustine insists that in those things where God has made his will explicit — through Christ, Scripture, and church (in general), and here (in particular), through the visions of Monica which accorded with the former – God will not contradict himself. "For you deigned ... even to become a debtor to [your own] promises for those to whom you forgive all debts" (V,xi,17).[88] On the basis of this confidence Augustine concludes that God, in fact, "did all things in the order in which [he] had predestined that they ought to be done" (V,ix,17).[89]

His unwillingness to be baptized also shows the state of his soul. Augustine explains why he refused Catholic baptism. He did so because of his objection to the Incarnation. As he says in the next chapter, "I feared therefore to believe in the Incarnation lest I should be compelled to believe that Christ was defiled by the flesh" (V,x,20).[90] Because the Manichees understood matter as evil – and to this point Augustine agreed with them – they insisted that Christ's flesh was only apparent and consequently that his death too was only apparent.[91] From this docetic point of view the Catholic position was simply an ignorant superstition which confused God with his opposite – i.e., matter.[92] There was nothing new in this for Augustine – it was what he had thought on the subject for nine years. But this was just the problem – there was nothing new when there should have been.

What was especially "shameful" (V,ix,16)[93] and "mad" (V,ix,16)[94] in his refusal of baptism at this time was that, while he was on the point of death, he now knew that he did not really know if he was in a proper relation to the truth through Manichaeism. Perhaps he was – but then again perhaps he wasn't. What is certain is that in "ridiculing" (V,ix,16)[95] baptism in these circumstances and for this reason he showed that he preferred to die apart from the truth, should Mani be wrong, rather than having to entertain the notion that the truth was anything other than what he imagined it to be, or that he might have to come to it in any other way than through those teachings which "pleased his vanity" (V,ix,18).[96] The difference between this attitude and the deathbed repentance of his young Manichaean friend in very similar circumstances is striking.

V,x,18-20. The move towards scepticism

Augustine was staying in the house of a Manichaean Auditor in Rome when he fell ill. On his recovery he began to associate not only with other Auditors but also, and especially, with the Elect in the Manichaean community at Rome.[97] The point is significant because it shows that the hope for personal salvation was all that tied him to the Manichees. If silence is a legitimate argument in this case, he did not even trouble to find out if any of the Manichees in Rome could answer his questions about astronomy. Presumably this was because none of them appeared knowledgeable enough to bother asking – which meant that his only hope was that his soul might be put in a right relation to God through the mediation of the Elect.

> [I]t pleased my pride to be free from fault and when I had done some evil not to confess that I had done it ... but I loved to excuse myself and accuse I don't know what other thing which was with me but which was not me. ... and therefore at that time I used to associate with their *elect ones*. (Ps. 140:4).[98]

This refers to the Manichaean teaching that man is composed of a mingling of good and evil. What this meant, so far as his relation to God was concerned, was that by identifying his real self with the good part he became incapable of doing evil (which was the work of the evil part that was with him but was not himself), while on the other hand the good part had also to be separated from the evil. This was accomplished through the digestive processes of the Elect and his focus on personal salvation explains the new association he kept with them – in contrast with the less prominent role they played for him in Carthage where he was more interested in coming to an absolute knowledge of all things.

While this teaching pleased Augustine's vanity by freeing him from any responsibility for evil and seemed comfortable with a 'rational' view of things (i.e., that as good and evil are opposed they must come from two separate principles – with the consequences he outlines in V,x,20), he knew now that he did not know if any of this was true. Perhaps the good part of him could be rescued from its entanglement in evil through the Elect. But could he be sure of this? And without this knowledge he began to wonder whether there was any use in going along with these opinions. They could just as easily be a waste of time, which could have the most serious consequences if it should turn out that he had spent his life doing what the Manichees said the truth demanded while, in fact, it required something quite other.

Such thoughts could begin to fill his head once his association with the Manichees had been reduced from the promise of a universal knowledge to a simple question of his relation to God through the mediation of the Elect. And so here too he concluded that, since he did not know for sure if they were actually saving his soul, it did not matter if he didn't hold on to the doctrine with his old zeal. He says:

> [B]ut nevertheless [in spite of carrying food to the Elect] at that time I despaired of being able to get much advantage out of that false doctrine with which I had decided to remain content if I could not discover any better and I now began to be more remiss and negligent in holding it. (V,x,18)[99]

This negligence was a further distancing from the sect than the mere loss of interest after his meetings with Faustus. It led directly to the reflection that since he knew that he didn't know the truth or the way to it, perhaps the best thing was simply the frank admission that this was the case – instead of hoping to light on it by chance through believing what the Manichees, or anyone else for that matter, said on this score. Was this not in fact the only true attitude to take to the truth when he knew that he did not know it? Following directly from the previous quotation Augustine says:

> As a result indeed [of this new negligence] there arose in me the thought that those philosophers who were called Academics were more prudent than the rest in judging that all things ought to be doubted and in laying it down that man was not able to grasp anything of the truth. (V,x,19)[100]

The precise terms of Augustine's association with the thought of the New Academy (= Academics, the successors of Plato [in his Academy] = Sceptics) has been the source of controversy. Everyone recognizes that some form of scepticism was instrumental in breaking Augustine's attachment to the Manichees but how far he was a Sceptic, and in what sense, and how this led him to leave the Manichees, has proven hard to say.[101] The problem is complicated because Augustine distinguishes between what he then understood the Academics to say and what he later came to see as their real intention. He tells us that, at the time, he held only the *common opinion* that the Sceptics taught a universal doubt: "That this was clearly their teaching, which was the common opinion of it, I then believed even before I understood their real intention" (V,x,19).[102] Years before he wrote the *Confessions*, in the first book written after his conversion — *Against the Academics* — Augustine had provided both an appreciation and refutation of the position of the Sceptics. The arguments he uses there are often brought in to supplement the scant references to Scepticism which he makes in the *Confessions*.[103] Nevertheless, few as they are, Augustine tells us everything we need to know in the *Confessions* itself. As much as possible we will restrict ourselves to what we find there.

The thought that perhaps the Sceptics' doubt was the best attitude to adopt when he knew that he didn't know the truth was both attractive and repulsive to Augustine. On the positive side it promised to restore his self-esteem as a "wise" man on a basis over which he could have complete control. For the man who adopts this position accepts nothing from anyone and is certain to save himself from error by the simple expedient of never assenting to anything. This price was however too steep for Augustine since it would have meant that he would have had to abandon all hope of becoming truly wise in the knowledge of Wisdom. As nothing had proved that he could not come to the knowledge of God, he still refused to break with the Manichees. In fact, in a wretched contradiction, he continued to associate with them even though he did not hesitate to try and dissuade his host from what he then saw as an excessive confidence in their doctrines.[104]

The Manichees said they had the way to God but Augustine did not know if they were right. The Sceptics said that man could not know the way to the truth and ought not to pretend that he did. But was this right? Here too he did not know. Neither a convinced Manichee nor a Sceptic, Augustine was for the first time caught between two beliefs. Both seemed credible and yet they pointed in opposite directions. What was he to do?

Moved by this impasse he tried to see whether Catholicism offered a resolution in the form of a teaching about his relation to the truth which would be better than what either the Manichees or the Sceptics proposed. Here, once again, he met with a dead end. The Manichaean objections to Catholicism still seemed thoroughly justified.[105] "Whenever my soul tried to go back to the Catholic faith it was driven back because the Catholic faith was not what I then thought it was" (V,x,20).[106] The problem, as Augustine explains in V,x,20 was that Catholicism still seemed incredible and impious because it appeared to attribute evil to God in teaching that he is the sole creator of the universe which is evidently composed for both good and evil. Augustine is very precise about the reason why this Manichaean objection weighed so heavily with him. It was because the only reality he could think of was some kind of corporeal body. As good and evil were evidently opposed he was therefore bound to imagine both God and evil as two differing and opposed kinds of bodily substances.

> And because whenever I tried to think about my God I did not know how to think of anything except a corporeal mass — for that did not seem to me to be anything at all which was not a body — this was the greatest and almost the sole cause of the inevitable error in my thinking. (V,x,19)[107]

Given this premise Augustine continued to be unable to understand the Catholic interpretation of Scripture — in which God is not thought of as corporeal. This left him with nothing but the Manichaean account of Christianity which made it seem impious and unworthy. According to the Manichees, Christians said God was limited to the shape of a human body, created evil, and — by their insistence that he was born of the Virgin Mary and made flesh in the Incarnation — that he was necessarily polluted by this attachment to matter. The Catholic idea of the Incarnation seemed "very disgraceful" (V,x,19)[108] but Augustine's greatest problem was in arriving at a true conception of God considered as Father or creator.

> And because a kind of piety forced me to believe that a good God never created any evil nature, I made up two masses opposed to each other, both infinite, but the evil one smaller and the good one larger, and from this unsound starting-point there followed for me all the sacrilegious, impious conclusions which I drew. (V,x,20)[109]

It does not look as if Augustine had moved very far from the Manichees however much he might have lost his keenness for their teachings. Nevertheless in one important respect his situation was radically different from what it had been for the previous nine years — and on this account he was only a step away from leaving them altogether. The difference was that he now knew that he did not know whether Mani taught the truth.

V,xi,21. Catholicism and the literal word

After describing what he found incredible in Catholicism, Augustine goes on to say:

> At that time I thought it was not possible to defend what the Manichees criticized in your Scriptures but sometimes I had a real desire to discuss these matters point by point with some man truly versed in those books to find out what he thought.[110]

However much Catholic Christianity may still have seemed incredible to Augustine, he recalls here that he did "sometimes" want to find out what a truly learned Catholic would have to say about the points in Scripture which the Manichees derided. This desire was new. It came from not knowing what to believe. Were the Manichees right, or the Sceptics? He did not know. As for Catholicism, the apparent stupidity of their doctrines made him want to find out — in this new situation — how anyone could believe in them. This is a far cry from his earlier attitude that they were merely risible.[111] Now he was not so sure of this. What Catholics believed had become a question for him: not a big question, but a question all the same, and he wanted to hear them speak for themselves.

When he was still in Carthage, Augustine had already "begun to suspect"[112] that the Catholics might not believe what the Manichees said they did. There Elpidius, a Catholic apologist, had, in face-to-face discussions with the Manichees, countered their interpretations of the New Testament with other passages from the same text which argued a very different meaning from what the Manichees said. To this their answer, which they gave only in private to their disciples, was that the texts Elpidius used came from a corrupted version of Scripture. Nevertheless the

Manichees themselves never brought forward any examples of an uncorrupted copy, although they claimed to represent the true form of Christianity. The "feebleness"[113] of this reply had struck Augustine even in Carthage. Now that he really wanted to know what the Catholics said, it seems it would have been easy enough to find a learned spokesman and listen to his answers. But this is not what happened. Whatever efforts he intended to make in this regard were either never begun or else were inconclusive. "Mostly"[114] this was because he was

> bound and gagged, pinned down under those masses, I who only thought of things pertaining to bodies, and under their weight I was gasping and could not breathe in the clear and pure air of your truth.[115]

Because he could only think of bodily things in space and time he found he was blocked everywhere by the literal word of Scripture. It seemed inevitable to him that when, for example, Catholic Scripture said God made man in his image (Gen. 9:6) then it must follow that however big they might make him, they believed that God was a body with the shape of man's.[116] As he had already explained, it seemed "far more pious" (V,x,20)[117] to maintain, as the Manichees did, that God was not limited on every side by the form of a human body but that he was infinite in every direction except on the "side" where evil was set against him.[118]

Although Augustine could not make any more of the Catholic teaching than this sort of thing, he was no longer sure of the strength of the Manichees' position, or of the completeness of his grasp of Catholicism. All this was to change rapidly when he moved to Milan and met its Catholic bishop, Ambrose. For the time being his inquiry into Catholicism could go no further and he therefore turned to other concerns.

V,xii,22. Worldly interests

"Diligently therefore I began to put into practice that for which I came to Rome: namely, to teach the art of rhetoric."[119] Augustine presents this turning to worldly affairs as a consequence of his inability to make any headway in understanding Catholicism: this is the sense of the "therefore." He says this because he had been brought to a complete halt in his search for the truth. Of the three positions which he then saw as having any bearing on his relation to Wisdom, Catholicism still seemed superstitious, and between Manichaeism and Scepticism he could not choose. Since he did not think of himself as making any progress towards the truth he was left with no focus of interest except his worldly affairs. These centred about the teaching of rhetoric and the ambitions which arose from it: chiefly, the desire for money and position.[120]

Rome however had not turned out to be an ideal place to teach. True, the students there did not behave like the gangs in Carthage but he was "told" (V,xii,22)[121] that they were in the habit of banding together and changing masters just before they had to pay their fees. Augustine did not stay long enough to experience this himself — limited as he was to worldly interests, the mere threat of being cheated out of his rightful income was enough to make him look elsewhere.

V,xiii,23. Milan and Ambrose

Augustine now began a rapid advance in the world. It so happened that the city of Milan wanted a rhetorician and had requested a nomination from Symmachus, the prefect of Rome. Augustine put himself up for this position through the help of his Manichaean friends. He made an oration for this purpose which pleased Symmachus, a rhetor in his own right, and he got the position which included travel to Milan at public expense. He moved to Milan in the autumn of 384.[122]

"And I came to Milan where Ambrose was bishop."[123] This man greeted Augustine most cordially and treated him "in a fatherly way."[124] It can seem strange that Augustine should have had anything to do with the Catholic bishop but, as Courcelle notes, this was in all likelihood a formal exchange of "official politeness" between the bishop of the city and its new rhetor.[125] Yet regardless of the formal character of their meeting, Augustine tells us very clearly that: "From this time I began to love Ambrose. At first however not as a doctor of the truth, which I utterly despaired of finding in your church, but rather as a man who was benevolent towards me."[126]

Because of this kindness, and his own interest in Ambrose's reputation as a speaker, Augustine went "eagerly"[127] to hear him preach in church. At first he did this simply to test the bishop's eloquence and to compare it with that of Faustus, having no thought about what Ambrose was actually saying: "I hung intently on his words but as for the content I stood off disdainful and indifferent"[128] because he "utterly despaired"[129] that Catholicism held any help for him. Nevertheless this whole experience is seen as an example of the divine providence that led him to break completely with the Manichees and he says; "Unknowing I was led to him by you that through him I might be led to you, knowing."[130]

This text has a double signification when we recognize that Ambrose not only showed Augustine the credibility of Catholicism but also baptized Augustine into the Catholic church — and was thus the one who "led him to God, knowing." Augustine always speaks of his baptism as a rebirth and, both here and elsewhere, refers to Ambrose and Monica, respectively, as the father[131] and mother[132] of his second birth.

V,xiv,24-25. Ambrose, Scepticism and the final break
with the Manichees

V,xiv,24 — The long road Augustine had travelled from the time he read Cicero's *Hortensius* seemed to have come to a hopeless end. He stresses again that he had come to a point from which he despaired of being able to find the way to God. Catholicism seemed incredible, Manichaeism uncertain, and Scepticism unpalatable in its teaching that man could not find the truth.[133] Only his worldly interests remained and these offered small rewards compared to the Wisdom he had desired. Nevertheless, in listening to Ambrose's sermons a marvellous thing happened.

> For though I did not bother to understand the things which he said but aimed only to hear the manner in which he said them — since this empty care was all that in fact remained for me as I despaired that man could find the way leading

to you — nevertheless there came into my soul along with the words which I regarded highly, the content as well which I disregarded. (V,xiv,24)[134]

We know that Augustine had already learned to distinguish between eloquence and truth. His inability at this point to separate the words and their content was merely the other side of the same coin. Having once recognized this distinction he could no longer find eloquence alone in what he heard.[135] "Gradually" (V,xiv,24)[136] he found himself absorbing the content of what Ambrose said.

From these sermons it appeared, after all, that the Catholic faith could be maintained without absurdity in the face of the Manichees' objections which had, up to this moment, seemed insurmountable.[137] How was this accomplished? Augustine says that the Scriptures became credible when they were expounded "spiritually" while they had always seemed absurd to him when he had "taken them literally" (V,xiv,24).[138] We must be careful to understand this "spiritual" interpretation correctly. What it does not mean is that he came to recognize spiritual substance — intelligible being, every bit as real as the bodies whose existence he had always recognized. This did not happen until he read the books of the Platonists a year and a half later.[139] In Book V Augustine makes this perfectly clear by going on to say that with Catholicism now credible (in principle):

> I strongly turned my attention to see if I could in some way, by certain proofs, convict the Manichees of falsehood. If I could have been able to think of a spiritual substance all at once their fabrication would have been undone and thrown out of my soul. But I was not able. (V,xiv,25)[140]

Augustine explains the sense of the spiritual interpretation which he learned from Ambrose's sermons by the contrast he draws between the spirit and the letter.[141] What he discovered was that the Catholics did not believe what the Manichees said they believed. This came to him when he heard Ambrose explain "one or another" (V,xiv,24)[142] of the passages in the Old Testament which had always seemed impossible. The example which he gives in the next book (VI,iii,4-VI,iv,5) is the text from Genesis (9:6) which says that God made man in his image. Understood literally he had taken this to imply that God had a body in the shape of a man's body. Listening to Ambrose he discovered that the Catholics believed no such thing (VI,xi,18). Although he did not understand anything about the Catholic teaching that God was a spiritual substance, it became clear to him that they did not believe such "infantile nonsense" (VI,iv,5)[143] as that God, "the creator of all was confined in the space of a place, however great and high it might be, but limited in every direction in the form of a human figure (VI,iv,5)."[144]

Ambrose was certainly the key to Augustine's discovery of the credibility of Catholicism, but if he may be said to have heard the true Catholic position from him for the first time, this was not because he had never been exposed to it before — from Monica, from the Catholics he mocked and argued with, from Elpidius, or from his own study of Scriptures. That he could now see beyond the letter was due to the fact that he was no longer bound by the assumption that the Manichees knew what the Catholics taught. This freed him to move beyond their insistence on understanding the Scriptures in their immediate and literal sense and it was for this reason that he could now hear the true teaching when it was put before him by this Catholic of the highest authority and intelligence.

From this discovery it came to Augustine, especially in regard to the Old Testament, that what the Catholics taught about God could be maintained without absurdity. It was not that he made any particular study of the Bible, since he came to this realization simply from listening to Ambrose's sermons.[145] But in finding a resolution of the chief points on which he had always stuck because they made the Catholic notion of God (the Father) seem foolish, the way was finally opened for him to think of Catholicism as something more than a crude and silly superstition. It had become credible to Augustine for the first time. But merely because it was credible, it did not follow that it was right.

> Nevertheless I did not think that I was obliged to enter on the Catholic way simply on account of the fact that I now saw that it too could have intelligent defenders who were able to rebut objections fully and without absurdity, nor on the other hand did I think that I was obliged to condemn the way which I then held [Manichaeism] just because both sides were now equally defensible. For it seemed to me that if Catholicism was not vanquished, neither did it yet appear to be victorious. (V,xiv,14)[146]

Now that the positions of both the Catholics and the Manichees seemed equally credible he had to make some choice between them. He had found that the Manichees were mistaken in what they said of Catholicism so he turned to see if he could find "certain proofs" (V,xiv,25)[147] by which he could convict them of falsehood in their own teachings as well. He was quite unable to do this. When he wrote the *Confessions* Augustine attributed this to the fact that, at the time, he had no idea that God was not a bodily substance but a spiritual one. Formally speaking this is quite correct. The Manichaean conception of the deity is altogether excluded by the knowledge that the principle is intelligible and not corporeal. In fact Augustine was to come to a certain proof of the falsity of the Manichaean doctrines at an earlier point when, though still imagining God as a body, he nevertheless saw that he must be thought of as incorruptible, inviolable, and immutable.[148] At the time he knew neither of these things and was therefore unable to prove that the Manichees were wrong.

V,xiv,25 – Augustine's next step was crucial. He discusses it briefly in the last paragraph of this book. He once again compared the Manichees' account of nature to that of the secular scientists – but this time from a sceptical point of view. The result was that so far as nature was concerned he preferred the account of the philosophers and, as a consequence, decided to leave the Manichees altogether – even though he had no proof that Mani was wrong in what he said about the heavens. This left him with no religion and so, for his relation to the truth, he turned to the (now credible) alternative and decided to consider himself as a catechumen in the Catholic church.[149] So much comes together here that it is best if we have the whole text before us. Continuing directly from the observation that he was not able to prove the Manichees wrong because he could not conceive of a spiritual substance, he says:

> Nevertheless concerning the body of this world and of all of nature which the senses of the flesh are able to perceive, I now judged, after much consideration and comparison, that the opinions of very many of the philosophers [i.e., the natural scientists] were a great deal more probable [than those of the Mani-

chees]. Therefore, in the manner of the Academics — as they are commonly thought to do, doubting all things and floating amongst all things — I determined that I at any rate ought to abandon the Manichees, thinking that I, in that time of my doubts, should not remain in that sect above which I preferred the teachings [on nature] of no small number of philosophers [natural scientists]. However as far as these philosophers were concerned [i.e., the Academics] I altogether refused to place in their care the cure of my languishing soul because they were without the health-giving name of Christ. I resolved therefore to remain a catechumen in the Catholic church, where I had been entrusted by my parents for my soul's protection, until something certain should appear by which I could direct my course.[150]

What happened here is not easy to see unless we follow Augustine very closely. After listening to Ambrose and determining that the Catholic faith was credible in what it said of God, Augustine was in the following position. Manichaeism and Catholicism — both claiming to have the truth and the way for men to come to it — were equally believable. Yet he could not prove that either was right or either wrong. Against both was what he took to be the position of the Sceptics who held that man could not find the truth and therefore recommended a universal doubt as the only proper attitude to adopt in this situation — refusing to commit oneself to any dogma so long as it was not certain. All three elements were brought together in a coherent whole in Augustine's resolution. He arrived at it in this way.

Although he had no certain proof that the Manichees were wrong in what they said about God or nature, he was sure that the philosophers' account of nature seemed much more probable than that of the Manichees.[151] Knowing that he didn't actually know which account of nature was right or true, as between the Manichees and the philosophers, the new-found credibility of Catholicism had at least freed him to "prefer" (i.e., actually to choose and adopt)[152] what he had long considered the more probable account — and he did so for sceptical considerations, "in the manner of the Academics." In the absence of certain knowledge Scepticism taught that man must take the next best course, which is prudence. And a prudential calculation required that Augustine give up the less probable where, as in the case of nature, there was a possibility of weighing greater and lesser probabilities. This he could now do because he was no longer bound to keep alive a hope that the Manichees' teachings about nature could somehow be shown to be as probable as those of the philosophers, which was the position he had had to maintain as long as the Manichees seemed to have the only credible account of God.

What was involved in preferring the natural philosopher's account of nature? Not only did it means that Augustine finally abandoned Mani's astronomical teachings, but, more generally, that he gave up the whole Manichaean account of nature.[153] Specifically this meant that he gave up the Manichaean notion that natural objects were simply composed of a mixture of the contraries of good and evil.

We recall that in the Manichaean account nature ought not to be. It was a production of the evil principle when he captured particles of the good. Consequently, as all things were composed in the beginning out of the two principles of light and dark and would be separated into these two in the end, no particular sensible thing had any substantial independent identity of its own.

For an example we have only to look at Augustine himself. As a Manichee he thought of himself as nothing but a sensible body since all that is, was corporeal. Yet he never identified himself with the body which his senses revealed. He was only the "good" part. The rest was an "evil" part which was literally unthinkable. It was something which "was with me but was not me" (V,x,18).[154] Here, the real Augustine, who was thought of as a sensible body, was not identified with the body which the senses revealed — for certainly no sense of Augustine's ever saw these good or evil parts: he could not crush a hair or a fingernail or whatever and find the bits of good and evil.

At the time Augustine did not know that the Manichees could not possibly have a science of nature, because the result of assuming that the principles were separate was that nature was not anything on its own: it was only a mixture of light and dark (as images of being and non-being). These alone were substantial, these alone existed. And since the universe which is actually revealed by the senses had no theoretical existence, it could not be an object of knowledge because there was no finite sensible individual to know. But what he did know, when he measured the Manichees' teachings about nature against those of the secular scientists, was that the account of these philosophers seemed "a great deal more probable." Although he could not have said so at the time, the ground of this preference lay in the fact that the natural scientists started from the assumption that there were indeed concrete finite beings — that nature, as revealed by the senses, was in fact a real substantial entity. On this hypothesis the philosophers of antiquity had constructed a science of nature which was not imaginary, and which accorded with the evidence of the senses and the principles of number such that their astronomy could accurately predict heavenly events. It was on the basis of this accord that Augustine had long considered their view of nature the more probable and now, in preferring it definitely he had, in the most literal sense, come to his senses.

But once Augustine had determined that improbability was a sufficient cause for rejecting the Manichees' account of nature (which he knew to be a different thing than actually proving it was false), he was at the same time and for the same reason forced to reject their account of God and of the way to him since Mani had insisted that his teachings about nature were one with his teachings about God and religion. He could not abandon the Manichees' account of nature as composed of a mixture of the two principles without at the same time giving up the two principles themselves. This is just what he did. "I determined . . . that I, in that time of my doubts should not remain in that sect above which I now preferred the teachings of no small number of philosophers." In coming to this sceptical appraisal of nature, where there are only probabilities, Augustine had finally freed himself from Manichaeism even though he had no certain knowledge that Mani was wrong in what he taught about nature or God.

But why did he adopt a sceptical position only at this point although he had known about it at least from the time he was in Rome — and probably long before, through his acquaintance with Cicero's works? The answer is that he could be moved by these sceptical considerations — to prefer the more probable account of nature — only after Catholicism had become credible. This is proven by the fact that he now decided to consider himself as a catechumen in the Catholic church at the same time as he was a sceptic. This can look extremely confusing. Without knowing that the Manichees were wrong, Augustine gave up his belief in one set of teachings from sceptical reasons, only to turn around and consider himself as a learner in another set (Catholicism) under the same influence. The problem evaporates when we recognize the modified form of Scepticism which he adopted.

Ancient Scepticism presented itself – and was understood by Augustine – as having two chief teachings. One of these, which he accepted, was that insofar as a man did not actually have any certain truth – whether about nature or God – then he ought to doubt all things and refuse to give his assent to any doctrine which claimed to have it. As applied to the "body of this world and the whole of nature which the senses of the flesh are able to perceive" this is what had moved him to prefer – not merely to remain undecided about, but actually to prefer, to choose – the account of the natural philosophers. And indeed, because the senses cannot provide any certain indubitable knowledge, this part of Scepticism, applied to nature, is perfectly true. With respect to any knowledge which comes through the senses we can only have a greater or lesser degree of probability. Augustine has already discussed the argument which leads to this conclusion in his criticism of the secular scientists at the beginning of this book (in V,iii,3-6).

There was however another part of the Sceptical position which Augustine did not accept. This was the dogmatic opinion with respect to our knowledge of God which "judged that no truth can be grasped by man" (V,x,19).[155] Here the Sceptics claimed that man's good lay in his own hands. In this view, wisdom consisted in the absence of error and happiness in the imperturbability which would necessarily result if a man refused to assent to any doctrine – for in this way he would free himself from every possible error or disappointment if what he believed turned out to be false. This position offered man worldly contentment but at the price of making disappointment his *modus vivendi* since, as a matter of principle, he must ever despair of coming to a certain knowledge of God (= Wisdom).

So long as Augustine's choice was between Manichaeism, as the only credible way of coming to God, and a scepticism which required him to give up any hope of finding him, he would have nothing to do with the latter. However, once Catholicism had become another credible teaching which offered a way to the truth in the place of Manichaeism, the truth of the Sceptical position about the natural could come into play and by it he was finally moved to abandon the Manichees forever. All the same he "completely refused" to put the care of his soul in the hands of the Sceptics.[156] This was the other side of their teaching with which he would have nothing to do and for which there was no basis other than their dogmatic assertion that we are unable to find the truth. Augustine expresses this reason by saying that he refused to place the care of his soul (i.e., its relation to God) in the hands of the Sceptics, "because they were without the health-giving name of Christ." We recall that from the time when he first came to desire Wisdom through reading Cicero's *Hortensius* he had refused any teaching about God which did not refer to Christ. During all the years that he considered himself a convinced Manichee he had thought of Manichaeism as the true and purified form of Christianity. With Manichaeism gone and Catholicism credible he therefore resolved to consider himself – what he had long been in a purely formal sense – a catechumen in the Catholic church.[157] But he was a catechumen or a learner only. He did not know whether Catholicism was right in what it taught about God – and so long as he did not know for sure he refused to give himself to it lest the belief prove deceptive.[158] This too he took from the Sceptics, thinking it the only right attitude to take to the truth when he knew that he did not know it. Yet he was not a Sceptic who refused to search for the truth. He thought of himself as a catechumen who looked to the Catholic church, as a learner, to see if it had the truth and the way which actually led to God. Thus, on the religious side, we see that he became a sceptic only to the extent that he decided not to become a Christian until he was certain that Christianity was right. He refused to become a Sceptic — in the dogmatic sense which affirms that man cannot find God and must live without him — because he had no proof that this was true.

There is no name for Augustine's position in the repertoire of ancient philosophy, nor does he give it one. For the sake of convenience we will call it scepticism, but with a small "s." Had he become a Sceptic in the ordinary sense he would not have continued to search for Wisdom nor looked to the church to see if it had it. Instead he would have aimed to acquire the state of indifference, calmness or imperturbability which the true Sceptics promoted.[159] His scepticism, on the contrary, left him in a horribly divided state. His ignorance of the truth left him squarely in the world, while at the same time the world was a totally unsatisfactory place because of his hope that he could still find the truth — and ever since *Hortensius* this truth (the divine Wisdom) had attracted him as infinitely preferable to anything the world had to offer. The next book shows the exact form, and the miserable consequences, of this division in his soul.

NOTES

1 See V,iii,3 *Proloquar/meae* (78/8).
2 See V,xiv,25 *manichaeos/decrevi* (97/23-24).
3 V,i,1 *Accipe/tuo* (76/20-77/1). The "bones" which need healing are the same that had not been humbled in IV,xv,27 — see above, Chapter Four, n. 92. This *ossa* (76/22) should thus be seen as a quotation from Ps. 50:10 — a text not noted by G. N. Knauer (*Psalmenzitate in Augustins Konfessionen*, Göttingen, Vandenhoeck und Ruprecht, 1955).
4 *Et/integrum?* (77/11-13).
5 *Convertantur/tuam* (77/22-24).
6 *Non/tua* (77/3-4) and *ut/mirabiliter* (77/5-8). Notice the order: from nature to God.
7 *multa philosophorum legeram* (78/18-19). In IV,xvi,31 Augustine states that he read and understood these works without the help of any teacher — *Quid/enodati* (75/28-76/1): comp. IV,xvi,28 *legi/intellexi?* (73/28-29), and *quam/cognoveram* (74/3-4).
8 In V,iii,6 Augustine speaks of the works in question as *libris saecularis sapientiae* ("books of the wisdom of the age [i.e., as opposed to eternity]" — the English "secular" has much the same sense = "books of secular wisdom" — i.e., knowledge of secular = worldly = natural things). In V,xiv,25 Augustine says that the philosophers he was reading concerned themselves "with the sensible matter (*corpus*) of this world and with all nature perceived by the senses of the body" (*de/attingeret* — 97/18-19) which, as Solignac notes (*BA*, Vol. 13, p. 92), would mean "physics" in the ancient sense of the word.
9 See V,iii,6.
10 See *CFM*, XVIII,7, and XXII,12.
11 See *Letter*, LV,6.
12 See *CFM*, XX,6.
13 See *CFM*, XX,9.
14 See Alfaric, *L'évolution*, Vol. 1, p. 235.

15 See *CFM*, XV,6-7 and XX,10 describing the Eons who assist the Demiurge in the mainte-
    nance of the world — these complicated passages are somewhat clarified in Alfaric
    (*L'évolution*, Vol. 1, pp. 107-108). *CFM*, I,9 shows the scientific pretension of the Mani-
    chees about astronomical matters: "Mani . . . taught us about the structure of the world, why
    and whence it was made, and who made it; he taught us whence the day and whence the
    night; he taught us about the course of the sun and the moon."
16 There is room for question about which books Augustine read on astronomy. Alfaric
    (*L'évolution*, Vol. 1, p. 324) thinks certainly the sixth book of Varro's *Novem disciplinarum
    libri* which is traditionally regarded as being on astronomy (but see Solignac's reservation in
    "Doxographies et manuels," pp. 123-24), some of Cicero's works including the *Dream of
    Scipio*, and Apuleius' (lost) *On Astronomy*. Marrou (*Saint Augustin et la fin*, p. 248) argues
    that nothing proves Augustine ever studied astronomy directly, but Solignac (*BA*, Vol. 13,
    p. 90, n. 1 and p. 89, n. 1) judges that Augustine must surely have known at least enough to
    prefer, as more probable, the account of the philosophers.
17 *Ibi/erat* (80/26-28).
18 *Et/sciunt* (79/10-12).
19 *et/illi* (78/21-22). See also V,xiv,25 *Verum/iudicabam* (97/18-21).
20 *incertum* (83/1-2).
21 *auctoritatem/sanctitatem* (83/3-4). On Mani's claim to speak with the voice of the Holy
    Spirit see above, Chapter Three, n. 81. See also the text from V,v,9, quoted below, n. 46.
22 *regulas* (79/6).
23 78/28.
24 For the same reasons Augustine also speaks of this knowledge as an "art/skill/science" (*ars*)
    as well as a *peritia* — in distinction from a true science (*scientia*): see his description of the
    books in question, *omnes libros artium, quas liberales vocant*, in IV,xvi,30 (74/28-29) — "all
    the books of the arts which are called liberal." Augustine's definition of the character of a
    truly scientific knowledge (*scientia*) is given in *CA*, I,vii,19, quoted above, p. 94
25 On the truth of the positions of the secular scientists see V,iii,5 *Et/dicunt* (80/5). This is
    repeated in V,iii,6 and again in V,v,8. On the falsity of the Manichees' teachings about
    nature see V,v,8 *Itaque/deprehenderetur* (83/3-4) and also V,v,9 *quis/convinceretur* (82/24-
    25).
26 *fabulis* (78/21).
27 *possent/invenerint* (78/23-24).
28 *et/vident* (79/12-15).
29 Augustine did not know this in his 29th year. He did not discover that the knowledge of
    nature could lead to a knowledge of the truth until he came across the books of the Platon-
    ists: see VII,ix,13f.
30 See V,iii,5 "or, if they found [the truth], knowing God" — *aut/deum* (80/7-8).
31 *ut/saeculum* (78/22-23).
32 *Et/creatori* (80/5-18). This text from Romans 1:17f. is used often by Augustine in the *Con-
    fessions* as may be seen by consulting the *Index Scriptorem* (*BA*, Vol. 14, p. 676). I discuss
    its interpretation in Chapter Seven in connection with VII,ix,14f.
33 *Sed/numerant* (79/24-27).
34 See V,iii,3 *qui/astrorum* (78/22-29).
35 *Non/eorum* (79/30-80/5).
36 *homo fidelis* (81/11).
37 *Infelix/nesciat* (80/30-81/2).
38 *inhaerendo tibi* (81/12).
39 *sed/fortiter* (42/3-5).
40 *inter/habitandam* (149/25-27).
41 For references to Augustine's appreciation of the benefits of natural science, see Solignac,
    BA, Vol. 13, p. 475, n. 2.
42 *Sed/posset* (81/18-23).
43 See above, Chapter Three, n. 81.

44 *abditiora* (81/28).
45 See *cum/falsa* (82/6-7).
46 *In/iudicaret?* (82/21-26).
47 *nondum liquido conpereram* (82/27). M. Pellegrino (*Les Confessions de saint Augustin*, Paris, Éditions Alsatia, 1960, p. 129) argues that Augustine left the Manichees altogether because he saw that their teachings about nature were false. He says, ''In the books attributed to Mani, who claimed to have the Holy Spirit, there were long passages on astronomy which are not indispensable to the religious spirit: but they did not give any valid account of natural phenomena and taught theories manifestly contradicted by science. Obviously this fact also compromised their religious doctrines since, in this system, the scientific position was one with the religious problem.'' The difficulty in this way of arguing is that it takes no account of the fact that Augustine left the Manichees long before *he* discovered that they were wrong.
48 *Et/fabulis* (78/18-21).
49 See V,v,9 *sed/praeponerem* (83/3-4).
50 I understand that Augustine had no interest in astronomy except as it related to the search for Wisdom — but this should not be taken in Marrou's sense that he had no knowledge of the actual calculations used by astronomers. On this point I agree with Solignac against Marrou: see above, n. 16.
51 *manichaeorum episcopus* (78/9).
52 See V,vi,10 *Ceteri/expedirentur* (84/7-12).
53 *Et/Faustum* (83/5-7). On Faustus see the brief account in Solignac (*BA*, Vol. 13, pp. 673-74: see also the chapter (III) on Faustus in Decret, *Aspects*, pp. 51-70.
54 *conantes/nihil* (85/16-17).
55 See V,iii,3 *Quam/intuebar* (78/11-15). Augustine repeats this in V,vi,10 *Iam/eloquium* (83/16-20). In the image Augustine uses, he had learned to distinguish between the ''plate'' (V,iii,3 *vasculo* [78/13] — recalling his description, in III,vi,10, of the books of the Manichees as glorious plates in which they served him fictions), or ''cup'' (V,vi,10 *poculorum* [83/15], *vasis* [84/4]), and their contents. Augustine had used the same image in I,xvi,26. He attributes his awareness of this distinction to divine providence — to God's ''wonderful and secret ways,'' *miris/modis* (83/26) — since he had been brought to this conclusion although he had not set out to find it.
56 *adprime/eruditus* (78/17-18).
57 See V,vi,10 *Illi/loquens* (83/20-22).
58 Solignac (*BA*, Vol. 13, p. 203) has Faustus arriving in Carthage in the summer of 382 in Augustine's 28th year) because he was ''already'' (*iam* 78/8) in Carthage at the start of his 29th year (V,iii,3) — i.e., after his 28th birthday on 13 November 382. O'Meara (*The Young Augustine*, p. 103) lists various pieces of anti-Manichaean legislation and suggests that Faustus came to Carthage, from Rome, to flee the law of March 382 in which Theodosius imposed the death penalty on any Manichee who attempted to live in a religious community. Courcelle (*Recherches*, p. 179, n. 1) gives references for the existence of a Manichaean monastery in Rome — to which Faustus might have been attached.
59 Augustine does not hesitate to testify to Faustus' eloquence and pleasant character: see V,vi,11 and V,vii,12. In V,xiii,23 he judges his manner of speaking — though not the content — even more ''engaging and delightful'' (*hilarescentis atque mulcentis* [96/9]) than that of Ambrose. In V,vi,11 he says that Faustus' eloquence was more natural than formally trained (*delectabatur/occurrentibus* [84/7-9], and *aderat/naturali* [84/23-26]). This can also be seen from the fact that Augustine began to teach him (V,vii,13).
60 See V,vii,12 *Quae/inveniebam* (85/12-25).
61 See V,vi,11 where Augustine lists the extent of Faustus' prior learning: *expertus sum/conscripta erant* (84/17-23).
62 See V,vii,12 *Libri/confiteri* (85/6-15).
63 *Nam/dissolvere* (85/1-4).
64 *Refracto/apparuit* (85/26-86/1).

65 *Ceterum/eluceret* (86/5-11).
66 *laqueus mortis* (86/12). Compare V,iii,3 where Faustus is called "a snare of the devil" — *laqueus diaboli (1 Tim. 3:7 and 6:9)* (78/10). See also above, Chapter Three, n. 66.
67 *Manus/meam* (86/14-15) and *et/fecisti?* (86/17-21). See also V,vi,11 *Coram/odissem* (84/27-31). The providential nature of Faustus' coming to Carthage is clear from the argument. If he had not happened to arrive Augustine might have continued as a Manichee for an indefinite time. Without Faustus, or news of his death, Augustine had no reason to give up hope that he would some day understand Mani's astronomy.
68 *Egisti/praedicanda est* (86/22-27).
69 See V,viii,14 *Non/permiserit* (86/27-87/7).
70 *Sed/matri* (88/1-2).
71 See V,viii,15 *Amabat/amplius* (88/25-27).
72 *reliquarium Evae* (88/30).
73 In V,ix,16 Augustine speaks of the bond of original sin as the cause of death — *originalis/morimur* (89/7-8).
74 Of the consequences of the fall that result from the particular nature of man (as distinguished from woman when she is considered in her particular natural capacity), Augustine has already spoken of the necessity that the sons of Adam must, in labour and sorrow, create and maintain the government of man: see I,xi,14 and my discussion of this text.
75 *carnale desiderium* (88/24-25).
76 See *ALD*, art. *desiderium*.
77 *cum/pepererat* (88/30-89/1).
78 See V,viii,15 *Et/sineres?* (88/16-17).
79 See V,ix,16 *Non/pepererat* (90/2-5), and V,ix,17 *Huiusne/sui* (90/17-20). See also I,xi, 17, III,xi,19, and IX,viii,17.
80 See V,ix,16 *Et/absens* (89/18-19). O'Meara (*The Young Augustine*, pp. 104-105) is probably correct in seeing an intentional echo of the story of Dido and Aeneas (*Aeneid* IV) in the way Augustine handles his own flight from Monica.
81 V,viii,15 *Sed/petebat* (88/17-20); see also *cum/vapularet* (88/23-25).
82 V,ix,16 *Neque/confessus sum* (89/22-25). The earlier incident is recorded in I,xi,17-18.
83 *Non/eius* (90/6-7).
84 *ad inferos* (89/5).
85 *in ignem* (89/17).
86 *visionibus et responsis* (90/24). On Monica's visions, see above, Chapter Three, n. 153.
87 *nequamquam, domine* (90/21).
88 *Dignaris enim . . . eis/fieri* (90/27-91/2).
89 *et/faciendum* (90/22-23).
90 *metuebam/inquinatum* (93/30-94/2). Solignac (*BA*, Vol. 13, p. 493) gives a list of other references to the docetic nature of the Manichaean Christology. See also his longer note on the subject, pp. 674-76. In V,ix,16 Augustine speaks of the unreality of Christ's death on a "phantom cross" (*in cruce phantasmatis* [89/11]) in a caricature of the Manichees' views.
91 See *CFM*, XX,14-15 and XXI on the Manichean teaching about the evil of matter — also called ὕλη, in what Augustine scorns as a pretentious use of Greek. The Manichees identified this with the second principle which was the opposite of God. See *CFM*, XXVI-XXIX on their refusal to accept the reality of Christ's flesh or death because God would not voluntarily mix with his opposite — i.e., matter.
92 See V,ix,16 *Quomodo/credebat* (89/11-15).
93 *dedecus* (89/25).
94 *demens* (89/26).
95 *irridebam* (89/26).
96 *delectabat superbiam meam* (91/12).
97 See *Et/vocant* (91/5-10).
98 *et/fecisse* (91/12-14), *sed/essem* (19/15-16), and *et/eorum* (91/26-27). In the Latin translation of the LXX of Ps. 140:4, the last three words of the quotation, *cum electis eorum*, refer to

"men doing evil." Augustine took them as applying to the Manichaean Elect. See also *EP*, CXL,10.

99 *sed/retinebam* (91/27-92/4).

100 *Etenim/decreverant* (92/5-9).

101 For a brief account of the literature of the New Academy, its history and doctrine, and a review of the possible sources of Augustine's knowledge of these positions, see Solignac, *BA*, Vol. 13, pp. 94-100. For Augustine's relation to Scepticism, see J. A. Mourant, "Augustine and the Sceptics," *Recherches Augustiniennes*, 4 (1966), 67-96. This article reviews Augustine's statements about his relation to Scepticism. Mourant concludes that Augustine never was a Sceptic in the accepted sense of the word but wrongly attributes Augustine's interest in their teachings to their value in combatting what Mourant sees as a persistence of Manichaean ideas — long beyond the point where Augustine says that he had given up on the sect altogether. I do not think it is necessary to alter the record in this way nor that Augustine's interest in Scepticism can have been for its "opposition to philosophical materialism" (p. 96) — when it was precisely under its influence that he developed the strongly materialist conception of God which he describes in the first part of Book VII.

102 *Ita/intellegenti* (92/9-11). See also the *sicut existimatur* of V,xiv,25 (97/22). It is not necessary for our understanding of the *Confessions* that we examine the view which Augustine later came to hold on the real intention of the Academics' teaching. He explains this in *Against the Academics*, especially in the third book where he argues that their scepticism was designed to hide a secret Platonism which they wanted to keep from the unworthy: see *CA*, III,xx,43. A full discussion of the justice of Augustine's views on the "secret doctrine" of the Academics is found in D. House, "A Note on Book III of St. Augustine's *Contra Academicos*," available only in Spanish translation, in *Augustinus*, 26 (1981), pp. 95-101.

103 Apart from the first two sentences of V,x,19, the only other specific references to the Sceptics are found in V,xiv,25, VI,i,1, and VI,xi,18. Augustine's ambivalent attitude towards the Academics — partly favouring them, because of the positive role their tenets played in freeing him from the Manichees, while spurning the dogmatic side of their teaching which laid it down that we cannot know God — is underlined by the different titles he gave to *Against the Academics*. In *Retr.* (I,i), he calls it *Contra Academicos* or *De Academicis*. The work is dedicated to Romanianus — Augustine's friend and wealthy patron from Thagaste, the father of his student Licentius (who was with Augustine at Cassiciacum when he wrote the work), a relative of Augustine's best friend Alypius and, possibly, a distant relation of Augustine's father (on the last two points, see Brown, *Augustine*, pp. 54, 21). Augustine describes the tenor of Romanianus' life in *CA*, I,i, and, with gratitude, the help he received from him (II,3-4). Augustine had persuaded Romanianus to become a Manichee but, by 386, Romanianus had suffered serious reverses in his worldly affairs which had brought him to leave the Manichees and adopt a Sceptical attitude about the possibility of finding the truth. Augustine wrote *Against the Academics* to show Romanianus what was true and what was false in Scepticism in order to move him away from the world towards philosophy — and ultimately to Christ as Wisdom Incarnate.

104 See V,x,19 *Nec/quaerere* (92/11-18).

105 See, V,x,19 *praesertim/averterant* (92/18-21).

106 *Cum/arbitrabar* (93/9-12).

107 *Et/mei* (92/24-28).

108 *multumque/videbatur* (92/21-22).

109 *Et/sequebantur* (93/4-9).

110 *Deinde/sentiret* (94/5-8).

111 See III,x,18 *inridebam/tuos* (50/30-31). See also Augustine's scorn of the "medicine" of the Catholic faith in V,ix,16 *medicinae/inridebam* (89/26).

112 *movere me coeperant* (94/11).

113 *inbecilla* (94/13).

114 *maxime* (94/18).

115 *captum/poteram* (94/19-22).

116 See V,x,20. Compare III,vii,12, and VI,iii,4.

117 *magis/videbar* (93/12).

118 See V,x,20 *Et/finiri* (93/12-17). See also *CEF*, XX,22-XXVII,29 for an account of the Manichaean conception of the spatial relation of good and evil.

119 *sedulo/rhetoricam* (94/23-24).

120 This is the general tenor of Augustine's comments in V,xii,22. Courcelle (*Recherches*, p. 83) speaks correctly of Augustine at this point as "arriviste."

121 *inquiunt* (94/29).

122 This date is "unanimously accepted" according to Courcelle (*Recherches*, p. 79, n. 1). It is determined by the time when (Quintus Aurelius) Symmachus entered office as *praefectus urbis*, known to be between 11 June 384 when he was not yet prefect and 9 November 384 when he was. For a brief account of Symmachus and his position in relation to Augustine see O'Meara (*The Young Augustine*, pp. 92-93), or Brown (*Augustine*, pp. 66-67, 70 – see also p. 81 where Brown notes that Symmachus was a cousin of Ambrose). Courcelle (*Recherches*, pp. 78-87) suggests that Symmachus – a distinguished conservative Roman patrician who is generally seen as the great defender of paganism against Christianity – appointed Augustine to the job in the imperial city because he was not a Catholic and thus might be useful against the Catholic "party" in Milan and against Ambrose, its leader. It seems to me that the likelihood of this is lessened by the fact that so far as Augustine was anything, he was known as a Manichee and as such would have been an easy target against whom the Catholics could have invoked the anti-Manichaean laws – the most recent of which had been issued two years previously (*Recherches*, p. 71, n. 5). Courcelle himself recognizes that, for his part, Ambrose either knew nothing of any anti-Catholic plot in which Augustine was, knowingly or unknowingly, involved, or else "pretended" to take him for a believer (*Recherches*, p. 89). A brilliant statement of the general relation of paganism and the church in the fourth century is found in J. J. O'Donnell, "The Demise of Paganism," *Traditio*, 35 (1979), 45-88. He gives a fine account of the motivation and interests of Symmachus and his mentor, the great Vettius Agorius Praetextatus (pp. 65-83). O'Donnell's position on the nature and character of the so-called pagan revival in the 380s is that "there simply was no [pagan] 'party' for . . . Symmachus to lead" (p. 81). O'Donnell's conclusions argue strongly against Courcelle's interpretation of Symmachus' supposed anti-Christian activities.

123 *Et/episcopum* (95/21-22).

124 *Suscepti me paterne* (95/27). Courcelle (*Recherches*, p. 86, n. 2) says of this *paterne* that Augustine calls his baptism a rebirth, "and never fails, in the works where he cites Ambrose, to call him his father." Thus we see that as Augustine regarded Monica as the "mother" of his spiritual rebirth (see the texts listed below, n. 132), so did he regard Ambrose as its "father." This is no mere rhetorical flourish but is intended as an accurate statement of their respective roles in his conversion. Monica "laboured" in spirit to bring him to that rebirth. Ambrose provided the spiritual "seed." In another sense, as the events of Book VIII will show, the old priest Simplicianus provided another kind of "seed," equally important to Augustine's final conversion – a "seed" not for his understanding but for his will. Courcelle (*Recherches*, p. 173, n. 6-7) notes a number of places where Augustine speaks of Simplicianus as a father. Noteworthy also is the fact that as Ambrose was the "father" of Augustine's conversion, so had Simplicianus been the "father" of Ambrose's conversion – see VIII,ii,3 *Perrexi/Ambrosii* (154/13-14). Sister B. Beyenka, "The Names of St. Ambrose in the Works of St. Augustine" (*Augustinian Studies*, 5 [1974], 19-28) gives a long list of the same and says that "Augustine does not ever call him [Ambrose] *pater*" (p. 25), i.e., does not use this precise word. This may be true but Augustine nevertheless understood their relation in the sense described above.

     I understand the phrase *peregrationem meam satis episcopaliter delexit* (95/28-29) in the sense of "he approved my coming in a manner befitting a bishop" – this is the sense of O'Meara's translation, "[he] showed me an episcopal kindness on my coming" (*The Young Augustine*, p. 117). For other references to the phrase, see Solignac (*BA*, Vol. 13, p. 507, n. 1).

125 Courcelle (*Recherches*, p. 86). The rest of Courcelle's account of the relations of Augustine
    and Ambrose (pp. 85-92), which has Augustine "hostile" (p. 90) to the bishop, is forced and
    unconvincing. Not only does it disregard what Augustine expressly says of their good rela-
    tions but it depends on supposing that Augustine was still a convinced Manichee — as the
    source of his hostility — when this was no longer the case: see VI,i,1 *non/manichaeum*
    (98/21). Augustine's official duties would have included speeches in praise of important
    people, such as the one he mentions in VI,vi,9.
126 *Et/me* (95/29-96/2).
127 *studiose* (96/3).
128 *verbis/adstabam* (96/6-8).
129 *prorsus desperabam* (96/1-2).
130 *Ad/ducerer* (95/26-27). See also *Sed/nesciens* (96/13-15).
131 See above, n. 124. Courcelle (*Recherches*, p. 86, n. 2, pp. 212-12) notes that Augustine does
    not specify anywhere in the *Confessions* that Ambrose baptized him. Texts where this is said
    are the *Letter* (to Casulanus), XXXVI,xiv,32, the *Letter* (to Paulinus), CXLVII,xxiii,32, and
    CJI, VI,21. Courcelle would be mistaken if, as I suggest, the phrase *ut per eum ad te sciens
    ducerer* — "so that through him [Ambrose] I might be led to you [God], knowing"
    (V,xiii,23 — 95/26-27) — is taken to refer to Augustine's baptism at the hands of Ambrose.
132 The texts relative to Monica's role as the mother of Augustine's spiritual birth: I,xi,17,
    III,xi,19, V,ix,16, V,ix,17, and IX,viii,17.
133 See *DUC*, VIII,20 where Augustine says of this same period that he had not given up the
    hope that he could come to a knowledge of God (= Wisdom) — which was the position of the
    Sceptics — but only that he had not yet found the right method (*modus*) to come to it.
134 *Cum/neglegebam* (96/16-21).
135 See V,xiv,24 *Neque enim ea dirimere poteram* (96/21) — "Indeed I was not able to keep
    them apart [i.e., the form and content of Ambrose's teaching]." In the previous chapter
    (V,xiii,23) Augustine spoke of Ambrose as a "doctor of the truth" (*doctorem veri* 96/1),
    dispensing, amongst other spiritual foods, the "sober drunkenness of [God's] wine" —
    sobriam vini ebrietatem 95/25 — in contrast to those "drunken with Manichaean
    vanities" — *manichaeis vanitatibus ebrios* 95/18-19. Compare God's entering our hearts and
    making us drunk (I,v,5) — in a holy sense — and, on the other side, the "wine of error" dis-
    pensed by teachers whose only interest was worldly — such as the ones mentioned in
    I,xvi,26.
136 *gradatim (quidem)* (96/23-24). Courcelle (*Recherches*, pp. 93-138) discusses the question of
    which of Ambrose's sermons Augustine might have heard. His conclusions are now widely
    accepted — but see the reservations noted in O'Meara (*The Young Augustine*, pp. 116-25).
137 See V,xiv,24 *Nam/existimabam* (96/24-27).
138 *cum/spiritaliter* (97/1-2).
139 See VII,x,16f.
140 *Tu/poteram* (97/13-17).
141 See V,xiv,24 *maxime/posse* (96/27-97/6). See also VI,iv,6 *Et/ignorarem* (104/8-15).
142 *uno atque altero* (95/28).
143 *infantiles nugas* (103/27).
144 *creatorem/contruderet* (103/28-104/3). On Augustine's ignorance of spiritual substance
    at this time see the text from V,xiv,25, cited above, n. 140. See also VI,iii,4 *quamquam/
    suspiciabar* (102/28-103/1).
145 See V,xiv,24 where Augustine speaks of the *scriptis veteribus* — "the ancient writings"
    (97/1) — and of the "law and prophets" — *legem et prophetas* (97/4-5). See also *DUC*,
    VIII,20 where he specifically mentions the Old Testament in the same context. In VI,iii,3
    Augustine describes how he could never get a chance to talk with Ambrose about the things
    he wanted to ask him because, although he would sit in the room where the bishop was read-
    ing silently, he never "had the heart to disturb him when he was so engrossed in study"
    (trans. Pine-Coffin) — *quis/auderet?* (102/2-3). This passage is ignored by Courcelle in his
    speculations about Augustine's supposed "hostility" to Ambrose at this time: see above

n. 125. Its tone supports what Augustine had said earlier about loving Ambrose from the
start (V,xiii,23).
146 *Nec/appareret* (97/6-12).
147 *certis . . . documentis* (97/14).
148 Augustine shows how he came to the sure knowledge of the falsity of the Manichaean idea
of God in VII,ii,3.
149 Augustine refers to the "sacrament of catechumens": signing with the cross and contact
with blessed salt, done first at his birth (see I,xi,17, III,iv,8, and VI,iv,5). Solignac notes (*BA*,
Vol.13, p. 303, n. 1) that this "sufficed for such a one to be considered as a catechumen." It
is interesting that Augustine speaks of his "parents" – *a parentibus* (V,xiv,25 – 98/3), i.e.,
Monica and Patricius – as having done this. See the same words in the text from *DUC*,
VIII,20, quoted below, n. 157. Presumably this means that Monica insisted that Patricius be
present at the ceremony since, at the time, he was still indifferent to her religion: see above,
Chapter One, n. 59-61. There is no stronger confirmation that Augustine was never seriously
influenced by pagan religion than in the fact that, at this point in his life when he was searching for an acceptable relation to God, he never for a moment considered any of the pagan
forms. This is supported by the conclusions of Mandouze, "Saint Augustin et la religion
romaine."
150 *Verum/dirigerem* (97/18-98/4). Augustine states his relation to the Manichees' teachings at
this point in his life in VI,iv,5 *Quod/accusabam* (103/19-24).
151 See V,iii,3 *Et/videbantur* (78/18-21).
152 *praeponebam* (97/26-27).
153 See V,xiv,25 *Verum/iudicabam* (97/18-21).
154 *mecum/essem* (91/16). We have already seen how this same result was involved in
Augustine's grief over the death of his young friend in the fourth book.
155 *nec/decreverant* (92/8-9).
156 See V,xiv,25 *quibus tamen philosophis/recusabam* (97/27-98/1). There is a certain difficulty
in determining the antecedent of *quibus philosophis* – "to which philosophers." It could
refer to the natural scientists, clearly mentioned as "philosophers" in the line above, or to
the Academics, or both. The grammar gives no clue but I understand it to refer to the Sceptics alone – viewed as teachers of the truth – since the qualifications that they were without
the saving name of Christ and that he refused to place the cure of his soul in their hands
make no sense in reference to the natural scientists.
157 See V,xiv,25 *Statui/dirigerem* (98/1-4). Compare VI,xi,18 *Figam/veritatis* (117/1-3). Augustine says the same thing in almost the same words in *DUC*, VIII,20: "I decided to remain a
catechumen in the church to which I had been handed over by my parents, until such time as
I might find what I wanted or should persuade myself that it need not be sought." The natural implication of the phrase *tamdiu esse catechumenus* – which occurs both here and in
V,xiv,25 – is that at the time "Augustine considered himself to be still a catechumen"
(Gibb, *Confessions*, p. 135). The meaning of this phrase has been much discussed. It is
involved in the "historicity" question to the extent that this is seen as a matter of deciding
when Augustine turned to the church. From an Augustinian perspective the question admits
of only two answers. Properly speaking one only becomes a Christian through the conversion of the *will*, of which baptism is the objective expression. Augustine insists on this in
Books VII-IX. From this point of view we must be very cautious in speaking of an "intellectual" conversion to Christianity. This has been the widespread tendency in recent years in
the works of those scholars who have conflated Christianity and Neo-Platonism. Thus, for
example, the statement of M. Pellegrino (*Les Confessions de saint Augustin*, p. 161) that the
text from V,xiv,25 "confirms . . . that the conversion of his intelligence to Catholicism took
place even before his encounter with Neo-Platonism." When Augustine tells us that he
decided to "remain a catechumen" in the Catholic church this does not mean that at this
point he thought the Catholic idea of God was true nor that he believed it. It means only that
he was willing to look to the church because it now seemed at least possible that it might
have the true idea of God – and this is not what Pellegrino intends by calling this an "intel-

lectual'' conversion. On the other hand if the sense of the question is, ''At what point did Augustine become unwilling to trust his soul to any doctrine from which the name of Christ was missing?'' the only answer is, never. He had always insisted on this from the earliest time he could remember (see III,iv,8).

158 See VI,iv,5 *Tanto/recusabam* (103/15-24).

159 For a statement of the doctrine of the Sceptics — ἀταραξία as the end, and ἐποχή as the means — see Sextus Empiricus, *Outline of Pyrrhonism*, I,xii,25-30 and I,xiii,31-35. Cicero, who was largely responsible for the creation of the Latin philosophical vocabulary out of Greek, translates ἐποχή (i.e., the suspension of judgement, as the means to imperturbability or ἀταραξία): ''ἐποχή , *id est adsensionis retento . . .*'' (*Academia*, II,xviii,59). Augustine uses the same word to describe his effort at the time: see VI,iv,6 *Tenebam cor meum ab omni adsensione* (104/15-15) — ''I kept my heart from all assent.''

Chapter Six

COMMENTARY ON BOOK VI

Book VI is divided in two parts. Augustine begins by explaining his new position more fully because the argument at the end of the last book was very condensed. He then describes the practical consequences which resulted from it (I and II below).

MATURITY: VI,i,1-IX,xiii,37

I. VI,i,1-Vi,v,7. Augustine's scepticism and Christian belief

VI,i,1-VI,ii,2. Monica and Christian belief

The opening words of the book are quoted from Psalm 70:5, "*My hope since my youth.*"[1] In using them Augustine indicates that he is speaking of a new period in his life — *iuventus* — which covers the period of youthful maturity from one's early 30s to the 40th or 45th year.[2] Spirituality as well as physically Augustine regarded himself as having come to a new stage because he had come into a new relation to the truth. "I had not yet reached the truth but I had been torn away from falsity" (VI,i,1).[3] He could not now make any progress toward the truth but at least he was no longer going away from it.[4] On the other hand, from the point of view of his higher aims, according to which he not only wanted to find the truth but also to be able to hold on to it,[5] his new position was a further descent into the abyss. This is why he says, "I was coming to the bottom of the deep" (VI,i,1).[6] That is, he was coming towards a bottom that he would only reach when he arrived at the certain knowledge of God through reading the books of the Platonists. In Book VII we will find that in the same moment that he came to the indubitable knowledge of God he also discovered that he was utterly cut off from the God he knew. That is, he recognized, in the same vision and with equal certainty, that he lived in another world than his God — in a "region of unlikeness" (VII,x,16).[7] Augustine will eventually show that the only way of overcoming this unlikeness between himself and God was through faith in the promises of Christ. For the time being such a belief was just what his sceptical position made impossible. The purpose of the first part of this books (chs. i-v) is to explain why this is so.

He begins by recounting three episodes from his mother's life which showed capacities he found remarkable at the time and which indisputably arose from her belief. He does this in contrast to his own inability to believe which, while done for the sake of the truth, nevertheless resulted in the impotence and misery which he describes in chapters vi-xvi. The three stories correspond to the same general headings under which he later treats his own impotence: he shows that Monica had

---

Notes to Chapter Six appear on pages 162-68.

a power, a knowledge, and a love which he entirely lacked. In Augustine's idiom such a trinity comprehends the entire spectrum of created goods.

Monica is first described as "[my] mother, strong by reason of piety" (VI,i,1),[8] which sets the frame of the discussion: it is about her faith. She followed Augustine to Milan some time in the spring of 385.[9] The first episode concerns her crossing of the Mediterranean: "during a crisis at sea, she consoled the sailors themselves — from whom inexperienced voyagers on the deep are accustomed to look for reassurance when they are scared" (VI,i,1).[10] By calmly assuring the crew of a safe landing, Monica seems to have prevented a panic. How did she know they would not perish? "Because you [God] had promised her as much in a vision" (VI,i,1).[11] This is the third of Monica's visions or dreams which Augustine has reported.[12] It derived solely from her faith, it was a far cry from the certain knowledge he desired, and yet she could act with an astonishing power that he lacked.

The second episode concerns the knowledge born of Monica's faith. When she got to Milan, and Augustine told her that he had left the Manichees but not yet come to the church, she did not respond with the wild joy he expected. Why not? It was because she firmly believed — on the basis of her earlier visions — that before her death she would see him a true Catholic. On these grounds she refused to be impressed by anything less. Knowing how fervently and how long Monica had prayed that he would leave the Manichees, Augustine was surprised by the "totally calm" (VI,i,1)[13] manner in which she took his news. Moreover, instead of slacking off in her prayers because he was, as he thought, closer to the truth than when he had left her in Carthage, she "redoubled her efforts" (VI,i,1).[14] As she saw it, the most critical time lay ahead. The sequel justified her view. The source of her reaction was in the faith Augustine refused for the sake of the truth. Yet Monica, who was left neither too cold nor too hot by his condition, discerned where her son stood far more exactly than he did himself.[15] In retrospect it was clear that Monica's faith "knew" the truth in a way which was far beyond Augustine's capacities when he refused to believe because he did not know whether the Catholic faith was true or not.

Finally, in the second chapter, Augustine shows an instance of the love which was born of her faith. According to the usage of the North African church she had carried offerings of bread and wine to the tombs of the saints. She was turned away by a gatekeeper because this was not the custom in Milan. But, says Augustine,

> [W]hen she learned that the bishop [Ambrose] had forbidden her custom she accepted his judgement with so much piety and obedience that I myself was surprised at how easily she came to accuse her own custom rather than dispute with his prohibition. (VI,ii,2)[16]

Augustine was surprised because Monica never drank too much of the wine: "She sought piety there, not pleasure" (VI,ii,2).[17] As her own usage was innocent she could have objected that the prohibition should only have been directed against those who abused it, yet she "most willingly" (VI,ii,2)[18] gave it up without any fuss. Ambrose justified the prohibition by saying that her practice gave occasion for abuse by the intemperate and because it too closely resembled pagan practices. Augustine judged that Monica was less moved by these reasons than by the fact that she loved Ambrose *"like an angel of God* (Gal. 4:14)"[19] for his role in freeing her son from the Manichees. He reflected that it must be a powerful love that would make her quietly give up the innocent custom to which she was so strongly attached.[20]

Power, knowledge, and love: Monica clearly possess all three even though she "merely" believed and had no knowledge of the truth. On the other hand, Augustine, who refused to believe because he thought this brought him closer to the truth, will show that he was unable to grasp any of them.

VI,iii,3-VI,v,8. Augustine's scepticism and the credibility of Catholicism

These three chapters explain Augustine's scepticism and also why he refused to become a Catholic. He is interested in those aspects of the new position that account for the contradictions he suffered in his practical affairs as he describes them in the rest of the book.

VI,iii,3-4. Augustine and Ambrose — At the end of the previous chapter Augustine reported that Ambrose often congratulated him on having a mother of such remarkable piety: "little knowing what kind of a son she really had, who doubted all these things [i.e., what Monica believed, what the church taught, and what Ambrose himself said], and supposed that man was not at all able to find *the way to life* (Ps. 15:11 and Acts 2:28)" (VI,ii,2).[21] All the same he did want to have a chance to question Ambrose about Catholic belief in order to find out whether it was true. The opportunity never presented itself, for the reasons he explains in VI,iii,3,[22] yet he did go to hear Ambrose preach "every Sunday" (VI,iii,4).[23] From this he was further confirmed in his discovery that the Catholics did not hold the silly doctrines which he supposed they held on the say-so of the Manichees.

VI,iv,5-6. Augustine's scepticism — When Augustine says that he thought that he was not able to find the way to life[24] we must distinguish this from the position of a real Sceptic which he had only partly adopted. He has already told us that he "utterly refused" (V,xiv,25)[25] to "commit [to the Sceptics] the cure of the troubles of my soul" (V,xiv,25).[26] He would not accept, as a principle of knowledge or action, the position that we cannot grasp any certain truth. This was the cardinal tenet of ancient Scepticism which maintained it not only about the sensible but also about the possibility of knowledge itself — since they noted that all sciences have axioms which are assumed and that all proof moves from premise to conclusion, so the premises themselves require proof and so on *ad infinitum*.[27] From this the Sceptics concluded that we could not grasp any certain truth and so ought always to withold our judgement. By refusing to assent to any position they sought to avoid the error and disappointment which would result from believing something which was actually false. They did this to secure the only real happiness of which they thought we were capable — a state of imperturbability which was secure against anything being taken away from them because they refused to attach themselves to anything in the first place.[28]

Augustine's first book, aside from the lost *On the Beautiful and the Fitting*, was

Against the Academics, composed in November 386 at Cassiciacum right after his conversion. In it he provides a full refutation of Academic Scepticism.[29] If we find no such thing in the *Confessions* it is because Augustine himself was never "in" the radical doubt of the Sceptics. We can see this both in relation to the sensible and the intelligible.

The Sceptics argued that since the senses could provide no certain knowledge they could not be relied on as a guide to the truth. Augustine's scepticism had precisely the opposite effect for, as he tells in the following chapter (VI,v,7-8), he came to see "how innumerably many things I believed which I had not actually seen . . . which, unless they were believed, we should be able to do absolutely nothing in this life" (VI,v,7).[30] "Doing nothing in this life" was the aim of the Sceptic: this was the apathy for which he strove. Augustine would have none of it. The reason is important. It is contained in the text just quoted, for we see that he did not doubt the things he had "actually seen." Far from shunning the senses because they did not yield certain knowledge, Augustine had come to rely on them as the source of opinion. In *Against the Academics* he points out that it is certain that what appears to me through the senses appears to me as it appears to me.[31] In this sense the senses are an infallible guide to appearance and the appearances which they present to the mind are the source of opinion – which can be either true or false.

On the other hand where the Academics also doubted the possibility of knowledge even if it did not come through the senses, Augustine did not. Although he did not yet know of a spiritual or intelligible reality as the proper object of thought he did hold, in the case of mathematical propositions, that they were quite certain.

> In fact I wanted those things which I did not see to be made as certain as I was certain that seven plus three makes ten. For I was not so far gone as to suppose [with the Sceptics] that even this could not be known. But as I was certain of this, so did I desire to be made certain of other things as well, both bodily things which were not before my senses and spiritual things about which I did not know how to think except in a corporeal manner. (VI,iv,6)[32]

Augustine regarded the certainty of mathematics as the norm he desired in all things. He could think of its propositions as certain – granted the axioms of number, addition, and subtraction, etc. – just because they were beyond every possibility of being disturbed by the sensible since they did not derive from it or depend on it in any way. As he says in *Against the Academics* (III,xiii,29), "No matter what condition our senses are in, these things are true in themselves."

The radical doubt of the Sceptics, both about the sensible and about the certainty of mathematics, did not affect Augustine and for this reason he neither rehearses nor refutes their position in the *Confessions*. He was never a Sceptic as the position was understood by the ancients. The reason lies in his experience with the Manichees. For nine years he had adhered to a position which had, in effect, refused the evidence of the senses and ignored the principles of number. Coming as he did from the presumption of a certain knowledge, which he now saw that he had never actually possessed, the discovery of the limited certainty of the senses and of mathematical propositions – the one limited to appearances and the other to its axioms – was for him a liberation from the fantastic and a clear advance over it. To the Sceptics, on the other hand, any probability was a restriction. It was merely a second-best in relation to the notion of certain knowledge — although it was a second-best with which, they insisted, we must learn to be content.

With this we are brought back to Augustine's own answer, and the only one he gives in the *Confessions*, about why he did not become a Sceptic. It was because they "lacked the health-giving name of Christ" (V,xiv,25).[33] The Sceptics gave no certain reason to deny the possibility of a knowledge of God, and Augustine, who had wanted this above all things since he had first read the *Hortensius*, would not assent to this dogmatic aspect of their teaching. His doubts were simply about his ability to find a way to come to this knowledge, and here the problem centred around the question of whether the teachings of Christ were the way to the Wisdom of God.[34] He says of himself that "my spirit was altogether bent on seeking [Wisdom] and making inquiries about it" (VI,iii,3).[35] This "anxiety" which "gnawed at my guts" (VI,iv,5)[36] was the very opposite of the imperturbability which a true Sceptic cultivated.

Augustine wanted to find out, with the same kind of certainty that he knew that 7 + 3 = 10, whether or not the Christian idea of God was true. He was eventually to find what he was looking for but for about a year and a half, between the time he decided to leave the Manichees at the end of 384 and his discovery of the Platonist doctrine of God in the early summer of 386, he was unable to do so.[37] During this period he "doubted all things and judged that it was not at all possible for man to find the way to life" (VI,ii,2);[38] he "floated" (VI,v,8)[39] amongst all things; he "kept [his] heart from all assenting, fearing a fall" (VI,iv,6);[40] and his judgement was "in a suspended state" (VI,iv,6).[41] All this is exactly the behaviour of a convinced Sceptic: the vocabulary is drawn from the Sceptics and yet Augustine was not one of them. While the Sceptics regarded all this as final, for Augustine it was merely provisional. They adopted these positions because they had given up looking for the truth, but he adopted them because he was looking for it. The Sceptics refused to assent to any belief because they presumed that no certain knowledge was possible. Augustine did so because he was not yet sure this was true. Despite all the apparent similarities the two positions are worlds apart.

As for Augustine's relation to the church, his new position entailed consequences which pulled him in opposite directions. He refused to accept the Catholic faith while at the same time Catholic belief seemed daily more acceptable to him. He discusses the first at the end of VI,iv,6 and the second in VI,v,7-8.

Of the first, he says,

> And I could have been cured by believing as, in this way, the sight of my soul would have been directed in a certain way towards your truth which always remains and is lacking in nothing. But, as it often happens that one who has had the experience of a bad doctor fears to place himself in the care of even a good one, thus it was with the well-being of my soul which, although it could in no way be cured except by believing yet, lest it should believe false things, refused to be cured, resisting your hands who have prepared the medicines of faith and spread them on the fatal illnesses of the whole world and have given them so great an amount of authority. (VI,iv,6)[42]

Since Augustine does not give proof of this statement until Book VII it will be best if we simply say what it means. After he had come to the certain knowledge of God (the Father) through the Platonists (Book VII) — which knowledge they shared with Christians — Augustine was to discover with an equal certainty that the "cure of his soul" could only be accomplished by a divine mediator and that the only adequate mediator — Christ — could only be appropriated in faith. Since the essence of the soul's well-being lay in this faith — which one can have with or without a scientific knowledge of God — the cure is available to us at any time. It does not require that we first make the long and arduous ascent to the intellectual vision of God. The Christian idea of God will, in the end, be shown to be true, and so Augustine says that if he could have believed his sight would at least have been pointed in the right direction. But at the time his scepticism prevented him from assenting to any position unless he was certain it was true, and this meant that he could only come to Christianity through the prior discovery that its notion of God was the right one. In the end he would also be brought to see that even with this knowledge he could not get to God apart from the belief in Christ as the way — which is what distinguished Christianity from Platonism — but until he knew God this way was blocked and he was left squarely in the world of the probable.

VI,v,7-8. The credibility of Catholicism — Augustine's argument now turns to the increasing probability which he began to attribute to the Catholic position. His inquiry into the truth of Christian belief led him to go to hear Ambrose's preaching every Sunday.[43] Partly what he took from Ambrose was the confirmation of his discovery that the Catholic faith could be maintained without absurdity. On the other hand the new-found credibility of Catholicism led him to consider certain questions about the nature of belief itself, as a result of which he came to see the place of belief in the world.

> All the same [i.e., in spite of the fact that he refused to believe the Catholic faith], from this time I preferred the Catholic doctrine and I recognized that it was more reasonable and not at all deceiving when it ordered that some things must be believed which were not demonstrated — either because there was a proof which not everyone could grasp, or else because no proof existed — than the rash promise of science [of the Manichees]. (VI,v,7)[44]

"Next of all, little by little" (VI,v,7),[45] Augustine was led from this to recognize that belief was not to be scorned. For "unless [some things] were believed we should [be able] to do nothing at all in this life" (VI,v,7).[46] How could we even know who our parents were unless we believed the report of others, since none of us remembers the moment of birth? How, unless we believed, could we have any knowledge of past time or other places — none of which we had seen with our own senses? Augustine came to see that the conduct of life would be impossible without a belief in appearances which we had not actually experienced ourselves, and so he concluded that belief in a God not yet known was not to be scorned merely because it was not a certain knowledge.

> [You, O Lord] persuaded me that it was not those who believed your Scriptures, which you have established with such great authority amongst almost all peoples, but those who did not believe them who were guilty of error. Nor ought they to be listened to who said such things as: "How do you know that those books were given to human kind by the Spirit of the only God of truth and of perfect truth?" (VI,v,7)[47]

It was not that Augustine only began to believe in God at this point. In one way or another he had believed in him from the time he had first heard of him as a young boy — and explicitly since he had begun to search for him after reading the *Hortensius*.

> [A]lways however I believed that you were and that you cared for us even if I did not know either what ought to be thought about your substance or what is the way which leads, or which releads, us back to you. (VI,v,8)[48]

What is new here is not that Augustine believed in the existence of God but that belief itself had become a possible relation to God. He didn't know whether the Catholics were right or wrong but he was now willing to acknowledge that one could in principle come to God through belief. At this point Augustine recognized two ways of approaching God: through belief or through knowledge. Between them he concluded that,

> [S]ince we might be unable to find the truth by pure reason and on account of this there was need of the authority of Holy Scripture I now began to believe that you would not in any way have accorded to the Scriptures an authority so prominent over all the earth if you had not willed that you were to be believed and sought through them. (VI,vi,8)[49]

As Augustine had recognized that it was not necessarily a superstitious folly to be related to the truth through belief, the logic of his scepticism could now come into play. That is, where belief was seen as an acceptable relation to God, he was bound to accept the most probable account of God as the most believable. Weighing the probabilities he determined that it was more likely than not that the Scriptures were the word of God and that they taught us what he wanted us to believe about him. The evidence? their preeminent reputation. Of course this proved nothing — but the world-wide reputation of Scripture argued strongly in favour of the supposition that they were indeed divine. Otherwise it would follow that the God whom Augustine presumed to care for us had allowed most of mankind to believe what was not his word. From this point of view the "most simple and humble" (VI,v,8)[50] style of Scripture, which made it available to all, now seemed an argument in favour of its authority.[51] This was the opposite of what he had thought when he first turned to the Bible after reading Cicero's *Hortensius*.

Nevertheless Augustine refused to believe in the Catholic faith. He thought that unless he knew for certain that it was true he should not risk going astray again — as he now believed he had done with the Manichees. Because, in the end, his soul could only be cured by believing — i.e., by faith in Christ as mediator between us and God — he says of his refusal to believe that "by hanging in suspense I was more completely killed [than had I believed]" (VI,iv,6).[52] This is true — but at the time he could only have given his assent to the Catholic doctrines by denying the same sceptical argument which had made belief itself a credible way of seeking God. He had seen this much under sceptical influence and it was the logic of the sceptical position that now propelled him forward. He either had to come to a knowledge of the truth or else to a knowledge that we cannot know it. Truth itself demanded that he should not rest in belief at this point — and in the end the truth did not fail him. This is why he ends the section in this way:

> I was thinking about these things [the credibility of the Catholic faith] and you were with me, I was begging for [the truth] and you heard me, I was drifting about and you guided me, I went by the broad way of the world and you did not desert me. (VI,v,8)[53]

All the same, until he found the proof that the Catholic idea of God was true, he was a divided man. He was caught between a belief in Catholicism which he could not accept, and a knowledge which he did not possess. This left him torn between the many worldly goods on the one hand and the absolute good on the other. His scepticism forced him into the world because he refused to believe in the church — which was the only credible way he knew about that offered to lead him out of it. At the same time, because his scepticism was determined to look for the certain knowledge of God, he could not be reconciled to accepting the world. The rest of this book shows how this unfortunate position worked itself out in his life.

II. VI,vi,9-VI,xvi,26. The practical consequences of Augustine's scepticism: honours, wealth, and marriage

> I longed eagerly for honours, wealth and marriage and you only laughed. In these desires I suffered the most bitter difficulties and your favour towards me showed itself so much the greater insofar as you less allowed anything to grow sweet for me which was not you. (VI,vi,9)[54]

Augustine announces here that he is about to discuss the life he led during this period. He does this under three headings: the pursuit of honour, of wealth, and of marriage.

The structural features of the *Confessions* are beginning to come clear. We have seen that such triplets keep reappearing each time he turns to discuss the practical consequences of the various positions he held. This is so here. It was so earlier in this book when he spoke of Monica's belief. It was so in Book IV where he spoke of his life as a Manichee under the headings which we called the pursuit of power, love, and glory. It was so in the first three chapters of Book III where he showed the life he led as a result of the theft of pears, and the same was true of Book I when he spoke of his early and later childhood. What do these recurring triplets mean? The answer is that in Augustine's thought these triads of power, knowledge, and love are the various (perverted) images of the Trinity into which he fell at different stages in his life. His thinking is so thoroughly imbued with the orthodox trinitarian understanding that, for him, the only complete discussion is the one which treats of every position in its relation to the Trinity. As the Trinity is both the beginning and end of all creation, all human error is, in some form or other, a perverted imitation of that Trinity. In Book III, where he first made this point explicit, he said:

> These are the [three] sources of iniquity: things which come from the desire of ruling [= power], or from the desire of seeing [= knowledge], or from the desire of feeling [= love] — either from one or from two of them or from all together. (III,viii,16)[55]

In the most profound sense this trinitarian approach determines the structure of the whole of the *Confessions*. It determines the content and the relation of each of its three parts (Books I-IX, Book X, and Books XI-XIII) — and again within each of these parts the same thing reappears. By the end of this work we will be in a position to see this — at least in relation to the internal logic of Books I-IX.

VI,vi,9-VI,x,17. The pursuit of worldly honour

VI,vi,9-10. Augustine and the drunken beggar — On a day when, in his capacity as rhetor of Milan, Augustine was struggling to prepare a laudatory oration for the emperor "in which I was going to make a lot of lies and from which I would gain, as a liar, the favour of the crowd which knew they were lies" (VI,vi,9),[56] he saw a drunken beggar. The encounter aroused the strangest thoughts because he suddenly saw the beggar as far happier than he was. This kind of contrast was forced on him by his sceptical position.

Insofar as he did not know the truth he had only worldly happiness to aspire after. His aim in making this oration was to win glory in the eyes of men. But if worldly happiness was his goal, why not act like the beggar who had a far surer happiness from a little cheap wine than Augustine had from all his anxious learning? The happiness he sought depended on the hopelessly uncertain task of pleasing men: the beggar's on the certain intoxication which came from wine. Viewed simply from this point of view there was absolutely no reason why he should not prefer the beggar's way. It may have been dishonourable and inglorious, but that man was happy while Augustine was not. And the beggar was at least filled with real wine as a result of wishing well to passers-by, while Augustine was only filled with empty pride as a result of making the elaborate lies of his profession. Of course when viewed from the standpoint of the truth, as Augustine does in the final paragraph of this section (VI,vi,10), the beggar's joy was as false as the glory Augustine sought, yet the former at least slept off his drunkenness overnight while Augustine's errors went on and on, "behold, for how many days!" (VI,vi,10).[57]

But if Augustine could find no reason why he should disparage the happiness of the drunk, neither could he follow the man's actions.

> And if anyone had asked me whether I preferred to rejoice or to fear I should have replied, "to rejoice." And yet if he had gone on to ask if I would rather be as the drunk was or as I then was, made up of worries and fears, I still would have chosen myself — but this would have been a perverse preference. Could there be any reason for it? No, for I ought not to have preferred myself to that man, even though I was more learned, since my learning gave me no joy. (VI,vi,9)[58]

Given the side of his scepticism that had only worldly happiness as its goal this decision *was* perverse and could not be justified. On the other hand, insofar as he was also looking for a truth which would give a happiness quite other than worldly joys of any kind, he could not adopt the beggar's position. His position was very wretched and this is just what he says of it: "How miserable I was" (VI,vi,9).[59] Such thoughts "often" (VI,vi,10)[60] came to him during this period and he often discussed them with his friends. But nothing was ever concluded except that he became increasingly conscious of his misery – to the point that he was even loath (VI,vi,10)[61] to grasp at any good fortune because, like the beggar's drunkenness, it would flee as soon as he grasped it. Although he did not know it at the time his scepticism would not permit of any other conclusion. He was rooted, unable to move, in a position he could neither accept nor escape, where his misery could only increase. This is why, at the start of the chapter, he speaks of this misery as the sting of a beneficent providence moving him towards itself by making his false position untenable.

VI,vii,11-VI,x,17. Augustine's friends – These four chapters are mainly devoted to a sketch of the character of Augustine's best friend Alypius – first mentioned here by name. There is good reason to suppose that they are connected with the historical genesis of the *Confessions*. Alypius later became the bishop of Thagaste and we know that when he was bishop he wrote to Paulinus of Nola, whom he had never met, asking if Paulinus could send his some texts of Eusebius of Caesarea. Paulinus sent off one of the works and asked Alypius in return if he would oblige him with a history of his life. Alypius had a good will to do so but was reluctant lest he seem to boast about himself, and so handed the task to Augustine who accepted and eventually (sometime after the summer of 386) sent off a little biography. It is likely that parts of this were revised by Augustine and included at this point in the *Confessions*. Probably the biography began with the second sentence of chapter vii, "Alypius was born in the same town as I, where his parents were of the first ranks. He was younger than I" (VI,vii,11).[62] As Courcelle notes, "There is every reason to suppose that Paulinus, his appetite whetted by this little work, requested Augustine to narrate the story of his own life."[63] Such a request was likely the immediate cause which moved Augustine to begin the first part of the *Confessions*.[64]

However this may be, our task is to try to understand why Augustine included parts of Alypius' biography at this point in the *Confessions*. Part of the answer is easy since each of the four episodes which Augustine relates – one to a chapter – is designed to show Alypius' character – both the "great natural virtue" (VI,vii,11)[65] he possessed as well as the peculiar problems that he had to face. The four stories go together as two couplets (vii and viii, and ix and x).

Chapter vii illustrates what Augustine found to be Alypius' amazing capacity to do the good. He does this in the description of the manner in which Alypius suddenly and completely gave up his strong addiction for the games of the circus (the Roman chariot-races) while they were both still living in Carthage.[66] Chapter viii shows the problems that Alypius suffered as a result of this virtue. In an incident which occurred in Rome, years later, Alypius is shown trying to exhibit his strength of character by ignoring the cruel gladiatorial spectacle which he detested, but to which he had been dragged by some rowdy friends, only to discover that he could not. The reason, as Augustine says, is that he was "bold ... rather than steadfast" (VI,viii,13).[67] Not knowing the source of his goodness he presumed, without thinking, that it lay in himself and that he could therefore use it to glorify his reputation as a good and principled man – just as Augustine assumed the same of his intellectual powers. But in desiring to show this virtue Alypius had already lost it since what he really sought was not virtue but the applause of the world. Thus he said, "Though you drag my body to that place [the amphitheatre] you can never force me to give my mind and eyes to those shows'' (VI,viii,13).[68] Yet when the crowd roared at a particularly gory sight he, whose heart was already given to the world in wanting its praise, found he was no less interested than the rest. Indeed, having once lost the appearance of virtue he had nothing to gain by staying away and so became a worse lover of such sights than those who had dragged him there in the first place.

The second couplet makes the same point from the other side. Chapter ix describes an incident in Carthage when Alypius was falsely accused of stealing and narrowly escaped imprisonment or worse. Here was a clear case in which real innocence was something far different from what the world took it to be. Augustine cites the incident to point out what it reveals of Alypius' character. For Alypius, who later in life was to become a bishop, "a dispenser of your word and a judge of many cases in your church" (VI,ix,15),[69] took from this experience the recognition that "in coming to the knowledge of causes a man ought not to damn another on the basis of a rash credulity" (VI,ix,14).[70] From this we may infer that such a "rash credulity" — the tendency to judge things too quickly, as if he knew where the right lay — was the peculiar problem of Alypius' active and unintellectual character. It also shows how the lessons of history and experience were the things that moved Alypius who went away from the episode "more experienced and instructed" (VI,ix,15).[71]

But much as Alypius lived amongst practical concerns where virtue and vice are easily and often confused, Augustine concludes (in ch. x) by pointing out again to his friend's remarkable "native" (VI,x,16)[72] virtue which did not prefer gold to innocence however easy the former and however hard the latter. When he came to occupy a minor position in the court system of Rome, Alypius refused both the bribes and threats of a powerful senator who wanted him to bend the law. The senator was accustomed to getting such favours from small officials like Alypius and even from judges such as the one for whom Alypius worked — who agreed with Alypius but dared not take his stand against the man. Similarly Alypius — with that interest in a good library which is often found in those who admire intellectual things without being intellectuals themselves — refused to have the court scribes copy books for himself at public expense though others in a similar position often did do. Especially in this matter it seems he was really tried and "almost" (VI,x,16)[73] succumbed to the temptation, but in the end refused it because it was wrong.

These four chapters have a wonderful symmetry. They start (in ch. vii) with Alypius' natural virtue and strength of will when the good of his soul required him to give up evil habits. From here they move to the problems of this virtue considered on the subjective side (ch. viii). Next Augustine shows the problems that Alypius' kind of virtue faces objectively in the world (ch. ix), and finally (ch. x) he moves back to the strength of Alypius' adherence to the good in the face of external threats and temptations. In the compass of these four chapters Augustine has shown the strengths and weaknesses of Alypius' character on both subjective and objective sides.

A picture emerges of two friends with strikingly different characters who nevertheless loved in each other just what they lacked in themselves. Where Augustine sought God primarily through his desire for a knowledge of the truth, but found difficulties in doing the good he knew, Alypius sought the same end in the practical form of doing the good, and with him the problem lay in knowing what good he should do. This view is confirmed where Augustine tells us why Alypius became a Manichee with him in Carthage. Alypius was drawn to the sect not by the promised rationalism which drew Augustine but by the Manichees' "show of continence which he took to be real and true" (VI,vii,12)[74] — that is, he became a Manichee because their holy men seemed to lead good lives with a visible display of their sanctity.[75]

Augustine regarded Alypius as having an unusual capacity and will to do the good. This contrasted sharply with his own weakness in such matters — as for example in the incident he describes at the end of this book where he says that he was too weak-willed even to follow the example of a woman — his nameless concubine — when he reluctantly forced her to leave him and she vowed never to know another man. He wanted to do the same — while waiting to be married — but instead gave in at once and found another mistress to satisfy his lust.[76] Likewise, what Alypius loved in Augustine was just what was lacking in himself — the capacity for scientific knowledge. Although Alypius was both converted and baptized with Augustine and the two were like twins in spirit (in IX,iv,7 Augustine calls him "the brother of my heart"[77]), there is no evidence that he ever came to the philosophical knowledge of God, and he was always in awe of Augustine's learning on which he depended to show him where the good lay.[78] Here is Augustine's own summary of their relationship from its earliest days in Carthage when Alypius was Augustine's student: "[H]e loved me greatly because I seemed to him to be both good and very learned. And I loved him on account of his great inborn virtue which was very remarkable in one of no great age (VI,vii,11)."[79]

The answer to the second part of our question — why Augustine introduced Alypius at just this point in the Confessions — is given in the final paragraph of this section (VI,x,17). As Alypius had first followed Augustine into Manichaeism, so later did he also become a sceptic with him — being content, as it were, to follow Augustine's lead as to where the truth lay.[80] These two were joined by their mutual friend, Nebridius, who had come from North Africa "to Milan for no other cause than to live [with Augustine] in the most passionate search of truth and wisdom" (VI,x,17).[81] Nebridius too had, by this time, become a sceptic, as Augustine indicates when he says "together with me he sighed [for the truth], together with me he floated about, an ardent researcher of the blessed life and a very gifted examiner of the most perplexing questions" (VI,x,17).[82]

At the time these three friends were all in the same sceptical position. All longed after the same end and all suffered the same difficulties. But for the first time in Augustine's adult life such friends could and did appear as substantial, independent figures rather than simply as extensions of his own subjectivity (in the gang), or the imaginary fictions of his Manichaean days (compare his false understanding of the young friend who died). He could only have friends in this sense once he had left the Manichees behind and so it is with a perfect logic that his friends are introduced as persons, with their names, only at this point in the story.

From this point on the spiritual careers of Augustine and Alypius weave in and out in a kind of antiphony through the time when they were both converted in the garden and later baptized by Ambrose. By reflecting on their common course in spite of their different characters, Augustine broadens the *Confessions* beyond his own private experience to show something of how the same God who moved him in his particular circumstance also moved others, of very different talents, to the same end by other roads.[83] Nebridius receives less attention because his character was similar to Augustine's and because his career did not so closely parallel Augustine's as that of Alypius. He followed them both to the church but only at a later date.[84] At the time of which Augustine writes in Book VI all three were together and he sums up their position in this way.

> There were three starving mouths which in turn gasped out their need to each other and which waited on you *to give them their food at the right time* (Ps. 102:27 and 144:15). And when, in all the bitterness which, by your mercy, followed our worldly affairs, we looked to the end for which we suffered these miseries we saw only darkness and so we turned away groaning to ourselves and saying: "How long will this last?" This we often said to ourselves but in saying it we did not give up those worldly things because we did not find anything certain which we could grasp if they were let go. (VI,x,17)[85]

VI,xi,18-20. The pursuit of worldly wealth

At this point Augustine reflected that he was then in his 30th year and that a long time had passed since that day when he was 19 and had first been inflamed with the desire for Wisdom. At that time he had promised himself to give up the world once he had found the truth, yet here he was, years later, still "sticking in the same clay" (VI,xi,18).[86] In this perspective the question first came into his mind about what his prospects might be if death were suddenly to carry him off. Such thoughts could not bother him when he was still a Manichee because he then thought that he was on the way to the truth. He did not think this any more and so death had become a problem. He asked himself, "Where will we have to learn the things which we neglected to learn here? Or rather, will we not have to pay for this negligence with punishments?" (VI,xi,19).[87] Of course, it might be that death was simply the absolute and final end of our existence, in which case there was no problem. Yet, as he did not know for sure that it was so, "this question also [i.e., is death simply annihilation?] demanded an answer" (VI,xi,19).[88] He had no certain knowledge of the immortality of the soul but he refused to count on the possibility that death was just the end of us. It might be true but it seemed foolish to act in this matter on a mere presumption and open himself to the possibility, if he was wrong, of terrible future punishments. Moreover the great authority of the Catholic faith, which maintained that the soul was punished or rewarded beyond death, seemed to be an evidence which he could not now lightly disregard. If so many the world over believed this, what did he have to put against them? Nothing certain.

To Augustine and his friends the conclusion they ought to draw was as clear as it was unattainable.

> Why do we delay any further? Let us cast aside hope of this world and give ourselves over totally to the search for God and the happy life. But wait! Even these worldly things are pleasant, they have no small sweetness of their own: we ought not lightly to cut off our interest in them since it would be shameful if we had to come back to them again. (VI,xi,19)[89]

The worldly things of which Augustine is speaking are his hopes for a modicum of wealth and power, "some position of honour" (VI,xi,19).[90] He specifically refers to the office of *praesides*, a governor of a province of the lowest rank, which he thought he might be able to obtain through the help of the many powerful friends whom he cultivated in Milan.[91] If to this he could add a wife "with some money" (VI,xi,19),[92] what more could be desired? The answer was nothing – except Wisdom itself.

Augustine had no certain knowledge of the primary good. He refused the relation to that good which was offered by Catholic belief and yet he was driven to look for this knowledge because "fleeting" (VI,xi,18)[93] worldly goods did not satisfy him completely. What he needed to discover was the relation of particular goods to the good itself. His sceptical position made this demand but it could not give him the answer. He was not satisfied with worldly goods since he knew they were not primary, nor could he relinquish them since he had no certain knowledge of the good itself. He was trapped in a position in which he was on both sides equally. Much as the three friends scorned the pursuit of worldly riches and power in favour of a detached search for the truth, they wanted the same power and riches to gain the time and freedom they needed to search for the truth. Augustine laments:

> All the morning hours are filled up by our students. What shall we do with the rest? Why not go about looking for the truth? But when could we visit our powerful friends whose approbation we need? When could we prepare the lessons which our students buy? When could we recreate ourselves by relaxing the soul from the strain of cares? (VI,xi,18)[94]

Once again Augustine shows how his scepticism had chained him to a vicious circle which became more painful the longer he remained in it.

> While I spoke of these things the winds kept changing and drove my heart first one way then another. Time passed but I delayed *to be converted to the Lord* and *from day to day* (Eccles. 5:8) I put off living in you, but I did not put off dying in myself. Loving the blessed life I feared it in its own seat and fleeing from it I sought it. (VI,xi,20)[95]

VI,xii,21-VI,xv,25. The pursuit of worldly love

The chief worldly good which Augustine was convinced that he could not live without was the love of a woman – understood in the sense of sexual gratification.[96] Augustine affirms over and again that he felt he had "no power to be continent" (VI,xi,20).[97] So strong was this desire that Alypius, who was naturally continent after one "snatched and furtive" (VI,xii,21)[98] experience in early adolescence, began to wonder "what kind of delight it was without which my life – which seemed pleasant to him – seemed to me no life but a punishment" (VI,xii,21).[99] Moved simply by this curiosity Alypius tried again, thinking that he could turn back at will since he was not moved by lust. But this uncritical recklessness, so like what he had done at the gladiatorial games, was the peculiar fault of his character.[100] And by this thoughtless flirting with a danger he did not have to face, he himself was caught by the same lust which held Augustine. Alypius was to remain in these "sweet snares" (VI,xii,21)[101] until his conversion.

At this same time Augustine was strongly urged by his mother to get married. He agreed, sought a bride who pleased him, and the girl was promised to him by her parents.[102] As she was almost two years short of marriageable age he could not have her at once but was obliged, because of their engagement, to send back to Africa his mistress to whom he had been faithful for some fifteen years.[103] His mother's interest in the match was her hope that once he was married he would soon be baptized — from which we can take it that the girl came from a Christian family.[104]

Augustine's own interest in agreeing to the marriage is less clear. Immediately it meant that he had to send away his old mistress because he could not be openly living with one woman when engaged to another. This, he says, hurt him greatly.[105] And because he thought he could not do without some woman he had to find another for the interim. He did this at once — though presumably he came up with a less obvious, if "more fierce" (VI,xv,25),[106] arrangement. Furthermore he was clearly troubled about whether he should get married at all, since he asked Monica to ask God to give her a vision on the subject — which God did not do.[107] It seems that Augustine agreed to marry because he would be able to satisfy his sexual desires, and a bride would bring with her some money so that his own would not be depleted in keeping a woman — as it had been with his mistress. In this way it would be easier for him to find time to look for the truth. This, at any rate, was part of the plans and dreams which he had in mind at the time.[108]

But if the desire for love and for enough money to be at ease moved Augustine towards marriage, his equally strong desire to devote himself wholly to the search for Wisdom led in the opposite direction. The two could not be reconciled. In VI,xiv,24 he tells of his plans, shared with Alypius, Nebridius, their wealthy patron Romanianus and some six others, to form a community devoted to the search for Wisdom. The idea was that all their goods would be pooled and that two members in annual rotation would look after the others who would be left in peace and quiet to pursue the truth.[109] These plans were "well along"[110] when the whole proposal was wrecked once it was recognized that the "little women"[111] — the wives and mistresses some had and others wanted — would certainly not tolerate any such arrangement.[112]

The contradiction was everywhere the same. In these chapters on worldly love we should notice how Augustine continues to weave his counterpoint on the relationship between his character and that of Alypius. Augustine defended the compatibility of marriage with the pursuit of Wisdom,[113] yet he wrecked the plans for a community devoted to Wisdom by his unwillingness to live without a woman. Alypius insisted that Augustine not marry so that they could live together in the pursuit of the truth, but became tied to the lust he deplored in Augustine. Their scepticism had bound them both to a wretched course. Augustine ends the chapter by noting once again that in the pursuit of worldly love — as when he sough wealth and honour — he and his friends found that they could neither tolerate their actual lives nor could they do anything to improve them.[114]

VI,xvi,26. Summary: Epicurean pleasure and the fear of death

In the final chapter Augustine sums up everything he has said on the practical consequences of his sceptical position. He does this by drawing what would have been
seen as a stark contrast between his approval of Epicurus and his own fear of
death. Here his scepticism reached its logical conclusion in an intolerable contradiction which he attempted to resolve in the new idea of God described at the
beginning of the next book.

On the one side, because he was checked everywhere in his search for the truth,
Augustine says that he had almost given it up and was ready to "give the palm [of
victory]" to Epicurus as the wisest philosopher and the one to follow. Epicurus'
philosophy had developed to the fullest the practical consequences which would
follow if one held that the totality of our existence was comprehended by this life,
and that the gods — whether they existed or not — did not concern themselves in
any way with human affairs.[115]

Augustine says little by way of explaining Epicureanism since his readers
would have had to same general idea of the teaching as we have of a position like,
say, Marxism.[116] Epicurus' doctrine was a determined worldliness. All things
were composed of matter — of atoms and the void — including the human soul,
which was simply annihilated in the dissolution of its material elements once they
were no longer held together by the body. Sense-perception, produced by images
streaming off the surface of things, passing through the senses and imprinting on
the soul, was true and indubitable. Error did not come from perception but from
our judgement when we form, from the known, an opinion of the unknown. The
truth or falsity of opinion was determined by experience. Good and evil were simply pleasure and pain — although by pleasure Epicurus meant the pleasures of the
entire person and an entire life, both bodily and mental. He understood pleasure as
the absence of pain since, on his view, it consists chiefly in the satisfaction of a
need and thus the removal of pain. With this in mind he scorned any involvement
in worldly affairs beyond what was strictly necessary to secure our bodily needs,
and observed moderation in all things since excessive indulgence in any pleasure
led to an excessively painful reaction. The goal for the Epicurean wise man was,
as with the Sceptics, a state of imperturbability — although Epicurus understood
this primarily in relation to life rather than thought.[117]

Even in antiquity this exclusively worldly view had earned Epicurus an
undeserved reputation as a hedonist who sought only pleasure. This was true — but
not in the sense that he was a libertine — although this was how Augustine understood his teaching. It was the inevitable conclusion of one side of Augustine's
scepticism that he should be brought to this position. Because he could make no
headway in his search for the truth he was ready to give it up and devote himself
wholly to the world and its pleasures: "Nor," he says, "did anything call me back
from [falling into] a deeper gulf of carnal pleasures."[118]

But this was only half his situation. He concludes the last sentence by adding,
"except the fear of death and of your future judgement."[119] On this side Augustine found that no worldly position, not even that of Epicurus, was a possible
resting-place for his soul. "It turned and turned again, / on its back, on its sides
and on its belly, / and it found all places hard."[120] He could not adopt the Epicu-

rean way because "Epicurus refused to believe"[121] in the life of the soul after death or in future rewards and punishments. Augustine's belief in these things was at an opposite extreme from Epicurus, for whom the denial of any divine concern in human affairs was the cornerstone of his philosophy. Not that he proved that the gods do not exist. His point was simply that if they did exist their own bliss would not be troubled by any concern for what went on in this world and so in either case — whether they existed or not — for us it was best to act as if they did not. His position was intended to free us from what he regarded as a superstitious and debilitating belief in such things which ruined our prospects for happiness in this life by creating worries about the next. Augustine has already shown why he refused to act as if there were no God who had any interest in mortals or that the death of the body was simply the end of our existence and this, as he says here, was what prevented him from adopting the Epicurean way.[122] He had no proof that he was right — but then neither did Epicurus.

Fear of death and of God's future judgement made it impossible for Augustine to find any rest and contentment in the world, and this was just as much the logical conclusion of his scepticism as was the other side. His failure to know the truth was no longer a matter that could be put off while he enjoyed the world — as if the question could be taken up at some later date. It was itself the reason he could not adopt Epicureanism. Both sides weighed equally and they tore him in opposite directions.

So far as he had any idea of immortality he could only think of its joys in worldly terms and yet he could not live happily in this world because its pleasures were fleeting and he wanted a permanent bliss. "And I asked if we were immortal and if we lived in the perpetual enjoyment of corporeal pleasures, without any fear of losing them, should we not then be blessed or what else should we want to seek."[123]

On the other hand he was ready to throw himself into a "raging abyss"[124] of carnal pleasures because he had no hope of finding any higher good — and yet he could not do this because he feared a life after death and the judgement of the higher good he could not find. At this point the division between reason and nature seemed absolute, yet Augustine found that he was on both sides at once. As a rational being he found that he was subject to natural needs and desires: as a sensitive animal he found that he had rational aspirations which nature could not satisfy.

His position was utterly wretched and intolerable. Nevertheless, from the standpoint of the truth towards which he was moving, his very wretchedness was what saved him. This is what he had said at the beginning of this chapter where the contradiction of his sceptical position was brought to its highest pitch in the opposition between the fear of death and Epicureanism.

> To you be praise, to you be glory, O fountain of mercies! I became more miserable and you drew closer. Thy right hand was ready at that very time to snatch me out of the mire and to wash me clean, and I did not know it.[125]

In the last words of this book Augustine blames these miseries on the fact that he still could not think of any reality or substance which was not corporeal.[126] This will be his starting point for the seventh book, where he first describes how he attempted to resolve this contradiction between nature and reason in terms of a corporeal notion of an immutable god and then how, from its inadequacies, he was able to move swiftly to the true and certain knowledge of God.

NOTES

1 *Spes/mea* (98/6). See also VII,i,1 where, in describing the notion of God that he developed in this period, Augustine again specifies that he had come to a new stage in his life — *iuventus* rather than *adolescentia*: *Iam/iuventutem* (124/2-3).
2 On the ages of life see Chapter One, n. 38.
3 *veritatem/ereptum* (99/3-4).
4 Recall the epitome of his Manichaean days from III,vii,12 *recedens/videbar* (45/25).
5 See the *adsequor, teneo*, and *amplexor* of III,v,9 (42/4-5).
6 *veneram/maris* (98/11-12). Augustine uses this image in contrast to Monica who was safe on the sea because of her faith in Christ's church which, by metonymy, = faith in the cross, = wood = the ship by which we may safely cross over the tempestuous seas of this life (see I,xvi,25 *Quousque/conscenderint?* [19/8-10]).
7 See the *regio dissimilitudinis* of VII,x,16 (141/8) which I discuss in Chapter Seven.
8 *mater pietate fortis* (98/13).
9 Courcelle (*Recherches*, pp. 86-87) proposes a date in early June 385 soon after the annual opening of the normal trans-Mediterranean shipping season (27 May). Solignac (*BA*, Vol. 13, p. 141, n. 1) prefers a date in the early spring of 385 since Monica found Augustine "at the height of [his] sceptical crisis," which, he estimates, should have been in the winter/spring of 385. Courcelle himself notes that ships did cross the sea before the end of May although the crossing was not considered safe (*ibid.*, p. 86, n. 6).
10 *Nam/solent* (98/15-17).
11 *quia/pollicitus eras* (98/18).
12 In V,ix,17 Augustine mentions that, of Monica's visions, he has recorded some and omitted others. The visions recorded are the dream of the wooden ruler of III,xi,19-20, and the bishop's answer in III,xii,21. In V,xiii,23 Augustine mentioned that Monica said she was able, in some unknown way, to distinguish between visions which came from God and mere dreams. "For she said that she could distinguish by I don't know what kind of taste, which she was not able to explain in words, what difference there was between a revelation which came from you and the dreams of her own soul" — *Dicebat/sominantem* (121/1-3). By Augustine's use of *sapor* ("taste"), with the same root as "wisdom" (*sapientia*), he suggests that his mother had a kind of divine wisdom in making these discriminations.
13 *placidissime* (99/6).
14 *studiosus* (99/12).
15 Monica had a remarkably accurate judgement of the Sceptics as "epileptics" — see *DBV*, II,16. Her use of the vulgar term *caducarii* — "those who fall" — is a perfect representation of the situation of those who talk about the truth while claiming it can't be found. Monica may not have had any philosophical culture but she certainly was not blind.
16 *ubi/effecta sit* (99/25-27). For extensive references to this custom, called the *refrigerium* or *parentalia*, see Courcelle (*Recherches*, p. 87, n. 1) and also Solignac's note in *BA*, Vol. 13, pp. 676-77. Courcelle (*ibid.*, p. 91) supposes that Augustine raised the question of the *refrigerium* in the same meeting with Ambrose at which he discussed Monica's questions fasting on Saturdays — mentioned in the *Letters* to Casulanus (XXXVI) and to Januarius (LIV). Because of this he assumes that the *Confessions* is not strictly accurate in how Monica is pictured as agreeing with Ambrose's decision. "Augustine presents things as if Monica conformed to the ruling at the outset, on the simple injunction of the porter once he invoked the episcopal interdiction" — whereas Courcelle maintains she did so only later, after Augustine had his interview with Ambrose as reported in the two letters. Solignac is correct when he says, against Courcelle, that "nothing proves ... that Augustine consulted

the bishop about the offerings to the dead on the same occasion [that he asked about fasting on Saturdays]" (*BA*, Vol. 13, p. 139, n. 2). Moreover, we are not obliged to think that it was only through her son that Monica learned about Ambrose's ruling about the *refrigerium*. The Latin only says "when" (*ubi*, 99/23 and 100/12) she heard that the prohibition was from Ambrose she obeyed gladly. This could mean "from the porter" or it could mean "as soon as she heard" that it was Ambrose's ruling — with no specification given as to when this was. I think that the first *ubi* (99/23) refers to her initial agreement when I suppose that the porter simply told her that the bishop had forbidden the practice, and the second *ubi* (100/12) to the confirmation of this acceptance when she had a fuller explanation (from Augustine or another) of Ambrose's reasons which are given in the text which follows. In neither case do we have grounds to doubt Augustine's presentation of the event in the *Confessions*.

17 *pietatem/voluptatem* (100/11-12).
18 *libentissime* (100/17).
19 *sicut angelum dei* (99/14-15).
20 See VI,ii,2 *Sed/diligebat* (100/23-28).
21 *nesciens/putabam* (101/5-7).
22 See VI,iii,3 *Non/animum* (101/19-25), and VI,iii,4 *Sed/audiendum* (102/15-17). Augustine's amazement at Ambrose reading to himself comes from the fact that the normal practice was to read out loud — even to oneself. See the references in Courcelle, *Recherches*, p. 155, n. 2.
23 *omni die dominico* (102/21).
24 See the text from VI,ii,2, above, n. 21. See also below, n. 34.
25 *omnino recusabam* (98/1).
26 *curationem/recusabam* (97/28-98/1).
27 A catalogue of such objections is found in the "Ten Pyrrhonian Tropes" of Aenesidemus contained in the life of Pyrrho; Diogenes Laertius, *Lives of Eminent Philosophers*.
28 The Stoic position is described in Cicero's *Academica*. For a brief modern account of ancient Scepticism see H. H. Long, *Hellenistic Philosophy*, London, Duckworth, 1974.
29 I think the best account of the argument of *Against the Academics* is that of House ("A Note on ... *Contra Academicos*." See also O'Meara's Introduction and Notes to his translation of the work in *ACW*, Vol. 12. Along with Mourant ("Augustine and the Sceptics"), O'Meara recognizes that Augustine was not a convinced Academic in the accepted sense of the term but both authors miss the important sense in which Augustine's scepticism was a total view — a comprehensive position which he adopted — and which could therefore be an adequate replacement for the Manichaeism he had abandoned.

  The question of Augustine's scepticism illustrates one of the great difficulties in the recent enthusiasm for searching out the sources of Augustine's thought. This only makes sense on the assumption that we are looking for something that already existed and which Augustine could therefore have used as a source. But this makes for difficulties in understanding what was really going on when Augustine's position does not fit with any known source because it was peculiar to himself. I maintain that this was the case with his scepticism. The failure to recognize this leads to the very awkward fit which we find in both the above mentioned authors as they try to make Augustine's position accord with a source from which it did not really derive. They are forced to see Augustine's declensions from the "source" of Academic Scepticism as meaning that he never was a Sceptic — which is true — but it does not mean, as they conclude, that he did not have a complete position in that form of scepticism which he invented on his own.

  O'Connell (*St. Augustine's Early Theory of Man, A.D. 386-391*, Cambridge, Mass., Harvard University Press, 1968, pp. 236f.) argues that there is no refutation of Academic Scepticism in *Against the Academics* because Augustine saw it to be one with the acceptable teachings of the Platonists in its "secret doctrine." House shows what is wrong with this view: "O'Connell's argument only makes sense if one distinguishes between a pure form of Scepticism, which Augustine attributes to the Academics in his 'secret doctrine,' and an impure form which he attacks in the rest of the book." But, as House notes, "Augustine does not maintain that the 'secret doctrine' is historically accurate [see *CA*, III,xx,43 — i.e., that

Augustine ever heard the content of the 'secret doctrine' from an Academic source] – but that it is theoretically sound [i.e., that one can come to Platonism from a refuted Scepticism]."

30 *quam/viderem* (105/12-13) and *quae/ageremus* (105/17-18).

31 See *CA*, III,xi,26f.

32 *Volebam/nesciebam* (104/17-23). In *CA*, I,iii,8 Augustine recommends to Romanianus that he should not think he knows something unless he knows it as he knows that 1, 2, 3, and 4 added together = 10.

33 *quod/essent* (97/27-28).

34 See the text from VI,ii,2 quoted above, n. 21, where his doubt was only about his ability to find a way to the truth. Augustine repeats this in *DUC* (XX), where, speaking of the same period, he says: "I thought that the truth lay not hid, save that in it the way of search lay hid, and that this same way must be taken from some divine authority" (trans. *NPNF*).

35 VI,iii,3 *sed/meus* (101/9-10). See also VI,xi,18 where Augustine makes clear that he rejected the Sceptic's counsel to despair of knowing the truth – *O/desperemus* (116/26-28).

36 *cura/mea* (103/15).

37 For the dates see Solignac, *BA*, Vol. 13, pp. 204-205.

38 *dubitabam/putabam* (101/5-7).

39 *fluctuabam* (106/25).

40 *Tenebam/praecipitium* (104/15-16).

41 *suspendio* (104/16). This is the Sceptic's ἐποχή: see above, Chapter Five, n. 159.

42 *Et/tribuisti* (104/24-105/2).

43 See above n. 23.

44 *Ex/scientiae* (105/3-8).

45 *deinde paulatim* (105/10).

46 *nisi/ageremus* (105/17-18).

47 *persuasisti/ministratos?* (105/21-26). For other Augustinian references to this argument, see Solignac, *BA*, Vol. 13, p. 531, n. 1.

48 *semper (tamen)/te* (106/25). The same thing is said a few lines above at the end of VI,v,7 *Id/pertinere* (105/26-32).

49 *cum/voluisses* (106/5-11).

50 *aperitissimis et humillimo* (106/18).

51 See VI,vi,8 *eoque/promptu* (106/14-16).

52 *suspendio magis necabar* (104/16-17).

53 *Cogitabam/deserebas* (106/23-26).

54 *inhiabam/tu* (106/27-107/1).

55 *Haec/omnibus* (49/8-11).

56 *die/scientibus* (107/9-11). Courcelle (*Recherches*, pp. 78-83) has a long discussion of the nature and possible occasion of this oration.

57 *vide quot dies!* (108/16).

58 *Et/gaudebam* (107/29-108/6).

59 *Quam ego miser eram* (107/7-8). Augustine says the same thing of his soul a few lines above, *quam miser erat* (107/4).

60 *saepe* (108/23).

61 *taedebat* (108/24).

62 *Alypius/natu* (109/1-3).

63 Courcelle, *Recherches*, p. 31.

64 For details of the correspondence between Paulinus/Alypius and Paulinus/Augustine see Courcelle (*Recherches*, pp. 29-32) and Solignac (*BA*, Vol. 13, pp. 27-29). On the "first" *Confessions* see Courcelle (*Recherches*, pp. 269-90, and *Les Confessions*, pp. 559-607).

65 *magnam virtutis indolem* (109/6-7).

66 See VI,vii,12 *Etenim/accessit* (110/23-111/2). Courcelle (*Recherches*, p. 59) sees this account of the conversion of Alypius as "arranged" to conform to the parallel account of the conversion of Polemon by Xenocrates – but see the judicious reservation of Solignac (*BA*,

Vol. 13, p. 543, n. 1), who finds no reason to do any more than note the analogy.

67 *audax ... potius quam fortis* (112/12-13).

68 *Si/intendere?* (111/19-22). In the phrasing of this paragraph Augustine makes it clear that Alypius went along merely to prove his virtue: see *ac/superabo* (111/22-23) and *quasi/vincere* (112/6-7).

69 *dispensator/examinator* (114/21-22). See also VI,vii,12 *non/tui* (109/27-28). Solignac (*BA*, Vol. 13, p. 541, n. 1) gives a note on the dates of Alypius' episcopacy.

70 *non/credulitate* (113/6-7).

71 *experientior instructiorque* (114/22-23).

72 *indolem* (109/6-7).

73 *paene* (115/14).

74 *ostentationem/putabat* (111/6-7).

75 This point is important because it shows that Manichaeism could be just as attractive to men of action, like Alypius, as to intellectual spirits such as Augustine who were drawn by its promise of knowledge. On the side of action, Faustus, for example, claimed to have fulfilled the beatitudes of Christ (*CFM*, V,1). Brown ("Manichaeism in the Roman Empire," in *Religion and Society*, p. 112) describes the powerful effect which the unwashed elect with their followers must have had on arriving in a town: "the arrival in the forum, or in front of the Christian church, of a group of pale men and women, clasping mysterious volumes and dressed with ostentatious barbarity, was a sight to be seen." The "mysterious volumes" attracted Augustine – the "ostentatious barbarity" (i.e., the appearance of holy austerity), Alypius. The Manichees were no better in adhering to this side of their teachings than they were at fulfilling their promise of knowledge. In *DMM*, XIX-XX, Augustine describes a number of instances in which he had knowledge of the Elect secretly fornicating, eating meat, drinking wine, and going to the baths and theatres – all of which were prohibited by their religion.

76 See VI,xv,25.

77 *fratrem cordis mei* (185/14).

78 See for example, Alypius' insistence (in IX,iv,7) that Augustine's early works should carry a scholarly fragrance. From this point of view also we should understand Augustine's statement in VI,x,16 that Alypius almost succumbed to the temptation to have books copied for himself at public expense. This is the desire of a man who wants and admires knowledge but must settle for books.

79 *et/eminebat* (109/5-7). Augustine adds the qualification that Alypius' virtue was especially remarkable *given his tender years* because this kind of self-control normally comes only through the experience of a lifetime. Throughout the *Confessions* Augustine continues to stress Alypius' capacity to do the good. Even in the last mention he makes of Alypius he added the parenthetical remark that, during the winter at Cassiciacum, Alypius, to subdue the body, went barefoot on the frozen soil – see IX,vi,14.

80 *Talis/modus* (115/24-26).

81 *nullam/sapientiae* (116/2-4). See also VIII,vi,13.

82 *pariter/acerrimus* (116/4-6). Nebridius' character, with this strongly intellectual bent, was much closer to Augustine's than that of Alypius.

83 It is often remarked (though to my knowledge, nowhere better than in O'Donnell, "The Demise of Paganism") that by the fourth century the chief distinction between Christianity and Paganism was not so much in the worship of different gods – since the pagan cults were "fast departing from the Roman scene" (p. 65) – as in a difference of attitude. The Christians were intolerant in their claim that "theirs was the only acceptable form of worship [and] that it was incumbent upon all mankind to accept the tenets of their creed" (p. 50), while the pagan attitude, best expressed in the famous line of Symmachus that "it is not possible that there should be only one way to come to so great a mystery [as God]" (quoted by O'Donnell, p. 73), is summed up as the tolerant view that religion was largely a private matter – or, if public, perfunctory – where a variety of creeds and cults could exist side by side. O'Donnell puts this attitude in this way: "I worship my god [determined by family tra-

ditions, one's city, aims, enthusiasm and experiences], you worship yours, and we may both be doing the right thing, for there are many different ways in which man can profitably come into contact with divinity" (p. 50). This is quite true but — going beyond anything O'Donnell actually says or suggests — we must guard against the conclusion that Christianity's intolerance had the sense that it was a monolithic unit in which all differences were reduced to conformity. *Within* the one way of the church the whole variety and multiplicity of mankind reappeared. Augustine insists on this both at the practical level — as here, where the great differences between his character ar. ، that of Alypius were both to find a place in the church or, for example, in the many classes of people he saw in the vision of Continence (VIII,xi,27) — and on the intellectual level where he argues, in XII,xxv,34, that there can be a number of different interpretations of Scripture, all of which are true.

84 See IX,iii,6. On Nebridius' career, see Brown, *St. Augustine*, pp. 68, 133-36.

85 *Et/adprehenderemus* (116/6-16).

86 *in eodem luto haeistans* (116/22).

87 *Et/luenda?* (117/20-22).

88 *Ergo et hoc quarendeum* (117/23).

89 *Quid/redire* (118/2-7).

90 *aliquis honor* (118/7-8). The *honor* refers to the *cursus honorum*, the stages of public office through which Romans aspired to rise from the lowest office to the consulship and senate.

91 See the *amici maiores* of VI,xi,18 (117/13) and VI,xi,14 (118/9). Courcelle (*Recherches*, p. 83, n. 5) suggests that Mallius Theodorus, a Platonist, was one of these "important friends." See also pp. 153-56 for Courcelle's suggestions about the relations of Augustine and Theodorus. A brief account of this man is found in Solignac, *BA*, Vol. 13, p. 533-34.

92 *cum aliqua pecunia* (118/11).

93 *fugientibus* (116/23).

94 *Antemeridianis/curarum?* (117/11-16).

95 *Cum/eam* (118/15-21).

96 See VI,xii,22 *Magna/excruciabat* (120/13-15), and VI,xv,25.

97 *quarum/conscius* (118/25-26). See also VI,xii,22 *ut/degere* (119/20-22) — "I used to say, whenever we [Augustine and Alypius] used to discuss the question [sex] that I was in no way able to be celibate."

98 *raptim et furtim* (119/24-25).

99 *quidnam/videretur* (120/3-5).

100 See VI,viii,13.

101 *dulces laqueos* (119/16-17). In the last sentence of VI,xii,22 Augustine specifies that he and Alypius remained unchaste until their conversion — *Sic/modis* (120/16-18).

102 See VI,xiii,23 *Instabatur/expectabatur* (121/3-6).

103 See above Chapter Four, n. 12 on the length of this relationship.

104 Augustine does not say expressly that the girl was Christian but I take this for granted. In VIII,i,2 he contemplates his projected marriage in the context of the Christianity which, by that time, he actively wanted to embrace: *nec/obstringebar* (153/16-23). If the girl had not been Christian it is unlikely that he could have thought of a pagan marriage as satisfying both his sexual desires and the desire to become a Christian — although this is not impossible as there were still many mixed marriages like that of Monica and Patricius (see O'Donnell, "The Demise of Paganism," pp. 62-63). But when this is taken with the words of VI,xiii,23 that Monica "hoped that once I was married I would receive the health-giving washing of baptism about which she rejoiced to find me better disposed as each day went by and saw that her prayers and your promises were being fully realized in my faith" (*quo/amimadvertebat* 120/21-23), I regard it as established. Monica's hope would thus have the definite sense that a Christian wife could do for her son what she had been able to do for Patricius — i.e., bring him to baptism.

105 See VI,xv,25.

106 *auctior* (122/18), trans. Watts (*Loeb*).

107 See VI,xiii,23.

108 See VI,xi,19 *Et/gravet* (118/10-12). In *Sol*, I,x,17, in painting a picture of the "ideal" wife,
 Augustine imagines such a girl as beautiful, chaste, obedient, educated or educable, with
 enough dowry to keep her from being a burden on his resources or leisure, and no trouble!
 We should not too easily condemn Augustine for the "callous" dismissal of his mistress. For
 a properly historical view of his behaviour see O'Meara (*The Young Augustine*, pp. 128-29),
 or Solignac (*BA*, Vol. 13, pp. 677-79) who gives a brief review of the legal status of concu-
 binage in Roman and early church law. See also Brown (*St. Augustine*, p. 63, n. 4 and 5, and pp.
 88-89).

109 See VI,xiv,24. On the idea of this community Solignac (*BA*, Vol. 13, p. 567, n. 1) sums up
 the present state of the question. Three "sources" are suggested: it is based on (*i*) a Manichaean monastery founded in Rome by the auditor Constantius; (*ii*) a Platonopolis mentioned by Porphyry in his *Life of Plotinus*; or (*iii*) on a Pythagorean community discussed by
 Iamblicus. Because Augustine had already abandoned the Manichees, I see no likelihood in
 the suggestion that this community had anything to do with them. As against the other
 proposals – that it derived from Neo-Platonic or Pythagorean sources (which Augustine
 nowhere says he knew at this time) – it seems to me far more probable that he and his friend
 had in mind the establishment of an Epicurean "Garden." He tells us (VI,xvi,26) that in
 practical matters he was ready to give the palm of victory to Epicurus who, like the Sceptics,
 saw imperturbability as the proper goal of the wise man's life (see Diogenes Laertius, *Lives
 and Opinions*, X,128). To this end Epicurus scorned any involvement in worldly affairs
 beyond what was necessary to secure bodily needs and this is just what Augustine's scepticism also desired (see VI,xiv,24 *Et/moliti* – 121/7-10). Epicurus set up his "Garden" as a
 tranquil resting-place, parallel to the *sedes quietae* of the gods, mentioned by Lucretius (*De
 Rerum Naturae*, III,18-24), where a wise man might find peace in the company of like-
 minded friends. See A. A. Long (*Hellenistic Philosophy*, p. 45): "The Gods, like true Epicureans, dwell in *sedes quietae* [tranquil resting-places] enjoying a life free of all trouble." See
 also *ibid.*, pp. 15-17, pp. 71-72 on the life of the Epicurean garden community. This quiet is
 just what Augustine and his friends sought in their proposed community: "And our idea was
 that each year two of us would act as magistrates, taking care of all the necessaries, leaving
 the rest in quiet" (VI,xiv,24 *Et/quietis* – 121/22-24). Diogenes Laertius (X,119) notes also
 that Epicurus taught that the wise man will not marry or raise a family and it was on just this
 question that Augustine's community foundered: see VI,xiv,24. I do not mean to suggest that
 Augustine and his friends were Epicureans – which they were not because their idea was to
 look for God which no real Epicurean would have done – nor that the Epicurean "Garden"
 was in any direct sense the "source" of the planned community (see above n. 29). But, so
 far as they adopted any existing pattern, it seems likely to me that we should look to a
 modification of Epicurus' teachings – whom Augustine mentions in this book – rather than
 to a Neo-Platonic or Neo-Pythagorean model since there is no direct evidence that, at the
 time, he was moved by either of these systems while he specifically mentioned that he had
 considered Epicureanism.

110 *paene iam firmaveramus* (121/9).

111 *mulierculae* (121/25).

112 See VI,xiv,24 *Sed/abiectum est* (121/24-28).

113 See VI,xi,19 *Multi/fuerunt* (118/12-14). See also VI,xiii,21 *Ego/aberam* (119/7-11). Courcelle claims that Augustine was thinking of Mallius Theodorus as an example of a man who
 was both married and a philosopher: see *Recherches*, pp. 179-80, 281-86. In *Sol* (I,x,17),
 written *after* his conversion, Augustine sums up his thinking on the relation of a real marriage (i.e., one entered for the sake of children) to philosophy. He says: "So if it is part of the
 duty of the Sage (which I have not yet learned) to have children, anyone who has intercourse
 with a woman for this purpose only seems to me worthy of admiration rather than imitation.
 The danger of attempting it is greater than the happiness of achieving it. Accordingly in the
 interests of righteousness and the liberty of my soul I have made it my rule not to desire or
 seek or marry a wife" (trans. *LCC*).

114 See VI,xiv,24 *Inde/benedictione* (121/28-122/6).

115 On the source of Augustine's knowledge of the Epicureans, which does not seem to have come through Cicero, see Solignac, *BA*, Vol. 13, p. 572, n. 1.

116 For an ancient account of the life and teachings of Epicurus, see Diogenes Laertius, *Lives and Opinions*, X. A modern review may be found in E. Zeller, *Outlines of the History of Greek Philosophy* (13th ed. [1931], rev. Nestle, trans. Palmer, New York, Dover, 1980, pp. 230-41) or, for a more detailed treatment, see Long, *Hellenistic Philosophy*, pp. 14-74.

117 There is a sense in which the Sceptical suspension of judgement — at least in the Pyrrhonean tradition — can be regarded as moral in the primary sense of breaking down all vanity. In refusing assent the Sceptic overcomes the presumption that we (mortals) control or can do anything — thus opening us to God's mercy. I am indebted to Dennis House for this observation.

118 *Nec/gurgite* (122/26-27).

119 *nisi/tui* (122/27-28).

120 *Versa/omnia* (123/21-22).

121 *Epicurus credere noluit (123/5-6).*

122 See VI,xiv,26 *Nec/noluit* (122/26-123/6).

123 *Et/quaereremus* (123/6-9). Augustine notes that he would have been miserable without the friendship of his friends and that this friendship itself was not a body — however much he thought that all pleasures were bodily: see *Nec/voluptatum* (123/13-17).

124 *gurgite* (122/27).

125 *Tibi/ignorabam* (122/23-26).

126 *Nesciens/sentiebam* (123/9-19).

Chapter Seven
COMMENTARY ON BOOK VII

The seventh book is devoted to Augustine's final progress to the certain knowledge of God and to his discovery of the way by which we may come to him. It is divided into three parts. In the first (chs. i-vii) he describes the inadequate idea of God which he developed out of his sceptical position. In the second (chs. viii-xvi) he tells how, from these inadequacies, he was led by the books of the Platonists to the true knowledge of God. In the third (chs. xvii-xxi) he shows the deficiencies in this knowledge which moved him towards Christianity.

I. VII,i,1-VII,vii,11. The God of Augustine's scepticism

VII,i,1-VII,ii,3. God as incorruptible, inviolable, and immutable

VII,i,1-2. God the creator — At this point Augustine still believed that he could find the way to God since he had seen nothing in the opinions of the Sceptics or Epicureans which proved otherwise.[1] But his rejection of the views of the Manichees and his refusal to believe what the Christians taught about God meant that, in the matter of what he should think of God, he was quite on his own. This is just how he describes things.

Later in this book he reviews the three false ideas of God which he held before he finally found the true notion in the Platonists: that is, opinions coming from (*i*) the theft of pears (*ii*) his Manichaean days, and (*iii*) his scepticism. He says of the last one:

> And coming back from there [i.e., the Manichaean "opinion of the two substances"] it [his soul] made for itself a god spread throughout the infinite spaces of all places and him its had supposed to be you, and him it had set up in its heart and again it had become the temple of its own idol, abominable to you. (VII,xiv,20)[2]

The first section of Book VII explains this false idea of God that he developed by himself and tells where it led him.

He begins by stating the problem that doomed his efforts to failure.

> Already my wicked and impious adolescence was dead and I was going on into my mature years, and as much as my age was the greater so much was the falseness of my thinking the more despicable — I who was unable to think of any substance unless it was of such a kind as these eyes see. (VII,i,1)[3]

He goes on to say that he rejoiced to have found that the Catholics did not think of God as contained in the form of a human body[4] but his problem was just that "[he] did not know what else [than a body] to think that God was" (VII,i,1).[5] He could not break free from this false premise but he did not fall back into the Manichees' dualism.

The reason was that in giving up the Manichees' position he was freed for the first time to appreciate the certainty of mathematical propositions. It was not that he had not long recognized their stability. Indeed we have seen that it was as much because of the Manichees' inability to provide a mathematically sound account of the movement of the heavenly bodies as by the fact that their account did not conform with the evidence of the senses that he first questioned and then rejected their teachings. But mathematics, in itself, had nothing to do with his relation to God – and as long as he thought Mani had a certain knowledge about that, he needed nothing else. On leaving the Manichees the certainty of mathematics became the model he desired in all things. Such a knowledge had nothing to do with God but it did have the certainty he desired. Although he could not have said so at the time,[6] what gave mathematical propositions this character was the fact that in relation to nature they were unchangeable. They had a self-identity which was beyond anything nature or the senses could alter because they did not derive from either. Such an inner stability which was proof against every possible externality was what Augustine now saw that he must ascribe to God if his demand for an absolutely certain knowledge was to be satisfied.

> And I, a man, and such a man, was trying to conceive you, the supreme and only and true God, and I believed you to be incorruptible and inviolable and incommutable[7] with all my innermost being because, not knowing whence or how, I nevertheless saw clearly and was certain that that which was able to be corrupted was worse than that which was not able to be corrupted, and what could not be violated I preferred without hesitation to that which could be violated, and what suffered no mutation I knew to be better than that which was able to change. (VII,i,1)[8]

The fact that Augustine insists in one and the same sentence that he believed God to be thus and that he knew him to be so is no confusion. That God must be so, if we are to know him, was a certain knowledge. That he is so, that such a God exists, could only be believed at this point in Augustine's life.

From these considerations Augustine had come to think of God as the absolutely self-identical. But a self-identity which is absolute must be supposed to have nothing outside of itself which could conceivably disturb it. All things other than itself – that is, all things corruptible, violable and mutable – must therefore be thought to be in God and referred to him as their *creator*.[9] This is what he now maintained – but he had to do it while also thinking that God was some sort of a body.

> Because whatever I deprived of such spaces seemed to me to be nothing – and absolutely nothing rather than merely the void which would occur if a body were taken out of its place and the place remained free of all body whatsoever, whether earthly, watery, airy, or heavenly, but nevertheless remained an empty place, a kind of spacious emptiness. (VII,i,1)[10]

But if everything real had to be in space, and everything in space had to be a body, then God, though infinite and containing and creating all things, had to be a body in space. The result, for Augustine, was the following.

> Thus indeed I thought of you, O life of my life, as a greatness which existed throughout infinite space and which penetrated the whole mass of the world and outside of the world existed in every direction through immense spaces without limit so that the earth possessed you, the heaven possessed you, all things possessed you, and all were contained in you but you were not limited anywhere. Just as the light of the sun is not blocked out by the body of the air – I mean this air which is above the earth – so that it cannot get through it, and just as the light penetrates the air without bursting or ripping it but by filling it completely, so in the same way I thought that the body not only of the heaven and the air and the sea but even of the earth also was passible to you and that you could penetrate all the parts of these bodies, both the greatest and the smallest parts so that they could receive your presence since, as I then thought, by a secret inspiration both inwardly and outwardly all things are governed which you have made. (VII,i,2)[11]

We see that Augustine had been driven to conclude that if it was possible to have a certain knowledge of God then God must be supposed to be incorruptible, inviolable, and unchangeable – that is, that he has an absolute self-identity which nothing could conceivably disturb. This in turn implied that nothing could be outside God or separated from him – which meant that he must be the creator of the corruptible, the violable, and the mutable.

So far Augustine's scepticism had led him to believe in the existence of an incorruptible God who was the creator of corruptible nature. Everything should have been clear but it was not. On the one hand he discovered a problem in separating this God from nature: how was God's substance actually distinguished from nature's? His solution is discussed in VII,i,1-2, and then in VII,ii,3 he shows the positive benefit (the proof that the Manichees could not know God) which he got from the partial correctness of his answer. On the other hand he found an equal difficulty in holding both sides together: how could the actual existence of evil be explained in a universe which was wholly created by God? This is discussed in VII,iii,4-VII,v,7 and again, in VII,v,8, he shows the positive benefit (the proof that astrology was no science) which resulted from his partially correct answer. At the time Augustine could not find the final and completely true answer to either question. In the opening lines of the book he blames this on the fact that he was unable to think of any other substance than sensible bodies. By assuming that God was corporeal, Augustine found that God's nature became unintelligible, just as he found no answer to his questions about evil because he assumed that it too was sensible.

Augustine first discusses the problem he found in thinking of the distinction between God and nature. His answer was ingenious but wrong. He concluded that the identity of God and nature lay in the fact that God, like nature, was a corporeal substance – i.e., matter in space, a body. The difference between the two lay in the fact that God's body was infinite, incorruptible, inviolable, and unchangeable, while natural bodies (from the smallest speck to the whole universe itself) were finite, corruptible, violable, and mutable. The relationship between them was the God penetrated and was present in all nature while also extending infinitely beyond it in every direction. As he describes it in a later chapter (VII,v,7), God was like an infinite sea diffused in every direction through all space – and nature, or the natural universe, was like a huge but finite sponge plunged in the middle and pervaded throughout with the divine sea.[12] Augustine thought that with this idea he had managed to preserve the absolute difference between God and nature. He could distinguish between them, as between the incorruptible and the corruptible, without denying their identity. But this did not work on two accounts.

Subjectively, he found that he was unable to fix his thoughts on this God.

> My heart cried out violently against all my imaginings and with a single blow I tried to drive away from the glance of my spirit the evermoving host of impure [i.e., because composed of contraries] images [in order to look at God]: but scarcely had they been sent away when, *in the twinkling of an eye* (1 Cor. 15:32) behold, gathered together, they were back again and they pressed on my sight and clouded it over. (VII,i,1)[13]

This is a vivid statement of Augustine's difficulty. He was by now certain that God had to be thought of as incorruptible if he was to have a certain knowledge of him. He also knew certainly that the one incorruptible God was infinitely "preferable" and "better" (VII,i,1)[14] to mutable nature and its many goods – that is, "better" and "preferable" from the point of view of his rational soul with its demand for certainty and the consequence need of a stable unchanging object. He tried to fix his thoughts on God but found that the images of corruptible nature kept intruding. They could do this because he knew they were implied in God as their creator. He tried to clear them away "with a single blow" by concentrating on the absolute distinction between God and nature which would exclude them: God was unchanging, they were subject to change. But no sooner had he done this than "in the twinkling of an eye" they were back again, rushing in to fill the void in his notion of God which, at this point, was only abstractly distinguished from nature as the incorruptible from the corruptible. What he needed was some way of concretely distinguishing God from nature – but he would not be able to do this until he came to recognize that God and nature were not composed of the same substance.

On the objective side, although he did not notice it at the time, the distinction which he invented "was false" (VII,i,2)[15] because if God was an incorruptible body then there would be "more of God in the body of an elephant than in the body of a sparrow" (VII,i,2).[16] In this the infinite God would be subject to finite distinctions which contradicted the principle of their difference – God was infinite and they were finite.

In trying to preserve God's incorruptibility *vis-à-vis* mutable nature, Augustine had only succeeded in making the incorruptible, corruptible. He had not yet discovered that the substantial and concrete difference between God and nature was not merely the abstract distinction between the incorruptible and the corruptible, but was rather the distinction between corporeal and intelligible reality. As long as he assumed that God must be some kind of a body, not only would the hidden problem of the elephant and the sparrow remain unresolved, but his notion of God would be inadequate to his own requirements because of his inability to fix his thoughts on God in concrete distinction from mutable nature. A solution was possible but he had not yet found it. Thus he says in the final words of this first chapter, "It is not thus [that God is present in nature yet different from it]. But you had not yet illumined *my darkness* (Ps. 17:29)."[17]

VII,ii,3. The certain proofs that the Manichees could not have a knowledge of God: Nebridius' argument appreciated — The recognition that God must be thought of as incorruptible, inviolable, and unchangeable — if he was to be known by us — did not, by itself, lead Augustine to the true knowledge of God. But it did at last provide him with a sure proof of the falsity of the Manichees' claim to know God.[18] Now he was able to see the decisive force of the question which Nebridius used to put when they were still in Carthage: "What could the imaginary Race of Darkness, from the opposite mass [than God], which the Manichees opposed to you, have done if you had been unwilling to fight with it?"[19]

This question had been "striking"[20] to all who heard it in Augustine's circle. At the time none of them took it as proving that the Manichaean idea of God was wrong, although Augustine now saw it as doing just that. Why? The answer is that it did not necessarily disturb the hypothesis that good and evil were separate. No Manichee would have said that the race of darkness could have harmed God — who was inviolable just because he was utterly separated from evil. Thus the question could be taken in the sense of "Why is there a mixture of the contraries if the principles of good and evil are separated? In other words, the real force of the question while Augustine was still a Manichee was not, "Is God really incorruptible?" but, "Why is there the mixture of good and evil — i.e., why is there nature?"

By this logic Augustine's inability to find an answer at the time was taken not so much as a proof that the Manichees' idea of God was wrong as a difficulty in the way of their idea of nature being right. But this difficulty was not pressing because nature was before them. In this sense the question was beside the point, a striking problem but of no practical significance, since they were actively engaged in the war of good against evil. As long as they were content to suppose that nature was this mixture of the contraries then the sense of the question could only be, "Why is there the war?" and not "Is there the war?"

So long as they assumed that the war existed they could easily suppose that an answer was possible. Of course there *must* be an answer since the war that the reason would explain was real — and it had to be real because they were fighting it. Since an answer was theoretically possible it did not much matter if no one actually knew it. They had more pressing practical concerns in the struggle to separate themselves from evil, and Augustine, Nebridius, and the others turned to them at the time. And very cannily too, because the minute an answer is sought the contradictions in the position became manifest. Augustine shows how this was so in his work *On the Customs of the Manichees* (XII,25). There he reports that a Manichee who foolishly attempted an answer proposed that God himself chose to be subject to evil or that, because of his goodness, he decided to come to the aid of the evil to pacify it — both of which plainly contradict the assumed separation of good and evil.[21] For these reasons, at the time, Nebridius' question only posed a curious problem rather than a fatal dilemma.

But once Augustine had understood that if we were to have a certain knowledge of God then God must be thought of as incorruptible, inviolable, and unchangeable — in the precise sense that nothing could be supposed to exist apart from him which he had not created — then the Manichaean assumption that the divine incorruptibility simply meant God's separation from the corruptible no longer made any sense. It is from this point of view that the dilemma posed by Nebridius' question became decisive. This also explains why Augustine recalled it at just this point in his life and why he reports it here in the *Confessions*. The Manichees denied that God was corruptible or that the separated principle of evil could harm him in any way.[22] But by this denial they were thrown squarely on one horn of Nebridius' question and the whole of the rest of their teaching was reduced to nonsense. For if the war of evil against the good did not exist – because God could not possibly be harmed by evil – then the struggle of the faithful Manichee to separate the one from the other was simply inane. Or else, if the war was real, it must follow that God could actually be harmed in his substance, which was a position to be rejected outright even on the Manichees' own account. But because they did not consistently maintain this – by their insistence that the war was real – Augustine saw that their God was in fact corruptible and that consequently it would be impossible for them to have the certain knowledge of God which they claimed to possess. Here at last was the certain proof that their teaching about God was false.

So far we have seen three main stages in Augustine's escape from the Manichees. First there was his initial disenchantment following his meetings with Faustus (V,vi,10). Second, his determination to leave the sect even though he had no proof that they were wrong in what they taught about God or nature (V,xiv,25). And now, thirdly, his discovery of the proof that they were wrong. All the same we should note that, so far, this is only a proof that *if* we are able to have a certain knowledge of God then the Manichaean position cannot possibly be true – and so we should also include, as the fourth and final stage, the certain and altogether unhypothetical knowledge that such a God does exist. Augustine finally came to this through his discovery of Platonist philosophy (VII,x,16).

VII,iii,4-VII,v,7. The problem of evil

VII,iii,4-5. Free will – The recognition that God's incorruptability meant that nothing could be opposed to him, raised a question about the origin of evil. If there was nothing but God and his creation where did evil come from? This is exactly the question Augustine faced since he was now certain that the Manichees were not right when they taught that evil was a separated substance.

> So I bent my efforts to see and understand what I had heard[23] – that the free decision of the will was the cause of the evil which we do and that your just judgement was the reason why we suffer. But I was not able to understand this clearly. Thus, while trying to raise the aim of my mind out of the deep, I again fell back and trying often I fell back again and again. For this lifted me up to your light, that I now knew that I had a will as surely as I knew that I was alive. Thus when I willed or nilled something I was most certain that I and not another willed and nilled and here, as I now saw, was the cause of my sin. (VII,iii,5)[24]

For the first time Augustine had really encountered the problem of evil, which can only appear if one is not obliged to remain with its abstract separation from the good. For the Manichees there was no problem since any evil that a man did was supposed to have been willed by the separated evil principle which was in him but was not a part of himself and over which he had no control.[25] Such a view gratified Augustine's determination to insist on his natural innocence but it could only do so at the cost of maintaining that God was corruptible. But if God was incorruptible, in the sense that he was not opposed by another (evil) principle, then the only possible source of evil would have to lie somewhere in God's creation.

Here Augustine began to discover the existence of human freedom. It is a necessary corollary to the divine incorruptibility, as he indicates when he says that he was now "most certain" (VII,iii,5)[26] that he had a will and that he and no other was the author of all his actions. The exclusion of dualism means that there is no independent reality which does not belong to the rational principle and which could be regarded as the (separated) source of evil. But since evil cannot be referred to God, as the absolute good, it must therefore be supposed — of the evil which we do — that we do it freely. From this recognition Augustine came to the certain knowledge that the Manichaean teachings about human nature — that it is incorruptible and naturally innocent — were as wrong as their teachings about God — that he is corruptible and suffers evil.

> [A]nd I was certain that it was not true what the Manichees said — from whom I fled with my whole soul — because I saw that in seeking the cause of evil they were themselves full of evil because they preferred to assume that your substance suffered evil rather than that their own did evil. (VII,iii,4)[27]

We can now see that chapters ii and iii go together as a couplet. They explain first how Augustine came to the certain knowledge of the falsity of the Manichees' teaching about God (ch. ii) and secondly how he came to understand where they were also wrong in what they said about human nature (ch. iii). To say that he knew that he willed all that he willed, good and evil alike, is to say that Augustine knew himself as a particular finite substance — an indivisible concrete and corruptible being who was capable of both good and evil. Again, everything should have been clear but it was not.

He found that if he looked to God as the incorruptible and omnipotent creator he could not explain how there could be any evil in himself. On the other hand when he looked to his evil deeds he found that he could not understand his relation to God. Just as his effort to come to a true understanding of God's nature was thwarted by the fact that he had only the most abstract grasp of the difference between God and nature (incorruptible/corruptible), so here his problem in understanding the nature of evil arose from the fact that he had only the most abstract view of their relation. His position was incapable of bringing the two together in the face of what he perceived to be the corporeal reality of evil. Where could this substance have come from?

In seeking an answer to this problem Augustine determined that although he knew he was the responsible author of all his actions, he distinguished between his good and evil deeds in the following way.

> What I did against my consent, that I seemed to suffer rather than to do, and that I judged not to be my fault but my punishment, which punishment I immediately acknowledge that I did not unjustly suffer since I thought you to be just. (VII,iii,5)[28]

The similarity between this position and that of the Stoics is striking. Nowhere in the *Confessions* does Augustine mention the Stoics by name nor does he ever claim that he was one. Nevertheless he certainly knew what they taught and his own position can be usefully compared to the Stoic teaching, if only to show where he differed from it.[29]

Like Augustine the Stoics held that the universe was governed by a single rational, incorruptible, omnipotent, and corporeal divine principle. Like Augustine they also concluded from this that our will was free. And like Augustine they said that we must acknowledge the evil things in life as a just punishment for our own sinful acts. Whatever seems evil to man — the class of "things done against his consent" — must be understood as a punishment for having unknowingly, but voluntarily, contravened the divine order. The Stoic sage accepted any suffering or evil in his life as a deserved punishment for having somehow stepped out of line — a punishment which he was therefore willing to endure "stoically." By this willingness to regard any suffering as a just punishment the Stoic, like Augustine, acknowledged his sin in such a way that he ignored his own evil nature. What he confessed was not a sinful nature but sinful acts — moments in which he unknowingly contravened the divine order. By this simple expedient of resolving not to rail against God, the Stoic established his fundamental innocence and freed himself to pursue his worldly goals to the exclusion of all else so long as he did not complain when they went wrong and brought him to grief.

For the Stoic there was no problem of evil. He knew that it certainly did not come from God, that it could not have come from another principle, and so must have come from himself. Yet, by his will to suffer in patience what he could not control — the class of things "done against his consent" — he did not see himself as responsible for preventing evil but only for putting up with it. He did this by regarding it as a just punishment. In this way evil did not have to be explained — it had only to be endured.

Augustine's position was identical — except that his final step made all the difference. He would not rest here but demanded to know why and how there could be evil in a universe made by God. Like the Stoic, Augustine regarded his sufferings as a punishment for evils he acknowledged he had done without knowing what they were. "What I did against my consent, that I seemed to suffer rather than to do and that I judged not to be my fault but my punishment." But, unlike the Stoic, Augustine insisted on knowing how it was that there could be the evil which he assumed was the hidden cause of any suffering he experienced — detracting from his happiness in what he regarded as a divinely established order.

> Again I asked myself, "Who made me? Was it not my God who is not only good but goodness itself? From whence then does it come that I can will evil and nill good? Whence does it come that there is a reason why I justly undergo punishment? Who put this in me and planted in me this seed-bed of bitterness since I was wholly made by my most sweet God?" (VII,iii,5)[30]

Perhaps, Augustine thought, it was the devil who did this? But this line of questioning brought him to a dead end. If he supposed that the source of his capacity to will evil lay in some very high and powerful creature, like an angel of God gone wrong, the same problem simply reappeared at another level.

If the devil was the author where did the devil himself come from? For if, from the good angel [that he once was] the devil became the devil by a perverse will, whence did this evil will come into him too — which made him into the devil — seeing that he was made altogether a [good] angel by the very best creator? (VII,iii,5)[31]

There was no resolution to the problem in this direction and Augustine ends the chapter with a resumé of his position at the time. He could not find an adequate answer to his questions about evil but neither did he try to avoid the problem by returning to the supposition that God was constrained to suffer evil — in which case God would not be unchangeable, which carried with it the inevitable consequence that he would then have been unable to have any certain knowledge of him.

> By such thoughts as these I was once again cast down and stifled but I was not seduced into that hell of error [of the Manichees] where no one confesses to you because one thinks that it is rather you who suffer evil than that it is man who does it. (VII,iii,5)[32]

VII,iv,6. Divine incorruptibility and the nature of evil — If the insistence on the divine incorruptibility prevented Augustine from relapsing into Manichaeism, his failure to insist on it sufficiently prevented him from finding a resolution to the problem. As he points out in this chapter, he ought to have sought to understand the nature of both God and evil from his certain knowledge that the good was absolutely incorruptible, which meant that it could not be harmed by any will, by any necessity, nor by any unlooked-for chance — such as he had to suppose if he could step far enough out of line to deserve the punishments he thought he suffered. Had he stuck with this starting point (good = incorruptible), he would have seen the connection between evil and corruptibility on the one hand and, on the other, the fact that from the divine standpoint evil can have no existence. He could not do this because he still assumed that evil, like God, was a corporeal substance.

VII,v,7. Evil and matter — "And I was seeking the source of evil but I sought ill and did not see the evil in this very inquiry of mine."[33] What was this evil? It lay in his refusal to acknowledge that his own free will was itself the only cause of his evil deeds. This is shown by his efforts to discover a cause for his evil will. In trying to understand why he suffered in a universe which was made by God he turned to his false conception of the relation between God and the world (the sea and the sponge). Where could evil come from? Nowhere, it seemed. God was good and what he created was good. Then maybe there was no such thing as evil? But this could not be. If evil were supposed not to exist,

> Why then do we fear and beware of that which is not? If we fear on no account this fear itself is evil, this fear by which the heart is tormented and distressed for no cause: and so much the greater is the evil as that which we fear is not and yet we fear it. Therefore either there is evil which we fear or this is evil, that we fear.[34]

Evil was real, it could not come from God or the devil — understood as an angel of God gone wrong — nor could it come from the separated principle of the Manichees which was excluded by his supposition that God was incorruptible. Augustine still refused to think that its ultimate source lay in himself which meant that the only remaining place to look for its cause lay in matter — in the sponge — which he thought of as other than God but controlled by him. So he asked, "Was it that the matter out of which God made the good creation was somehow evil and that he formed and ordered it but left some evil in it which he did not turn to good?"[35] But why would God do this? Did he not have the power to turn it all to the good? Of course he did if he was omnipotent. Or again, if the matter was evil why did God not annihilate it altogether and simply be alone? Could it exist against his will? No. Again, if one supposed that it was somehow good that the finite should exist as well as God, why did he not first destroy the evil matter and then make some good so that there would be no evil in his creation? Augustine had no answer.

Given the presupposition that evil is a corporeal entity and that its ultimate source did not lie in his own free will — when this is taken along with his certainty that God must be thought of as incorruptible and omnipotent — there are no possible answers to such questions and Augustine did not find any. "Such things I turned over and over in my wretched breast which was filled with the most biting cares by the fear of death and by the fact that I could not find the truth."[36] The sponge theory of the concrete relation of God and nature could not account for the reality of evil. Starting from this premise, Augustine found that he could only understand evil by making the corruptible, incorruptible (matter was somehow independent of God and resistant to his touch), or the incorruptible, corruptible (evil was somehow present to God and suffered by him just as it was by Augustine). He knew very well that neither of these could be true yet he could not think how things could be otherwise. His situation here — "while trying to raise the eye of my mind out of the deep I again fell back, and trying often, I fell back again and again." (VII,iii,5)[37] — is exactly the same as he experienced in his earlier efforts to fix his thoughts on God where he said, of the images of nature, that "scarcely had they been sent away when, *in the twinkling of an eye* (1 Cor. 15:32) behold, gathered together, they were back again and they pressed on my sight and clouded it over" (VII,i,1).[38]

Desperate for a knowledge of the truth, terrified that he might die before he found it, and not knowing where to turn, Augustine found his situation intolerable. The faith of the Catholic church, its belief that Christ was the way to the truth and salvation, became "daily"[39] more attractive. Yet still he refused to give his assent to Catholicism until he knew for certain whether it was true or not. He had not yet found a way beyond his scepticism.[40]

VII,vi,8-10. Firminus' story and the refutation of astrology

The proof that astrology was no science follows directly out of the questions of the previous chapter, where Augustine asked whether the origin of his evil will could be attributed to matter. At the time he could find no answer to this question but his certainty that his own will was free ruled out the astrologer's claim that human affairs were determined by external and material causes such as the motion of the stars. He had already pretty well come to this conclusion; he tells us that even before his meeting with Firminus he was "almost" (VII,vi,8)[41] persuaded that the claims of astrology were vain and ridiculous. The episode with Firminus made this explicit.

We recall (from IV,iii,4) that Augustine had become interested in astrology almost as soon as he had fallen in with the Manichees. At the time, in North Africa, the kindly old proconsul Vindicianus (now mentioned by name) and Augustine's friend Nebridius had both argued that any success which the astrologers had was due solely to chance and was not the result of any skill or knowledge.[42] Augustine had been unmoved in Carthage because,

> I had as yet found no irrefutable argument such as I sought by which I could know, without ambiguity, whether the things that they truly said in their predictions happened by luck or lot rather than by the art of observing the stars as they claimed. (IV,iii,6)[43]

Augustine's interest in astrology evidently continued through the whole intervening period since we find him here being consulted by his friend Firminus, who has asked him to cast his horoscope even though Augustine himself was by now openly sceptical about the whole business. To counter Augustine's doubts, Firminus "providentially" (VII,vi,8)[44] told Augustine a story which he had heard from his father, an avid believer in astrology. Firminus himself did not see how far the story served to overthrow the pretension that astrology was a science but Augustine saw it immediately. The story concerned what Firminus evidently considered to be an amazingly correct foretelling of the fortunes of two children (himself and the child of one of his father's friend's servants) who were born in the same instant but whose fortunes — one good, the other mean — turned out just as predicted.[45] Here, for Augustine, was an irrefutable proof which he could now at last appreciate. If the actual course of events had been truly foretold then the contrary fortunes of the two children would have been ascribed to the same constellation of stars — and it was clearly no knowledge which ascribed differing effects to the same efficient cause.

But even if Firminus had got the story wrong, Augustine reflected that it would still be true in the case of twins — like the biblical Jacob and Esau — whose careers were opposite. In such situations, where the time difference between the births was inconsequential in the charts of the astrologers, the different fortunes had to be attributed to the same constellation. Any astrologer who foretold these differences truly could not therefore have done so from his knowledge of the effects of the stars — which were the same for both — but must have done so from his knowledge of worldly things such as the rich and noble family of Firminus and the mean and poor family of the slave. This meant that the astrologers' pretension to any kind of science was "vain and ridiculous" (VII,vi,8).[46]

Firminus' story contained nothing very extraordinary and the fact that Augustine himself sharpened its point by the consideration of twins should lead us to ask why he had not been able to come to this conclusion earlier. The answer is the same — from the other side — as in his discovery that the Manichees could not possibly have a knowledge of God. By itself the story did not rule out the possibility that astrology was a science. We see this clearly in Firminus himself who told it to shore up Augustine's wavering belief and who was apparently unmoved by Augustine's attempts to explain its significance.[47]

Such a case would not disprove that astrology was a science if one assumed that our will was actually governed by some external necessity. On this hypothesis a successful prediction — especially in the most difficult case of simultaneous births — could be seen as an evidence of the astrologer's very great skill, while an unsuccessful one would simply be attributed to the "imperfection of the art" (VII,vi,9).[48] This was the state in which Augustine had been for years. What was needed to move beyond this uncertainty was to abandon the assumption which made it possible. Augustine had been moved to do so by his desire for a certain knowledge of God. As he now saw this carried with it the necessity that if God could be known then he must be incorruptible, and if incorruptible then he could not be thought to suffer evil from some separated principle nor to be its ultimate author — which would be the case if human affairs were determined by some necessity in the stars which God had created.[49] As soon as the will was recognized as free, the force of the contradiction in Firminus' story could be seen as a certain proof that astrology was no science. This is just what happened to Augustine and from these considerations he says that he

> concluded very certainly that whatsoever things were said truly from the consideration of the constellations were not said by art but by chance, and what things were said falsely were not false because of the imperfection of the art, but from the uncertainty of chance. (VII,vi,9)[50]

VII,vii,11. A summary of Augustine's problems

Although Augustine was sure that the cause of his evil deeds could not lie in matter — and on this account he had been freed from astrology — he was still quite unable to find any answer to his questions about the origin of evil: "and I sought the cause of evil but there was no solution."[51] His torment was intense. This was not a question which he could lay aside to examine at some later date. Until he found an answer he knew he did not know the truth, while at the same time he feared that at any instant he might die and he was not at all confident that if this happened it would go well with him.[52]

He repeats here what he has said several times before. The heart of the problem lay in his inability to think of anything real or substantial which was not a body. He was shown how this led him on the one side to imagine God as a body and, on the other, to his futile efforts to understand evil in terms of matter. In all of this his attention was only directed outwards to sensible objects while his intelligence itself, that asked such questions about the immutable good, completely escaped his notice. And yet, as he has already pointed out, the very thought by which he sought these things certainly existed and was not nothing even though it was not a body in space.

> Thus my thought[53] was very gross. It could not even see its own self and whatever was not stretched out, or diffused, or brought together, or lumped up through a certain amount of space, or which did not take on such a form, or could not take on such a form, I judged to be altogether nothing. Such forms as my eyes were accustomed to go over were the images my mind ranged through nor did I see that this same thought[54] which itself formed these very images was

not something like them [a corporeal substance] and yet it could not have formed them unless it were some great thing. (VII,i,2)[55]

Here he repeats this point which, once he had recognized it, would be instrumental in bringing him to the certain knowledge of God.

> [T]he light of my eyes was not my own (Ps. 37:11). For that light was inward but I however outside, nor was it in a place. But the whole of my intention was directed towards those things that are in places and there I did not find anywhere to rest nor did the things in places so receive me that I was moved to say, "This is enough and this is good," neither did they let me turn to where, for me, "enough" would have been "good." For to those things I was superior while to you, inferior."[56]

There is only one possible resolution to this problem — the discovery of intelligible being. Augustine was only a step away from it, which is why he has said that God's hand was "even at that moment" (VI,xvi,26)[57] poised to snatch him from the pit though he did not know it.

He concludes the treatment of his sceptical period by insisting that his difficulties stemmed from the same source he has already shown to be the cause of both previous false conceptions of God (i.e., after the theft of pears and in Manichaeism). At bottom all three errors arose from his pride which blinded him to the truth. So long as he refused to relinquish the arrogant aim of grasping the truth immediately and directly so that he could put it to the service of his private ends, he was bound to conceive of God as a corporeal substance. The truth would thus be something to which his mind was superior and which he could consequently manipulate and dominate while at the same time he would be free from any subordination or service owed to it.

But the truth was not corporeal and all his insistence would not make it so. All he accomplished was to render himself unable to see it. He closes this section by recalling an image he had already used in II,iii,8. He ascribes his blindness to an improper attention to the sensible which pampered the fleshly man (by which he understands both the body and the mind that thinks only in bodily categories) and, as it were, puffed up the skin of his cheeks until his sight was blocked — or, as we could also say, which prevented his rational powers from attaining their proper end. He says: "And these things grew out of my wound (vulnere) because you have humiliated the proud like a wounded man (Ps. 2:11), and by my tumor (tumor) I was separated from you and by a great swelling of the face my eyes were closed."[58]

II. VII,viii,12-VII,xvi,22. The vision of God

VII,viii,12. Divine mercy

Nothing moved Augustine towards the truth so much as the misery of his inability to find it as long as he held on to the false premise that God was corporeal.

> You indeed, O Lord, remain in eternity (Eccl. 18:1) and in eternity you are not angry with us (Ps. 84:6, see Eccl. 17:31) because you had mercy on what was dust and ashes[59] and in your sight (Ps. 18:15) it was pleasing [to you] to reform my deformities. And by internal torments you drove me on so that I might not be able to bear it until you were certain to me through an interior sight. And my

tumor subsided under the secret hand of your doctoring and that troubled and
darkened sight of my mind was healed from *day to day* (Ps. 60:9) by the burning ointment of health-giving griefs.[60]

VII,ix,13-15. The Books of the Platonists

In the final chapter before he describes the vision of the truth, Augustine makes
the famous reference to the "books of the Platonists" — the *libri Platonicorum*
(VII,ix,13) — by which he was "admonished" (VII,x,16)[61] to turn inwards and
away from the sensible and was thus assisted to come at last to the vision of the
truth.

Modern scholars have produced an immense literature aimed at discovering
precisely what books of which Platonists Augustine read, and to determine what
he took from them by showing possible correspondences between passages in the
Confessions and this or that Platonist source.[62] Whatever particular source or
sources have been promoted, almost all are agreed that by the "books of the Platonists" Augustine intended certain Neo-Platonic works, either of Plotinus himself or of one or another of his disciples, imitators or translators.[63]

We shall not involve ourselves in the discussion. For the purpose at hand this
search for Augustine's sources is unnecessary. In order to understand the argument of the *Confessions*, Augustine himself did not think it necessary for the
reader to know the authors or the precise content of these works. Not only does he
refuse to refer to them by name — which he could easily have done[64] — but he
finds it perfectly adequate to describe their content solely in terms of the same
teachings which are contained in the Scriptures. Moreover, the effort to locate his
sources can be very misleading because it is just this method of working from
clues in Augustine to the discovery of his sources and thence back to Augustine
that has led to strained interpretations, as Augustine's works are forced to conform
with the source that is presumed to explain them. This, I believe, is a difficulty
with the Neo-Platonizing defenders of the historicity of the *Confessions*, whose
chief proponent is Pierre Courcelle.

Augustine could have come to the vision of the truth from an understanding of
any number of ancient texts (Platonic, Aristotelian, Neo-Platonic or, as he himself
makes clear, from an understanding of either the Old or the New Testament).[65] It
is a vision which is in principle available to all mankind. In the *City of God*
(VIII,9), he allows that all people can acquire this knowledge by the exercise of
their rational powers and he cites — moving roughly around the Mediterranean —
the wise men from the Libyans of the Atlas, Egyptians, Indians, Persians, Chalde-
ans, Scythians, Gauls, and Spaniards as examples of those who are reputed to have
come to it. We shall not therefore attempt to determine which texts Augustine read
but rather — confining ourselves to the argument of the *Confessions* where everything needed is present — bring this whole long process of coming to the certain
knowledge of God to its proper end by coming ourselves to see the same truth
which Augustine saw. To do this we must follow him as closely as possible.

To begin, we must take note that he prefaces his remarks about the books of the
Platonists by insisting that while they do contain a true and certain knowledge of
God they nevertheless belong wholly to the world of human pride.

And so, first wishing to show me how *you resist the proud and give grace to the humble* (1 Ptr. 5:5 and Jas. 4:6), and with what great mercy you have shown to men the way of humility, that *your Word was made flesh and dwelt* (Jn. 1:14) amongst men, you procured for me through a certain man inflated with monstrous pride[66] certain books of the Platonists translated from the Greek tongue into Latin. (VII,ix,13)[67]

Augustine insists from the first that while the Platonists do have the true idea of God, this idea, taken by itself, merely serves human pride. He will subsequently show that even their true and certain knowledge could not possibly put him in a proper relation to God if he would not also humble himself by believing in Christ as the way to God. This is the point of the chapter's repeated antiphony between the things he read in these books — i.e., the true knowledge of the eternal Word or Wisdom of God — and the things he did not read there — i.e., that the same eternal Word was also incarnate in time and is the only way by which we can come to God. He places this antithesis before us at the very beginning of his discussion and we must recognize it from the outset if we are to understand the distinction which he draws between Platonism and Christianity, between pride and humility, between presumption and confession.

At the end of chapter vii[68] Augustine had distinguished between (*i*) the fundamental "wound" (original sin) by which he was separated from God as a result of his nature in which reason and nature were at odds, and (*ii*) coming from this, but distinguished from it, the "tumor" (the local swelling of his face which blocked his sight) that grew out of his efforts to pamper the flesh by insisting on a corporeal, sensible God. The Platonists were able to cure the latter swelling inasmuch as they led him to recognize intelligible substance from which he came to the certain knowledge of God. But the original and deep-seated wound remained untouched. And, on account of it, he continued to be separated from the God whom the Platonists would teach him to know. In time he was to discover that this wound — his pride — could not possibly be cured by the Platonists because they refused the way of the Word made flesh.[69] Here he merely states what he found and what he did not find in the books of the Platonists. And what he did not find was any mention of the Incarnation.

Augustine holds that it was providential that he did not come to look to Christianity as a cure for his wound until after he had come to the vision of the truth. In this way he came to know and experience the inadequacies of the vision by suffering the consequences of the pride which the Platonist knowledge does not cure but rather aggravates.[70] It was therefore through the inadequacies of the Platonists, and not by their teachings, that he finally came to Christianity.

VII,x,16. The vision of God

What Augustine took from the teaching of these books can be simply stated. He was already sure that if he was to have a certain knowledge of God then God must be incorruptible, inviolable, and immutable. Now "having been admonished by the books of the Platonists, I returned to myself and I entered into my inner being, led by you [God]."[71] On the advice of the books of the Platonists he turned the attention of his mind away from sensible bodies and inward towards his thought itself. He asked himself about the mind or intelligence which knew that if it could know God then God must be thought of as incorruptible. How did he know this? What was the ground of his certainty that this was true? His attention was finally directed towards his intelligence itself, which had the idea of an infinite, universal, and incorruptible good as the proper object of a certain knowledge. Here at last, as he now saw, in the certainty of this thought itself, was something which was real but which was not a body in space. From this moment everything fell swiftly into place.[72]

Augustine was forced to turn upwards from his own mind in looking for the incorruptible principle of both the corporeal universe and what he now saw as the incorporeal reality of his own thinking, neither of which he had made. There was nothing else to do: he had exhausted every other possibility. His thought itself could not be the immutable principle because, as he had long recognized, it, like all else in creation, was mutable. Already in the fourth book he had remarked that "this was manifest to me because I desired to become wise, that out of a worse condition I might become better" (IV,xv,26).[73] From this point it followed of necessity that if God was to be thought of as incorruptible, inviolable, and immutable, then he must also be incorporeal. Otherwise he would not be the immutable creator — not only of corporeal reality — but also of what Augustine now saw as his own mutable but incorporeal intelligence.

> I entered and I saw with the eye of my soul — such as it was — above this eye of my soul, above my intelligence, the immutable light: [it was] not this ordinary light which is visible to all flesh, nor a sort of light of the same kind which was greater, as if this ordinary light were to shine much more brightly and filled all with its greatness.[74] No, it was not thus but other, altogether other than any such light. Nor was it above my mind as oil floats on water nor as the heaven is above the earth [i.e., by place], but it was superior because it made me and I was inferior because I was made by it. Whoever knows the truth knows this light and he who knows this light knows eternity.[75]

Here at last was the true idea of God which Augustine had so long been seeking. He had been converted to Platonism. He is clear that this was no mere belief but a certain knowledge about which it was impossible to be mistaken. He says that he could not doubt that God was thus (incorruptible and intelligible) and that he existed.

Why is this so? It can perhaps seem that the whole argument to this point is merely hypothetical and that Augustine has not shown any necessary connection between what we must think about God, if we are to have a certain knowledge of him, and the actual existence of such a God. But this is not the case. It is true that Augustine started from the hypothesis that *if* he could have a certain knowledge of God, then God would have to be thought of as incorruptible. From this he went on to recognize that if God were the incorruptible creator of corruptible nature — both corporeal and intelligible — then he would have to be thought of as intelligible being: otherwise Augustine would fall back into the insoluble problems of the first section of this book. We might object that this does not prove that such a God exists. It only shows that he must be so if we are to know him, and if there is to be an answer to the problem of evil. This is true, but it is not all the truth. It is not the case that the requirements of human thought impose any necessity on God — as if the demand that God must be thus if we are to know him compelled such a God to exist. But, on the other hand, these requirements of our thought do impose an absolute necessity on the mind which has come to understand them. They demand that it recognize the objective existence of such a God.

Since it is true that for us a certain knowledge of the truth is only possible if the truth is incorruptible and intelligible, the objective existence of such a principle is established beyond any possible doubt in the moment that both these conditions are recognized – because our thought itself exists subject to these limitations. Unless this principle existed *above* our thought there would be no such limitation on it. If the limitations were certain and objective, as Augustine knew they were, then such a God must certainly exist. The hypothesis with which the argument began therefore dissolves into the certain and true knowledge of God's existence in the same instant that Augustine recognized the necessity that God be thought of as both incorruptible and intelligible. This is exactly what he says.

> ... and I said,
> "Is truth then nothing at all
> Since it is not diffused through finite or infinite spaces of places?" [i.e., since it cannot be thought of as corporeal].
> And you called out from far off:
> "Verily indeed, *I AM THAT IS*" (Ex. 3:14) [i.e., the only perfectly real existent is the immutable, intelligible being of God].
> And I heard, as one hears in the heart[76]
> And indeed there was *absolutely no ground whence I might doubt* [emphasis mine]:
> Indeed, I might more easily have doubted that I lived than that the truth was not,
> Which is seen *having been understood through those things which have been made* (Rom. 1:20).[77]

The existence of the incorporeal and incorruptible God as the absolute principle, or Creator, of the corruptible universe – both corporeal and incorporeal – was thus established beyond doubt through the existence of the world. Once seen, the existence of this first principle can only be called into question by doubting the existence of the creatures through which it was revealed. But, as he says, this was impossible: to do so would have required him to doubt his own existence as a finite intelligence. This was excluded by the law of non-contradiction and God's existence was therefore established beyond any possibility of error.

With this conclusion we see that the hypothesis has moved, as it were, to the other side. God's existence turns out to be the only thing we can know with an absolute certainty because God is the only object of our intelligence in which thought and being are necessarily united. God is no longer assumed but known. On the other hand the whole of the created order in time and space, whose existence and intelligibility have no necessary connection for us, turn out to be not known but only assumed – these things exist and we sense them or think about them but we do not know them as having to be.

For Augustine this was not a proof for the existence of God in the medieval or modern sense of the word. He never speaks of it as anything other than a vision or knowledge of the truth. If, in his own image, we think of God as a distant but now visible city (see VII,xxi,27), we see that what he has done in the *Confessions* is to

describe the path he took from the time of his birth, somewhere in the midst of
what he imagines as a dark forest, to the point when he finally came out in a clearing on a "wooded hilltop" (VII,xxi,27)[78] and saw the City of God in the distance.
To anyone still caught in the forest, the account of Augustine's vision will not be a
proof for God's existence — transporting him instantly to the clearing and to the
knowledge of God. To such a one the story of Augustine's journey will only
appear as a traveller's tale which he may either believe in or not. We can therefore
say that while the demonstration of God's existence was indubitable for Augustine, it is not an indubitable demonstration unless we have followed him every step
of the way. But this does not mean that his knowledge of God was peculiar to
himself — a private vision he attained through some special revelation in such a
way that he was unable to explain the road which led him to it. Throughout the
Confessions he has at every point explained where he was and how he got there.
He has done this in such a way that we can all follow the path he marked from the
depths of the forest at his birth to the sight of the city. Of course not everyone will
make this journey, nor is it necessary that all do since we can be related to the
same God through belief. In principle however every one of us can do as he did. In
this sense the certain knowledge of God is a knowledge that all can possess since it
is derived from our rational powers and "is seen, *having been understood through
those things which have been made* (Rom. 1:20)." As these are the same for all of
us, as are the laws by which our thought is governed, all can follow where Augustine went.

But although this knowledge of God was certain it did not, in itself, reveal anything about God's inner nature. The city was seen but only at a great distance and
from without. This contrast between the existence of God, which is known in the
vision, and the inner nature of God which is not or, to put it another way, the contrast between the vision of the outside of the city seen at a great distance and from
another country, and the inner life of that city experienced from within, is the
sense of this passage in which Augustine says:

> You are my God.
> For you I long *day and night* (Ps. 42:2).
> And when I first came to know you
> You raised me up so that I might see
> That what I was seeing exists
> And also that I was not yet
> One who might know it [i.e., as my home].
> And you beat back the weakness of my sight
> Shining with tremendous force on me
> And I shook all over with fear and dread.[79]

Between Augustine and the city was an impassable gulf. It was not, so to speak,
contiguous in a bodily sense with the hill on which he stood. There was no road or
connection, from the side of the sensible world where he stood, to the city in the
distance because that city was intelligible rather than sensible. He saw it with the
"eye of my mind"[80] rather than with the eyes of his flesh. This is what he means
when he says that it was above his mind not in space or place but in kind[81] or,
again, when he says "I found myself to be far away from you in a place of a dissimilar kind."[82] He has much more to say about these things but first he draws

out the corollaries of this knowledge with respect to the relation of God and the world.

VII,xi,17 — VII,xvi,22. The true relation of God and world

VII,xi,17— The previously insoluble problem of evil found its resolution as soon as Augustine had seen the immutable and intelligible God as the primary reality. This was the cause both of the sensible being he had formerly taken as the only reality and of his own mutable intelligence which he now recognized and knew to be other than the sensible (because intelligible) and other than God (because mutable). On the one hand, Augustine saw that the true reality of all mutable creation — both matter and mind — was its intelligibility — its likeness to God who alone was really real. On the other hand, so far as creation was mutable, corruptible, and violable it was unlike its principle and unreal.

> And I looked closely at the rest of things below you and I saw that they neither are absolutely nor are they absolutely not. They are indeed because they are from you, however they are not because that which you are they are not. For that truly is which remains unchangeably. *For me then to inhere with God is the good* (Ps. 72:28), since if I will not remain in him neither will I be able to remain in myself [since I am not unchangeable]. He however *remaining in himself renews all things* (Wis. 7:22) and *you are my Lord since you do not need my goods.* (Ps. 15:2).[83]

VII,xii,18-VII,xiii,19— From this it followed that in the entire universe all that is, is good. Consequently, evil could not be a substance as he had formerly assumed. In the light of the vision it could have no substantial independent being since all that is, so far as it is, is good. Evil therefore had to be thought of as depending on a prior good of which it was the corruption. It could not exist for God nor for creation as a whole. It could only exist for man and for other intelligent creatures who can both know the absolute good (God) and will some lesser (created) good.

VII,xiv,20 — In comparison with this "more sane" (VII,xiii,19)[84] judgement, Augustine now reviews the three stages of error through which he had passed on the way to the vision of the truth. These correspond, as it were, to three distinct levels of the forest through which everyone will go who makes the ascent to the vision of God, although not everyone will make the complete journey. Some live their entire lives in one or another of these errors, and others who never come to the knowledge of God — who never reach a clearing from which the truth can be seen — may still hold on to the same God through belief.[85] Augustine says:

> *There is no sound reason* (Ps. 37:4 and 8) in those to whom some part or other of your creature is displeasing, just as there was none in me when many of the things which you have made were displeasing. And because my soul did not dare to allow that my God should be displeasing to it, it would not allow that anything which was displeasing to it should be yours [Augustine's first wrong idea of God: the error from birth to the moment before Manichaeism, epitomized in the theft of pears]. And from there my soul had gone to the opinion of the two substances but it found no rest and was raving [second error: Manichaean dualism]. And coming back from there it made for itself a God spread

throughout the infinite spaces of all places and him it had supposed to be you and him it had set up in its own heart and again it had become a temple of its own idol, abominable to you [third error: the God of his sceptical period]. But after that you ministered to the needs of my head unbeknownst to me and you closed *my eyes so that they might not see vanity* (Ps. 118:3) and I rested from myself somewhat and my insanity was put to sleep. And I awoke in you and saw you to be infinite in another way (*aliter*) and this vision was not derived from the flesh.[86]

VII,xv,21-VII,xvi,22 — In these last chapters Augustine draws out the nature of the difference between the substance of creation and the substance of God. The finite sponge in the infinite sea was false. It was not the case that God was an infinite corporeal body. Rather, all creation was thought to be in God insofar as it was intelligible. Everything in the universe was present in God but the manner of the existence of created things "in" God differed (*aliter* — last sentence of VII,xiv,20, and again in the first sentence of VII,xv,21) from the manner of their existence "outside" God where creation exists under the conditions of space, time, and motion. These three are themselves created by God since they depend on the abiding reality of the divine principle to connect their various moments — but God's substance is other than that of creation in that it is not subject to time, space, or change. Creation thus exists in two forms: as the eternal, immutable, and intelligible reasons of things in the Word of God — and also mutably, in time and space, as finite individuals.[87] The former are the ground and cause of the latter.

In this distinction, Augustine found the true explanation of evil. So far as things are in God there is no evil. Everything is as it ought to be and cannot be otherwise. So far as things exist outside God in time and space, where they are mutable and can turn to or away from him, evil appears for and through intelligent creatures in any voluntary turning from the highest good to a lower (i.e., created) good. For God there is only good. For created intelligences, capable of voluntary actions there are, of necessity, both good and evil. Common experience showed Augustine that the point of view made all the difference. The same bread which was good to the healthy palate seemed evil to a sick one. The bread was not different, the difference lay in the subject.

> And I looked back at the other things [i.e., the whole universe other than God] and I saw that they owe to you that they are and that in you are all finite things together, but differently (*sed aliter*), not as if in a place but because you are holding them all in hand in the truth, and all things are true insofar as they are, neither is falsehood anything except when it is thought that something is what it is not. And I saw that they do agree, not only each to their own places but also to their times, and that you, who alone are eternal, did not begin to work after innumerable spaces of time, because all spaces of times, both those which have passed by and those which are yet to come, would neither go nor come except by your working and remaining. (VII,xiv,21)[88]

> And I knew by experience that it is not to be wondered at that bread is offensive to the distempered palate which bread is pleasant to the sound one, and that light is odious to sore eyes which light is amiable to clear eyes. Even so does your justice displease the iniquitous, as do the viper and little vermin which things you have created good and fit for the lower parts of your creature to

which the iniquitous themselves are fit insofar as they are dissimilar to you, though fit also to the higher parts inasmuch as they can come to be similar to you. And I sought out what iniquity might be, and I did not find any substance, but a turning from the highest substance, you O God, into lower things, a perversity of the will throwing away its *inner parts* (Eccl. 10:10) while swelling up outwardly. (VII,xv,22)[89]

All this Augustine took from the Platonists, and all this Platonism shares with Christianity. Beyond this however the two positions have nothing in common, as he was soon to discover.

III. VII,xvii,23-VII,xxi,27. After the vision. The necessity of a Mediator

The final chapters of this book are very important for understanding Augustine's argument. In them he shows the failure of this vision in its own terms — that is, its failure to put its possessor in a right relation to the truth known. They establish the difference between Christianity and Platonism (or, more generally, the true knowledge of God to which the natural man can arrive). Augustine does this by showing the inadequacy of the vision of the truth and the manner in which this limitation is overcome in Christ and in Christ alone.

VII,xvii,23. The habit of the flesh

Augustine had come to a certain and unmistakeable knowledge of God but he immediately found himself faced with a problem which he describes in this way:

> And I was astonished that although I now loved you and not a phantasm instead of you, I did not remain in the enjoyment of my God but while on the one hand I was being ravished to you by your beauty, on the other hand I was soon ripped away from you by my weight and I fell down into these lower things with groaning. And this weight was the habit of the flesh. But with me was the memory of your and I was not in any way doubting that there existed one to whom I should cohere (*cohaero*) but that I was not yet a one who might do so: for *the body which is corrupted weighs down the soul and the earthly habitation presses down the mind with many thoughts* (Wis. 9:15).[90]

Armed with the memory of his vision Augustine recollected the various considerations by which he had ascended to the knowledge of the truth in the first place. But the memory of the vision was not the same thing as the vision itself, any more than the scent of food was the same as food itself. He concludes the chapter with the lament he had already raised in chapter x. Here he says:

> Then indeed [i.e., in the vision] I saw your *invisible parts which have been understood through those things which have been made* (Rom. 1:20)[91] but I did not have the strength to keep my gaze on them and, my weakness being beaten back, I was returned to my usual thoughts carrying with me nothing but a memory of things to be loved and the scent, as it were, of things desired which I was not yet able to savour.[92]

The problem with this vision was just that it was only a vision. In itself, his new knowledge did not give Augustine the power to "adhere to" (*cohaero*) God — which is where he wanted to be. It only brought to light his separation from God with the utmost clarity. This can be understood in two ways.

On the one hand, considered as a knowledge possessed by a subject, the vision merely illuminated the absolute distinction between Augustine, the concrete individual who possessed the vision, and the divine principle which was the object of his knowledge. He was not the object which he knew: he was not God. Thus he says, of the moment after he had come to the vision, that he found that he was far away from God "in a reign of utter unlikeness" (VII,x,16).[93] In the vision all particular things are known as being in God — yet they are seen to be there apart from the categories of time, space, and motion. This is the sense of the *aliter* of VII,xiv,20 and VII,xv,21. But the person who has the vision is a particular mutable individual existing in time and space and as such has no part in the all-encompassing harmony and unity seen in God. In other words Augustine, the particular individual, who began to look for Wisdom because he wanted its completeness in preference to the fleeting goods of this world, now discovered that he was utterly unlike the absolute good he both knew and desired. This left him with nothing but the certain knowledge of his separation from God and the recognition that the world was no adequate resting-place for his soul because it was not the absolute good. He was part of the changeable, divided world of time and space while God, beyond time and space, was unchangeably whole — and there was nothing Augustine could do to overcome the division.

On the other hand, the individual who has risen to a thinking activity and actually enjoys the vision of God is, *qua* knower, in a unity with God. But here again the same problem reappeared from the other side. For the individual who is actually knowing God is not simply this activity but is also a rational *animal*. He may rise to the vision of God after much effort but he cannot long stay in this state because he is an animal also. The "habit of the flesh" — hunger, fatigue, the distraction of a mosquito bite, the need to relieve oneself, etc. — soon asserts itself. Such demands, which cannot long be ignored, are the weight by which we are ripped away from the intellectual activity of contemplation and turned again to our involvement in the world. The actual vision — as distinct from the mere memory of it — can be regained. But only at the cost of the same great labour by which it was generated in the first place — and this requires circumstances (freedom from interference, provision of external necessities, health, etc.) which nature and human society only rarely provide, and then to but a few, and which in any case can last for only a moment which we are powerless to prolong.[94]

These are the necessary and inevitable consequences of this knowledge. Augustine's problem was to find a solution to this difficulty and he did not find it in any of the forms of antiquity. The Neo-Platonic philosopher, Plotinus, faced with the same situation, sought to regain the vision as often as he could. He is reported by Porphyry, his disciple and biographer, to have achieved this end four times during the five years Porphyry was with him.[95] Augustine's response was very different.

VII,xviii,24. The need of a Mediator

Augustine did not attempt to regain the vision. The problem with this ecstatic knowledge was just that it was bound to be temporary. It was inevitable that the "habit of the flesh" would tear him away after a brief moment and force him to return with groaning to this world which could only offer its divided and partial goods. No matter how often he might return to the vision such a programme offered no solution to his desire to be united with the absolute good beyond any possibility of falling away from it.

In his own words what he needed was to get from where he was to the God he knew, to the glorious city he had seen in the distance. And for this he had to find "a way" (via),[96] a road, some form of mediation to unite himself — as a mutable being who knew the immutability of the good — and the immutable good itself. There was no longer any question about where he should go: he had found God and had thus, in a certain sense, completed the first of the tasks, outlined in III,iv,8 after the *Hortensius* had enflamed him with the desire for Wisdom. His whole problem now was to find a way and the strength to actually get there. He needed to find a road he could "follow up to" (III,iv,8)[97] the God he knew. "And I looked for a way which would provide the strength that was necessary in order that I might be with you."[98]

If it turned out that there was no such way then he would have to settle for a life — or a series of lives (as Plato and Vergil taught)[99] — lived wholly within the conditions of creation in which, at the very best, he could hope for a limited number of ecstatic visions. But Augustine had no proof that this was the case nor was he prepared to assume that it was. What he did know, because it was revealed in the vision, was that he was quite unable to unite himself with God by his own power since his nature as a mutable creature was precisely what separated him from the immutable God. He therefore began to look about for a mediator. In retrospect he says that he was prevented by his pride from finding the true and only way which was before him. "For I was not humble enough to hold to my God, the humble Jesus, and I did not know what his weakness was meant to teach."[100] The result was that he did not at once find what he was looking for — "I could not find [the way to God] until I embraced *the mediator between God and man, the man Jesus Christ* (1 Tim. 2:5)"[101] — and he refused to embrace Christ because he saw only a man.

VII,xix,25. The false mediators of Platonism

Augustine has not yet shown why Christ is the only solution to this impasse. The proof will come at the end of this book. What he does first is to show why he could not see this at the time. It was because the idea of Christ which he then held was incapable of providing the necessary mediation. When he thought of Christ he did not think of him in terms of the orthodox definition of Nicaea but in an Arian manner.[102] It was not that he was an Arian but rather that he supposed that the church thought of Christ in an essentially Arian sense — and he knew this was inadequate to the mediation he desired. "What mystery there was in the *Word made flesh* (Jn. 1:14), of this I was not able to form even the slightest idea."[103]

That is, he did not know that the church taught that Christ was himself God or, in words of the Nicene formula, "of the same substance as God." As a result Augustine assumed that Christ was simply a creature and as such he knew that he could not be the mediator who united God and creation.

Starting from his sure knowledge of the immutability of the divine Word he supposed, when the church said that the eternal and immutable Word of God was united with the flesh of the man Jesus, that this could not have happened in such a way that the eternal Wisdom of God had, as it were, replaced either the human soul or both the soul and mind of Jesus. In this case the mutable activities of Christ's life would be inexplicable.

> This much I was certain of from those things which were written about Christ
> and passed down to us, namely, that he ate and drank, slept, walked about, was
> glad and sad. I was certain that the flesh was not joined to your Word without a
> human soul and mind. Everyone knows this who knows the immutability of
> your Word which I now knew as far as I was able to, nor was there any way
> whatsoever in which I could doubt it.[104]

It was perfectly clear to Augustine that Christ possessed a mutable mind and soul if the Scriptural account of his life was true. To eat and sleep, to walk here and there, to rejoice and to be sad were clearly "properties of a soul and mind that can change."[105] From this it followed that Christ must have been a "perfect [i.e., total, whole, complete] man."[106] He clearly was "not the body of a man only, or with the body a soul without a mind,"[107] as if the eternal Word had replaced either the human mind, or both the mind and soul in Christ.

Augustine therefore concluded, falsely, that the church must teach that because Christ was a complete man he was simply a creature. It seemed obvious that Christ could not possibly be the immutable Word of God since he was mutable like Augustine himself.

The only other alternative was to doubt the account of the Scriptural record, but Augustine saw no grounds for doing this. Ever since he had left the Manichees he had recognized the necessity of belief in certain situations and for certain people and he regarded the great authority which the Scriptures enjoyed the world over as strong evidence of their credibility.[108] Nothing in the Platonic vision changed any of this and so he refused to doubt what the Scriptures said about Christ because he would then have abandoned his only viable hope that God cared for us and had not left us on our own: "If the things which were written about Christ [that he ate, talked, walked, etc.] were false then all the rest would be in danger of being a lie nor in the rest of those writings would there remain any safeness of faith for humankind."[109]

But if the record was true and Christ did all the many things he was said to have done, then Augustine was sure that he must be a complete man. And therefore if the Scriptures venerated him it could only be because he "participated the divine wisdom more perfectly"[110] than any other creature and not because he was the immutable Wisdom of God.

> I only thought of Christ, my Lord, as a man of excellent wisdom to whom no
> one could be equal — chiefly because he was miraculously born of a virgin to
> give an example of how temporal things ought to be scorned in order to come to

immortality – and because of this divine care for us [i.e., because God had certified his spokesman by the miraculous virgin birth] his teachings seemed to have deserved their great authority.[111]

The point about the virgin birth is simply this. The Scriptures say that Christ was born of a virgin (Mt. 1:18 and 25, Lk. 1:26-38, etc.). This was perfectly possible to the God Augustine now knew. He who had created all things could certainly do this much if he had wanted to use this miraculous means of giving authority to Christ as his chosen spokesman – and Augustine was ready to grant that the teachings of Christ were the most divinely inspired account of how God wanted us to live in this world. But because Christ was simply a creature – albeit the wisest and best of men and the closest to God – there was nothing here which could help Augustine get from where he was to that far city, on another plane of existence, which he knew as his proper home. He was certain from the vision that it was impossible for any mutable creature to unite itself with the immutable God. If Christ were only a creature that he too would stand in need of the same mediation as Augustine required. This is exactly what he concluded.

> [This] complete man [Christ] I thought worthy of being preferred before all other men, not because he was the very person of the truth [i.e., the actual Wisdom of God], but because I saw in him a unique excellence of human nature and a more perfect participation of wisdom [i.e., than in any other man].[112]

In the idiom of the church this view, to which he came on his own, was essentially identical to the heretical position of Arius or, more exactly, to that of Photinus.[113] Yet Augustine was not a heretic of either sort as he never thought of worshipping this Christ by giving him the honour and glory that belonged to God alone.[114] Such a Christ might well "participate wisdom" more perfectly than any other man and on this account Augustine was prepared to think that his teachings should be "preferred before [those of] all other men," but he was not the "very person of the truth." Because of this Augustine concluded that he should not be worshipped as God, and also that the church did not possess the mediation he required.

In the last sentences of this chapter Augustine mentions the opposite, and equally false, view of Christ which Alypius held at the time and which he too, from his own standpoint, rejected as an inadequate mediator. This sounds again the counterpoint between their two careers. Alypius' chief problem was to know who was a trustworthy teacher to tell him what he should do. The very best guide was God himself. This is what he thought that the Catholic church claimed about Christ – i.e., that Christ was God in the flesh. But when he came to think how this could be, he supposed the church taught that "besides God and the flesh, there was not in Christ a human mind and soul."[115] As both Augustine and Alypius were to learn "later"[116] this was not how the church understood that God was present in human flesh – replacing, as it were, the mind and soul of the man Jesus with the divine Wisdom. This was the heretical view of Apollinarius.[117] But because Alypius supposed that this was what the church understood of Christ and because he also agreed – no doubt through Augustine's discussions on the point – that if what was recorded of Christ in the Scriptures were true then he would have to be a complete man with a rational mind and soul, he was forced to reject, as impossible, the claim of the church that Christ was God in the world.[118]

In time both were to recognize the falsity of their various assumptions and both were to come, from their different directions, to the same Christ of orthodox Catholicism. Augustine was to learn that although Christ was a complete man, the church also claimed that he was fully God: and Alypius was to discover that the church taught that he was fully God in spite of the fact that he was also a complete man.

VII,xx,26. The failure of Platonism: presumption and confession

A few weeks passed before Augustine turned to the New Testament to check his assumptions about Christianity — and discovered that they were quite false.[119] He judges that during this period he did not act as he should have and he regards this as a deadly fault which arose from his pride.)

> I carried on altogether as if I were highly expert and, had I not sought for your way in *Christ our Saviour* (Tit. 1:4) [i.e., had he not looked for, and found, the orthodox Catholic Christology], I should not have been skilled but killed.[120] For I had now begun to wish to seem wise and full of my own punishment I did not weep and, over and above this, I was puffed up with my knowledge.[121]

Augustine's insistence on the error of the same Platonism that had led him to the true knowledge of God may seem confusing but it is absolutely essential to understanding the radical difference he sees between Platonism and Christianity — a difference which is central to the logic of the remainder of the *Confessions*. Those scholars, like Courcelle, who have sought to defend the historicity of the text by showing the identity of Neo-Platonism and Christianity, have little to say about the substance of Augustine's teaching in these passages.[122] The reason for this silence is clear — given the thesis they are defending — but their one-sided emphasis on the identity leads us far from Augustine's complete teaching.

What then was the error of the Platonists and what was Augustine's relation to it? In this chapter he distinguishes between Platonism and Christianity as the difference between: "presumption and confession, between those who see where they ought to go but do not see how to get there, and the way leading to the blessed homeland which man was not only intended to look at but in which he was also intended to dwell."[123]

To understand this presumption we must return to two sections we earlier glossed over (VII,ix,14 and 15). There, having told what he read in the books of the Platonists and what he did not read there, he went on to speak of the failure of Platonism, which has two forms. Subjectively it consists in our pride at having come to the true knowledge of God (VII,ix,14). Objectively it consists in the worship of false — i.e., created — mediators (VII,ix,15).

We have already seen that Augustine rejected the objective error in his refusal to worship the (Arian/Photinian) Christ but it will be worthwhile to explain more fully what this means. In so doing we can see how his was a stricter and true Platonism than that of the books he was reading.

This error did not lie in the Platonists' knowledge. They had the true idea of God and Augustine had come to the same knowledge through their works. This he freely allows. The difficulty lay in what came after this knowledge — in how one reacted to it. As Augustine has shown in the preceding chapters (xvii-xix), the sole question after the vision is how we are to get to the city seen in the distance. Both Augustine and the Platonists knew for certain that a mediator was required, and both knew what a true mediator would look like since this was determined by the terms to be united — mutable creation and the immutable creator. The error of the Platonists was that the mediators they proposed were inadequate according to the logic of their own position, and in this their wisdom turned to folly.

In the *City of God* Augustine points out that "Plato is reported as saying 'Gods never mix with men.' "[124] Because the immutable God was known to be other than mutable creation, the Platonists looked to certain intermediary powers — half-way between man and God — to act as mediators who could lead us to God. They worshipped these things but, as Augustine knew and as the Platonists themselves must have known, such creatures could not possibly provide the necessary link. What was revealed in the knowledge of God was the absolute otherness of *all* creation from its creator. So far as these *daimones* were thought of as created beings, which they must be if they were to have any connection with us, they could not mediate between God and us because, as creatures, they themselves were in need of the same mediation we required. So far as they were one with God they could not "mix with men" and again could not be mediators. In the *City of God* Augustine gives a very thorough consideration of all the possible combinations of God and man such as he found in the Platonism of Apuleius (Bk. VIII) and Porphyry (Bk. X). In every case he comes to the same conclusion. The mediators recommended by the Platonists were inadequate according to the logic of Platonism itself.

In VII,ix,15, using the language of St. Paul's text in Romans (1:23), Augustine says that such Platonists had turned their wisdom into folly because they had exchanged the glory of the incorruptible God, as the proper object of their worship, for these corruptible creatures which were, so far as their capacity to mediate was concerned, simply fantastic products of their own imaginations. They ended up serving their own creations — in *"the likeness of the image of corruptible man and birds, quadrupeds and serpents* (Rom. 1:23)" (VII,xi,15)[125] — rather than the creator they knew. If we ask why they did this the answer is pride: a pride which refused to come to God if this could only be done through the humiliating dependence on a mediator who was not our creation and whom we must obey, and a pride which insisted that what was true for us was also true for God as if he were subject to the same limitations as we are — i.e., which claimed that because of the unlikeness between God and man it was not possible for *God* to join himself with his creation *because* it was not possible for us to join ourselves with him.

Augustine says, "I found these things there [i.e., in the books of the Platonists] but I did not eat of them" (VII,xi,15),[126] and "I had not given my mind" (VII,ix,15)[127] to them. We know this is true because he refused to worship the Photinian Christ — as an inadequate mediator who, although fully man, was not the "person of the truth" (VII,xix,25)[128] — yet he did not abandon the hope of finding an adequate way to God because nothing in the Platonic knowledge excluded the possibility that such a way could exist. The strict logic of the vision showed beyond doubt that it did not lie in the power of any mutable creature to come up to the immutable God. But while this was the truth for human thought, nothing showed that God was subject to the same limitations. Nothing ruled out the possibility that he could unite himself with his creation even though it was certain that creation could not unity itself with him — and Augustine was unwilling to make this assumption. In terms of the Platonic knowledge it was as unfounded and illogical to limit God in this way as it was, on the other side, to suppose that any being which was merely created could act as a mediator.

Nevertheless for a short while Augustine was trapped in nature without any way to God, until he discovered that what the church believed about Christ meant that he was the true mediator. During this time he continued to do the same as he had done since infancy. He attempted to use the universal — here in the form of his certain knowledge of God — for his own private ends, as an instrument to gain love, power, and glory for himself. This is the sense in which, from a subjective point of view, he succumbed to the vain pride of the Platonists by refusing to adopt a proper relation to the God he knew. He speaks of this proper attitude as "weeping," "charity," "humility," and "confession" — that is, the truthful recognition of his wretched condition as one who knew the absolute good yet was unable to achieve the good he knew. In Augustine's idiom this right relation was the position of the righteous men of the Old Testament — who were in the same situation as he, i.e., who knew God but did not know Christ as the mediator — and it is summed up for him in Job's words that *"wisdom is the fear of the Lord"* (Job 28:28).[129] At the time he wanted none of this. Instead, along with the Platonists and as illogically as they, he attempted to pervert the knowledge of God to his own selfish ends.

> For now I had begun to wish to appear wise and full of my own punishment I did not weep and over and above this I was puffed up with my knowledge. Where indeed was there that love which builds on the foundation of humility which is Jesus Christ? Or when could these books have taught this to me? Indeed I believe that you willed that I should come across these books before I considered your Scriptures in order that the effects which the books of the Platonists wrought in me would be imprinted on my mind so that when afterwards I was tamed by your books and my wound (*vulnera*) was touched by your curing fingers I might be able to discern and distinguish what a difference there was between presumption and confession.[130]

Having once seen the truth Augustine could never again mistake anything else for it — as he had in the various errors he had made about God on his way up to the vision. However, he now pretended to have a knowledge he did not possess by adopting the presumptuous "puffed-up" position that besides God he knew other things as well. His thoughts ran this way. He had actually been to the top of the hill and had seen God — which most have not — so if not through him (and other "wise" men like himself), then through whom could the truth be brought into the world? He knew that the "gods never mix with men" so who was better than a philosopher to tell the order of all things in the world and give them their rank and place? This is what he now presumed to do, and this was pure presumption.[131] The knowledge of these matters was not given in the Platonic vision which only shows the interrelation of all things as they are in the principle — i.e., apart from the conditions of this world. But Augustine refused to accept the logical conclusion that, as he did not know God's mind about the things of this world, he should live humbly in the avoidance of evil and in the fear of his inscrutable judgements. Instead, wanting to seem wise and to get some worldly advantage out of his knowledge, he now pretended that he knew how God regarded worldly things. In this form his fantasies, creations of his own imagination, once again made their appearance after the vision of the truth — though on this side they were mistaken for the truth of creation rather than for the truth about God.[132]

What prevented him from staying long with this presumption was that although he refused to weep for the iniquity which actually separated him from God, neither could he ignore it — for this was revealed in the vision with the same certainty that he knew about God. In VII,x,16 the same verb (*cognovi*) is used for both.

> When first I knew (*cognovi*) you, you lifted me up so I could see that what I was looking at [really] existed and that I, who saw, did not yet [really] exist. And you beat back the weakness of my sight shining most brightly on me . . . it was if I heard your voice from on high: "I am the food of grown men: grow and you will feed on me. Nor will you change me into yourself as with the food of your flesh but you shall be changed into me." And I knew (*cognovi*) *that [it was] on account of his iniquity that you have corrected man and had made* my *soul wither like a spider's web* (Ps. 38:12).[133]

To stay where he was — however attractive the presumption that through him the divine truth was to be brought into the world — meant that he would have to abandon his desire for union with God and settle for the recognition that his sinful nature could neither approach nor enjoy the absolute good. Nothing had yet proven that a true mediator did not exist. There was still one possibility and he now turned to it as the last resort. He regards it as providential that he did not turn to the Scriptures until after he had actually experienced the hopeless situation which is the price of the Platonists' presumption, because in this case he might either have been attracted by the worldly advantages of seeming wise or else supposed, since the Platonists taught the same God as the Christians, that they also shared their piety.[134]

VII,xxi,27. The true mediator, Jesus Christ

At this point Augustine turned to the Scriptures to make sure of what the Catholic church taught about Christ as the mediator and the way. Perhaps the Platonizing mediation of Photinus was not the true Christian position? "Most greedily therefore I laid hold on the venerable writings of your Spirit, and foremost amongst these, on the writings of the apostle Paul."[135] Here at last he found, in addition to the true idea of God which he had from the Platonists, an adequate mediator in Christ.

From Paul, Augustine learned that Jesus Christ was not only understood as a complete man with a rational soul and body — which he had already recognized (VII,xi,25) — but he also discovered that this same Christ was acknowledged as the truth in person, God with God, the co-eternal and co-equal Word of the Father, the Wisdom of God incarnate in the flesh.[136] Here at last was a truly adequate mediator between man and God — one who was fully God and fully man — in whom God himself united himself with his creation.[137] Here was the way he had been seeking which could lead him to the heavenly city, the fatherland, the *patria* he knew as his proper home.

While Augustine claims that the orthodox Catholic teaching about Christ is the only one which meets the requirements of a true mediation, this does not mean that those who do not know of it — either because they lived before Christ or had not yet heard him preached — cannot be in a right relation to God. This is not the case. He already found fault with his failure to adopt a right relation to God even before he learned what the church really taught about Christ and he returns to this point at the start of the next book where he says:

> For certain all those men are vain in whom there is no knowledge of God and who are not able to find him who is from these [visible] things which are good (Wis. 18:1). I myself was now no longer in that vanity. I had gotten beyond it and by the testimony of the universal creation I had found you, our creator, and your Word with you, God and together with you one God through whom you made all things [i.e., this is what he had learned from the Platonists]. But there is another kind of impious people who, *knowing God have not glorified him as God nor given thanks* (Rom. 1:21). Amongst these men I had also fallen [i.e., the form of the Platonist presumption to which he did succumb] but *your right hand picked me up* (Ps. 17:36) and having been carried off from there you placed me where I might get well because you have said to man, *behold, piety is wisdom* (Job 28:28) and *do not wish to seem wise* (Job 28:28) because those who call themselves wise *are become fools* (Rom. 1:22). (VIII,i,2)[138]

In these words from an Old Testament text Augustine teaches that piety or the fear of the Lord (i.e., the humble repentance of our sinful and separated state) is the only true response to our own imperfection as this is discovered in the knowledge of God. Here was the true piety which is available to everyone even apart from the revelation that Christ is God. "Wisdom is the fear of the Lord" (Job 28:28) is therefore the highest and the only absolutely true relation which the natural man can have to the truth known.

It is at just this point which is, in a logical sense, the end of antiquity, that the Christian doctrine, preached and heard, presents itself as the only solution to the impasse of the natural man — i.e., the desire to be united with God on the one hand and, on the other, the acknowledgement that our own sinful nature is the obstacle to this union. But as much as the fear of the Lord is the proper response to our concrete separation from God, in itself this ancient form of piety does nothing to overcome that separation. Even in adopting this true relation to God we remain separated from the divine principle which is the object of our desire. If it is to be realized, if our hope is to be fulfilled, it is absolutely certain that it cannot be brought about by the agency of any being that is merely created — neither by the *daimones* of the Platonists, nor by angels, nor even by our piety itself.

The man like Job who has seen God and who lives without presumption in the fear of the Lord can know what constitutes an adequate mediator between himself and God — as did Augustine and as does everyone who has come to the knowledge of God — and in this sense we can see how the truth of the Old Testament waits for and finds its completion in the revelation of the New. By the accidents of time and place Augustine was born in a world where Christ had been preached and proclaimed and for him therefore the piety of Job — or the true relation to the truth known – necessarily involved a relation to Christ. There was no alternative once he had come to know that the Christ preached by the Catholic church was, beyond any doubt, an adequate mediator.[139] He had seen this through reading the epistles of "the least of your [God's] apostles."[140] There, in addition to the knowledge of God which the Christians shared with Platonists and with everyone who knew the truth, he also found the tears of confession, a troubled spirit, a broken and contrite heart – and God's response to these, the salvation of mankind and the cup of redemption.[141] "Those books [of the Platonists] had none of this."[142] Here was the new form of the right relation to God. Job's pious fear of the Lord in the face of God's inscrutable ways was now transformed into a new piety in the love of Christ. God's own will for man was no longer unsearchable but explicitly revealed – and his will and his love was to unite man with himself.[143]

Having come this far Augustine had gone as far as the natural man can go in terms of knowledge alone. He had come to the true knowledge of God and had found a true mediator between the human and the divine. This represents a conclusion to the quest for the truth towards which he had been moving from the moment of his birth. The end of Book VII is therefore the end of the first part of the first part of the *Confessions* (i.e., Books I-IX). But in spite of the fact that Augustine had to come to know both God and his Eternal Word, and also Christ, the Incarnate Word, as the Way to God, he was not yet a Christian nor does he say that he was. For out of this conclusion a new beginning was generated which centred on the will. Knowing Christ as an adequate mediator between himself and God was one thing – his own union with Christ was quite another and he found that he was still moved by a will which refused to follow him and which was at war with his knowledge that he was the way to the *patria*. In short he discovered a division between his knowledge and his will and he asks:

> even if a man is delighted with *the law of God with respect to the inner man* what will he do about that other *law which, in* his *members is at war against the law of* his *mind* and *leads* him *captive to the law of sin which is in* his *members*? (Rom. 1:22ff.)[144]

Augustine's will – the expression of his absolute particularity – remained to be brought within the mediated relation of the human and divine in Christ. Until this occurred – which is to say, until he believed – he would be no Christian. Why this was so and how it happened is the content of the next book. In it he turns from a consideration of the objective knowledge of God as revealed in creation, and of the knowledge of the way to God as revealed in the church, to his own subjective relation to Christ through will and belief.

NOTES

1 See VII,vii,11 *Sed/meo* (135/15-23).

2 VII,xiv,20 *Et/tibi* (144/8-13). The same point – that Augustine made this idea of God for himself without receiving it from any sect, philosophy, religion, or dogma – is found in VII,i,1 *Et conabar cogitare* (124/20), *cogitare cogerer* (124/25). See also the *constituebam* of VII,v,7 (129/4).

3 *Iam/solet* (124/1-6).

4 See VII,i,1 *Non/tuae* (124/6-9).

5 *Sed/occurrebat* (124/9-10).

6 See VII,i,1 *nesciens/quomodo* (124/13-14).

7 These three adjectives, which Augustine uses frequently throughout this book, seem synonymous but are in fact distinguished. God is incorruptible in that he cannot suffer decay (i.e., natural change); inviolable in that he cannot suffer hurt (i.e., some unforeseen alteration from without); and incommutable (immutable) in that he does not change (i.e., voluntary alteration). These three are related to Augustine's final trinitarian conception of God. Considered as the Father, the divine being is incorruptible, as the Son, the divine knowledge is inviolate, as Spirit, the divine will is unchangeable.

8 *Et/potest* (124/10-18).

9 This is a radical change from his Manichaean views where God was not the creator of the universe — which was caused by the evil principle when he captured particles of the light.

10 *Quoniam/nihil* (125/2-7). The terms in which Augustine discusses the impossibility he found in conceiving of non-spatial reality are probably related to the dualistic physical theory of the Epicureans who held that all things were composed out of two spatial principles — atoms and the void (i.e., images of being and non-being). For a statement of the Epicurean teachings — "nature consists in two things for there are bodies (*corpora*) and the void (*inane*)" — see Lucretius, *De Rerum Natura* 1, pp. 417-20. *Corpus* and *inane* are the two terms that Augustine uses.

11 *Ita/creasti* (125/16-126/1). Note that Augustine lists the four traditional elements of nature: heaven, air, water, and earth — on these four, see below, n. 12. As the first three are transparent, the analogy between God and light needed no modification for them. This was not so in the case of earth which is why he says that he imagined that "*even* (*etiam*) the body of the earth was passable to God" — but just here the image of the sea takes over as it is easy to imagine earth permeated with water.

12 Although Augustine was not a Stoic, and nowhere says that he developed this idea of God from Stoic sources, there are marked similarities between the two accounts. The difference is that the Stoics were content to rest with theirs while for Augustine its inadequacies made this impossible. Solignac (*BA*, Vol. 13, p. 579, n. 1) notes the similarity between Stoicism and the notion of God which Augustine describes. This has been noted by others as well: see G. Verbecke, "Augustin et le stoicisme" (*Recherches Augustiniennes*, 1 [1958], 67-89). Testard (*Saint Augustine et Cicéron*, Vol. 1, p. 117) also notes the resemblance between the view of God which Augustine describes in these chapters and the views of the Stoic spokesman, Balbus, in Book III of Cicero's *De Natura Deorum*.

For a brief modern account of the Stoic philosophy see Long (*Hellenistic Philosophy*, esp. pp. 152-58). Long states the problem — to which the idea of "pervasion" or "mixture" was the answer for both the Stoics and Augustine — in the following way. "According to Chrysippus, *pneuma* [the infinite, incorruptible, rational principle of the Stoics (God)] interacts with matter by permeating it completely. But both the *pneuma* and matter are corporeal, and it is an elementary principle of physics that two bodies cannot occupy the same space at the same time. How then is it conceivable that *pneuma* can completely permeate matter? The Stoics were aware of the difficulty, and they sought to overcome it by distinguishing between different modes of mixture" (p. 158: see also pp. 159-60 for Long's treatment of the Stoic notion of mixing). Augustine's image of the sea (God) penetrating every part of creation (the sponge) or of light (God) filling the air (creation) without ripping or cutting it are both efforts to resolve the same difficulty. A collection of texts relating to the Stoic notion of mixture is found in J. von Arnim, *Stoicorum Veterum Fragmenta*, Stuttgart, Teubner, 1964, Vol. 2, pp. 151-58. The four elements in the Stoic account of nature are earth, water, air, and *pneuma* — the latter alone is indestructible (*ibid.*, Vol. 2, p. 413). It is also called fire or aether and constitutes the soul or vital force in the universe = God or the divine principle. On these four elements see Cicero, *De Natura Deorum*, II,xxxiii,84. Cicero notes that the fire or aether is, in Latin, called "heaven" (*caelum* – *ibid.*, II,xxxiv,91). These four (*caelum, aer, mare, terra*) are the four elements that Augustine distinguishes in two places in the first chapter. See VII,i,1 *et/caelesti* (125/6-7), and VII,i,2 *sic/corpus* (125/25-26). I do not claim that Augustine was a Stoic at the time but it seems clear that he did borrow from Stoic sources — most likely in Cicero — parts of their system which he used to fashion his own idea of God.

13 *Clamabat/eam* (124/19-24).

14 See the text quoted above, n. 8.

15 *falsum erat* (126/2).

16 *ut/passeris* (126/4-5).

17 *Non/meas* (126/8-9).

18 See V,xiv,25. I presume that the recognition of the divine incorruptibility came to Augustine towards the end of his sceptical period because in the sixth book he says, of the time about which he was then writing, that he was not yet certain of the falsity of the Manichees' teachings — see VI,iv,5 *Quod/fuissent* (103/19-21). This would not have been true if he already insisted on the divine incorruptibility.

19 *quid/noluisses?* (126/14-17).

20 *concussi sumus* (126/14).

21 Solignac is, I think, wrong when he suggests that Nebridius' question shows that he "preceded" Augustine in finding the contradictions in Manichaeism (*BA*, Vol. 13, p. 133). By itself, the question Nebridius posed does not "make the Manichaean fables unthinkable" (*ibid.*). As I have explained, it was possible for Augustine to escape between the horns of the dilemma and there is no evidence that Nebridius did otherwise at the time. See also below, n. 42.

22 See VII,ii,3 where Augustine, speaking of the Manichees' own position, says that the notion that God is corruptible is to be "rejected outright" — *prima voce abominandum* (127/5-6).

23 Courcelle (*Recherches*, pp. 99-100, 106-20) suggests that it was from the sermons of Ambrose that Augustine "heard" that the cause of evil was in the free will. Solignac follows Courcelle (*BA*, Vol. 13, p. 148). Perhaps this is true but Augustine could just as well have heard it from some Stoic source. The freedom of the will was held by all who recognized the divine incorruptibility in the sense indicated — which included Christians, Platonists, and Stoics.

24 *Et/avertebam* (127/24-128/7).

25 See V,x,18 for a very clear statement of the Manichaean position. See also IV,xv,26 and V,x,20.

26 *certissimus eram* (128/6).

27 *et/facere* (127/19-23).

28 *Quod/fatebar* (128/7-10).

29 On Augustine's relation to the Stoics, see above, n. 12.

30 *Sed/meo?* (128/10-16).

31 *Si/esset?* (128/16-20).

32 *His/putatur* (128/20-23).

33 *Et/malum* (129/22-23).

34 *Cur/timemus* (130/18-24).

35 *An/converteret?* (130/27-131/2).

36 *Talia/veritate* (131/18-20).

37 *aciem/iterum* (127/27-128/2).

38 *vix/eum* (124/22-24).

39 *in dies* (130/24).

40 See VII,v,vii *stabiliter/inhibebat* (131/20-25). Augustine recalls his scepticism by using the word *fluctuans*, "floating."

41 *prope iam* (132/27).

42 In VI,x,17 Augustine describes Nebridius as a "most acute examiner of the most difficult questions" — *quaestionum/scrutator* (116/5-6). Nebridius' talent seems to have lain in asking the right questions — as for example in his early suspicions about Manichaeism (see VII,ii,3) and astrology (VII,vi,8). On the other hand he does not seem to have come to the correct solutions any faster than Augustine and indeed appears for the most part to have fol-

lowed after him — as when he went from Carthage to Milan (VI,x,17) simply to be with Augustine in a search for the truth. He was also converted at a later date than Augustine (see IX,iii,6).

43 *nullum/dici* (58/10-13).

44 *procurasti ergo tu* (132/14).

45 On the expression which Augustine uses to describe Firminus' happy circumstances (*dealbatiores vias* — "whitened roads"), see above, Chapter Two, n. 16.

46 *ridicula/inania* (132/28). Augustine frequently uses the case of Jacob and Esau both in his discussion of grace, as in his reply to Simplicianus in *DD7*, I,iii,3, and in the refutation of astrology, as in *DCD*, V,1-7.

47 See VII,iv,9. I say that Firminus was apparently unmoved because Augustine says only that he "attempted to recall" (*conatus sum . . . revocare* — 134/3-4) him by means of his own story. Had he been successful, surely he would have said, "I recalled him."

48 *artis inperitia* (134/18).

49 See IV,iii,4 where Augustine states the argument that leads to this conclusion — *Quem/ordinator* (56/15-20).

50 *certissime/mendacio* (134/15-18).

51 *et/exitus* (135/14-15).

52 Augustine's belief in a judgement to come is stressed here (see the text quoted above, n. 36) and was mentioned and discussed already in VI,xi,19, and VI,xvi,26.

53 See Solignac's note on this "heart" (*cor*) = "thought" (*BA*, Vol. 13, p. 579, n. 2).

54 See Solignac's note on this *intentio* (*BA*, Vol. 13, p. 581, n. 1).

55 *Ego/aliquid* (125/8-16). See also the text from VII,i,1 quoted above, n. 10.

56 *et/inferior* (136/6-12).

57 *iam iamque* (122/24-25).

58 *Et/meos* (136/24-27). In *DCD*, XIV,1-6 Augustine explains how the sins of the flesh include defects of *both* the body and the mind.

59 By recalling the opening lines of the confession of his past life from I,vi,7 — *Sed/loquor* (5/11-14) — Augustine indicates that he is coming to the end of this first long segment of his career, dominated by the effort to come to the certain knowledge of God.

60 *Tu/sanabatur* (136/28-137/6).

61 *inde admonitus* (141/17). On the intellectual character of this admonition see *ALD*, art. *admoneo*, "to bring to one's mind . . . by influencing more directly the reason and judgement; while in *adhortor* the admonition is addressed immediately to the will." See also VII,xx,26 where *admoneo* is again used in the same sense.

62 For the explicit references to the Platonists see VII,ix,13-15, VII,x,16, VII,xx,26, VII,xxi,27, VIII,i,2, and VIII,ii,3. See also the two other brief accounts of the effects of the *libri Platonicorum* which are found in *CA*, II,ii,5 and *DBV*, I,4. For my account of the debate that has gone on over Augustine's relation to Platonism at the time of his conversion, see the Appendix, "An Essay on the Historicity Debate."

63 Before the *Enneads* of Plotinus came to be widely known through the translations begun in the mid-nineteenth century by M. N. Bouillet (*Les Enneades de Plotin*, 1857-1861), Harnack had supposed that the *libri Platonicorum* referred to the works of Plato himself: see "Die Hohepunkte in Augustins Konfessionen" (repr. in his *Redens und Aufsätze*, Vol. 1, part 2, Giessen, Ricker, 1904, pp. 51-79). This supposition is not implausible. In a passage in *DBV* (I,4) where Augustine speaks of his discovery of what, in the *Confessions*, he calls "the books of the Platonists," he says, "Moreover, I read a very few Platonic books" (*Platonis libris* — i.e., of Plato himself). Harnack's assumption has now been replaced for a century by the view that Augustine actually means the books of the Neo-Platonists — chiefly Plotinus and Porphyry. Recent scholarship has been to some trouble to show that the *Platonis* of *DBV* is really a copyist's error for *Plotini* — notably in Henry's *Plotin et l'Occident*, Louvain, Spicilegium sacrum Lovaniense, 1934, pp. 82-89. Du Roy in *L'intelligence* (p. 69, n. 1) says that "Henry . . . has established the reading *Plotini* as absolutely certain." O'Connell is more circumspect (*Saint Augustine's Early Theory*, p. 6): "The manuscript tradition presents strong

arguments for a copyist's error at this point; it seems so probable that the original reading was *Plotini* that one may safely take it as practically certain." In the historicity debate (see reference above, n. 62) the defenders of the historical truth of the *Confessions* have taken the line that there is an identity between Christianity and Neo-Platonism. By the early 1930s the question had arisen as to precisely which Neo-Platonists Augustine read. In this connection see especially W. Theiler, *Porphyros und Augustin*, Halle, Niemeyer, 1933, who argues that the books in question refer exclusively to the works of Porphyry; see also his critique of Courcelle's objections to this position (*Gnomon*, 25, part 2 [1953], 113-21). On the other hand Henry (*Plotin et l'Occident*), argues that the books of the Platonists refer to the *Enneads* of Plotinus. Courcelle (*Recherches*, pp. 93-174) thinks Augustine was mostly, but not exclusively, influenced by Plotinus. O'Meara in *The Young Augustine* (pp. 131-55), in "Augustine and Neo-Platonism" (*Recherches Augustiniennes*, 1 [1958], 9-11), and in *Porphyry's "Philosophy from Oracles" in Augustine* (Paris, Études Augustiniennes, 1959) thinks the influence of Porphyry was preponderant. For a brief account of the history of these efforts see O'Connell's *Saint Augustine's Early Theory* (pp. 6-10) and, for his own thoroughly Neo-Platonic interpretation, his *Odyssey*. Solignac understands that Augustine read both Plotinus and Porphyry (*BA*, Vol. 13, pp. 100-12, 145-49, 679-93): see also his "Réminiscences plotiniennes et porphyriennes dans le début du *De ordine* de s. Augustin," *Archives de Philosophie*, 20 (1957), 446-65. Solignac discusses the Neo-Platonic "circle" at Milan in *BA*, Vol. 14, pp. 529-36. The existence of such a group was first shown by Courcelle in his *Lettres grecques en Occident, de Macrobe à Cassiodore*, 2nd ed., Paris, de Boccard, 1948, pp. 119-29. For an account of the life and thought of these philosophers see A. H. Armstrong, ed., *The Cambridge History of Late Greek and Early Medieval Philosophy*, Cambridge, Cambridge University Press, 1967.

64 The reason why Augustine did not specify which books he got hold of but says only that he read "*certain* books of the Platonists" (*quosdam Platonicorum libros*, VI,ix,13 — 137/13) is, I think, similar to the more or less parallel case of the "*certain* Cicero" of III,iv,7 (see above, Chapter Three, n. 43). That is, he did not expect a large part of his audience — faithful but unphilosophical Christians — to know of, possess, have access to, or be capable of reading these texts. He refuses to name the books he read to prevent these people from trying to do so for themselves — as if they had to do this to discover the true idea of God. He says this is unnecessary because he testifies, by transcribing their teaching in the words of John, that the same idea of God is found in the Scriptures of the church which they already knew. For those readers who were philosophically cultivated, whether pagan or Christian, any detailed reference was unnecessary as they would already have known which books contained the true idea of God. These might be the ones Augustine read or some others but this would make no difference since, as he says (in VII,ix,15 and VII,x,16), this truth is the same no matter from whom it is taken or how arrived at.

65 Although the major Scripture texts which Augustine uses to explain the content of the books of the Platonists are from the Prologue to the *Gospel of John*, those parts of the Johannine text which he says are in accord with the teachings of the Platonist books are just the ones which John draws from the Old Testament (especially from Genesis and Psalms). The reason Augustine uses the Johannine text is that John adds something that is found neither in the Old Testament nor in the books of the Platonists — namely, that the Word was made flesh. In *DBV* (I,4), Augustine mentions that the books of the Platonists which he read at the time were "very few" (*paucissimis libri*). Courcelle speculates (*Recherches*, p. 202, n. 1), rather wildly it seems to me, that — because in IX,ii,2 Augustine uses the phrase *paucissimi dies* (181/2-3) for the "very few days" that remained before the end of the term (which he specifies as about 20) — this means that, when he uses the same adjective of the number of Platonist books which he read he could have had as many as 20 in mind! The dangers of an exclusively philological approach seem well illustrated here. In *CA*, II,ii,5 Augustine uses the same work where he likens the texts of the Platonists to a "very few drops" (*gutas paucissimis*) of the most precious perfume — but surely in this case *20* drops of perfume is not "very few" but a great many?

66 Courcelle supposes that this man was Falvius Mallius Theodorus. See *Recherches*, pp. 153-56, and also pp. 281-84 where he tries to resolve certain difficulties in this attribution which is not widely accepted. See O'Meara's reservations on this score in *The Young Augustine* (pp. 125-26) and his own suggestion that the phrase should be referred to Porphyry (p. 152). See also Solignac's reservations in *BA*, Vol. 13, pp. 101-103 and, on Theodorus, *BA*, Vol. 14, pp. 533-34.

In VIII,ii,3 Augustine says that he told Simplicianus that he "had read certain books of the Platonists translated into Latin by Victorinus" (*legisse/Victorinus* — 154/16-17). On the impossibility of determining the content of the Platonist translations of Victorinus, see P. Hadot's *Marius Victorinus*, pp. 199-210. Hadot affirms the conclusion Solignac had arrived at, a decade earlier (*BA*, Vol. 13, p. 110, n. 3), when he says "I think therefore, in conclusion, that it is not possible to determine with absolute certainty the exact content of the *libri platonicorum* of Victorinus" (p. 210).

67 *Et/versos* (137/7-14).

68 See the text quoted above, n. 58.

69 This is what Augustine teaches in the third section of this book (VII,xxvii,23-VII,xxi,27) where he discusses his movement from the vision of God to the discovery of the true mediator. Augustine's constant teaching is that Christ alone, who is both God and man, is able to heal our wound — i.e., original sin — by which we are separated from God. See IX,xiii,35 (in the final chapter of the first part of the *Confessions*) where he says, "*Hear me* (Ps. 142:1) through him who, hung on the wood [of the cross], is the medicine for our wounds (*vulnerum nostrorum*) and who, sitting *at* your *right hand beseeches* you *for us* (Rom. 8:34)" — *Exaudi/nobis* (207/11-13). In *DT*, IV,xv,20 Augustine distinguishes between Platonists and Christians in the same terms as he uses in the *Confessions*. He says: "For those persons [i.e., Platonists] promise themselves cleansing by their own righteousness for this reason, because some of them have been able to penetrate with the eye of the mind beyond the whole creature [i.e., all of nature], and to touch, though it be in ever so small a part, the light of the unchanging truth; a thing which they deride many Christians for being not yet able to do, who, in the meantime, live by faith alone. But of what use is it for the proud man, who on that account is ashamed to embark on the ship of wood [i.e., the cross of Christ], to behold from afar his country beyond the sea? Or how can it hurt the humble man not to behold it from so great a distance, when he is actually coming to it by that wood upon which the other disdains to be borne?" (trans. *NPNF*).

70 See VII,xx,26 *In/didicisset* (149/18-150/6). The verbs Augustine uses to describe his discovery of the Platonist books (*incurro* 149/19-20 and *incido* 150/2) are the same as those used for his fall into Manichaeism — see above, Chapter Three, n. 66.

71 *inde/te* (140/17-18).

72 In *CA*, II,iii,5 Augustine likens the effect of the books of the Platonists to a very few drops of the most precious perfume sprinkled on the smouldering coals of his heart which caused the most incredible flame. The image is that of an almost instantaneous reaction.

73 *et/fierem* (72/23-25).

74 This point is made against the imaginary extrapolation of visible light which the Manichees claimed was God.

75 *Intravi/aeternitatem* (140/19-141/1).

76 On the heart as the seat of intelligence, which is the sense here, see Solignac, *BA*, Vol. 13, p. 579, n. 2.

77 *et/conspicitur* (141/14-21). This transformation of a hypothetical starting point into the unhypothetical knowledge of the divine principle is stated by Plato in the *Republic* (511b). The Pauline text from Romans 1:18-25 was *the* Scriptural text with the church fathers not only for "justifying the affirmation of the existence of God as a consequence of the existence of the world" (Solignac, *BA*, Vol. 13, p. 619, n. 1) but also for clarifying the presumptuous errors to which this knowledge often led (the failure to honour God or thank him, and the worship of false mediators). Augustine uses the text in this sense in VII,ix,15 — i.e., not with but *against* the Platonists. As here, Augustine frequently combines Romans with the

Prologue to John's Gospel. For a very careful and thorough analysis of Augustine's use of these texts see Madec, "Connaisance de Dieu et action de grâces. Essai sur les citations de *l'Ép. aux Romains*, 1:18-25 dans l'oeuvre d'Augustin," *Recherches Augustiniennes*, 2 (1962), 273-309.

78 *de silvestri cacumine* (151/27-28).

79 *Tu/horrore* (141/2-7).

80 *oculum animae meae* (140/20).

81 See VII,x,16 *Intravi/ea* (141/19-29).

82 *inveni/dissimilitudinis* (141/7-8). See Solignac's subtle note on this much discussed *regio dissimilitudinis* — the "region of unlikeness" — *BA*, Vol. 13, pp. 689-93) and Courcelle's long discussion and thorough bibliography in *Recherches* (pp. 405-40) and in *Les Confessions* (pp. 623-45). See also above, Chapter Two, n. 89.

83 *Et/eges* (141/22-142/2).

84 *saniore* (144/3).

85 See the text from *DT*, IV,xv,20 (quoted above, n. 69) for a particularly clear statement of what the Christians achieve by means of their belief in Christ in contrast to those philosophers who have a knowledge of the city but are not on the way to it. O'Meara provides a collection of texts (in English) which illustrate this point from a wide variety of Augustine's works (*The Young Augustine*, pp. 143-51).

86 *Non/trahebatur* (144/4-18).

87 In the Christian idiom the distinction between God as the first principle and as containing the eternal uncreated reasons of all things is spoken of as the distinction between God (the Father) and the eternal Word, Mind, or Intellect of God (the Son). Both of these were known in the Platonist knowledge of God, as Augustine indicates by saying that they knew what John knew — i.e., that *"the Word [the Son] was with God [the Father] and was God"* (Jn. 1:1). Augustine makes the same point in *DCD*, X,23 where he says, "we know what Porphyry, as a Platonist, means by the 'principles.' " He refers to God the Father, and God the Son, whom he calls in Greek the Intellect or Mind of the Father. About the Holy Spirit he says nothing, or at least nothing clear" (trans. Bettenson, Penguin — see also X,29). What the Platonists either did not know or would not acknowledge was that the eternal Word of God was also incarnate in time. This is not revealed in the philosophical knowledge of God and they refused to accept it on the testimony of the church.

88 *Et/manente* (144/19-24).

89 *Et/foras* (145/1-11).

90 *Et/cogitantem* (145/12-21). Augustine's aim is "being with God" ("coherence") and the distinction he draws here — "[God was the one] to whom I should cohere, although I was not such a one who could cohere [with him]" (*cui/coharerem* 145/17-18) — is the same thing, from the side of existence, as he had earlier noted from the side of knowledge — "[God raised me up] so that I could see that what I saw existed but that I was not such a one who could see [him continuously]" (VII,x,16 *ut/viderem* 141/4-5). In both cases God, as the absolute goal of knowledge and existence, is given — as well as the discovery that we cannot be with God because we are unlike him, being separated by our nature as (fallen) rational animals in whom nature and reason are not reconciled — i.e., by the wound of original sin.

91 On Augustine's use of the text from Romans 1:18-25, see above n. 77. See, in the *Loci sacrae Scripturae* (*BA*, Vol. 13, p. 676), a list of the many places in which Augustine uses this text in the *Confessions*.

92 *Tunc/possem* (146/17-22). On Augustine's image of God as the food of the soul see the etymological connection between *sapientia* (wisdom) and taste noted in Chapter Three, n. 138. In nature we turn the food we eat into ourselves, whereas Augustine says that in the vision he saw (heard) that *if* he had the strength to stay with God and feed on him he would rather be changed into God — see VII,x,16 (*tamquam/me* (141/8-12). This transmutation of the creature into God is to be understood in the precise sense in which he describes the Heaven of Heavens (= the City of God) in Books XII and XIII. See, for instance, this passage from XII,xi,12: "In my heart, O Lord, I have also heard your voice telling me loud and clear that

not even the Heaven of Heavens, your creature, is co-eternal with you. Though it delights in you alone and enjoys your savour with untiring purity, at no time and in no way does it shed its mutability. But being always in your presence and clinging to you with all its love, it has no future to anticipate and no past to remember, and thus it persists without change and does not diverge into past and future time" (trans. Pine-Coffin, Penguin) — *Item/distenditur* (301/7-14). See also XII,xv,18-22 where Augustine explains the distinction between the true eternity of God, which he alone possesses, and the created likeness of that eternity ("sempiternity"), enjoyed in heaven by creatures who are mutable by nature yet, through grace, are actually beyond time and change in the constant contemplation of God's eternity and absolute immutability.

93 *in regione dissimilitudinis* (141/8). On this phrase, see above, n. 82.

94 Doull ("Augustinian Trinitarianism," p. 143) makes the same point. "The relation of God and man is mediated by a thinking relation of man to nature. But this mediation contains a division between thought and sensibility — the necessary and the contingent — whose unity is beyond the mediation itself. If by the human is understood the being who is at once mutable and knows the immutability of the ideas — or, stated in relation to the practical, knows a binding and rational law and is moved by desires and their concentration in the spirited part (τὸ θυμοειδὲς) — then the human falls outside the divine-human relation taken strictly."

95 See Porphyry (*Life of Plotinus*, 23) on Plotinus' ecstatic visions — which Plotinus himself describes in the last words of the *Enneads*: "This is the life of Gods and of godlike and happy men, liberation from the alien which besets us here, a life taking no pleasure in things of earth, the flight of the alone to the Alone" (VI,ix,11) — I have slightly altered the translation of S. MacKenna (*Plotinus, The Enneads*, London, Faber and Faber, 1969, p. 625). In Chapter IV of his *Recherches*, in a section (III) entitled "Vain efforts at Plotinian ecstasies" (pp. 157-67) Courcelle argues that Augustine immediately attempted to regain the vision (p. 160) only to discover that he was prevented by his "poor moral health" (p. 167). The problem with this view — which results from forcing Augustine into a Plotinian mould recommended by the sources Courcelle has discovered — is that if moral turpitude prevented Augustine from regaining the vision, how then did he come to it in the first place? Courcelle cannot answer such a question. Augustine does not say that he attempted to regain the vision. Instead he began to search for a mediator right after the vision (see VII,xviii,24, "And I was looking for a way..." — *Et quaerebam viam* 146/23 which can only mean that he had already decided it was fruitless to regain it. Even when, for a while, he supposed that the church did not have an adequate mediator his response was not to return to the contemplation of God but rather he "began to wish to seem wise" (VII,xx,26 — *coeperam/sapiens* 149/14) — i.e., to use his knowledge for worldly ends.

In his *Odyssey*, O'Connell takes Courcelle's line to its logical conclusion. He understands Augustine to be teaching pure Plotinian theology — the soul must get rid of the body and return itself to the place whence it descended. This view cannot be reconciled with Augustine's insistence on the Incarnation and the resurrection but O'Connell explicitly discounts both points at the beginning of his book (p. 24). The result brings the *Confessions* into line with Neo-Platonism — but are these *Confessions* any longer Augustine's?

96 *[Et quaerebam] viam* (146/23).

97 *adsequor* (42/4). I say that at this point Augustine had only completed the first task of "seeking" God (see IV,iv,8 *quaereo* 42/4), "in a certain sense" because the quest was not really finished until he had not only found the end or goal but also the way to it. In the central section of this book (VII,viii,23-VII,xvi,22) he has told us how he found God (i.e., the true goal). His search for the way to that goal (see the text quoted above n. 96) is the content of this final section (VII,xvii,23-VII,xxi,27) and as such it belongs to the first task. The altogether different problem of actually getting himself on the way once he had found it, and of "following it" (*adsequor*) towards God, is the content of Book VIII.

98 *Et/te* (146/23-24). The expression *comparandi roboris* (146/23-24) — "to provide the strength" — in using the word *robor* which means, literally, a very hard kind of oak, calls to mind Augustine's frequently used image of the wood of the cross as the ship by which we

are transported across the bitter sea of human life to our proper home. Augustine uses the images forest/road and sea/ship interchangeably. The forest and sea are both images of the chaotic, impassable wilderness of this world and the road or ship (= Christ) is the divine way which leads from this world to God. On these images see above, Chapter One, n. 44 and 87. See also the text from *DT*, IV,xv,20 (quoted above, n. 69), and *TJ*, II,4.

99 See the myth of Er at the end of the *Republic* (X,614b), and Book VI of the *Aeneid*.

100 *Non/noveram* (147/4-6).

101 ... *nec/Iesum* (146/24-26).

102 At the time Augustine probably knew little more of the Arians than that they were opposed by Ambrose (see IX,vii,15). He would have had no clear idea about the Arian controversy nor of its upshot in the Council and Creed of Nicaea (325) which became the definitive statement of orthodox belief. What happened was that on his own he assumed (from such things as he already knew) that the church taught a Christ who was in fact logically similar to that of Arius (or rather Photinus) — in that he was a creature and not the very person of God. He recognized that such a being could not be an adequate mediator between creation and God if he was only a creature. In this connection I think Solignac goes too far when he suggests that Augustine "probably got this [view] from Photinians who were living at the time in Milan" (*BA*, Vol. 13, p. 694). There is no need to suppose this and it seems unlikely that, if Augustine was associated with people who knew themselves to be "Photinians," he would have been ignorant of this fact. Finally, through Paul, he discovered an adequate mediator who, as he eventually learned, was the same Christ as affirmed by Nicaea. On Augustine's relation to the Nicene faith, see B. Studer, "Augustin et la foi de Nicée" (*Recherches Augustiniennes*, 19 [1984], 135-54).

103 *Quid/poteram* (147/22-24).

104 *Tantum/dubitabam* (147/24-148/1).

105 *propria/mentis* (148/4-5).

106 *totum hominem* (148/8).

107 *non/animum* (148/9-10).

108 See VI,v,7-8.

109 *Quae/remaneret* (148/5-8).

110 *perfectiore participatione sapientiae* (148/12-13).

111 *tantumque/videbatur* (147/16-22).

112 *totum/arbitrabar* (148/8-13).

113 See VII,xix,25 *Photini falsitate* (148/24-25) — "the error of Photinus." It is curious that Augustine mentions Photinus (bishop of Sirmium, *c.* 340), and not the better known Arius, as the one whose Christology he had unknowingly supposed that the church taught. Like Augustine, both of these men held that Christ was not God: Photinus seeing in him the wisest man, and Arius a being infinitely better than all other creatures (the highest angel) but still a creature himself in relation to the Father. In two articles which appeared in 1954 — "Litiges sur la lecture des 'libri Platonicorum' par s. Augustin" (*Augustiniana*, 4 [1954], 225-39), and "Saint Augustin 'photinien' à Milan" (*Richerche di storia religiosa*, 1 [1954], 63-71) — Courcelle noted that Augustine connects Photinus and Porphyry's *Philosophy from Oracles*. O' Meara (*Porphyry's Philosophy from Oracles*) later picked up on the point and maintained with Courcelle that the reason Augustine mentions Photinus was that he "wants to show his dependence at the time on Porphyry" (p. 159). This view is based on the fact that Porphyry, like Augustine at the time, both recognized the need for a mediator and rejected Christ because he was not God. This "dependence" has been rightly contested by Hadot in "Citations de Porphyry chez Augustin (à propos d'un livre recent)" (*Revue des études augustiniennes*, 6 [1960], 205-44; see also O'Meara's reply, 245-47), and in Solignac's excellent note, "La christologie d'Augustin au temps de sa conversion" (*BA*, Vol. 13, pp. 693-98).

There is no evidence that Porphyry maintained the virgin birth of Christ, as did Augustine, and unlike Augustine, Porphyry did not acknowledge the need for a mediator for anyone, such as Augustine, who was capable of the intellectual vision of God (see *DCD*, X,27). The mediator was only for the mass of mankind who "were incapable of raising themselves to a life of intellectual contemplation," for whom he saw the necessity of "some mediator between the Father and mankind, some commanding authority, some universal way of the soul's deliverance" (O'Meara, *The Young Augustine*, p. 143 – in dependence on *DCD*, X,23-32: compare DCD, XIX,23). If the thesis of Courcelle and O'Meara cannot be sustained, the question remains as to why Augustine characterized his error as Photinian rather than Arian. The answer lies in the link he made at the time between the excellence of Christ's wisdom and the virgin birth – the latter being, as it were, the seal of the former. Photinus had held this position whereas Arius did not: see *Letter*, CLVII,vii,19. See also *LDH*, I,44-45 where the teaching of Photinus is likened to that of Paul of Samosota – with which, compare what Augustine says about Arius, (I.49). In *Ser*, LXXI,3 Photinus is said to have denied that there was a Holy Spirit and this too is different from Porphyry. In *DCD* (X,23) Augustine concludes that, although in a confused way, Porphyry nevertheless maintained that there was a Holy Spirit who was not inferior to the Word of God in the manner of Plotinus' "world soul."

114 This is the sense of Augustine's comments in VII,ix,15 about the things which he found in the Platonist books but did not take from them – i.e., that aspect of their teaching which recommended the worship of false mediators in the cult of created idols and demons.

115 *ut/hominis* (148/14-16). In *CA*, III,vi,13 Augustine states what I take to have been Alypius' general position: "You, Alypius, have told us who can point out the truth ... for you said that only some deity could reveal to man what truth is."

116 *postea* (148/20). It was "somewhat later still" – *aliquanto posterius* (148/22-23) – that Augustine learned that the Christology he ascribed to the church was actually like that of Photinus.

117 On Apollinarius, see Solignac, *BA*, Vol. 13, p. 698.

118 See VII,xix,25 *Et/est* (148/17-22). I think that the *bene persuasum* (148-17) means, "having been well persuaded [by me – i.e., Augustine]." In other words Alypius became convinced that Christ could not be God (because he was mutable) in discussing the matter with Augustine.

   In the last sentences of this chapter (*inprobatio/infirmos* – 148/25-29) Augustine points out, on Scriptural authority (1 Cor. 11:19), that the value of heretical opinions was that in the discussion which led to their rejection the church was able to clarify its own belief.

119 Solignac (*BA*, Vol. 13, p. 205) places the reading of the *libri Platonicorum* some time in May-June 386 and the reading of the Pauline texts in July 386.

120 So Watts (*Loeb*) for Augustine's *non peritus sed periturus essem*.

121 *Garriebam/scientia* (149/11-15). Augustine accuses himself of two things – first, that although he was cut off from God ("full of my own punishment") he did not weep and lament over this condition – and secondly, and worse, that he "began to wish to seem wise" refusing to use his knowledge to honour God but pretending instead to know things which he really did not know, i.e., that he had a knowledge about worldly things (*quasi peritus* – 149/11-12) as well as his knowledge of God. On the latter point see also below, n. 132.

122 Courcelle's position is as subtle as it is learned and there is no doubt that he recognizes, with Augustine, that the worship of false mediators, as recommended in the Platonist books, was "illogical" (*Recherches*, p. 177) according to their own lights. The difficulty is that all his arguments are aimed at supporting the view that Augustine recognized a pure, intellectual, and "logical" form of Platonism – which rejected magic, theurgy, and the cult of idols – and which Augustine saw as being essentially identical with the position of the Catholic church. In a sense this is true since Augustine does maintain that any Platonist who is true to the knowledge of God *must* become a Christian according to the logic of his own position. What Courcelle fails to see is where Augustine also teaches that even though he refused the worship of false mediators he was not yet a Christian and that the only way of becoming one was to leave Platonism behind and submit his will, in faith, to Christ and his church (this side of things is discussed in Book VIII where also my disagreement with Courcelle is sharpest).

The failure to do this was just as proud and "illogical" as was the worship of false mediators and those who acted in this way were no more Christians than the others. For Augustine any Platonist — even one who rejected the worship of false mediators — who had heard the orthodox teaching about Christ and yet refused to join the church and submit to its authority was, by definition, a presumptuous man who had turned his wisdom into folly.

123 *praseumptionem/habitandam* (149/24-27). See also the text from *DT* (IV,xv,20 — quoted above, n. 69) for the aqueous version of this image as well as above, n. 98.

124 *DCD*, VIII,18. See Plato, *Symposium* 203a, and also Apuleius, *De Deo Socratis* 4 and 6 as sources for the quotation.

125 *in/serpentium* (139/20-23).

126 *Inveni/manducavi* (140/4).

127 *non adtendi* (140/13).

128 *persona veritatis* (148/11). The Word of God is the Mind, Intellect, or Wisdom of God — i.e., what Augustine had been seeking since he first read the *Hortensius*. He distinguishes between the highest kind of *human* wisdom which he attributed to Christ — highest, because he allowed that it participated the divine Wisdom more perfectly than any other — and the actual *divine* Wisdom itself which he calls here the "person of the truth."

129 In VIII,i,2 (quoted below at n. 138) Augustine uses the text *ecce pietas est sapientia* (Job 28:28) — "behold piety is wisdom." In the Vulgate, this appears as *ecce timor Domini ipsa est sapientia* — "behold the fear of the Lord, that is wisdom." They mean the same.

130 *Garriebam/confessionem* (149/11-24). Notice again that while the Platonists could cure the tumor that grew out of his wound and prevented him from seeing the truth, they could do nothing to heal the wound itself. Here the wound — i.e., the sin by which his nature was separated from God through its imperfect relation of reason and nature — can only be cured by God's healing hand — i.e., by Christ.

131 The whole 22 books of the *City of God* arise from Augustine's observation in the Preface that the problem with the Romans (i.e., natural man as opposed to Christians), is the presumptuous claim that it belongs to them to mediate the divine truth to the world — not in the negative sense that they knew themselves as subject to the divine law but positively, as if they knew how God sees and rates temporal things. In this context Augustine quotes Vergil (whose teachings he regards as Platonic — *DCD*, XIV,3) where he says that Rome's task is "To spare the conquered and beat down the proud" (*Aeneid* VI, 853). Augustine however insists that "This is God's prerogative" since even in the true knowledge of God we see nothing about these temporal things (see below, n. 132). Augustine adopted this presumptuous attitude in his desire to seem wise when he should rather have feared God and repented his sinful nature.

132 A passage from *DT* (IV,xxi,21), in which Augustine speaks of the philosophers' rejection of the resurrection of Christ, explains this side of the Platonist presumption very clearly. The Catholic doctrine of the resurrection of the flesh is the same teaching as the Incarnation looked at from the side of humanity. In it the claim is made that our mutable flesh is made immutable by grace just as in the Incarnation the immutable Word of God is said to have become mutable flesh. From the standpoint of Platonism the idea of the resurrection is as foolish as that of the Incarnation: it is simply the expression of an ignorant arrogance of the part of Christians to suggest that corporeal nature can become like the incorporeal God. See, for example, the outrage of Plotinus (*Enneads* II,ix,46-60) against what he regards as the blind arrogance of those who claim that man can transcend what he is by nature; this is directed against the Gnostics but, *mutatis mutandis*, it applies equally to Christians. Augustine says: "These philosophers censure us [Christians] for believing in the resurrection of the flesh and would rather that we believed them in these matters. As if, because they have been able to understand the heavenly and immutable substance *through those things that have been made* (Rom. 1:20), they ought also to be consulted concerning the changes of mutable things or about the arranged order of times. Though they discuss most truly and persuade with the most certain proofs that all temporal things come to be according to the eternal reasons, does it follow that they are able to penetrate into these reasons themselves or to

see into them so that [like God] they can deduce from them how many kinds of animals there
are, what are the seeds of each at their growth, what are the numbers of their conceptions,
births, ages, settings, what motions there are in their desiring those things which are according to nature and fleeing those things contrary to it?'' The answer to this rhetorical question
is a definite no. The philosopher's knowledge of God cannot answer a single one of these
questions. One might say that they can know for certain that all mice are from God and in
him but they cannot discover, by looking at God, how many mice are in their own houses.
The sources of the philosopher's knowledge about these things are the same as for the rest of
us: observation for present things, history for the past, prophecy for the future — and none of
these has any claim to *infallible certainty* so in these matters they are no wiser than anyone
else in spite of the fact that they know God. This is the kind of knowledge Augustine falsely
pretended to have when he ''began to wish to seem wise.'' Had he stayed with what he
really knew he could only have wept for his separated condition and given humble thanks to
God for the mind by which he had come to know him — that is, recognizing his subjection to
the divine law and his own inability to fulfill it, he ought to have lived humbly in the fear of
God.
133 *Et/vehementer* (141/5-7), and ... *tamquam/meam* (141/8-14).
134 See VII,xx,26 *Nam/didicisset* (149/27-150/6).
135 *Itaque/Paulum* (150/7-8). In *CA* (II,ii,5), Augustine mentions that at this time he read the text
of St. Paul ''from one end to the other, very intently, very religiously.'' Gibb (*Confessions*,
p. 216) notes that '' 'The Apostle' usually formed one codex,'' thus all of the letters would
have been in one volume. This was the book Augustine had open at the time of Ponticianus'
visit (see VIII,vi,14).
     Courcelle (*Recherches*, p. 169) says bluntly that ''The *itaque* is unintelligible,'' referring
to the first word of VII,xxi,27 — ''*Therefore* I turned [to the Scriptures etc.].'' This is only so
if one supposes that for Augustine his Platonism and Christianity were the same. In this case
there would be no intelligible reason for Augustine to turn to Scripture since he already had
the essence of Christianity from his Platonist knowledge. Abandon this supposition and the
itaque makes perfect sense — which is exactly why Augustine used it. That is, he turned to
the Scriptures *because* they were the only place he knew to look for the mediator he needed.
Courcelle also (*ibid.*, p. 113, n. 4) surmises that Augustine only learned of the orthodox
Christ from Simplicianus. But this disregards Augustine's explicit words in VII,xxi,27 where
he says that he found the true mediator in Paul and it is disproved in the following chapter
(VIII,i,1) where he says that he was already ''pleased with the way of the saviour himself''
(*placebat/salvator* 152/25-26) and that only then, because he was loath to actually get on the
way and follow Christ, he decided to seek the help of Simplicianus. In other words there can
be no doubt that he had already recognized Christ as the true mediator before he went to
Simplicianus, and before he became a Christian by willing and obtaining Christian baptism.
136 See VII,xxi,27 *Quis/nobis* (151/7-14). Here, once again, Augustine's final answer is in the
form of a rhetorical question.
137 See Augustine's statement of the requirements of a true mediator in VII,xviii,24 — i.e., fully
God and fully man. The role of Christ in Augustine's (eventual) conversion has been studied
by M. Lods, ''La personne du Christ dans la 'conversion' de saint Augustin'' (*Recherches
Augustiniennes*, 11 [1976], 3-34), who reviews the relevant texts and concludes, with Courcelle, that at the time Augustine saw no contradiction between his conversion in the garden
(Book VIII) and his Neo-Platonism (Book VII). W. Mallard, in what I think is a more balanced account, ''The Incarnation in Augustine's Conversion'' (*Recherches Augustiniennes*,
15 [1980], 80-98), discusses Augustine's idea of the ''person'' of Christ, here, and in the
Cassiciacum *Dialogues*, and concludes that, at the time of his conversion, he had ''crossed a
genuine boundary of belief in affirming the divine participation 'downward' in human
affairs'' (p. 98) — by which he means that Augustine had understood the doctrine of the
Word made flesh as essential to an adequate mediation.
138 *Vani/sunt* (153/26-154/10).

139 It is accidental from a human point of view that Augustine was born within the orbit of the
     Christian world, that his mother was a Christian, and that he was raised in a Christian man-
     ner. We should recall the great importance which he places on the role of a preacher (I,i,1) in
     the economy of Christian salvation — i.e., on the temporal proclamation of the "good news"
     about Christ's birth and resurrection. That the Word of God was Incarnate or that Christ was
     resurrected cannot be derived from the philosophical knowledge that God is the immutable
     intelligible. It is an historical matter which can only be transmitted in an historical
     manner — through a chain of preachers going back to witnesses.
140 *minimum apostolorum tuorum* (152/7). The Pauline humility — in calling himself the least of
     God's apostles (see 1 Cor. 15:7) — is contrasted with the presumption of the Platonist philos-
     ophers which, Augustine teaches, is the inevitable position of those who have heard Christ
     preached and yet refuse to follow him as the way to God. This is because their own knowl-
     edge of God shows them both the need of a mediator and that the Christ of the orthodox
     church is the only one capable of the task. The refusal to follow him can therefore have no
     other sense than that they either scornfully reject the possibility of union with God because it
     can only be achieved in dependence on God's grace, or else because they proudly, but illogi-
     cally, pretend they can come to God without the mediation of Christ (see *DT*, IV,xv,20 —
     partly quoted above, n. 69).
141 See VII,xxi,27 *Non/parvulis* (151/14-27). On the sense of this *parvulis*, see above, Chapter
     Three, n. 64.
142 *Hoc/habent* (151/14).
143 See VII,xxi,27 *Et/supplicium* (151/27-152/6).
144 ... *etsi/eius?* (150/21-151/1).

Chapter Eight
COMMENTARY ON BOOK VIII

The book is divided into two parts: in the first (chs. i-v) Augustine sets out the new problem he faced, and the second (chs. vi-xii) shows its resolution.

I. VIII,i,1-VIII,v,12. The problem
VIII,i,1-2. Introduction: "To walk on the way of God"

This book deals with Augustine's final conversion to Christianity. It tells how he overcame his reluctance to get on the way which led to the *patria* he had glimpsed from afar in the Platonist vision. He immediately makes it clear that the "bonds" (VIII,i,1)[1] which kept him from the church were not a matter of ignorance but of will. They had nothing to do with the truth of the Christian idea about God or about Christ as the mediator.

> Concerning your eternal life I was certain even though I had only seen it *darkly* and as if *through a mirror* (1 Cor. 13:12): but all the same every doubt about incorruptible substance, because from it came every substance, had been taken away as far as I was concerned, nor did I desire to be more certain about you but only more firmly fixed in you. (VIII,i,1)[2]

At this point Augustine was only "fixed" to God by the single tenuous thread he had established in the moment of ecstatic vision. All the rest of his temporal existence had no connection to him:

> On the other hand concerning my own temporal life all things faltered[3] and my heart had to be purged from the old passion. At one and the same time I found acceptable the Way, the Saviour himself, but I was still reluctant to go along his strait road. (VIII,i,1)[4]

When Augustine says that Christ was acceptable or pleasing to him, it meant that he knew that the Christ of orthodox Catholic belief met all the requirements of a mediator between temporal creation and the eternal God. But knowing this and following Christ were two very different things. Augustine distinguishes between them in the image of a man who knows the Way which leads to the *patria* and yet refuses to set his foot on the path before him, because he is reluctant to leave the trackless waste in which he has grown up. He knows that if he stays in that familiar forest he can never get to his proper home, but in the forest he was free to roam about and satisfy his natural desires while the Way, by its straitness, promised to impose a very different kind of life.

Augustine knew the goal and he knew the way to it. He had only to step on the

---

Notes to Chapter Eight appear on pages 237-45.

path directly in front of him (in the Catholic church) — and yet he held back. If we recall the list of verbs from his account of the effect of the *Hortensius* where he had first learned to love God, we will see that he had now completed the first task — he had sought and found both God and the Way to him. The third verb characterizes his present problem. He had actually to follow the Way which led to the patria.[5] Since the Way was Christ, this meant that he had to follow Christ by obeying his commands — but this was what he was unwilling to do. Until this was done he could not be a Christian. This is Augustine's clear and inflexible teaching. The difficulty lay in his will which forms the whole content and focus of the eighth book.

In recent years an important school of interpreters has argued that Augustine was converted to Christianity with his intellectual conversion to a Christianized Neo-Platonism. But in regarding Augustine as already a Christian in virtue of those intellectual things Christianity shared with philosophy, these scholars can only see, in the discussion of Book VIII, a conversion of his morals and way of life which followed as a secondary issue, and more or less automatically, from the prior intellectual conversion. O'Connell puts this in its strongest form in his *Odyssey*. Concerning Augustine's difficulties at this time, he says:

> The question which confronts him now is that of choosing one of the several ways he finds men treading *inside* the *Catholica*. Both the married life and the life of celibacy, he is assured by St. Paul, are legitimate and permissible for Catholics *in general*, the question is, which one is appropriate for one "affected" like himself? [i.e., by strong sexual desires] [p. 91]. . . . He no longer seeks intellectual illumination, he desires spiritual counsel on the style of life he should adopt as a Catholic [p. 93]. . . . The "second stage" of his conversion, then, is not to Catholic Christianity as such, but to the contemplative — and therefore celibate — "way" of Catholic Christian life. [p. 94 — italics O'Connell]

It seems to me that this reading ignores much of what Augustine says. His problem was not the choice of an appropriate style of life from amongst those approved by the church, but what he perceived as the necessity of submitting his will, totally, to that of Christ. This was the prerequisite to *any* form of Christian life, celibate or otherwise, and until this happened he could not think of himself as a Catholic. The reason is contained in the argument he has presented so far.

He knew the eternal God and says that he did not desire to have any more certain knowledge about him. He also conceded that the Christ taught by the Catholic church could provide the needed mediation to get him from where he was in this world to the heavenly city where he wanted to be. But this knowledge that Christ was an adequate mediator is a strict knowledge (a *scientia*) only in the most abstract sense. Humanly speaking it is only a conditional knowledge that *if* Jesus really was the Incarnate Word — in the sense maintained by orthodoxy — then he would be a mediator and the Way which united us to God. But was he? Was this man what the Catholics claimed he was? Augustine knew for certain that there was no way of proving that this was the case.

The reason is not far to seek. If the eternal Word of God was truly Incarnate then he became subject to the conditions of creation just like every other created moment — and as Augustine had long known there could be no certain knowledge of what exists in time and space. So far as he looked to the historical Jesus his knowledge of the man was limited by the credibility of the record – and even among the Apostles themselves nothing they experienced could possibly establish with absolute certainty that this man was God. How could it, insofar as their experience depended on the senses and the senses, which are tied to the particular, cannot beget a certain and universal knowledge?

Viewed from the other side Augustine also knew that his indubitable knowledge of the eternal Word of God derived its certainty from the fact that the Word was known as an intelligible and immutable substance. But no possible examination of this side could ever show that he was also Incarnate in time because there was nothing mutable in the God he knew.

The conclusion was that it is impossible to *know* that Christ was the Word of God. But if our relation to God through the mediation of Christ could not be established as a knowledge how could anyone enter into the mediated relation? How, in other words, could Augustine have any concrete relation to Christ if his knowledge could only go so far as to affirm, abstractly, that *if* Christ was what the church said he was, then he would be the mediator? There was only one way and that was through the immediate relation of one particular individual with another – through an act of will, through faith. In short, Augustine had to believe what he had no possibility of knowing – and if he failed to do so he would voluntarily be placing himself outside the only mediation he recognized as capable of uniting him with God. The logic of orthodox Christianity demanded the move from knowledge to belief, and in general that is why no one can be born a Christian:[6] to become such requires an act of will, made explicit in baptism, and this must be done whether or not one has come to the philosophical knowledge of God.[7]

The necessity of believing in order to establish a concrete relation between each individual and Christ – who was, in turn, the link between this mutable world and God's immutability – places the Christian in a dependent relation on Christ. What he teaches and commands us to do, through his church and Scriptures, becomes absolutely authoritative – and, in relation to the end of uniting ourselves with God, we become utterly dependent on a will other than our own. This dependence is what the Platonists refused and in so doing they, like Esau, sold their birthright (union with God) for a mess of pottage (such worldly benefits as they could wring out of their knowledge of God).[8] This is the ground of the distinction Augustine has frequently drawn between the false pride of natural reason, epitomized by the Platonists, who reject the submission of belief – wanting to be free from any external authority – and the humility of the faithful whom he likens to little birds who cannot yet fly on their own. Dependent in this world on the milk of divine truth which they get through Christ's church, these "little ones"[9] are nourished on a spiritual food and acquire from it – i.e., from the mediation of Christ – the strength to return to God and to become his adopted sons. This divine "food" transforms them into the likeness of God which they neither have, nor can get, by nature.[10]

For Augustine the actual content of what he must will was both clear and objective. But exactly here was his problem. At the time he partly wanted to do so – "I found acceptable the Way, the Saviour himself" – but partly also he did not – "but I was still reluctant to go along his strait road" (VIII,i,1).[11] Until he did so, until he actually stepped on the road in front of him, Augustine knew that he was not yet a Christian and could have no part in the mediation promised by Christ. The reason for this should be clear and with it we can return to the first chapter of the book.

Augustine's problems centred around his temporal life because he found that he was unwilling to follow the commandments of the person whom he regarded as the mediator. In his case the difficulty was very specific:

> [T]he desires of the hope of honour and money now no longer were inflaming me where they formerly had . . . for now these things did not delight me instead of your sweetness and *the beauty of your house* [i.e., the heavenly city] which *I loved* (Ps. 25:8), but I was still very strongly bound by [the attractions of] women. (VIII,i,2)[12]

Here is the familiar trinity of the love of worldly honour, power, and love. Augustine was free of the first two but was still bound by the most immediate, the least rational, and for him the most powerful of the three: his natural sexual desires and the consequent need of a woman's love (= sex). He saw that the church allowed a variety of sexual conduct, counselling chastity but permitting marriage.[13] He though he could not live without a woman and so, desiring also to be a Christian, realized that if he was going to enjoy sex and be a Christian, he could have both in a marriage such as the one to which he was already engaged.[14]

Once again everything should have been simple but it was not. Two things prevented him from solving both problems by joining the church and marrying: one was worldly and the other religious. On the side of his worldly interests he could not adopt this solution because he found that he could not face the "other things" (VIII,i,2)[15] such a marriage entailed. He does not say what these were but it is not difficult to guess. The girl to whom he was engaged was still about 18 months short of marriageable age[16] which meant that if he joined the church at this point he would have to go for almost a year and a half without sex.[17] He was "unwilling to endure this" (VIII,i,2).[18] But even if he had been able to marry at once this would not have been a solution to his problems since he could not disguise from himself that his only interest in marrying was to satisfy his sexual desires.[19] He had understood from Matthew and Paul that marriage was only a second-best way of being a Christian since a wife, taken for even the best of reasons (i.e., for the sake of getting children), would prevent him from devoting himself entirely to God.[20] Such a total dedication is what he found enviable in the situation of Marius Victorinus when this man had been forced to give up his teaching by the decree of the emperor,[21] and this is also what he saw to be desirable about the solution of Anthony and the friends of Ponticianus whose examples were before him on the day of his conversion.[22] In his own case the marriage he contemplated was an unauthorized compromise with his lust and he could not settle for any half-way measures, since anything that left him "torn two ways" (1 Cor. 7:34) would offer no resolution. This division in himself was precisely the problem he expected Christianity to resolve.[23] For this reason his sexual desires were, as he says, the chief impediment to his becoming a Christian at this point: "on account of this alone [his sexual desire] I was turned upside down in other aspects of my life: an ill man and one wasting away with decayed cares" (VIII,i,2).[24] He had found in

Christ the way to the *patria*: he ought to have given up all other things to follow him — yet he did not.[25] Doing so would have meant giving up once and for all the joys of sex — which he thought impossible. Or else, if he was to satisfy those desires in the context of marriage, he realized that his Christianity would only be nominal and then what would become of his relation to God? "And I had now found that good pearl and to have bought it I ought to have sold all that I had, but I hesitated" (VIII,i,2).[26] Augustine was in a quandary about what to do and decided to seek the advice of the old and venerable priest, Simplicianus, about what he should do to overcome this reluctance to "walk on the way of God" (VIII,i,1).[27]

VIII,ii,3-VIII,iv,9. The example of Victorinus' conversion

VIII,ii,3-5. Simplicianus and the Victorinus story — My disagreement with Courcelle's efforts to show the identity of Neo-Platonism and Christianity becomes very marked in the interpretation of this episode. Courcelle understands that Augustine went to Simplicianus because he was discouraged by the failure of his efforts to recapture the ecstatic vision in the manner of Plotinus' repeated flights of the "alone to the Alone."[28] He says, "Augustine addressed himself to Simplicianus not only to lay before him his moral disarray but with an eye to instructing himself in Christian Neo-Platonism."[29] He did so because Simplicianus was at the centre of the Christian Neo-Platonic circle in Milan. Simplicianus had learned his Neo-Platonism from the famous Roman rhetor and philosopher, Marius Victorinus, and had in turn taught Ambrose.[30] Courcelle supposes that "The ordinary subject of their discussions [between Augustine and Simplicianus] was the rapport between the Neo-Platonic system and the Prologue of John."[31]

Augustine's argument points to a very different reason. He went to Simplicianus not to learn about the rapport between Christianity and Neo-Platonism but for help in that which distinguished them. As he has told us, he was not interested in learning anything more about the eternal things of God which were known equally by Christians and Neo-Platonists, but he did need help in bringing his temporal life into line with the commandments of Christ. This is reflected in the words he uses to describe the visit to Simplicianus. Augustine went to see him not because of his reputation for philosophy but because he was "greatly experienced in following your ways" (VIII,i,1);[32] not because he had taught Ambrose his Neo-Platonism but because he was the "father" through whom Ambrose had accepted grace — i.e., baptism in the church.[33] Simplicianus undoubtedly had great philosophical attainments but, as a letter from Ambrose shows, his chief virtue in the eyes of Ambrose lay in his ability to distinguish between Christianity and Neo-Platonism. Ambrose, writing to Simplicianus, says of him: "you understand intelligibles with unusually keen wit seeing that you are accustomed to demonstrate how far the books of the philosophers have gone from the truth and how far they are for the most part vain (*Letter*, LXV,1)."[34]

This is precisely where Augustine needed help: not in that which linked Christianity and Neo-Platonism but in that which distinguished them. He needed help in following the way of the Word made flesh, not in knowing the eternal Word. This is just what Simplicianus gave him by recounting the story of the conversion of Victorinus.

Augustine laid before Simplicianus the "compass of my errors" (VIII,ii,3).[35] Evidently he told him that he had come to the knowledge of God and of his Word through reading "certain Platonist books which Victorinus – formerly rhetor of the city of Rome, who, I had heard, died a Christian – had translated into Latin" (VIII,ii,3).[36] Simplicianus congratulated Augustine on having come to the true knowledge of God which he acknowledged was contained in the Platonist writings[37] – but this was not the main point. He recognized that Augustine's difficulty did not lie in his knowledge of God but in his inability to submit his will to that of Christ. Seeing the similarity between the cases of Victorinus and Augustine, he told him the story of Marius' conversion.[38] He did so not to show the rapport between Christianity and the philosophical knowledge of God but to show the absolute difference between the two relations to this knowledge, embodied in the philosopher's presumption and the Christian's humility, as well as the considerations which had moved Victorinus to reject the one and choose the other. The whole story is placed in the context of the will, of humility, and of exhortation – as opposed to knowledge, pride, and instruction. "Then, in order to exhort me to the humility of Christ which is hidden from the wise and revealed to little ones, he told the story of Victorinus" (VIII,ii,3).[39]

Marius Victorinus was an influential and celebrated rhetor and philosopher who had for years publicly defended pagan philosophy and practice against Christianity. However, by dint of close study of the Scriptures in the course of his polemic, he had become convinced that Christianity and the best of pagan philosophy (i.e., Neo-Platonism) taught one and the same God. Thereafter, as a friend of Simplicianus, he used often to say to him, though only in private conversation, "I want you to know that I am already a Christian" (VIII,ii,4).[40]

This would have been true if Christianity were simply a matter of knowing the true God or of recognizing, intellectually, that Christ met the formal requirements of a mediator between man and God. But, as we have seen, the Christian position demands more. It demands the total submission of the will which is expressed in a certain definite and objective order of life – i.e., that commanded by Christ. At first Victorinus did not see this but Simplicianus knew better. He knew that Victorinus would have to acknowledge – not merely intellectually but in his practical and temporal life as well – that Jesus Christ was the eternal Word of God. This meant he had to show his willingness to obey Christ in those things which he asked of his followers – first amongst which was the demand that they seek baptism.[41] Thus his reply to Victorinus: "I will not believe it nor will I count you amongst the Christians unless I see you in the church of Christ" (VIII,ii, 4).[42] This is not a flat statement that Victorinus was no Christian, since Simplicianus had no way of knowing the inner state of his will.[43] It does however contain the certainty that unless Victorinus had subjected his will to Christ – of which his professed membership in the church would be the visible, though by no means infallible, sign – then for certain he was no follower of Christ and no Christian. Victorinus did not understand and answered with a flippant question, "Is it therefore the walls which make a Christian?" (VIII,ii,4)[44] – with the implication that this was sheer nonsense.

This state of affairs went on for some time with Victorinus continuing to maintain that he was a Christian simply in virtue of what he knew.[45] He thought he could be such without being obliged to offend his powerful pagan friends by openly repudiating their religious practices or having to face the storm of ignominy and derision he feared would break on him if he did — the great philosopher has joined those simpletons who worship the Jewish carpenter whom our fathers crucified![46] This unreconciled division between his knowledge and his will evidently rankled in Victorinus who, by "reading and desiring" (VIII,ii,4),[47] came to see and feel the falseness and duplicity of his position, inasmuch as he wanted the benefits Christ promised but would not submit to the demands he made, "and he feared to be denied by Christ *before his holy angels* (Lk. 12:9) if he was afraid to confess him *before* men (Mk. 8:38)" (VIII,ii,4).[48] At last he "gathered his courage" (VIII,ii,4)[49] to scorn whatever worldly consequences might ensue in order to obtain the kingdom of heaven through Christ's mediation and so resolved one day to join the church by going "inside the walls." He went to Simplicianus and said: "Let us go into the church, I want to become a Christian" (VIII,ii,4).[50] After a brief instruction in the first elements of the Christian revelation Victorinus made a splendid public profession of his new faith and was baptized.[51]

The logic which made it necessary for Victorinus to make this movement of the will in order to become a Christian is clear and inescapable. Victorinus saw it, Simplicianus did, and so did Augustine who says, "as soon as your man, Simplicianus, had told these things about Victorinus, I burned to imitate him: and of course it was for this purpose that he told [the story]" (VIII,v,10).[52]

The conclusion to Courcelle's discussion of the Victorinus episode is that: "Without a doubt we shall never know why Simplicianus raised the objection [that he would not count Victorinus a Christian until he was within the walls of the church] or why Victorinus was suddenly moved to inscribe himself for baptism."[53] To Courcelle these are simply irrational and insignificant details lost in the mists of history. But surely there is something very wrong with any interpretation of Augustine's Christianity which makes the decision for baptism an irrelevant and unintelligible matter of secondary importance. By following Augustine's argument we have seen that there *were* reasons why Victorinus had to go within the walls of the church in order to become a Christian and that we can *know* them. Courcelle cannot see this because of the external manner in which he approaches the work.[54] By his method of comparing texts — of which he is truly a great master — he misrepresents the Christianity to which Augustine was moving and ends up conflating it too closely with the Neo-Platonism from which, on this central and all important question, both Augustine and the church differed radically.

The misleading character in this philological method can be seen as clearly as anywhere in Courcelle's long discussion of the literature on the "walls of the church."[55] This is aimed at proving that Victorinus could have considered himself a Christian in good faith even though he did not go to church. In fact it only goes to prove — what is not in any way in question and least of all for Augustine — that merely going to church and performing the externals of the Christian liturgical life is no sure sign that anyone is a Christian.[56] The church did maintain this, as Courcelle says, but what he does not see is where Augustine also teaches that no one can be a Christian who could join the church (having heard Christ preached), but who refused to do so. This is what Victorinus both saw and willed. He knew that if he was to follow Christ he would have to enter the walls of the church although it was not the walls but the will which made him a Christian. Courcelle knows nothing of this — working only with externals he sees only walls.

VIII,iii,6-8. God's relation to the world — On considering the great joy in the church over Victorinus' conversion, Augustine asks:

> what makes it happen that a man rejoices more for the salvation of a soul for which hope had been given up, or one freed from a greater danger, than if there had always been hope for him or if the danger had been lesser? For indeed you also, O merciful Father, rejoice more *over one sinner who repents than over ninety-nine just men who have no need of repentance* (Lk. 15:7). (VIII,iii,6)[57]

The question may seem like a digression unless we recall the passage in Luke from which Augustine takes all three of the parables he mentions here to explain the joy of the church at the conversion of Victorinus. The parables are: (*i*) The shepherd who searched for the one lost sheep out of a flock of a hundred (Lk. 15:3-7); (*ii*) The woman who looked for the one lost coin out of ten (Lk. 15:8-10); (*iii*) The Prodigal Son (Lk. 15:11-32). All three were told by Jesus in response to the Scribes and Pharisees who had complained against him that "This man receives sinners and eats with them" (Lk. 15:2). The implication in this Jewish criticism was that if any man ignored the decrees of the divine law — by keeping company with sinners — then the true response of God-fearing men was to cut him out of the holy community and leave him to God's wrath which, they rejoiced to think, he would soon and remorselessly visit upon him.

According to this abstract view each particular individual in a group of 100 was worth 1/100th of the whole, so the defection of one was no great loss compared to the 99 who remained true. Or, looked at from the other side, one could say that the sheep was the sheep of the shepherd, the coin was the coin of the woman, and the son was the son of the father, and thus, from an abstract point of view, the sheep, the coin, and the son all continued to "belong" to their respective owners whatever their actual temporal condition — whether lost or not. From this standpoint the actual disposition of the things in time and space does not matter. The parables of Jesus point out that in their worldly affairs men do not act this way and he teaches that with God it is the same: "Just so I tell you there will be more rejoicing in heaven over one sinner who repents than over ninety-nine persons who need no repentance" (Lk. 15:7).

That men act in this way was no revelation and Augustine adds more examples from everyday experience (VIII,iii,7) where pain and pleasure are connected as opposites, so that the greater the preceding pain or danger, the greater the pleasure on being rescued. That God and his church also look at things in this way, and rejoice more the greater the evil from which we are rescued, is a consequence of the Christian revelation. For the Pharisees, as for the ancients generally, God was thought to distinguish between the righteous and the wicked in terms of his law. He cares for the good, he does not care for the wicked. The end terms, good or evil, are all that appear *sub specie aeternitatis* and are alone thought to be what God regards. How we get into either camp is our own affair.[58]

With Christianity everything is different. By his Incarnation God reveals something about himself that cannot be deduced from any consideration of the divine law. He shows us that the temporal belongs to him as much as does the eternal. By making himself a temporal means to an eternal end God has shown that he regards our temporal situation just as much as our eternal status and thus — like us — cares about the evil man who has wandered away from him in time even more than he does for those who are already within the fold or those, like the holy angels, who have always been there (VIII,iii,6). But the joy of God is not conditioned by an preceding pain nor lessened by this involvement in the changing circumstances of this world (VIII,iii,8). It defies the canons of human thought to maintain both sides of this position, yet Augustine could confidently do so on the basis of his belief in the Christian revelation that the eternal God was also in time. It was because God cares for us temporally that the church acted properly when it reacted after the manner of creation (rather than as things appear simply according to the demands of the divine law where all are abstractly equal) in the joy it showed for the conversion of Victorinus.

VIII,iv,9. The world's relation to God — Having just shown that Christ and his church have regard for our temporal situation Augustine now turns the matter around. He notes that there are many who are converted to God from a "deeper hell of blindness"[59] than Victorinus yet who, if less well known, cause less joy in the church. The reason is not (as we might think from the preceding chapter) that the church sees things simply in worldly terms as if the famous and important were more welcome than ordinary men and women. Augustine says: "Let it never be the case that in your church persons of wealth are taken in preference to the poor, or the renowned and well-born in preference to the unknown and base-born."[60]

Viewed from the temporal side, the Christian economy of salvation is just the opposite as Augustine points out by quoting St. Paul where he says:

> You have chosen the weak things of the world in order that you might confound the strong ones, and you have chosen the lowly things of this world and the despised things and those which are nothing, as if they were something, in order that you might reduce to nothing those things which are. (1 Cor. 1:27-28)[61]

If the church showed greater joy in the conversion of the illustrious Victorinus than in an even more difficult conversion of a less well-known and powerful man, it was not *because of* Victorinus' standing in the eyes of the world but because he had *repudiated* that standing by becoming a little one humbly submitting to the "gentle *yoke* (Mt. 11:29) of Christ."[62]

> For the enemy is defeated more thoroughly [in the conversion] of a man whom he held more [tightly] and through whom he held many other men. And he holds more firmly the proud by reason of [their] illustriousness and through these he holds many more by reason of [their] authority.[63]

It thus became the church to rejoice because: (*i*) when many rejoice together, which happens in the conversion of a well-known man, the joy of each individual is greater, (*ii*) because where the famous lead others follow;[64] and (*iii*) because the enemy loses more when he loses the unusual talents of a man like Victorinus, "whose tongue like a powerful and keen weapon had slain many"[65] which,

cleansed and made serviceable to God by his conversion, can be set against the
devil himself and turned *"to every good work* (2 Tim. 2:21)."[66]

VIII,v,10-12. The two wills: the old and the new — The story of Victorinus has
"set" Augustine "on fire to imitate him" (VIII,v,10).[67] Ardour, example, and
imitation: these are the categories of the will. As Doull says, "The comparison of
himself with this well-chosen example awakened in Augustine the strongest division between his attachment to the universal good and all his particular interests."[68] And Augustine longed even more to do as Victorinus had done when
Simplicianus told him that Victorinus had given up his school of rhetoric rather
than his Christianity when, some time after his conversion, the apostate emperor
Julian forbade Christians to teach.[69] To Augustine, "he seemed to me not so much
courageous as lucky, because he had found the occasion to give himself over completely to your service" (VIII,v,10).[70] Augustine tells that "I longed to do the
same, bound as I was, not by the irons of another man, but by my own will"
(VIII,v,10).[71]

From the Victorinus story Augustine had come to see that he had to give up his
worldly interests if he was to follow Christ to the *patria*. He knew this, and he
wanted to do it, yet he did not do it.

> I no longer had that excuse on account of which I used to say to myself that I
> was not yet ready to give up the world to serve you because the perception of
> the truth was not certain to me: for now this truth was certain. (VIII,vi,11)[72]
> I had the certainty that it was better to give myself to your love than to yield
> to my lust: but while the former delighted and convinced, the latter drew and
> held [me] bound. (VIII,v,12)[73]

What held him back, seeing that he no longer had any doubt about the good or
the way to it? Indeed, what could hold him back since he *wanted* to follow Christ
and give up his worldly interests? He recognized that there was nothing outside his
will which was forcing him to will these things — and indeed how could there be,
since he himself no longer wanted (i.e., willed) them? But still he was bound. The
question was, why?

The only answer could be that he had tied himself to these ends by his own former will for them, now hardened by long usage into a "chain of habit." Doull
remarks that Augustine "gives the Aristotelian answer that these ends are
acquired, that their stability is that of habit. There is not in them a natural necessity
but a necessity which has its origin in the will itself."[74] Augustine says:

> The enemy held my will and from this he made a chain for me and held me
> tightly bound. For from a perverse will lust was born and by giving into lust a
> habit was created and when this habit was not resisted it became a necessity. By
> which things, as if by small loops joined to one another — for which reasons I
> have called it a chain — he held me bound up in hard servitude.[75] But the new
> will which had begun to come to life in me that I might serve you freely and
> enjoy you O God, the only sure joy, was not yet equal to overcoming the earlier
> will strengthened by age. Thus two wills within me, one old and the other new,
> one carnal and the other spiritual, struggled violently amongst themselves and
> by their discord tore apart my soul. (VIII,v,10)[76]
> Thus I understood by my own experience that which I had read about how

flesh strives against spirit and spirit against flesh (Gal. 5:17). I was indeed on both sides but I was more in that which I approved in myself than I was in that which I disapproved in myself. Indeed for the most part I was not on the latter side seeing that I now rather suffered it unwillingly instead of doing it willingly. Yet all the same it was by my own doing that habit fought fiercely against me since I had come willingly [to this state] where I no longer wanted to be. (VIII,v,11)[77]

Augustine likens his state at this time to a sleeping man who is called to wake. He knows he ought to wake and he actually wants to wake, yet still he tries to hold on to a few more minutes of sleep, saying: "Soon," "In a minute," and "Let me sleep a moment longer." "But 'Soon and soon' had no limit, and 'Let me be a moment longer' turned out to be a very long time" (VIII,v,12).[78] The contest was between going the way of "God's love" or "yielding to [his] own lust" (VIII,v,12)[79] and he lost it – finding that he was unable to do what he really wanted to do.

In vain *did I delight* in your *law according to the inner man* since the other law *in my members* fought against *the law of my mind and led me as a captive into the law of sin which was in my members* (Rom. 7:22-23). For the law of sin is the impetuosity of habit by which the mind of man is drawn and held against its will, though deservedly since it fell into this state willingly. (VIII,v,12)[80]

Augustine was in a trap of his own making from which he could find no means of escape. His final sentence in this chapter is one of those questions which point to the direction in which the resolution will be found. It is the continuation of the quotation from Romans. He asks: "*Who* therefore could free wretched me *from this body of death* except your *grace through Jesus Christ our Lord?*" (VIII,v,12).[81]

II. VIII,vi,13-VIII,xii,30. The resolution

VIII,vi,13-15. Ponticianus and the discovery of monasticism

Augustine turns now to the resolution of this problem and shows how he was finally converted.

And so concerning the manner in which you delivered me from the chain of the desire of copulation by which I was very closely bound and from the bondage of the affairs of this world I will now tell and I will *confess to your name O Lord my helper and my redeemer* (Ps. 53:8 and 18:15). (VIII,vi,13)[82]

For a time after his meeting with Simplicianus, Augustine remained unable to bring himself to a decision and his misery grew steadily worse.[83]

I continued in the same situation with growing anguish and daily I longed for you, going to your church as often as I could get free from those [worldly] affairs under the weight of which I was groaning. (VIII,vi,13).[84]

On a certain day[85] – some time in the first week of August 386[86] – everything changed. The rest of the book is devoted to the events of that momentous day. At the time Alypius, Nebridius, and Augustine were all living in the same lodging-house in Milan[87] to which there was attached a small garden, of which, along with the unrented portion of the house, they had the use because the owner did not live there.[88] This garden seems to have been bounded on at least one side by the wall of a neighbouring house,[89] to have had a seat big enough for two[90] and, at a distance from the bench, a fig tree.[91]

On the day in question Alypius and Augustine were alone at home[92] when they were unexpectedly visited by a fellow countryman from Africa, a man named Ponticianus, who held high office in the imperial household.[93] Ponticianus had come on some business the nature of which Augustine had forgotten by the time he wrote the *Confessions*.[94] A Christian himself,[95] he evidently already knew Augustine slightly or by reputation — but only as a pagan rhetor inasmuch as he evinced surprise on discovering the codex of the Apostle Paul lying open on the table.[96] Seeing Augustine's interest in Christianity he, "smiling and looking at me in a congratulatory way, marvelled that this book and this book alone was unexpectedly lying open before my eyes" (VIII,vi,14).[97] Augustine told Ponticianus that he was studying these writings with the greatest care and, since he expressed this interest in the church, Ponticianus began to tell Augustine and Alypius about the great Egyptian, Anthony, born in the middle of the preceding century, the "father of monasticism," about whom neither had known until that moment.[98] Ponticianus then mentioned that monastic communities existed not only in Egypt but in the West as well. Indeed he told them of such a monastery, under the care of Ambrose, just outside the walls of Milan itself. Neither Augustine nor Alypius had had any idea of its existence.[99]

The quantity of modern commentary which has been generated by Augustine's account of this day is astonishing. In his *Confessions de saint Augustin dans la tradition littéraire* alone, Courcelle has over 100 pages on the material of these chapters — and there are scores of other monographs and articles on the same chapters which are thought by most to be the high point of the *Confessions*.[100] Courcelle's arguments, though not universally accepted, do represent the fullest achievement of a whole school of interpretation and his conclusions are still, on the whole if not in every detail, the most authoritative word on these questions — but I will leave my discussion (and criticism) of this material to the notes since it is possible to follow Augustine without reference to them.

Let us look to the *Confessions*. From Ponticianus Augustine learned for the first time of monasticism — that is, a concrete form of temporal life, existing and adopted by many, which was nevertheless devoted wholly to God and was thus free of the division between worldly and heavenly goals.[101] This discovery provided the last thing Augustine needed to move to his conversion because, for him, the way of Christian marriage was a compromise with his lust and could not have resolved the conflict.

Augustine and Alypius listened in silent amazement to the stories of Anthony.[102] Ponticianus continued with an account of Anthony's contemporary influence, describing in detail how two of his own friends, who had also been attached to the imperial court,[103] had made the decision to abandon the world and enter on a way of life like Anthony's.[104] In Trier one afternoon when the emperor was at the circensian games, Ponticianus and three friends had gone for a walk in a park by the walls of the city. During the course of the stroll the group split in half. The two who had wandered off from Ponticianus and his companion came across the rude shelter of some ascetics where they found a copy of the *Life of Anthony*.[105] One of them began to read it and was so astonished and inflamed by what he found that he himself began to think of imitating Anthony on the spot. He said to his friend words to this effect: "Why do we go on wearing ourselves out serving the world when the most we can hope from this service is to become 'friends of the emperor' (VIII,vi,15)[106] which at best, is a fragile and dangerous good. We can, if we will, become 'the friend of God' (VIII,vi,15)[107] at this very instant." Reading on in the text he decided to abandon all his worldly goods and hopes "*to follow Christ*" — after being moved by the same verse of the *Gospel of Matthew* (19:21) which had provoked the conversion of Anthony.[108] His friend then and there decided to follow him in conversion.

When daylight faded Ponticianus and the other man arrived at the hut, where their friends told them of their resolution and how they had come to it. The converts invited Ponticianus and the other to join them. But these, though moved to tears for their own state of life, were unwilling to do as much themselves and returned to the palace, their "hearts drawn to earthly things" (VIII,vi,15)[109] while the other two remained to join the ascetics, "fixing their hearts in heaven" (VIII,vi,15).[110] Ponticianus added that the fiancées of these two, moved by their example, afterwards "dedicated their virginity to God" (VIII,vi,15).[111]

VIII,vii,16-18. The loss of excuses and alternatives

Ponticianus' story had a revolutionary effect on Augustine. "Even while he was speaking" (VIII,vii,18)[112] Augustine found himself inwardly turned to face himself — and what he found was not pleasant but "base," "deformed," "sordid," "dirty," and "full of sores" (VIII,vii,16).[113] He is clear what made this revolution possible. He had exhausted every hiding-place and there was no longer anywhere he could turn to conceal his own wickedness from himself.

> And I saw and was appalled that there was nowhere I could flee from myself. And if I tried to turn my gaze from myself it fell on Ponticianus still telling his story and once again you placed me in front of myself forcing me into my own sight so that I should see my iniquity and hate it. Of course I had always known it but I used to pretend that it wasn't what it was and I pushed it away and forgot it. (VIII,vii,16)[114]

The reason Augustine could no longer lie to himself was that he now had in his hands — and knew that he had — all the pieces he needed to construct a new life. Ponticianus had provided the last one by showing him the existence of a concrete way of life in the world which was nevertheless not of this world but totally dedicated to God in its willing obedience to follow his (i.e., Christ's) commands to the exclusion of all other ends. Knowing this, Augustine could no longer tell himself that he could not give up the world because he did not know the form of the life for which he would exchange it. He now saw his whole life as a long series of excuses aimed at avoiding having to give up his own natural interests. He recalls that even from the beginning of his adolescence he had desired chastity but used to pray for it thus:

"Give me chastity and continence, but not yet." For I was afraid that you
would hear me too soon and would too soon cure me from the disease of earthly
desire which I preferred to have satisfied rather than extinguished.
(VIII,vii,17)[115]

The same was true of everything he had done in the twelve years since he first
came to desire Wisdom through reading Cicero's *Hortensius*, and especially of his
nine-year attachment to the Manichees.[116]

> I used to think that the reason why I had put off *from day to day* (Ecclus. 5:8)
> giving up hope in the world to follow you alone was that I did not see any cer-
> tain course by which I might direct my steps. But now the day had come when I
> was set naked before myself and within myself my own conscience accused me.
> "Where is your tongue? Beyond question you are the one who used to say that
> you were unwilling to give up the burden of vanity because you were uncertain
> about the truth. Behold the truth is now certain and yet still the burden of vanity
> holds you down. And wings have grown on freer shoulders for men who have
> neither worn themselves out in seeking [the truth] nor have spent ten years and
> more in making up their minds about these things." (VIII,vii,18)[117]

This last point is very important. To become a Christian did not require years of
learning nor certain knowledge of the truth which he now possessed. In spite of all
the time he had spent in search of God he saw that the two friends of Ponticianus
had gone further towards him in an instant than he had in twelve years. In fact
they stood on the way to the truth while he did not.[118] This is the sense of the criticism of his former life in the preceding section (VIII,vii,17). It was true that the
ascent to the vision of the intelligible good took years to achieve, as the ancient
philosophers well understood,[119] but what was it all worth since it did nothing to
put him on the road to the *patria*? Wherever Christ was preached, there the possibility of getting on the way was available to everyone at every moment: it had
only to be willed. This is what the friends of Ponticianus had done and this is what
Augustine saw clearly that he too must do. He wanted to follow where they had
led but found that he could not. Ponticianus eventually finished the story and his
business and Augustine was left with himself. He was repulsed and disgusted by
his inability.

> How did I beat my soul with the whips of [my] thoughts to make it follow me
> who was trying to follow after you! But it fought back. It was unwilling yet
> could offer no reason why it should not [go where I wanted it to]. All the rea-
> sons had been used up and shown false: all that remained was a mute trembling
> and it dreaded like death to be restrained from the course of habit by which it
> was being dissolved into death. (VIII,vi,18)[120]

Everything had been reduced to a pure and simple question about his will. This
is where the argument turns.

VIII,vii,19-20. The flight to the garden

Once Ponticianus had gone, Augustine, in great inner commotion, turned to
Alypius to ask why on earth they did not do the same as Ponticianus' friends.[121]
But, terribly wrought up, he could not continue any discussion and instead found

himself drawn out to the little garden to try to resolve the struggle within himself.[122] Alypius followed silently and the two sat down.

> I raged against myself in spirit, being angry with the most tempestuous indignation that I did not go over to your order and into your way my God, into which way *all my bones* (Ps. 34:10)[123] cried out for me to go and which they extolled with praises to the skies. And one does not get there by ships or by four-horse chariots or by feet nor even by the few [paces] I had taken to get from the house to the place where we were sitting.[124] For not only to go but also to arrive in that place was nothing other than to will to go but [to do this I would have] to will strongly and completely and not twist and turn here and there, a half wounded will with a part rising up struggling against a part falling down. (VIII,viii,19)[125]

Augustine's agony was complete. His own heart was divided against itself.[126] In explaining this condition he notes that he did many bodily actions in his turmoil: he tore at his hair, beat his forehead and, locking his fingers, hugged at his knees, and so forth. He remarks that he was able to do each of these things without the slightest difficulty merely by willing to do them. Yet in these cases his will was one thing while the power to act was another. This was evident because he could not have done any of them if, for example, he had been tied up. The mind could apparently move the body more easily than it could move itself — where the will and the power were one and the same thing — because in what he wanted, to will it was to do it, and still he could not.[127]

VIII,ix,21. "Whence this strange thing?" — the incomplete will

How could it be that he willed to follow Christ, which he then did, and yet have his will resisted, not by some external and alien thing, but by itself? "The mind gives an order to the body and is obeyed immediately: the mind gives an order to itself and it is resisted."[128] He asks, "What is the source of this strange thing? And why is it thus?"[129] He first suggests the direction in which the answer will be found: "let me ask," he says, "if perhaps the hidden recesses of the punishments of man and the most dark griefs of the sons of Adam are able to provide an answer."[130] The problem came from his being a son of Adam — that is, from his nature as a fallen rational animal.

When the will has some external end, as in the movement of a part of the body, it is determined by the immediate potencies of that end. The hand will move insofar as it can move unless it is impeded by exhaustion, bodily defect, or some external constraint. The hand itself has no explicit desire of its own which might conflict with the will and for this reason bodily motion is for the most part unconscious. Augustine recognize this when he says: "The soul orders the hand to move and it is so easily obeyed that the order can scarcely be distinguished from its execution."[131]

On the other hand Augustine had now experienced that it can happen that the mind orders itself to will, which it would not do unless it willed, and yet does not do what it orders. From this it appeared that the will had more power over something external to it, like the body, than it did over itself. Again he asks, "What is the source of this strange thing? And why is it thus?"[132] He finds the reason for this resistance of the conscious will to itself in the multiplicity of possible ends amongst which it can freely choose — none of which, however, is willed to the exclusion of all the others. This was the source of the strange conflict which the will put up against itself.

> The mind orders itself to will, which it would not order unless it willed, yet it does not do what it orders. But [this only happens because] it does not will completely therefore it does not order completely. For it only orders insofar as it wills and insofar as what it orders is not done, so far also it did not will — since the will orders that there be a will and it does this not to another but to itself. Therefore it does not order fully and consequently what it orders is not done. For if the will were total it would not order that it be total since it would be so already. Therefore it is not strange[133] partly to will and partly not to will but it is a sickness of the soul that does not wholly rise up, although supported by the truth, being weighed down by habit. And thus there are two wills because neither of them is whole — and that which is present in the one is lacking in the other.[134]

VIII,x,22-24. One soul, many wills

Augustine is conscious that in speaking in this way both he, and the Scriptural texts he follows,[135] can easily seem to be teaching the doctrine of the Manichees, "who, since they have noticed that there are two wills in deliberation, assert that there are two natures in two minds, one good and the other evil" (VIII,x,22).[136] He had already rejected this position as incompatible with the divine incorruptibility, but the discovery that his will was divided seemed to suggest that the Manichees were right after all in claiming that because "they see in one man two wills in conflict, two opposite minds from two opposite substances from two opposite principles are in conflict" (VIII,x,24).[137] But this was not the correct explanation of what he experienced.

> When I was deliberating about accommodating myself at last to *the Lord* my *God* (Jer. 30:9) — as for a long time I had proposed to do — it was I who willed and I who did not will: it was I [alone]. But I was neither willing wholly nor nilling wholly. Consequently I was struggling with myself and was torn in pieces from my own self and although this tearing apart happened against my will it did not show the nature of another mind [in me — as the Manichees said] but the punishment of my own. And likewise it was not now I who caused it *but the sin* which dwelt *in me* (Rom. 7:17) as the punishment of a freer sin because I was a son of Adam. (VIII,x,22)[138]

Against the Manichee's interpretation Augustine observes that the will may be divided not only between one good and one evil course but between any number of good or evil courses alone or between a number of good and evil courses mixed together. On the Manichees' account there was only one good and one evil principle in the universe as a whole and in each of us in particular. But what then could they say of a man who was deliberating whether he should do one of two things, both of which they considered to be evil? Either they must say that there were two evil wills and principles, "or they will be converted to the truth and will no longer deny that when anyone deliberates, a single soul is tossed about between contrary wills" (VIII,x,23).[139] And what if a person were deliberating between four ends? Must each come from a separate nature which in turn required a separate principle? But again this made nonsense of the premise that there were only two natures.[140] The conclusion to the *reductio ad absurdum* was inescapable: we must be thought of as being a single soul from a single principle with a will that can freely desire diverse ends which can be good or evil.

Because Augustine was certain that his divided will did not imply two minds this meant that any conflict he experienced was a division within his one soul. But if he knew that his will was free, in the sense that it was not constrained or limited by anything other than itself, he was not free in the sense that he could avoid making this choice. As he said, "this tearing apart happened to me against my will" (VIII,x,22) — and it would continue "until one [end, course, or way] was chosen on which the will, which is divided into many parts, bears one and whole" (VIII,x,24).[141]

He had to decide between following the temporal demands of Christ — which, as he now knew, called him to a life that was not partly attached to this world and partly to God but was totally dedicated to him — or else refusing to do so. There was no alternative. He could not procrastinate any longer claiming that he was not certain that Christ was the mediator. Since he knew that this could never be known, there was no point in the future at which he would ever discover any reason or any fact that could have any bearing on the matter beyond what he already knew. But if there was no reason to put off his decision,[142] further delay was no longer possible as an alternative to following Christ or refusing to do so. To stay where he was would either be simply irrational — which way lay madness if he remained for long in that troubled and divided state where he could not bring his will to bear on one course — or else, if with no reason and no excuse he simply chose not to choose, would amount to the irrational rejection of Christ. He insists that he had come to a point where he could not avoid the decision: "The tumult in my breast had brought me to this point where no one could halt the burning conflict I waged within myself until it was resolved, the [outcome] of which you knew [O God] although I did not" (VIII,viii,19).[143] This does not mean that his choice, once made, was irrevocable and could not be altered tomorrow. What it did mean was that further delay was excluded and that from this point on — unless he became mad by his inability to pick one to the exclusion of the other — he had either to be with Christ or against him.

He concludes the chapter by pointing out that he found himself caught in a division between his habits and his will for Christ. He says:

> [E]ternity attracts the soul upwards and the desire of a temporal good holds the soul below, it is the same soul which is not willing with a complete will the one or the other and therefore it is pulled apart with grievous vexation while it prefers the higher course in truth and the lower course it does not lay aside from familiarity. (VIII,x,24)[144]

But these contrary ends do not come from different wills, they are merely different aspects of his total will: "there are," as he said, "two wills because one of them is not total and what is present in the one is lacking in the other" (VIII,ix,21).[145] Once this division had appeared in his soul the argument has shown that his will could only achieve its integrity and his soul its composure by choosing one of the two ends completely. But since this conflict of the will with itself arose because his choice between the two temporal lives was mutually exclusive – if he chose the Way of God he would have to give up the rest of the world, and if he chose the rest of the world he would have to give up the Way of God – the question was whether the total will, which desired both the temporal *and* the eternal, could ever regain its integrity? The answer has two sides, one objective and one subjective, and Augustine treats them in turn in the last two chapters.

VIII,xi,25-27. Empty nothings and the vision of Continence

So long as Augustine's will was divided between these contradictory ends the difficulty could not be resolved by picking one side, suppressing the other, and simply getting on with his life. He wanted both: that was the problem. He was *both* his old habitual will *and* his new rational will, which meant that no matter which side he picked he would continue to be opposed, however feebly or strongly, by the other – and as long as this was the case his will would not be total. This is why he could neither made a decision nor avoid making it – as he describes his condition in the first section of the chapter. This is also why he turned to examine the objective ends between which he was "hanging suspended."[146]

On the side of nature in its independence from God were all his "old friends,"[147] the finite goods that had been with him throughout his life and to which he had attached himself by the chain of habit.

> My old friends, nonsensical trifles and empty nothings
> Held me back and picked at the robe of my flesh
> And murmured from below:[148]
> "Do you send us away?" and
> "From this moment we will never be with you for all
>   eternity" and,
> "From this moment on you will never be allowed to do this or that for all eternity."
> And what things did they suggest in the phrase "this or that" which I just used!
> What things did they suggest my God!
> May your mercy keep such things away from the soul of your servant!
> What sordid things they suggested, what shameful acts!
> But I heard them now much less than half as strongly.
> It was not as if they were freely contradicting me to my face
> But they were like things muttering behind my back
> And like things stealthily plucking at me to make me look back
> While I was going away from them.
> Nevertheless they held me who delayed from ripping myself clear
> And forcing myself off from them
> And leaping over to the place to which I was called,
> Since habit, a tyrant, said to me,
> "Do you think you can live without these things?" (VIII,xi,26)[149]

The problem with these finite goods was simply that they were finite. The difficulty was not that nature was evil as such, but that its goods were temporal and limited and in this way they were inadequate to his rational desire for the eternal and infinite good. If he was to become chaste by following Christ's way he would have to abandon such things forever. We must be clear that he is not speaking of great and unmentionable crimes or perversions. What was ''sordid'' and ''shameful'' about these things was only that they were so small, so insubstantial, so fleeting – and yet he could not tear himself from them to will wholly the absolute good he acknowledged in Christ. Augustine found himself held back from joining the church, where he wanted to be, by a lifelong habit of fornication – indulged through no natural necessity, and whose object was a few minutes of limited and doubtful pleasure. It was true that nature offered him these joys over and again but here was only the ''bad'' infinity of an endless repetition of finite goods. These ends had nothing of the absolute and eternal in their own proper natures and Augustine was cut off by his mortality from the infinite enjoyment of their finitude. The union of temporal and eternal that he could have on this side was false and the choice of nature's way was therefore irrational.

When he turned his glance from the broad way of the world to the other side, to the strait road of the church which lay at his feet, he saw the ''chaste dignity of Continence'' (VIII,xi,27).[150] Sexual desires were the main thing that held him in the world and so the forms in which he saw Continence were examples of sexual chastity. In principle, however, the contrast is between continence – i.e., holding oneself on a particular way – and the incontinence or dissipation of whatever sort to which each of us is prone – i.e., the unrestrained and irrational pursuit of an endless multiplicity of finite goods. When he looked to Continence he was presented with a specific and exclusive form of temporal life which also promised to lead him to the infinite good his rational will desired.

It must not be thought that this single way did not accommodate a whole variety of natural differences – as if everyone had to become identical in order to follow Christ. He stresses this in reporting that he saw with Continence all varieties and conditions of mankind.

> There were there so very many boys and girls,
> A multitude of mature people, and people of all ages,
> Both sober widows and virgins late in life.
> And in all of these was Continence herself,
> By no means sterile
> But the fruitful mother of children of joys from you,
> O Lord, her husband. (VIII,xi,27)[151]

All followed Christ according to their different natural capacities: what they had in common was that each had chosen Christ to the exclusion of all other ends.

As opposed to nature's way which urged Augustine to an infinite pursuit of finite goods, Continence (= the church)[152] invited him to follow a single way to the infinite good. These were the two choices between which he was torn. His consideration of each had now shown that, of the two, only the Christian way offered the unity and integrity he desired. Only on Christ's way was there any possibility that he could have everything he desired – a true and stable unity of finite and infinite goods. This was the only rational choice and at this point Continence asked him:

"Can you not do what these men and and women have done?
Or were these men and women able to do it in themselves and not in the Lord
  their God?
The Lord their God gave me [i.e., continence] to them.
Why do you [try] to stand on your own when on your own you do not stand?
Throw yourself on him without any fear: he will not withdraw so that you fall.
Throw yourself on him without fear: he will catch you and cure you."
  (VIII,xi,27)[153]

Augustine says: "I was terribly ashamed because I still heard the murmurings
of those nonsensical things and remained hanging suspended"[154] — but once again
Continence spoke, advising him: "Stop your ears against these unclear whisperings of your [bodily] members so that they may be reduced to death. They tell *you
of pleasures but not such ones as the law* (Ps. 118:85) of the Lord your God has to
tell." (VIII,xi,27)[155]

The discussion has moved from will to grace because Augustine saw in the
examples before him that to become a follower of Christ he would have to will
Christ without any reserve, without any conscious part of him, however weak,
wanting anything else. But how could he do this when he still "heard" — i.e., was
attracted by — nature's way? It was shameful that he still wanted these things
because there was no reason to desire them apart from the fact that he had bound
himself to them. But he had, and they were there, and there was nothing that he
could do about it. The solution could only lie in divine grace.

VIII,xii,28-30. Augustine's conversion

The argument shifts now to the subjective side. Only one thing remained to complete Augustine's liberation from nature: he had to cease to be moved by it or to
act according to it. He finally broke down in a storm of tears over his inability to
get rid of his former sins, and turned to God because he was unable to help himself. "For I felt that my sins still held me. And I was crying out with misery:
'How long, how long must I go on saying "Tomorrow and tomorrow"? Why not
now? Why should there not be an end to my base desires at this very hour?' "
(VIII,xii,18).[156] At this point he happened to hear from a neighbouring house the
voice of a child repeating a singsong refrain: "Pick it up and read it, pick it up and
read it" (*tolle lege, tolle lege* — VIII,xii,29). Moved by this voice he went back to
the table where he had left Paul's letters, read the first thing his eyes fell upon, and
was converted. These are the simple facts of the case — our problem is to arrive at
a correct interpretation of them.

The consideration of the two ends between which he was deliberating had
clarified that Christianity alone could provide the totality of all he desired. It was
the rational choice and yet he could not make it. He begins the last chapter by stating specifically that as a result of his consideration of the two ends, and because of
the irrational resistance he still experienced to giving himself entirely to the course
he both knew to be best and wanted to follow, a great storm broke within him.[157]
This brought on a deluge of tears which caused him to get up from where he was
sitting with Alypius and fling himself down under a fig tree where he could be
alone with himself.

His inability to go where he wanted was frustrating beyond endurance. He had struggled and fought and worn himself out trying to break his chain and still it held. There was, quite literally, no reason why it should hold and yet it did just because it was not amenable to reason.[158] He was in the grip of an irreducibly irrational power in his own soul. He knew he had reached his limit. At this point all he could do was to break down and appeal to God. *"And you, O Lord, how long, how long O Lord: will you always be angry?* (Ps. 6:4) *Be not always mindful of our ancient iniquities.* (Ps. 78:5 and 8)" (VIII,xii,28)[159]

What held Augustine was perfectly clear. His rational will could not act freely and without hindrance because of his "ancient iniquities" in the form of a lifelong acquisition of bad habits in which he had continually chosen ends that were a confused mixture of reason and irrational desire over those which were true and universal. A division had now appeared in his soul between his past choices of such ends and the now clear and explicit recognition that Christ's way was the true and universal end in the world. He knew he could only become whole and well by choosing this way without reserve, yet at the same time he discovered that the wrong or thoughtless choices of a lifetime had bound him to habits he could not break. His habits and his ways of acting now existed in him beyond reach of his reason. Insofar as their content was irrational and did not have the form of thought it contained something external and alien to the rational will which had once chosen them freely. In his case the example would be his choice of sexual intercourse not for its rational and objective end – in the procreation of the species – but simply because it felt good, or for whatever other irrational purpose. But having done this over and again he now found, with shame and frustration, that the habits he had introduced and cultivated in his soul could not be brought to want what he now knew to be the truth because they had been formed without regard to it and had no place in it.

When he speaks, in the Biblical language, of *"the law of sin* (Rom. 7:23) which was in my [bodily] members" (VIII,v,12),[160] or of the *"sin which dwelt in me* (Rom 7:17) as the punishment of a freer sin because I was a son of Adam [i.e., because he was a fallen rational animal]" (VIII,x,22),[161] it is not the body as such which is sinful but a lifelong habituation to the satisfaction of ends which were a confusion of reason and irrational desire. His deliberation, therefore, was not primarily about whether or not he should follow a celibate form of life – suppressing sexual desire in favour of the requirements of an intellectual life.[162] Many had done this without any intention of following Christ.[163] Such people imitated the lives of (some) Christians in this respect – but it was not celibacy, in itself, which would make Augustine a Christian since this could be chosen for any one of a number of reasons (natural preference, fear of the divine law, incompatibility with the life of the mind, etc.)[164] that had nothing to do with a dedication to Christ. It was true that Augustine would not become a Christian unless he became celibate, yet his primary choice was about whether he would remain with his old habits in the confusion of reason and nature or else come to a position in which they were reconciled and united. He had found such a union objectively present in Christ. But inwardly there was only division and opposition and there was nothing he could do about it because this division was presupposed in everything he did. His habits, however weak and unattractive they now seemed, would never consent to his going over to Christ – and without their consent he could not follow Christ with his whole will. He could not "order" himself to follow Christ because he could not "order" his old habits.

The argument of the *Confessions* has moved from Augustine's birth in nature which he called "a dying life or a living death" (I,vi,7),[165] to the point where he was about to be reborn in grace, "to die to death and come alive to life" (VIII,xi,25).[166] At just this moment he happened to hear:

> a singsong voice from the neighbouring house, as if the voice of a boy or a girl though I am not sure which, and this voice repeated many times, "Take it up and read it, take it up and read it." (VIII,xii,29)[167]

It sounded like the words of some child's game and, as such things happen, Augustine turned his attention for a moment from his own hopeless condition to wonder distractedly whether he knew of any games which included this refrain. Nothing came to mind which would, as it were, provide a natural explanation of the words.[168]

> And holding back a flood of tears I got up, interpreting this in no other way than as a divine order to open the book and read whatever I should find in the first passage I came across. (VIII,xii,29)[169]

Recollecting that he had just heard how Anthony had been converted by such chance words,[170] Augustine hurried over to where Alypius had left the copy of Paul's epistles. He snatched up the book. opened it, and read in silence the first passage he saw.[171]

> *Not in rioting and drunkenness, not in lust and wantonness, not in contentions and the assiduous effort to be first in all things, but put on the Lord Jesus Christ and do not make provision to satisfy the desires of the flesh* (Rom. 13:13-14). I had no desire to read further nor was it necessary. For as soon as I had come to the last words of this saying it was as if all the darkness of hesitation was put to flight by the light of security which had been poured into my heart. (VIII,xii,29)[172]

Augustine was finally converted to Christianity. The conflict in his soul was over and his will was wholly and completely intent on following Christ. He had stepped out of the wood and onto the high road which led to the *patria*. He would walk on it all the rest of his days.

In the same moment that he recognized that his rational will would be ceaselessly opposed by his own habitual nature – which he did in the deluge of tears that was the recognition and confession of a lifetime of wrong choices he was now powerless to undo ("the [only] sacrifice which is acceptable to you [O Lord]" [VIII,xii,28][173]: "acceptable" because this was the truth) – the way was finally opened to him to move beyond this division. The union of human and divine which he saw to be objectively present in Christ and which he could not achieve by any force of will could only be his if, inwardly and subjectively, he abandoned and renounced the hopeless effort to unite these aspects of his divided will by his own power. His habits were in conflict with his rational will. Neither could ever be fully satisfied nor could their conflict be truly resolved as long as he acted according to his nature, in which this division was now explicitly and self-consciously manifest. In terms of what Continence had told him to do he had "stopped his ears to the unclean whisperings of his bodily members [i.e., his habits] in order that they might be reduced to death."[174] That is, as the attempt to unify his will by his own effort was doomed it was not worth a moment's further consideration. Augustine did not give it as much and, as Continence had promised, God did not let him fall. He had done this much in the confession of his sin and impotence but this was all he could do. The actual restoration, the healing of his divided soul, if it was to come at all, would have to come from God.

This is the sense of the *tolle lege* incident. Because he had acknowledged the impossibility of healing the division in his soul by himself he was at last open to a restoration and cure that would be effected by divine agency — by grace. The ordinary words of an ordinary child heard over the real wall of the garden could thus be *taken* as a divine command: that is, he understood this ordinary event not merely in its natural significance — i.e., in its independence from God — but spiritually, as the word of the rational principle. Here was an end, immediately present, beyond the division of nature and reason and on which his total rational will could bear. Presented as a divine command, where he had either to obey or disobey, he could now at last choose definitively between his habits and his rational will since this order — which spoke only to his rational will — did not come from within and from what was merely a part of himself. It was a command he obeyed voluntarily. In doing so his will was wholly and perfectly free since it was at last moved by an end in which the division of reason and nature was not presupposed and from which their confusion, which had characterized his entire life to this moment, was totally excluded.[175]

Taken as a divine command the voice of the child had a definite content. He interpreted it as ordering him not to read just anything but to "Pick up the Scriptures" and when he turned to them they too had a definite content ordering him to "Take no thought for nature and nature's appetites but put on Christ." The random reading of Paul's text therefore completed Augustine's conversion by making explicit the full content of the command he had first obeyed in turning to the Scripture — and once he had read this far he had no need to go further for "the light of confidence flooded into my heart and all the darkness of doubt was dispelled."[176]

In obeying these commands Augustine had therefore freely committed to God the cure of his soul — the healing of the wound or division in his innermost nature, the opposition between his animal and rational natures, the sickness in his bones.[177] Throughout the *Confessions* it has been his constant teaching that divine grace alone can cure us and he has now fully shown the logic which justifies this position. The command was Christ's and so was the way: from henceforth he would not look to himself for his salvation but to Christ.

As a result his sexual appetites were never again to trouble him at the conscious level. This was because he had not suppressed them in favour of reason while leaving them alive and independent in his soul. The whole threat and tyranny of his habitual desires had come from their independence from reason — but in the position to which he had been called, and which he had freely and consciously chosen, nature had no such independence since here, through divine grace, it was

perfectly united with reason in Christ. As long as he stayed on this way by his conscious obedience to Christ, then nature, in its independence from reason, could
have no power over him. This was the way "defended by the care of the heavenly
Commander [where] there are no deserters from the heaven's army to prey upon
the traveller, because they shun this road as a torment" (VII,xxi,27).[178] This is
what he says at the end of this chapter — bringing the book full circle by showing
the resolution of the difficulty with which he had begun: "For you had so converted me to yourself that I no longer sought a wife nor placed any hope in this
world" (VIII,xii,30).[179] We know what this means. It meant that he would live the
rest of his life without sex since he had no desire to get married for the sake of
children, nor for anything else which this world had to offer apart from Christ.
This is confirmed in Book X where he tells us that, from the moment of his conversion he was able "to decide once and for all to repudiate [fornication] and
never to embrace [it] again" (X,xxxi,47).[180] The continence which had been
impossible so long as he tried to achieve it by his own power had become actual in
the moment that he placed his whole confidence in Christ. Of course he did not
cease to be a rational *animal* and neither his hormones, nor his habits, had dried up
or disappeared. In the tenth book he tells us how he continued to be troubled by
these things in his unconscious and instinctive life — and would continue to be so
troubled until his flesh and memory were reformed and made spiritual in the resurrection. But that is another matter.

Alypius was converted at the same time and in the same way according to his
own particular nature. That is, Alypius, who found it easy to do the good once he
knew what it was, was content to follow Augustine, trusting that he could safely
follow if his friend had concluded that Christianity was the true and proper
course.[181] The two went into the house and told Monica what had happened. She
"rejoiced," "exulted," and "triumphed," for "You had converted me to you so
that I no longer sought a wife nor placed any hope in this world [as] I was [now]
standing in that rule of faith on which you had shown me to her so many years
before" (VIII,xii,30).[182]

This is the end of the second part of Augustine's first confession as found in
Books I-IX. Its trinitarian structure begins to emerge ever more clearly. As we
have seen, the first part (Books I-VII) was devoted to Augustine's relation to the
external and objective structure of the universe through his search for a true
knowledge of God as creator (the Father) and for a true mediator between us and
him. The knowledge of God was revealed through creation generally, being available in principle to all through the consideration of nature, and the knowledge of
the mediator was revealed through the church, being available to all who had
heard Christ preached. The second part (Book VIII) has turned on Augustine's
inner, subjective relation to Christ, believed to be the Incarnate Son of God. We
may expect the last part (Book IX) to deal with Augustine's relation to the Holy
Spirit as the third person of the Trinity where the objective and subjective, the
knowledge and the will of the first two parts, will be shown in their unity.

NOTES

1 *vincula mea* (152/13).

2 *De/cupiebam* (152/19-24). Augustine insists that he was certain he had come to the true idea of God. He says so twice in this passage and, further on in VIII,i,1, that he had found God and his Word (*inveneram/omnia* — 154/1-3), and that he had found the good pearl (God) (*Et/margaritam* — 154/10-11). In VIII,v,11 he says that the vision of God was certain to him (*iam/erat* — 162/15-16) and that he could no longer claim he did not know it (*Et/veritas* — 162/13-16). The same is repeated in VIII,vii,18 — *Ecce iam certum est* (168/20). Augustine uses Paul's image of seeing God dimly in a mirror — for the character of the Platonist knowledge of God — in a very precise sense. We should not think of the wonderful modern mirrors but of the poor reflection in a piece of metal or smoky glass sufficient only to show that something is there but not clear enough to see its details: compare VII,x,16 — *Et/viderem* (141/3-5).

3 *nutabant* (152/24) = to stagger or falter (in judgement = to doubt, to hesitate), or in faith (= to be faithless) – contrasted with the desired stability of the preceding sentence.

4 *De/pigebat* (152/24-27).

5 See III,iv,8 *adsequor* (42/4) and above Chapter Seven, n. 97.

6 This contrasts, for example, with Roman citizenship which, by Augustine's day, was extended to all freeborn men in the empire in virtue of the fact that, as free rational beings, they were thought to belong automatically to Rome – i.e., to fall under the rule of the universal reason expressed in her laws. Here no choice was thought necessary or possible.

7 This point becomes blurred in the strongly Neo-Platonic interpretations of Courcelle, O'Meara, and O'Connell, concerning which, see the Appendix. In his *Odyssey*, O'Connell (who takes this position as far as it can go) sees a two-stage Christianity where Christ does one thing for the ordinary man or woman, like Monica, and another for intellectuals like Augustine. He writes, ''Christ's function in this 'return' to the blessed fatherland Augustine conceives as twofold. First he contemplates the case of the man less intellectually endowed, 'who cannot see from afar off' as he has done. For such a one Christ constitutes the 'way' upon which he may 'walk . . . come to . . . see . . . and hold fast to (God)' (VII,27). For the Monicas of this world, then, Christ now provides an alternative to the intellectualist way of the 'disciplines.' But secondly, even for the intellectually endowed, there is a difference between glimpsing the fatherland and being strong enough to dwell therein, enjoy, endure the vision's splendour. Food of Truth mixed with flesh, Christ provides the 'strength' which makes the difference between a momentary glimpse and continued enjoyment of God'' (p. 79). The difficulty is that if O'Connell means that the philosophers can come to the same end as simple Christians, though without Christ, then Christ is not necessary for them and this is not what Augustine teaches – or else, if they do not and cannot, is it right to speak of two ''alternative'' ways to the same end? Augustine's constant teaching is that gaining the strength to live in the city seen in the philosophical vision, and walking on the way of the many, are one and the same thing. In other words there are not alternative ways to heaven but only the one way, which is Christ, and no one can be a Christian or come to God, including especially those philosophers who have seen him, who will not bow ''to the gentle *yoke*'' (Mt. 11:29) of Christ'' (VIII,ix,9 — *sub/Christi* — 160/20: see also IX,i,1). In XIII,xxi,29 Augustine says this explicitly: ''for there is no other entrance *into the kingdom of heaven* (Jn. 3:5) from the time that you [God] decreed that such [i.e., baptism] should be the way into it [i.e., since Christ]'' — *non/intretur* (350/14-15).

8 See VII,ix,15.

9 On these images see above, Chapter Three, n. 64.

10 This image is clearly Eucharistic. See also above, Chapter Seven, n. 92.

11 *et/pigebat* (152/25-27).

12 *non/pecuniae* (153/11-13), and *iam/femina* (153/14-16).

13 See VIII,i,2 *Videbam/sic* (153/9-10). See Solignac's note on this passage (*BA*, Vol. 14, p. 11, n. 1) which is related to the distinction between marriage and chastity in 1 Cor. 7:7.

14 See VI,xiv,24-VI,xv,25.

15 *aliis rebus* (153/21).

16 In VI,xiii,23 (at the start of 386), Augustine's fiancée was "nearly two years too young for marriage" — *cuius/erat* (121/4-5: compare VI,xv,25 where the time is simply "two years" — *biennium* — 122/14). In July of the same year she would still have been about one or one and one half years too young. For the dating of these episodes see Solignac, *BA*, Vol. 13, p. 205.

17 He was clear that he could not be in the church and have sex unless he were married — which meant that he would have to do without the interim mistress he had gotten to tide him over until he got married (see VI,xv,25).

18 *quas nolebam pati* (153/21-22).

19 See VIII,i,2 *Nec/locum* (153/16-19). In VI,iii,3 Augustine mentioned that he envied Ambrose's life — except for his chastity: *caelibatus/videbatur* (101/12-13).

20 See VIII,i,2 *Audieram/capiat* (153/23-26). Augustine quotes Mt. 19:12 which Paul echoes and expands in 1 Cor. 7:32-35 — "An unmarried man can devote himself to the Lord's affairs, all he need worry about is pleasing the Lord, but a married man has to bother about the world's affairs and devote himself to pleasing his wife: he is torn two ways."

21 See VIII,v,10 *non/tibi* (161/15-16).

22 See VIII,vi,13-15.

23 See also IX,iii,5 where Verecundus holds the same view. None of this should be taken to imply that Augustine opposed marriage in principle. Following Scripture, he insisted that it was a holy state. His defence of marriage is found in *DBC*, written in 401 at about the same time as the *Confessions*. A wider treatment is found in *DCD*, XIV. Even right after his conversion, Augustine did not urge Verecundus to give up his marriage although it was what prevented him from becoming a Christian — see IX,iii,5-6. An excellent study of Augustine's views on marriage is Clark's "Adam's only companion."

24 *et/marcidis* (153/19-21).

25 See VIII,i,2 *Vani/dubitabam* (153/6-154/12).

26 *Et/dubitabam* (154/10-12).

27 *ad/tua* (153/8). See also VIII,i,1 *Et/tua* (152/27-153/8).

28 See above, Chapter Seven, n. 95.

29 Courcelle, *Recherches*, p. 171.

30 See Courcelle (*Recherches*, p. 170) where Victorinus is called "the founder of Christian Neo-Platonism." See also pp. 171-72 on Simplicianus, where Courcelle remarks that Augustine "was probably not ignorant of the fact that Ambrose had gotten his Plotinian learning from Simplicianus." Solignac (*BA*, Vol. 14, pp. 529-36) briefly traces the known facts of Simplicianus' life along with those of the other members of the "Milanese circle."

31 Courcelle, *Recherches*, p. 172.

32 *sectandae/expertus* (153/4-5).

33 See VIII,ii,3 *patrem/Ambrosii* (154/13-14). Courcelle ties Augustine's visit to Simplicianus to his vain attempts to regain the Plotinian ecstacy which he reads in the end of Book VII (*Recherches*, pp. 157-74) — i.e., he understands that Augustine went to Simplicianus to try and regain the intellectual vision. If Courcelle and those who identify Neo-Platonism and Christianity tend to overplay the philosophical interest of Augustine's meeting with Simplicianus, others like Alfaric, who want to separate Christianity and Neo-Platonism, seek to minimize its moral interest. Since they maintain that Augustine was not converted to Christianity at the time but only to Neo-Platonism, they have to try and explain away the whole practical aspect of the visit. Thus Alfaric claims that Augustine played up the moral aspect in order to praise Simplicianus who was just replacing Ambrose as bishop of Milan when Augustine was composing the *Confessions* (*L'évolution*, p. 382, n. 1). For my account of this controversy, see the Appendix.

34 Ambrose, *Letter to Simplicianus*, LXV,1.

35 *circuitus erroris mei* (154/15).

36 *quosdam/transtulisset* (154/16-19).

37 See VIII,ii,3 *gratulatus/verbum* (154/19-23).

38 On Victorinus, see Solignac's note in *BA*, Vol. 13, pp. 532-33. For much greater detail see Hadot's *Marius Victorinus*.

39 *Deinde/est* (154/23-26). See above Chapter Three, n. 64 on Augustine's use of this image of Christians as "little ones."

40 *"Noveris/christianum"* (155/25).

41 See the text from XIII,xxi,29 quoted above n. 7.

42 *"Non/videro"* (156/1-2).

43 Augustine insists that in these matters of the will we are not competent to judge one another. He stresses this especially in Book X where he says (X,iii,3) that "no one *knows* amongst men what goes on in a man except the spirit of the man which is within him* (1 Cor. 2:11)" − *nemo/est* (210/22-24).

44 *"Ergo/christianos?"* (156/3).

45 As long as Victorinus saw Christianity to be simply a matter of knowing something he was not obliged to confess openly that he was a Christian and said so only in private to Simplicianus: see VIII,ii,4 − *non/familiarus* (155/24-25).

46 See VIII,ii,4 *Amicos/arbitrabatur* (156/6-10).

47 *legendo et inhiando* (156/10-11).

48 *timuitique/confiteri* (156/11-13).

49 *hausit firmitatem* (156/11).

50 *"Eamus/fieri"* (156/11-13).

51 On the Roman baptismal customs, see Gibb's brief notes (*Confessions*, pp. 206, 207).

52 *ubi/narraverat* (161/8-10).

53 Courcelle, *Recherches*, p. 391.

54 Courcelle describes this method − philology and the comparison of texts − on p. 12 of the *Recherches*. See the Appendix for my account of the difficulties and limits of this method and also below, Chapter Nine, n. 136.

55 Courcelle, *Recherches*, pp. 383-91.

56 In the *City of God* Augustine states often that the elect are not identical in number or person with the members of the visible church − see *DCD*, XVIII,49. Nevertheless he also insists that no one ever got into heaven "unless he had received a divine revelation of *the one mediator between God and men, the man Jesus Christ* (1 Tim. 2:5)" (*DCD*, XVIII,47). See also the text (from XIII,xxi,29) quoted above, n. 7.

57 *quid/paenitentia* (157/23-29).

58 This is the general position of the ancient world (i.e., the world apart from Christianity) and is common to Greeks, Jews, and Romans. Vergil puts the case in the famous words of the *Aeneid* (V, 709-10), where the prophet Nautes says to Aeneas: "O goddess-born, let us follow wherever the fates [i.e., God] push or pull us. Whatever will happen is our own power of endurance which must give us control over all fortune [i.e., the changing temporal circumstances]." Here God [*fatum*] irresistably disposes all things *sub specie aeternitatis*: it is for us to follow on our own and endure all obstacles − the side of *fortuna*.

59 *ex profundiore tartaro caecitatis* (159/26).

60 *Absit/nobiles* (160/10-12).

61 *infirma/evacuares* (160/13-17).

62 *sub lene iugum Christi* (160/20). As Gibb (*Confessions*, p. 211) notes, this "combines the Roman *sub iugum mittere* with an allusion to Mt. 9:29." The Roman custom of making a defeated enemy walk under the yoke is alluded to in the *hostis* of the following sentence (160/23) while the real enemy, the devil is mentioned a few lines further on (161/2).

63 *Plus/auctoritas* (160/23-26).

64 See VIII,iv,9 *Sed/ laetantur* (160/3-10).

65 *lingua/peremerat* (161/2-3).

66 *ad/bonum* (161/6-7).

67 *exarsi ad imitandum* (161/9).

68 Doull, "Augustinian Trinitarianism," p. 145.

69 On this law, see Gibb, *Confessions*, p. 212.

70 *non/tibi* (161/15-16).
71 *Cui/voluntate* (161/17-18).
72 *Et/veritatis* (162/13-16).
73 *ita/vinciebat* (162/28-163/1). Here again the same word, *placebat*, is used for Augustine's relation to the church as in VIII,i,1 — text above, n. 4.
74 Doull, "Augustinian Trinitarianism," p. 145.
75 On this *dura servitus* and its opposite, *libera servitus*, see Solignac (*BA*, Vol. 14, p. 29, n. 2). Notice the "chain" Augustine forges with his rhetoric.
76 *Velle/meam* (161/18-162/2). On the distinction between flesh and spirit, see *DCD*, XIV,1-6.
77 *Sic/perveneram* (162/3-11).
78 *Sed/ibat* (163/7-8). In VIII,v,12 Augustine likens his sleep to the sleep of death (*Non/paululum* — 163/1-6). using the text from Eph. 5:14 because his natural life was a "dying life or living death" (I,vi,7). The condition can only be overcome in the "rebirth" of baptism.
79 Text quoted above, n. 73.
80 *Frustra/inlabitur* (163/8-15).
81 *Miserum/nostrum?* (163/15-17).
82 *Et/meus* (163/18-22).
83 Courcelle claims that Augustine made a whole series of visit to Simplicianus on the strength of the imperfect verb (for habitual, repeated actions) in the words *solebamus audire* ("We used to hear") in a text from the *DCD* (X,29) — see *Recherches*, pp. 170-71, and *Les Confessions*, p. 69. Courcelle's general thesis requires Augustine to have made several trips to Simplicianus if the latter was to explain all that Courcelle says he told him (i.e., about the rapport between Neo-Platonism and Christianity) rather than the simple story of Victorinus. The *solebamus* need not indicate multiple visits at this time: all Augustine says is that he often heard Simplicianus tell the story of the Platonist who wanted the Prologue of the *Gospel of John* written in the churches and this could just as well have happened after Augustine's conversion.
84 *Agebam/gemebam* (163/22-25). Here we see Augustine "within the walls of the church" but as yet no Christian because he had not yet actually willed to conform his temporal life to the demands of Christ.
85 See VIII,vi,14 *quodam die* (164/16).
86 This date is known from the fact that in IX,ii,2 Augustine says that his conversion took place a "very few days" (*paucissimi dies* — 181/2-3) — which he specifies as less than 20 (IX,ii,4 *nescio utrum vel viginiti erant* — 182/18) — before the start of the annual "grape-gathering holiday" (IX,ii,2 — *vindemiales feriae* — 181/3). We know this extended from August 23 to October 15: see Courcelle, *Recherches*, pp. 201-202 and *Les Confessions*, pp. 120-22.
87 See VIII,vi,13 *Mecum erat Alypius* (163/25): VIII,vi,14 *Quodam/quidem* (164/16-18). I understand that Monica also lived in the same house because after their conversion in the garden Augustine and Alypius "went inside to my mother" (VIII,xii,30 — *inde ad matrem ingredimur* — 179/6-7) — the expression implies that she belonged there.
88 See VIII,viii,19 *Hortulus/domus* (169/17-19).
89 See VIII,xii,29 where the voice came, *de vicina domo* (177/22) — "from a neighbouring house." This reading is not in Sessorianus — the earliest and only pre-Carolingian manuscript (V-VIc) — which has *de divina domo*. Courcelle, who is opposed to reading the garden scene in its realistic sense prefers the unique reading of Sessorianus against the general tendency of all the editors except for Knoll in the *CSEL* ed. (who reversed himself in his *Teubner* ed.). For Courcelle's reasons, see *Recherches*, pp. 195-96, 299-306 and *Les Confessions*, pp. 165-68 (plate 1 in this volume reproduces the page of Sessorianus with the reading *divina*). Solignac's note (*BA*, Vol. 14, pp. 546-49) sums up the current state of the question: "in spite of Sessorianus the reading *vicina* remains the best attested and the best in accord with the context" (p. 548).
90 See VIII,xii,28. Augustine does not say that he and Alypius sat down on a bench (as opposed to the ground) but I understand this from the verbs he uses: *sedeo* (177/10, 178/8), "to sit,"

for what he and Alypius did at first (VIII,xii,28, and 29) and *sterno* (177/11), "to lie down, stretch out," for what he did under the fig tree (VIII,xii,28).

91 See VIII,xii,28 *Ego/me* (177/10-11). Courcelle, who argues that the whole scene in the garden is fictional rather than a realistic account of what happened, maintains that even if a real fig tree did exist it is mentioned by Augustine only "for its symbolic value" (*Les Confessions*, p. 191) and in *Recherches* (p. 193, n. 2) he claims that "in his account he transformed whatever kind of a tree was there into a fig tree." For Courcelle's reasons see below, n. 100.

92 See the texts quoted n. 87, and n. 93.

93 See VIII,vi,14 *cum/militans* (106/17-19). Nothing much is known about Ponticianus but see Brown, *Augustine*, p. 71, n. 4.

94 See VIII,vi,14 *nescio/volebat* (164/19-20).

95 See VIII,vi,14 *Christianus/erat* (164/27).

96 See VIII,vi,14 *Et/conterebat* (164/21-24). Compare the *tulit, aperuit, invenit* in this passage with the *arripui, aperui et legi* of VIII,xxi,29 (178/9-10). Gibb (*Confessions*, p. 216) says, "The Apostle usually formed one codex, the most usual division for the rest of the N.T. being the Four Gospels, Acts and Catholic Epistles, Apocalypse."

97 *arridens/conperisset* (164/25-27).

98 See VIII,vi,14 *Cui/latebat* (164/29-165/3). Courcelle (*Recherches*, p. 201, n. 1) supposes, perhaps correctly, that the reason Ponticianus began to speak about monasticism was that the book was open at Romans 13:13 where Paul speaks about continence.

99 See VIII,vi,15 *Et/noveramus* (165/13-15). Courcelle gives references to the existence of this monastery in *Recherches*, p. 180, n. 6.

100 *Solignac (BA*, Vol. 14, p. 548) writes, "Courcelle's interpretation [of the conversion scene] has raised a long controversy. These pages [i.e., of the *Recherches* (pp. 188-202)] have been the most controversial [in the book]." The argument has turned about Courcelle's radical suggestion that the whole garden scene is not to be understood as a realistic description of what happened but rather as a fictionalized version of the events of that day. This thesis was soon opposed by many scholars who defended the "realism" of Augustine's statements. For a history and bibliography of the controversy (to 1958), see the works mentioned by Solignac (*BA*, Vol. 14, p. 548 and Vol. 13, pp. 252-55). In 1963, in *Les Confessions*, Courcelle attempted to answer all these objections (pp. 91-197) in a remarkable tour-de-force in which he considered the scene from every possible angle except according to its internal logic — this is especially evident from the fact that little in all these hundred pages is concerned with the non-narrative parts of Augustine's text (i.e., chs. vii-x) where he explains the logic of what was happening to him. More recently W. Schmidt-Dengler has argued for the realism on stylistic grounds ("Der rhetorische Aufbau des achten Buches der *Konfessionen* des heiligen Augustin," *Revue des études augustiniennes*, 15 [1969], 195-208), and L. C. Ferrari, less convincingly, for its fictionalism ("Paul at the Conversion of Augustine," *Augustinian Studies*, 11 [1980], 5-20). Ferrari does not see that the same type of argument he uses against Schmidt-Dengler (p. 8) can be applied to his own thesis — i.e., that it is a distinct possibility that the reason Augustine does not make use of the text from Romans, except when describing his conversion in the *Confessions*, is simply because, in this respect, it had reference to himself alone. Courcelle's conclusions can best be presented in his own words from the *Recherches*. He says: "It is vain to look for a realist interpretation because Augustine takes care not to specify if it was the cry of a boy or girl and we know of no children's game in antiquity which used the refrain *tolle lege*" (p. 93). "I think the *tolle lege* is explained . . . by . . . concern for literary presentation" (p. 192). "In my opinion the fig-tree under which Augustine threw himself down to weep over his sins can only have a symbolic value: it is the same fig-tree under which, according to the gospel of John, Nathaniel lay at the moment when Jesus called him; because according to the constant exegesis of Augustine, the fig-tree of Nathaniel represents the mortal shadows of the sins of mankind, subject to concupiscence but justified freely by Christ" (p. 193). "The voice of a boy or girl who repeats *tolle lege* constitutes the conclusion of this inward dream [of Continence] and has no material reality." "I believe, with the editor of the *Vienna corpus* that one must adopt the reading *divina*. . . . It

is natural that the *tolle lege*, the cry of a boy or girl of Continence, comes from the *divine habitation*" (pp. 195-96). "Looked at closely, the scene in the garden of Milan appears as a simple doublet of the scene of 'conversion' to monasticism which occurred at Trier, also in a garden, and which Ponticianus had just related" (p. 197). "Like the converts of Trier, he conformed himself to the example of Saint Anthony who heard one day this verse of the gospel, attributed it to the force of an oracle and suddenly vowed himself to asceticism" (p. 198). "The scene of the garden of Milan appears thus to explain itself completely (except for the mention of the fig-tree which come from the episodes of Nathaniel) through the influence of the *Life of Anthony*. The divine cry of the chaste young people and the random consultation of the book merely constitute a colourful manner of presentation" (p. 200).

The whole point of this argument – which comes strangely from the pen of one who is defending the historical accuracy of the text – is intended to disprove that Augustine's conversion hangs on anything so trivial and external as the voice of a real child heard over a wall and the random reading of Scripture. To Courcelle this seems unworthy of the intellectual character of Christianity and reduces it to mere superstition. What he thinks he has to explain away is the raw elements of temporal particularity and chance (see p. 201) which, however, do belong to the Christian economy of salvation although they have no place in Neo-Platonism. Thus he turns the whole thing into an externalization of Augustine's inward state. The upshot is that Augustine's conversion becomes inexplicable in ordinary categories although Augustine's whole argument and purpose to this point has been to provide a comprehensible (i.e., rational) account of the journey from his birth to his conversion. In Courcelle's view Augustine had to abandon this purpose at the crucial moment as something special and unique happened to him which is certainly interesting, but which can have no application for the rest of us to whom such miraculous voices have not been granted. In Courcelle's words it is best regarded as a "sort of miracle" (p. 190) – which is to say that it is incomprehensible. But it can be objected that this "miracle," as the unmediated and inexplicable intervention of a *deux ex machina*, makes Christianity into the very thing he wants to avoid – a religion of fanatics who hear and obey voices not given to other men.

On the other side, though unreconciled with the above, Courcelle's explanation also insists that what happened in the garden was merely a natural event in which there was no divine intervention. This appears where he speaks of its upshot as Augustine's "heroic decision" (p. 201) to become celibate – done in order to facilitate the life of intellectual contemplation. But this is purely a natural exercise – i.e., the suppression of the side of passion in favour of reason – and was a course adopted by many without the slightest assistance from divine grace. In short, Courcelle's position is unable to bring the divine and human together in a manner that reflects the union which Augustine arrived at in his conversion.

101 See Doull, "Augustinian Trinitarianism," p. 145.
102 See VIII,vi,15 *et/tacebamus* (165/16-17).
103 The date of the conversion of these two friends of Ponticianus, which Augustine did not know (VIII,vi,15 – *nescio quando* – 165/17) was, presumably, before 381 when the emperor moved his residence from Trier to Milan (see Courcelle, *Recherches*, p. 181, n. 2 and p. 183). Trier, on the Moselle, had been "the capital of the West and the centre for the dominion of Gaul, Spain and Britain, the second Rome beyond the Alps, throughout the whole of the fourth century" (quoted in Gibb, *Confessions*, p. 217). Augustine specifies that both men held the office of *agentes in rebus* (VIII,vi,15 – 166/2). On this office see Solignac, *BA*, Vol. 14, p. 39, n. 1.
104 See VIII,vi,15.
105 On a possible connection between this ascetic community in Trier and St. Athanasius, the supposed author of the *Vita Antonii*, see Courcelle, *Recherches*, p. 181, n. 1.
106 On this title, *amici Augustii*, see Courcelle (*Recherches*, p. 182, n. 2) which reproduces and adds somewhat to the notes in Gibb (*Confessions*, p. 218).
107 See VIII,vi,15 *"Dic/fio"* (166/4-11).
108 Augustine says explicitly (VIII,xii,29) that Anthony's conversion was prompted by this verse from Matthew (*Audieram/conversum* – 178/1-7). On the parallels between the *Confes-*

sions account and the *Life of Anthony*, see Courcelle (*Recherches*, p. 198, n. 3 and p. 200, n. 3 and 4). Gibb with enviable brevity says of Anthony: "According to the traditional view Anthony was born in 251, spent twenty years in solitude, subsequently gathered disciples and founded settlements which are regarded as the beginnings of monasticism" (*Confessions*, p. 216).

109 *trahentes cor in terra* (167/6).

110 *affigentes cor caelo* (167/7).

111 *dicaverunt/tibi* (167/9-10). The conversion of the fiancée of a convert — by fidelity to one's lover — was a theme that strongly impressed the Middle Ages and was, with many variations, to have a long history: see, for example, Aude's relation to Roland (she dies of grief on hearing of his death because she had given herself to him so completely that there was no point in her living if he was dead: *The Song of Roland*, pp. 268-69) or Dante's relation to Beatrice in the *Divine Comedy*.

112 *cum/loqueretur* (168/24-25).

113 See VIII,vii,16 *Narrabat/ulcerosus* (167/11-16).

114 *Et/obliviscebar* (167/16-22).

115 *Da/exstingui* (168/6-10).

116 See VIII,vii,17.

117 *Et/meditati* (168/14-23). Gibb (*Confessions*, p. 220) refers the reader to Plato's *Phaedrus* for the source of this image of the wings. Courcelle (*Recherches*, pp. 106-32) finds its proximate source in Ambrose's sermon *De Isaac* and through this to Plotinus' treatise "On the Beautiful" (*Enneads*, I,6) — (see esp. p. 109, n. 1 and p. 126, n. 1). Whatever one thinks of these attributions it seems clear that Augustine was not using the image in a Platonic or Neo-Platonic signification. The wings he is thinking of are the wings of the "little birds" which have grown by faith in the nest of the church. They are the wings of grace and not those of natural reason since they grow on the shoulders of those who are not philosophers — see above, Chapter Three, n. 64 and 66 for a discussion of this image.

118 See VIII,viii,19 *Tum/sequi?* (169/5-12).

119 So Plato's teaching about the education of the philosopher in the *Republic*. The length and difficulty of the task is likewise stressed by Aristotle and Plotinus.

120 *Quibus/mortem* (168/27-169/4).

121 See the text quoted above, n. 118.

122 See VIII,viii,19 *Illuc/exiret* (169/19-21).

123 These are the bones mentioned already in VIII,i,1. Compare the two other references to this text in V,i,1 and IX,i,1.

124 Solignac (*BA*, Vol. 14, p. 49, n. 1; Vol. 13, p. 662) maintains that these phrases come from Plotinus and Plato. Courcelle (*Recherches*, pp. 107-12 and 126-28) finds them to be Plotinian/Ambrosian adaptations of the parable of the Prodigal Son. Gibb (*Confessions*, p. 212 and pp. 29-30) says: "Augustine has here fused together the parable of the Prodigal Son (Lk. xv,11f.) and a passage from Plotinus ... (*Enneads*, I,6,8)." But surely here too (as above at n. 93) the similarity to Plotinus is merely verbal. The argument has shown that Augustine is not talking about the soul turning away from corporeal things and inwards and upwards to the knowledge of God, but of the soul's willingness to leave nature in its independence from God and turning to the church by an unconditional reliance on Christ. This is not Plotinian doctrine. Compare the similar text in I,xviii,28 and see also above, Chapter Two, n. 89.

125 *Ego/luctantem* (170/2-12).

126 See VIII,viii,19, text above n. 118.

127 See VIII,viii,20 *Si/vellem* (170/17-24).

128 *Imperat/resistitur* (171/7-8).

129 *unde hoc monstrum et quare istuc?* (117/3).

130 *interrogem/Adam* (171/4-6).

131 *Imperat/imperium* (171/8-10). Compare VIII,viii,20 *faciliusque/moverentur* (170/26-27).

132 *Unde hoc monstrum et quare istuc?* (171/6-7, and again at line 13).

133 *Non est monstrum* — i.e., this is his answer to the thrice repeated question.

134 *Imperat/alteri* (171/13-26).

135 Gal. 5:17 in VIII,v,11; Rom. 7:22-25 in VIII,v,12; Rom. 7:17 in VIII,x,22.

136 *qui/malam* (171/27-172/3).

137 *duas/contendere* (173/16-19).

138 *Ego/Adam* (172/15-23).

139 *aut/aestuare* (173/13-15).

140 See VIII,x,24.

141 *donec/dividebatur* (174/13-15).

142 See VIII,vii,18 quoted above, n. 120.

143 *Illuc/non* (169/19-22). It is this aspect of Christianity that forces a decision and excludes indifference or delay once this point has been reached. This is the logic that provides the most profound explanation for the triumph of Christianity over the Roman empire, since the only alternatives available to the natural man who has heard the Gospel preached (including even, or especially, those who have the philosophical knowledge of God) are either presumption or conversion.

144 *aeternitas/ponit* (174/15-19).

145 *Et/alteri* (171/24-26).

146 *suspendebat* (175/12). Compare VIII,xi,27 *et cunctabundus pendebam* (176/18-19). This "suspense" or "indecision" is different from that of his sceptical period (see VI,iv,6): that was a refusal to will because of the lack of knowledge, this comes from an inability to will although the truth was known.

147 *antiquae amicae meae* (175/14).

148 Lewis and Short (*ALD*) know of the use of this word, *summurmuro*, from the *Confessions* alone. They translate it, "to murmur a little or in secret." I think a better sense may be deduced from the context of its use in VI,ix,14 where it describes the noise of the silversmiths, aroused under the roof at which a thief was hacking with an axe = "to murmur from below." This is what Augustine means here.

149 *Retinebat/poteris?* (175/13-28).

150 *casta dignitas continentiae* (176/3).

151 *Ibi/domine* (176/7-10). On the significance of the phrase *filii gaudiorum* see Courcelle, *Les Confessions*, p. 182. On the "auditory vision" of Continence herself, see *ibid.*, pp. 132-36.

152 Continence — holding oneself on the straight and narrow way of Christ (i.e., the church) — is connected with the wooden rule of Monica's dream of III,xi,19: see below n. 182.

153 "*Tu/te*" (176/12-17).

154 VIII,xi,27 *Et/pendebam* (176/17-19).

155 "*obsurdesce/tui*" (176/19-22).

156 *Sentiebam/meae?* (177/17-20).

157 See VIII,xii,28 *Ubi/lacrimarum* (176/26-177/3).

158 See VIII,vii,18 text above, n. 120.

159 *et/meae?* (177/14-20).

160 *lege/erat* (163/11-12).

161 *sed/Adam* (172/22-23).

162 Courcelle (*Recherches*, p. 201) claims that Augustine saw that he had to make "an heroic decision [because] the studious community about which he had dreamed for a long time would only be viable and would only bear fruit if her definitely gave up the hopes for his projected marriage, if he ripped himself away from the life of the flesh." O'Connell understands the events in the garden in the same way (*Odyssey*, pp. 91-94). Such talk of an "heroic decision" does away with the element of grace: it is difficult to understand in any other way than as the suppression of the side of passion in favour of intellect — but this would not bring about the unification of Augustine's will which is what he says happened.

163 In VI,xii,21 Alypius had urged Augustine to sexual continence for the sake of philosophy.

164 Alypius had been chaste for years from natural preference (see VI,xii,21).

165 *vitam/mortalem?* (5/17).

166 *mori/vivere* (175/7).
167 *vocem/lege* (177/22-24).
168 See VIII,xii,29 *Statimque/uspiam* (177/24-27).
169 *repressoque/invenissem* (177/28-178/1).
170 See VIII,xii,29 *Audieram/conversum* (178/1-7).
171 See VIII,xii,29 *Arripui/mei* (178/9-11). Courcelle (*Recherches*, pp. 188-89) compares the conversion scene in the *Confessions* with Augustine's other accounts of the same in *DBV* and *DUC*. See also O'Meara's article *"Arripui, aperui, et legi"* (*Augustinus magister*, Vol. 1, pp. 59-65) which makes similar comparisons with *CA* and in which O'Meara argues for a realist interpretation against Courcelle.
172 *non/diffugerunt* (178/11-19).
173 *acceptabile sacrificium tuum* (177/13). Over and again Augustine insists on the necessity of tears, humility, and a broken heart if one is to become a Christian. His favourite text in this context is Ps. 50:19 which he uses in IV,iii,4, V,ix,17, and, explicitly against the Platonists, in VII,xxi,27. It is to this text that these words about the "acceptable sacrifice" refer in VIII,xii,28.
174 See VIII,xi,27 *obsurdesce/mortificentur* (176/19-21).
175 See IX,i,1 *Tu/meus?* (180/3-11).
176 *quasi/diffugerunt* (178/17-19). Since Augustine was looking for the concrete content of what he had taken to be a divine command in the *tolle lege* it did not much matter where he happened to open Paul's text. Wherever it was he would only have had to read until he found something which he could have taken in this sense and, since Paul's teaching is the same throughout, he would soon have found a passage which stated what Christ demands of his followers.
177 See VIII,xii,30 *Convertisti/huius* (179/12-13). Augustine is very clear that God did the converting and he repeats this at the start of Book IX. Compare both these texts with VI,xi,20 and the chapters in Book VIII (esp. xi and xii) where he says that as long as he attempted to control his appetites by his own power he was unable to do so. This stands against Courcelle's understanding that the choice of celibacy was an "heroic decision" — i.e., something accomplished by nature. Such decisions do exist but could not have brought about the unification of Augustine's will as he describes it here.
178 *illuc/deseruerunt* (152/3-4).
179 *Convertisti/huius* (179/12-13).
180 *quod/potui* (224/22-23). See also the text from *Sol* (I,x,17), quoted above (Chapter Six, n. 113), which states Augustine's post-conversion position about marriage.
181 *Convertisti/revelaveras* (179/12-15). This refers back to Monica's vision in III,xi,19. L. C. Ferrari, "Monica on the Wooden Ruler," *Augustinian Studies*, 6 (1975), 193-205, gives a number of Augustinian texts which show that one of the chief functions of this ruler is that the "length of straightness which it embodies signifies lack of deviation to left or to right" (p. 199). The ruler of Monica's dream, on which Augustine was now standing, is that narrow and straight way or road which leads from the middle of the wilderness in this world to the heavenly *patria*. Recall the image of the way in VII,xxi,27. For Augustine to say that he was now standing on the rule (or within the rule — i.e., of faith = the church) is to say that he was now on the way: meaning that he had willed to become a Christian.
182 *convertisti/requirebat* (179/15-17).

Chapter Nine
COMMENTARY ON BOOK IX

If Augustine's purpose in writing this autobiography was to provide a full explanation of the steps that led him to Christianity, why did he add the ninth book at the end of his first confession?[1] Has he not already shown how he came to the church through the argument of the first eight books ending with his conversion? That was the point at which he freely willed to become a Christian. What more was there to add? Furthermore, the content of Book IX itself seems very arbitrary. It is divided into two parts. In the first (chs. ii-vii) he speaks of the events between his conversion and baptism. The second (chs. viii-xiii) deals with the life and death of Monica. What governs his selection of these episodes and what is their relation to one another?

The answer is that the content of this book is a description of the external life of the Christian in the world. If all Christians died on the day of their conversion there would be no temporal life beyond conversion. As it is their inner conversion demands a new relation to the external world. For this reason Augustine's account of his conversion was not complete until he had given some statement of the objective requirements and conditions of the new life to which he had been called. He had stepped out of the wilderness onto the narrow path: he still had to show what it meant to walk this road from rebirth to death. He does this in a paradigmatic form by showing his own life from conversion to baptism and then Monica's from baptism to her death.

IX,i,1. Introduction

As always, Augustine introduces the content of the book in the first chapter.

> O Lord, I am your servant,
> I am your servant and the son of your handmaid.
> You have broken my bonds.
> To you will I offer a sacrifice of praise. (Ps. 115:16f)
> May my heart and my tongue praise you,
> And may all my bones say:
> O Lord who is like you? (Ps. 43:10)
> Let them say this and you,
> Reply to me and say to my soul:
> I am your salvation. (Ps. 34:3)[2]

The ninth book is about Augustine and Monica as the servants of God. Here the content of the true knowledge found in the argument of Books I-VII, and the content of the free will found in Book VIII, are now united in the temporal life of the

---

Christian inasmuch as this is also a life which leads beyond this world to the eternal *patria*. This is the form in which knowledge (on the side of the eternal, universal, and objective) and will (on the side of the temporal, particular, and subjective) are brought together in a concrete unity for the Christian by the Holy Spirit.

Augustine uses a wonderful image to describe this union in the last sentence of the opening chapter: *et garriebam tibi* — "and I used to chatter to you." This may not seem like much until we think what an absolute difference there is between this *garriebam* and anything Augustine had experienced before. God is no longer a figure of infinite splendour on whom he cannot gaze (as in the vision of Book VII) nor of unrelenting anger (as in the moment before his conversion) but he (i.e., Christ) can be spoken to as one speaks with men — familiarly — and this without in any way departing from the absolute truth.

In a certain sense this book is also a return to the starting point of the *Confessions*. There Augustine showed how he was born into a world where he was "naturally" cut off from the natural and rational orders of the universe. Here he makes a fresh start through his spiritual rebirth and lays before us the new world where he was no longer cut off from either: "Now my soul was free / from the biting cares of striving to be first / and getting more and twisting about / and scratching the prurient sore of unlawful desires."[3]

I. IX,ii,2-IX,vii,16. Christian life between conversion and baptism

IX,ii,2-4. Augustine leaves his secular profession

As rhetor of Milan Augustine held public office and was, as he says, very much "before the eyes of all men" (IX,ii,3).[4] Now he wanted to give up every connection with what was merely worldly — i.e., whatever belonged to the world regarded in its independence from God. The first such thing was his official position which he now saw as a mercenary sale of his tongue for training young men to succeed in the courts of the world with no thought of the law or peace of God.[5]

Unlike his first infancy, Augustine, now inwardly reborn, did not act simply in terms of his immediate subjective desires: there were objective considerations. What action would best serve the name of Christ? He, Alypius, and their little circle of Christian friends decided that if he announced that he was a Christian and quit his post suddenly this would have the effect of turning everyone's attention to himself. They therefore concluded that any action which ostentatiously put him in the eyes of the world was not the best way to leave it and so he determined to make his retreat as quietly as possible.[6] To this end he decided to wait out the twenty-odd days until the end of term — and then, as he had a genuine illness, he could give this out as the reason why he would not return.[7]

All this looks ordinary enough, but a revolutionary change had occurred. Augustine was operating in a new world and in terms of a new principle. He was now able to distinguish between the certain and fixed requirements of the church (the necessity of humility and the avoidance of all that aimed at fame, power, and pleasure as the world understood such things) and his own uncertain opinion about how best to accomplish it. This is shown in the last words of the chapter where he allows that his decision to remain in *"the chair* (Ps. 1:1) of lies" (IX,ii,4)[8] for even a single hour beyond his conversion could properly be criticized by "your servants, my brothers" (IX,ii,4).[9] "I do not dispute it" (IX,ii,4)[10] he says — and the reason is clear. He knew his decision was open to question by spiritual men — his fellow Christians — on spiritual grounds. He did not presume to a knowledge he did not possess — i.e., that this course of action was the one which would do the most good for the cause of the church in the world. Temporal things of this kind — which depended on what people would have thought if he had left suddenly — he could not know with certainty and he did not pretend that he did. He was learning humility. He acknowledges that his resolve to stay on could be regarded as a sin, yet he was able to make up his mind to act in this way because, whether he stayed on or left at once, his inner submission to Christ was the important thing. It lay with Christ, and not himself, to bring good out of his actions, as it lay with Christ to redeem him from whatever sin was in this action, albeit unintentionally. Thus he ends, "But you, O Lord most merciful, have you not also pardoned and remitted this sin with the rest of the other horrible and mortal sins in the holy water [of baptism]?" (IX,ii,4).[11]

Augustine had also discovered Christian patience. He says that having lost all secular goals such as the ambition to make money — which had always enabled him to bear the burden of teaching — he would have been crushed by even the few weeks he had to wait until the holidays had he not found patience.[12] This patience was not the pagan virtue but a consequence of Christian faith. In the second part of the *Confessions* (Book X) Augustine shows the sense in which the whole of a Christian's life in the world is a trial. Since we are not yet in the *patria*, and will not get to it in this life, this life had to be borne with patience in faith, hope, and charity. For Augustine, who used to insist on an immediate possession of all the truth, this was a new attitude.

Finally we must note that for the first time in his life Augustine belonged to a community in which the actions he took to procure his soul's welfare were neither decided simply by himself, as in his sceptical and Platonist periods, nor simply by the arbitrary and subjective will of others, as in his existentialist and Manichaean days. He took counsel with his Christian friends and together they decided what was the best course for him to follow. He willingly subjected himself to their authority insofar as it could be shown to accord with the demands of the objective truth which all recognized in the will of Christ as interpreted by the *Catholica*. "Our plan was made in your sight: it was not made in the sight of any men except our own [i.e., the Christian friends of Augustine and Alypius] and we decided amongst ourselves not to divulge it to anyone at random" (IX,ii,2).[13] The change from the "I" of the preceding books to the "we" of the Christian community is very marked. God had pierced *"our* hearts,"[14] *"we* carried your words,"[15] *"our* thoughts"[16] were on the example of your servants which "set *us* on fire" (IX,ii,3).[17]

IX,iii,5-6. Friends and brothers: the cases of Verecundus
and Nebridius

Neither of these friends was converted along with Augustine and Alypius. At the time neither were therefore "brothers" in Christ along with the latter two. Both became Christians before they died. Augustine mentions them in this chapter to show the relation of the Christian community to non-Christians. In the cases of Verecundus and Nebridius, both of whom were very close to becoming Christian,[18] the relation was exclusively one of hope that the same grace which God had shown to those who had already been converted to the church would also be extended to those who had not yet turned from the merely natural.[19] Augustine says that he and his fellow Christians would have been intolerably "tormented" (IX,iii,5)[20] if Verecundus had not died as one of Christ's flock after the extreme "kindness" (IX,iii,5)[21] he had shown them.[22]

Verecundus, a Milanese citizen and teacher who had asked Nebridius to help him as an assistant,[23] offered his country house at Cassiciacum to Augustine and his friends as a place to escape from Milan once the term was over.[24] Since he himself was not yet a Christian this was not an act of Christian charity amongst brothers but simply one of benevolent *humanitas*. From Augustine's new position such natural goodwill and fellow-feeling could only find its fulfillment in the church[25] but his immediate response is telling. He and his friends did not in any way attempt to force or improperly persuade Verecundus to conversion. And how could they, who had so recently learned that one can only become a Christian if this is given in grace and willed in perfect freedom? Verecundus claimed that although he was married to a Christian wife he only wanted to become a Christian if he could do so entirely — which he, like Augustine, understood to mean as an unmarried celibate. But this way was blocked as he did not think it right to give up his wife.[26] Much as they desired him to come into the church, Augustine and the others recognized that all they could do was to pray for his conversion while insisting that in spite of their mutual desire to remain together he ought to remain faithful to the married state which was his lot.[27] It was preferable that Verecundus remain outside the church for the time being if the only way he could see of entering it meant that he would have to break "his marriage vow" (IX,iii,6)[28] when the church required no such thing. Those who consider Augustine's Christianity deeply misogynistic should consider the profound implications of a text like this.

As for Nebridius, that "most zealous searcher of the truth" (IX,iii,6),[29] though he did not come to conversion before Augustine left for Cassiciacum, remaining attached to his worldly interests in Milan,[30] he nevertheless was on the point of becoming a Christian[31] and was able "to rejoice in" (IX,iii,6)[32] Augustine's conversion as bringing him closer to the truth even though it meant that they would be separated.[33] Shortly after Augustine's baptism Nebridius was converted and baptized, returned to Africa, converted his whole family and died soon after.[34] In writing the *Confessions* Augustine rejoiced that his dead friend "*lives in the bosom of Abraham* (Lk. 16:22)" (IX,iii,6),[35] adding that, although his thirst for the truth must be fully satisfied there, he (Augustine) did not believe that even so Nebridius had forgotten him: "since it is you, O Lord, whom he drinks in there and you are mindful of us" (IX,iii,6).[36] Augustine saw, in the community which had its basis in Christ, a singly unbroken unity in which the temporal and the eternal were in communion. This is exactly what the logic of the Christian position made possible: it is precisely what Augustine did not find in the Platonists.

IX,iv,7-12. Cassiciacum

The end of term came at last and Augustine and all his company set out for Cassiciacum. As we know from other sources the little group included Monica, Augustine's brother Navigius, his son Adeodatus, two nephews of Monica (Lastidianus and Rusticus), his friend Alypius, and his pupils Licentius, son of Romanianus, and Trygetius, also originally from Thagaste.[37] Augustine was in Cassiciacum from early September 386 until early March of 387.[38]

Late in life Augustine looked back on his stay there as a "rest"[39] in God, far from the world and its troubles, in which he found for a brief space a sort of earthly paradise.[40] Here he says: "And when could I ever find the time to mention all your great blessings towards us in those days" (IX,iv,7).[41] By his own account he spent those months chiefly in "serving God" with his pen.

> What I did there in my writing which was indeed in your service although it still smelt of the breath of the school of pride, as if I could not stop panting from those exertions from which I had ceased, is witnessed in the books where I record the discussions I had with those present and with myself alone before you: the same is also testified to by my letters to Nebridius who was not with us. (IX,iv,7)[42]

The so-called Cassiciacum *Dialogues* which Augustine wrote at the time — *Against the Academics* (November), *Concerning the Blessed Life* (November), *On Order* (November), and the *Soliloquies* (winter)[43] — were the original cause of the modern dispute over the "historicity" of the *Confessions* since it was noticed by some critics that they are full of philosophy and make little reference to Christ, church, or the Scriptures as one would expect if Augustine had really been converted *before* he went to Cassiciacum.[44] In the *Confessions* itself, and without giving their titles, Augustine simply refers the interested reader to these *Dialogues* which he himself deprecates slightly as having too much the old air "of the school of pride." But is the conclusion of the critics correct? That is, do these works only reveal a concern with Neo-Platonic philosophy? And are they untouched by any real interest in Christian things as one would expect if he had been converted to Christianity? Or, perhaps, is our expectation about how he should have behaved a misleading assumption?

Where the critical side in the historicity debate maintained that Augustine "doctored the facts" in the *Confessions* by presenting himself as a Christian when he was really no more than a Platonist,[45] the defenders of the historical accuracy of the text have maintained that his Platonism was virtually identical with Christianity. The latter position is intent on finding, in the retreat to Cassiciacum, nothing but the attempt to establish a faintly Christianized philosophic community, which was essentially a Platonopolis, such as Augustine had earlier contemplated in the ancient tradition of *otium liberale*.[46] The problem with this is that Augustine himself, to the very end of his life, speaks of his time at Cassiciacum as a *Chris-*

tianae vitae otium (*Retractations*, I,i,1), "a rest of the *Christian* life" — i.e., as opposed to the *otium* sought by philosophers.[47]

The main problem of the *Dialogues* from the standpoint of both critics and defenders is their strongly philosophical tone and the very few references to anything identifiably Christian. The reason, as I understand it, lies in his peculiar status between the time of his conversion in the late summer and his baptism in the spring of the following year. Before his conversion there would have been no problem in writing about Christian things from the position of an outsider. Nor would there be any problem in writing about them from the standpoint of an insider once he had been baptized. But, in the period between August and April, Augustine was in neither position. His conversion ruled out any treatment of these matters from a profane and external viewpoint. Yet, as he had not yet been instructed in an authorized manner in the belief of the church and was not yet a member of it, it would have been presumptuous for him to speak out as a Christian on Christian matters during this period. It does not matter that there was probably not much in the formal catechism that he had not already learned from Monica, Ambrose, Simplicianus, or the Scriptures.[48] What matters is that regardless of how much one knows of the doctrine of the church, no one, not even a Victorinus or an Augustine, can become a member until these things have been given authoritatively and received as such.[49] Until this happened, at his baptism, Augustine, with the humility belonging to his status as a converted catechumen, did not attempt to speak as a Christian about Christian things.

But this did not mean that he could not use the time to serve the church in another capacity. While he warns us about the *Dialogues* as "panting" too much of the old air of the "school of pride" (i.e., ancient philosophy) he nevertheless insists that in spite of this failing they were written "in the service of God."[50] And for the converted Augustine this meant that they were written in the service of Christ. He reports that he had to convince Alypius — ever in awe of Augustine's intellectual prowess — that the name of Christ should appear in them at all.[51] "For he preferred that they should reek of the *cedars* of the schools which *the Lord had already broken* (Ps. 28:5), rather than the health-giving herbs of the church which are effective against serpents" (IX,iv,7).[52] That is, Alypius, "panting" after his own fashion from his former worldliness, wanted Augustine to include only the high and noble concepts of human philosophy rather than have them point to the lowly and humble herbs of the field (the sacraments of the church) by which our sin is cured.

But all of the *Dialogues* and the letters to Nebridius have the latter as their one aim. Each intends to show, by reason alone, how our nature, according to its own logic, leads inexorably to the recognition of the need for the mediation of Christ, which is to say, to the doors of the church. This was what Augustine had found from his own experience. In his works at Cassiciacum he presents this argument in a number of ways for the benefit of others.[53] This is philosophy given over to the service of Christ and the church — while preserving the absolute difference between itself and the matters of faith about which Augustine did not presume to speak. In this view we can see how he was converted to a Christianity which he understood to be absolutely different from philosophy and yet wrote the philosophical *Dialogues* right after his conversion. From this standpoint there is no contradiction between the evidence of the *Dialogues* and the *Confessions* and the original problem of the critics, as well as the newer one generated by the defenders, both disappear.[54]

Apart from the brief reference to the *Dialogues*, the burden of the description of Augustine's life at Cassiciacum is taken up with a long exposition of the Psalms, "songs of faith, those sounds of piety which exclude the inflated spirit [of pride]" (IX,iv,8).[55] This pride is what belongs to Platonist philosophy insofar as it rejects Christianity. In other words the whole account focuses on what distinguishes Christianity from Platonism rather than on what they share.

> What cries I made to you in [the words of] those Psalms and how I was set on fire for you by them and how I burnt to recite them, if I could, to all the world against the pride of the human species! (IX,iv,8)[56]

In the long recollection of how Psalm 4 affected him at the time, Augustine's whole point is about the solace he found in Christianity — "in those sacraments, in those medicines" (IX,iv,8).[57] He explicitly mentions the three persons of the Trinity, the real flesh of Christ, and the reality of his resurrection as the ground of his joy in the future as well as of his fear and shame over his past life.[58] In the same chapter Augustine also distinguishes the Christian position from the proud and fantastical lies of the Manichees. It can seem strange than on thinking of this Psalm Augustine should hark back to their errors, now so far behind him, rather than to the equally proud errors of the Platonists. The explanation is simple. It is precisely because the Incarnation and resurrection were the basis of his new position that he thinks to use the Psalm, in which he found them prefigured, not against the Platonists who rejected both outright, but against the Manichees who accepted both though in a form which denied them any substantial reality.

In the last paragraph of this chapter (IX,iv,12) Augustine recollects a terrible toothache that affected him at the time; the pain was so bad that he could not speak. The idea came to him that he should ask the others to pray for him. He wrote this message and scarcely had they put their knees to the ground when the toothache disappeared. Augustine confesses that he was "greatly terrified" (IX,iv,12)[59] since nothing like this had every happened to him. He had no explanation but only questions: "What was this pain? And how did it go away?" (IX,iv,12).[60]

The episode of the toothache looks like a digression or a *non sequitur* but it is not. Having just shown, in the exposition of the Psalm, the great comfort he drew from Christ regarding the health and cure of his soul, the toothache reminded him that he was also a creature of flesh and blood — and its cure, that God is the author of "every kind of health" (IX,iv,12).[61] The body no less than the soul is encompassed in the Christian economy of salvation and Augustine understood his cure as a direct consequence of his faith.

> And [in this way an evidence of] your power was gotten into me in the most profound way and, rejoicing in the faith, I praised your name, but that faith did not allow me to rest secure concerning my former sins which had not yet been forgiven me through your baptism. (IX,iv,12)[62]

It goes without saying that no such thing is possible in Platonist philosophy where God is known only in his separation from the pains which beset our flesh, and where such cures can only be understood in their natural signification.

IX,v,13. Leaving the world

At the end of the grape harvest holidays, or some time before the middle of October 386, Augustine, from Cassiciacum, notified his students that he would not be returning as their teacher. At about the same time he wrote a letter to Ambrose telling of his intention to seek baptism and asking for advice as to what he could best read to prepare himself. Ambrose replied that he should study Isaiah: "presumably," says Augustine, "because he foretells the gospel and the calling of the gentiles more clearly than all the rest."[63] At the time Augustine could not understand the beginning of Isaiah and put it away until he was "more experienced in the language of the Lord."[64] The patience and humility shown here are a world apart from his proud and disdainful reaction when he first looked at Scripture just before falling in with the Manichees.

IX,vi,14. Baptism

When the time came to "hand in their names"[65] for baptism, which was at the beginning of Lent — on March 10, 387 — Augustine and his group left the country and returned to Milan.[66] Alypius and Adeodatus inscribed themselves as *competentes* — postulant catechumens[67] — along with Augustine[68] and, after being "educated in your disciplines,"[69] they were baptized together by Ambrose in the baptistry beside the main basilica on the eve of Easter, April 24-25, 387.[70] "We were baptized and the anxiety for our past life fled from us."[71] Subjective faith and objective membership in the body of Christ were now perfectly united in Augustine.

> And I was not able to get enough in those days
> Of the wonderful sweetness
> When I thought of the greatness of your plan
> To save the human race.
> How much I cried
> When in your hymns and canticles
> The smooth tones of the voices of your church
> Struck me to the quick!
> Those voices streamed into my ears
> And the truth flowed clearly into my heart
> And from there boiled up a feeling of piety
> And my tears ran down
> And I was happy with them.[72]

A marvellous tradition of the church represents Ambrose and Augustine as improvising the *Te deum laudamus* in alternate strophes during the baptism. To this day it is called *Hymnus SS. Ambrosii et Augustini*.[73]

IX,vii,15-16. Ambrosian hymns and the discovery of the relics of Gervasius and Protasius

The last chapter before the eulogy to Monica occurred to Augustine as an afterthought at the time he was writing the *Confessions*.

Thanks be to you, O my God (Lk. 18:11). For what place and whither have you
led my recollection so that these things also I might confess to you which,
though great, I had forgotten and passed over? (IX,vii,16)[74]

The "great events" of which he speaks were Ambrose's challenge to Justina
which led to the introduction of hymns into the liturgy of the Western church, and
the discovery and "translation" to the Ambrosian basilica of the remains of the
martyrs Gervasius and Protasius.

The occasion of Ambrose introducing the singing of hymns and psalms by the
congregation[75] was the siege of one of the basilicas of Milan in February of the
preceding year (386). Ambrose did this to keep up the spirits of the people when
he had closed himself and his congregation in the church where they stayed day
and night to prevent it being taken over by the Arians. Justina, mother of the boy
emperor Valentinian, had demanded that Ambrose make available a church within
the walls of the city "for the sake of her heretic" (IX,vii,15)[76] Arians.[77] Monica
had played a considerable part in this resistance of the church to the demands of
the empire,[78] while Augustine who had not yet been converted — "with a soul still
cold, cut off from the heat of your Spirit" (IX,vii,15)[79] — took no part but was
still cognizant of these things going on in the terrified and disquieted city.[80]

The discovery of the location of the "uncorrupted" (IX,vii,16)[81] remains of the
two martyrs, revealed to Ambrose in a vision, and the miracles associated with
them, happened some months later in June of 386 and still before Augustine's
conversion in August.[82] Again there was much commotion in the city and without
doubt the episode would have appeared "to the Milanese as a judgement of God
in favour of Catholicism [i.e., against the Arians]."[83] At the time Augustine "did
not run" (IX,vii,16)[84] to witness the spectacle but he included these episodes in
his *Confessions* because, while they came unexpectedly to mind in connection
with his baptism, they seemed a perfect way of expressing the difference between
his condition before and after his conversion.

Here is the sense of his thoughts. In recollecting his baptism he recalled how
deeply he had been moved by the singing of hymns, canticles, and Psalms.[85] This
evidently led him,[86] at the time of writing, to consider the events which he knew
more or less at first hand,[87] introducing this practice into the liturgy. He first
remembered the siege of the basilica and from this his thoughts turned to the other
great event of the preceding summer, the "invention" of Gervasius and Protasius.[88] Now comes the important point. The contrast is between his actions at the
time when he was "unmoved by the fire of your Spirit" (IX,vii,15)[89] and so took
no interest, joy, or comfort in the affairs of the church — and his condition at baptism where the very things which had formerly left him cold had become the occasion of "as much heavenly air as is permitted to mankind in this world of straw"
(IX,vii,16)[90] — i.e., by their content which he now recognized as a divine presence
in this world.[91]

> At that time [i.e., of the siege of the basilica and the discovery of the martyrs —
> February to June 386], when the *sweet smell of your perfumes* blew across the
> land [in these mighty deeds of God in which the church triumphed over the
> world], we did not run *after you* (Song of Songs 1:2-4) [i.e., unlike the lover
> there who runs towards her lover being drawn by the sweet smell of his anoint-
> ing oils].[92] This then is the reason (*ideo*) why I wept so abundantly at your can-

ticles and hymns because at that time [i.e., of my baptism] I was breathing you
in: at last I was able to catch a breath of you as far as the breath of heavenly air
is possible in this passing world. (IX,vii,16)[93]

This is Augustine's expressed reason (*ideo*) for including these episodes. They
explain his joy in the psalms and hymns of the church by showing exactly where
he had come from — where such things were of no concern or consolation. If we
recall what he had said of his condition right after he had risen to the Platonist
vision — in another passage which alludes to these verses of the Song of Songs —
everything should be clear. There he had said of the vision:

> Then in truth I saw your *invisible [nature] having understood it through those
> things which have been made* (Rom. 1:20) but I was not able to keep my sight
> on it and my weakness was beaten back and I returned to my usual way of look-
> ing at things and I did not take with me anything except a loving memory and,
> as it were, a smell of things desired which I was not yet able to savour.
> (VII,xvii,23)[94]

What Platonism had not been able to give him — the strength "to savour"[95]
God — he had found at last through the baptism of the church.

From the fact that Augustine was not moved by these events in the church at
Milan in the months before his conversion, Courcelle concludes that his was "the
conversion of an intellectual individualist, a rebel from the enthusiasms and movements of the mob," who was "not touched by prodigies [but] contented himself,
in a corner of the basilica, to take in and assimilate inwardly the doctrine which
was both Plotinian and Christian that Ambrose developed in certain exegetical sermons."[96] This seems to me to miss the point. We have seen that Augustine's conversion was impossible at the time of these events for the very reason that he did
then hold the attitudes which Courcelle lauds. Courcelle is encouraged that Augustine was not moved by "prodigies," that he did not "run after" such vulgar
"spectacular ceremonies" which were appealing to the "mob," to the simple
"faithful or idlers," but instead came to another, higher, intellectual Plotinian
Christianity that placed no stock in such "miracles."[97] All this was doubtless true
of Augustine in the early summer of 386 when he had just come to the Platonist
vision of God and the church of Milan was astir with these happenings. The argument of the *Confessions* has shown how false it is of everything that happened
thereafter, when he discovered the deficiency of the Neo-Platonic position and its
correction through the conversion of his will and the baptism of the church. The
very thing he had formerly scorned, the simple faith of Monica in the concrete
union of God and world, was now the foundation of his new life, the basis of his
liberation from the sins and errors of his nature, and the ground of his confidence
in the life of the world to come. Augustine had truly come to where Monica had
always been.

This chapter on these events in the church at Milan also forms the necessary
transition to the final part of this book. It moves the argument beyond Augustine's
limited experience in the faith to that of Monica in whom he could see, as a para-
digm, the objective character of such a life from baptism to death.[98] This is where
he now turns to complete the first part of his *Confessions* and in so doing he will

show how, in a marvellous way, Monica's simple faith allowed her to come to where Augustine had also been: to the vision of God.

II. IX,viii,17-IX,xiii,37. Christian life between baptism and death

This section is a brief exposition of Christian piety from its start in time to its end in eternity. Chapter viii deals with Monica's life from her baptism to her marriage; chapter ix, with her married life; chapter x, with the vision at Ostia; chapter xi, with her death; chapter xii, with her burial; and chapter xiii, with Augustine's final prayer for her life in the world to come.

IX,viii,17-18. Monica's life from baptism to marriage

In turning to Monica at the end of the first part of his *Confessions* Augustine brings us back to its starting point, although the difference between the beginning and the end is absolute. In the first chapters on his own infancy we recall that Monica, not mentioned by name, was simply one of "the parents of my flesh" (I,vi,7).[99] Here she is considered not as the mother of his flesh but as the one who laboured to bring him to re-birth in the spirit where the human person gains an eternal substantiality beyond the limitations of nature.

> But I will not pass over in silence anything that my soul brings forth concerning that handmaid of yours who bore me both in the flesh, so that I might be born in this temporal light, and also in her heart so that I might be born in the eternal light. (IX,vii,17)[100]

Augustine contrasts Monica's childhood with his own: she grew up within the church whereas he did not. "The rod of your Christ educated her *in your fear* (Ps. 5:8), the rule of your only begotten Son educated her in a household of faith which was a sound member of your church" (IX,vii,17).[101] As an example of this education, which was largely in the hands of an aged servant, Augustine cites the stories his mother had told him[102] about how the old lady looked after Monica and her sisters with a "holy severity" (IX,viii,17),[103] telling them to go sparingly with water when they were thirsty lest they make free with wine when they grew up.[104] These were just the kind of limits on the disordered pursuit of natural pleasures which Augustine himself had lacked and which had allowed him to develop the chain of habit he had been unable to break in order to come to conversion. Here is the justification for the repeated remarks in which he has insisted on the great importance of growing up under the tutelage of the true authority of the church. It is the only possible defence against the formation of those perverse habits which bind the soul and prevent our will from moving freely when we grow up and come to recognize where our true good lies.

But in spite of this careful training at home, so unlike his own education in the public system where he was offered filthy, immoral, and intoxicating tales by masters drunk on the ways of the world, Monica slid into the bad habit of secretly drinking more and more of the wine she was entrusted to fetch as a girl — moving by slow imperceptible steps from her first innocent sip of a few drops which barely touched her lips, done merely "in sport" and out of the "superfluous excesses of youth" (IX,vii,18),[105] to the guzzling of a cupful at a time. Monica was saved, before things had gone too far, by the harsh taunt of a servant-girl who knew of her practice and one day called her a drunkard to get back at her for something or other: "By which goad she was so struck that she looked at her filthy [habit] and at once condemned and renounced it" (IX,viii,18).[106] That the servant should have made the taunt and that Monica was capable of being shamed by it, Augustine attributes to divine providence: "Can anything avail against our hidden disease except your medicine, O Lord, who watches over us?" (IX,viii,18).[107] This was the very thing he had wilfully ignored in his own youth when, for example, he was "ashamed to be shameless" (II,ix,17)[108] and blushed to accept his mother's admonitions.

IX,ix,19-22. Monica, Patricius and the family

The next stage of Monica's life began with her marriage. Her humble patience — which had its source in her unshakeable Christian faith — led to a life of such concrete and tangible virtue that it was the cause of much astonishment in those around her. She did not broadcast her Christianity, yet she never ceased to act according to it no matter how long she had to serve and suffer.

> [A]s soon as she had fully reached marriageable age she was given to a man whom she served like her master and she was continually trying to win him for you, speaking of you by means of her virtues by which you made her appear beautiful and respectfully lovable and admirable to her husband. (IX,ix,19)[109]

Monica had much to put up with: Patricius' infidelity,[110] his violent temper,[111] and his mother, whom the servants tried to set against her daughter-in-law — only to have her punish them due to her belief in Monica's good will.[112] In all of this she never wavered from the humble position to which she understood that she had been called in marriage.[113] She did her Christian duty cheerfully throughout her life, acting always as a peacemaker and never reporting malicious gossip.[114] Small things in one way, but very great in another — as Augustine points out when he says that the contrary behaviour is in fact the norm amongst mankind, the result of "a horrible widespread contagion of sins" (IX,ix,21).[115]

In the end she won Patricius for God. He was converted just before his death in about 370.[116] Her care for Augustine's salvation has been before us throughout the *Confessions* but the same was also true for the rest of her family. Here is Augustine's epitaph on her life: it is drawn from the description of a true widow in 1 Timothy.

> She had been *the wife of one man only* (1 Tim. 5:9),
> She had *repaid the duty she owed to her parents* (1 Tim. 5:4),
> She had run *her household religiously* (1 Tim. 5:4),
> She had *the testimony of good deeds* (1 Tim. 5:10),
> She had brought up her sons,
> So often labouring with them
> As often as she saw them turning away from you. (IX,ix,22)[117]

To her family and to all in the church she was ever "the servant of your servants" (IX,ix,22):[118] a mother to all in respect of her care for them, a daughter to all in respect to her service to them.[119] As she understood her labour, it would not be complete until she had done all she could to bring those to whom she was related into the church.

IX,x,23-26. The vision at Ostia

Sometime after his baptism in April and before his own birthday on November 13 in 387,[120] Augustine and Monica, along with Navigius, his brother,[121] Adeodatus, his son,[122] and a young Christian from Thagaste named Evodius,[123] decided to return together to Africa where they thought they could "more usefully serve God" (IX,viii,17).[124] This little group which had been "living together in holy purpose" (IX,viii,17)[125] in Milan set out for Ostia, the seaport of Rome, in order to return to Africa. Once there, they were forced to wait for the lifting of a naval blockade by the usurper Maximus.[126] Augustine and Monica found themselves alone one day and he says:

> we were standing leaning in a certain window which looked over the inner garden of the house where we were staying there at Ostia on the mouth of the Tiber, where far from the crowd after a long, laborious journey we were refreshing ourselves for the long sea trip. (IX,x,23)[127]

Here together they both came to the vision of God, Augustine for the second time in his life and Monica for the first.

This chapter has been the subject of the most extensive studies by modern scholars, all of which are indebted to Paul Henry's little book of 1938, *La vision d'Ostie*.[128] While not everyone has agreed with everything Henry said, this work has been seen to be of primary importance in "the solution to the problem of the opposition between Plotinianism and Christianity."[129] Certainly his was one of the first voices to be raised against the view of the critics of the historicity of the *Confessions*, that Platonism and Christianity are merely antithetical opposites. Henry's position is far from simplistic. It is, as Solignac says correctly, *nuancée*[130] — which has meant in effect that the totality of his view is somewhat vague and hard to grasp. Throughout the book he deals with three strands which he distinguishes in the *Confessions* — philosophy, authority, and life. He knows they are somehow one but he never manages to get them held together in anything more than a loose braid which easily falls apart in the hands of another. Courcelle, for example, sees chiefly that Henry has shown that the vision at Ostia has Plotinian sources. He says, "One cannot doubt, since the work of P. Henry, that the plot of the story [of the vision of God at Ostia] is constituted by the Plotinian treatises *On the beautiful*, and *On the three hypostases which are principles*."[131] What Courcelle wishes not to see is where (Chapter 8) Henry also quotes Augustine at length to the effect that while Plotinus and the Christians share the same notion of the perfect and blessed life, they differ completely in the estimate of how we can achieve it — the Platonists rejecting the Incarnation and the resurrection, while the Christians accept both and maintain that they alone can actually arrive at the goal where both want to be. Courcelle can hardly be blamed for getting only one strand since Henry writes from a position which does not prove the Catholic position but takes it for granted. He faithfully repeats all of what Augustine teaches but he does not explain the logic that Augustine has explicitly developed which justifies this position — and not knowing the logic he cannot show clearly and precisely what is uniquely Christian about the vision at Ostia and what it shares with the knowledge of the natural man. Because Henry's thesis is so full of qualifications by one strand on the others, I will not attempt to show where I differ from him in detail. It is enough to say that in general he makes the vision at Milan too Christian (Chapter 7) and the vision at Ostia too Neo-Platonic (Chapter 8). I think the best way to approach this much-disputed question is simply to state what appears out of the logic of the *Confessions*.

Plainly put it amounts to this. The vision at Milan is, as Augustine says, a Platonist vision. It is the vision of the invisible God which all men can achieve by their own natural powers through the consideration of creation. If Augustine expressed the content of the vision in Book VII largely in Scriptural terms, this was only because he was writing for a Christian audience in whom he did not expect to find any philosophical culture. It did not matter whether or not his readers knew anything of Plato or Plotinus. His point in Book VII was precisely that Christians shared the same notion of God the Father and of his eternally begotten Son — the eternal Word in whom all things were made — with the Platonists. Of course most Christians held these things by faith on the authority of the church — but Augustine testified, as one of the few who had actually risen to the knowledge of God, that the God of the Christians and the God of the Platonists are one and the same and he confesses that he first came to this true idea of God from Platonist philosophy.[132]

Furthermore, and in this Henry is correct, the conception of the proper end of the human soul, of its perfect bliss, as consisting in this vision of God is common to both Christianity and Neo-Platonism. Augustine is perfectly clear about this. The *City of God* is full of passages which say as much. Henry quotes Augustine's own words of approval on Plotinus (from the *City of God*, X,16).[133] Augustine says:

> For this vision of God is a vision of such beauty and altogether deserving of such love that Plotinus says without hesitation that a man who fails of it is altogether unfortunate no matter how richly endowed he may be with any other kind of goods.[134]

Here Augustine is referring to the treatise "On beauty" (*Enneads*, I,6) where Plotinus says:

> Here the greatest, the ultimate contest is set before our souls: all our toil and trouble is for this, not to be left without a share in the best of visions. The man who attains this is blessed in seeing that "blessed sight," and he who fails to attain it has failed utterly.[135]

Platonists and Christians have therefore an identical notion of God and share an identical understanding of the proper goal of the human soul as consisting in the direct vision of God. What the vision at Ostia shows is the nature of the difference between Platonism (or, more generally the true knowledge of the natural man) and Christianity. In saying this I don't in any way deny that the vision at Ostia is also

Platonist. Mandouze has noted that amongst themselves Henry, Courcelle, and Pepin have distinguished 21 Plotinian "sources."[136] The quotations around this last word — the *caveat* — comes from Mandouze himself who very properly notes that where so many "sources" have been identified we are faced with the dilemma that either Augustine is simply reproducing the thought of Plotinus or else that these "rapprochements, do not, properly speaking, constitute the *sources* of this unforgettable scene."[137]

Whatever we care to make of these "sources," it is clear that the vision of Ostia and the vision of Milan are both described by Augustine as being the direct knowledge of God *"in himself* (Ps. 4:9 and 121:3 LXX)" (IX,x,24),[138] as arrived at from the consideration of creation. In this respect they are identical. And, since the vision of Milan is Platonist on Augustine's own account, the vision at Ostia will be Platonist in the same sense. The question is whether this is all that can be said of the vision at Ostia, or if there is something more that lies altogether beyond the province and possibilities of human philosophy. To resolve this question we must look to the difference between the two vision. If, as I argue, Augustine included the little *vita* of Monica to show the character of the Christian life after baptism, then it will follow that he intended the vision at Ostia to be understood as specifically Christian — in contrast to the earlier vision at Milan. It can be shown that between the one and the other there is all the difference between presumption and confession, pride and humility. These differences are solely explicable in terms of the intervention of Christianity — of the Incarnation — in Augustine's life. To put this as bluntly as possible: the vision at Ostia is the Platonist vision of Milan now transformed by the necessary correction which the Christian revelation brings to the knowledge of God. The following nine points give an idea of what can be found once we know what we are looking for.[139]

1. Although Augustine shares in the vision, we should not forget that the description occurs in the life of Monica. This *vita*, I argue, is included to show the objective nature of the Christian life. In its two previous chapters (viii and ix) Augustine had described how Monica fulfilled the duties of her calling. In the chapter on her vision, and the subsequent one on her death, he shows its earthly rewards.

2. In the vision of Book VII we only know, by implication, that it took place in Milan — Augustine tells nothing about its physical setting. The character of the Platonian ascent — its ecstatic union of the mind and God by abstraction from all sensible conditions — makes these latter of no importance. In the vision at Ostia on the other hand these are carefully described. He and Monica were "standing leaning" against a window that looked out over an "inner garden of the house," "far from the turmoil of the world," enjoying a moment in which they could "renew," "repair," "celebrate," and "refresh" themselves (IX,x,23).[140] We are dealing here with an earthly anticipation of heaven which is the very opposite of Plotinus' "flight [from the world] of the alone to the Alone."[141]

3. Both accounts have also a spiritual setting and both are attributed to divine providence but there is a great difference. In bringing Augustine to the true knowledge of God, the vision at Milan is spoken of as curing the tumour which had prevented him from seeing the truth, yet the whole thing was placed squarely in the economy of pride — the pride of the man from whom Augustine got the

books of the Platonists, the pride of the Platonists in their knowledge of God, and the presumption that, for a while, this vision generated in Augustine himself.[142] There is none of this at Ostia: "There conferred we hand to hand very sweetly" (IX,x,23) is what Augustine says in the version of the 17th century translator William Watts.[143] He begins his account with this statement: "The day however was soon to come when [Monica] would quit this life — what day it was you knew, though we did not" (IX,x,23).[144] Here there are no tumors to be cured and, so far as anyone was to be cured of anything, Monica was going to be "cured" of this life where we can only see in part — but only to go to another, better life, where she would perpetually enjoy the vision of God face to face.

4. The whole account of the vision at Ostia is told in the first person plural. This is true not only of such external states as when Augustine says *we* were standing at the window and *we* talked together, but it also holds of the vision itself — *we* strove towards that goal and *we* attained to it.[145] Of course, one says, the reason is that Augustine and Monica were both there.[146] But what can this mean? We are not simply dealing with the extraordinary circumstance of two people coming to the vision of God in the same instant but of a union or community in their vision. They not only came to it at the same time, but *together* — that is, each knew that the other was there. But this is theoretically impossible according to Plotinus. It must be so for him because, in the One, all the distinctions of finitude are lost — including the distinction between "you" and "me," between Monica and Augustine. Or, to put it the other way around, one cannot be looking at the intelligible and immutable God and at the same time see the mutable things of this world: the two are unlike each other and are in different "places."[147] The philosophical vision is essentially solitary and those who come to it must do so alone — as was the case with Augustine at Milan. What then explains the difference between Milan and Ostia such that Augustine and Monica could have the vision together? This is only possible if finite distinctions are themselves present in God. Plotinus knows nothing of this but it is the meaning of the Incarnation.

5. At Ostia, the discussion which led to the vision was about the nature of the life of the saints — that is, about their life, sight, and delight in God in the world to come.[148] In other words, Monica and Augustine were inquiring after something which had been promised to them as their own and not, as with Augustine at Milan, after what was other than himself. The basis of this confidence was their belief in the promises of Christ. The suggestion that mutable man can be with the immutable God is, for Plotinus, the sign of an outrageous arrogance or ignorance.[149]

6. Henry insists that the object of the vision at Milan and Ostia is God himself, *in id ipsum*,[150] seen "without any intermediary" — which is "identically that [object] of the highest Plotinian contemplation."[151] This is true as far as it goes but it does not go far enough. The *id ipsum* towards which Augustine and Monica rose at Ostia is not simply the eternal Word of God in whom all things are made — which *was* the object of the Platonist vision in Book VII. Their vision is the vision of the same Word, but seen here as Incarnate, identified with the world and made available to us. In Milan he said, "I sensed the fragrance of the fare but was not yet able to eat it" (VII,xvii,23).[152] At Ostia they came to "that place of unending plenty where you feed Israel forever with the food of truth"

(IX,x,24).[153] This is only possible because God, *in id ipsum*, is not simply known in his otherness from the conditions of finitude but also in his (revealed) identity with them, and where the world, for its part, can actually feed on God rather than merely seeing him. But this is to say that the vision of Ostia is the vision of the true church, the heavenly Jerusalem, which sees God face to face because it is held to him by the God who is God and man.[154] Henry is wrong then when he says they came to the knowledge of God "without any intermediary" because theirs was rather the vision *of the Mediator*.[155]

7. The testimony of the whole of ancient philosophy, and of Augustine's own experience, was that it took years of training and considerable philosophical culture to escape the bonds of the sensible and rise to the vision of the intelligible God. Monica had none of this and yet she came to the vision as easily as Augustine. She could pass beyond the sensible in this way because the sensible to which she held in faith (i.e., Christ) was also the eternal Word of God.

8. Augustine says, "we sighed and we left there *the first fruits of the spirit* (Rom. 8:23) attached to it" (IX,x,24)[156] — that is, to the heavenly Jerusalem. This means that what they had glimpsed in the vision they understood to be a foretaste of what would be theirs forever on the resurrection of the body. This is what Paul teaches in the passage from which the phrase *primitias spiritus* is taken,[157] and Augustine explicitly points to the resurrection when he asks in a rhetorical question, "But when will this be? *Will it be when we all rise . . . ?* (1 Cor. 15:51)" (IX,x,25).[158] In Milan the body, the "habit of the flesh" (VII,xvii,23)[159] had been the inevitable and insurmountable obstacle to the continued enjoyment of God unless an adequate mediator could be found. At Ostia it is the necessary condition of its fulfillment. That this is so depends entirely on the mediation of Christ.

9. Finally, in the vision of God at Milan, Augustine discovered himself to be in a *regio dissimilitudinis*, "a place of utter unlikeness" to God — from which he had no hope of escape except in a temporal sense through repeated ecstatic visions. At Ostia, Monica and Augustine easily agree that where they have been, the *regio ubertatis indeficientis* — "the place of unfailing plenteousness"[160] — it was possible to be in forever and that this was the condition of the saints in heaven, Christian men and women who had died in the faith. Nowhere does Plotinus teach that temporal man can enjoy this vision eternally.[161] Without a true mediator, without Christ, the vision of God merely separates. With him it beckons us to our goal in the heavenly city, "which is meant to be no mere vision but our home" (VII,xx,26)[162] — and Monica's response was to answer this call, which she could do because she believed there was no further work for her to do in this world:

> [S]he said: "My son, so far as I am concerned nothing in this life now delights me. What I am to do here from this point on and why I am here I do not know, my hopes for this world are accomplished. There was one thing for the sake of which I used to desire to remain for a while in this life — in order that I might see you a Catholic Christian before I should die. My God has done this for me more than enough as I now see you, his servant, spurning temporal felicities. What is left for me to do here?" (IX,x,26)[163]

IX,xi,27-28. The death of Monica

We might ask what more there is to say. Augustine gives his answer in the last three chapters. His account will not be complete until he has shown the nature of a Christian death. Within about five days of the vision Monica took to bed with a fever[164] from which she died "on the ninth day of her illness" (IX,xi,28).[165] The purpose of this chapter is to show how Augustine's conversion and the vision at Ostia had brought Monica to a perfectly Christian relationship to her death. For long she had harboured what Augustine (the bishop) called the "vain" (IX,xi,28)[166] desire to be buried alongside her husband in Africa. This supposes she still thought that such natural dispositions were of some consequence and to this extent she was still tied to nature in its independence of God. In the light of the vision at Ostia Monica had actually seen that this world — in its immediate form — was in no sense her home and that the merely natural had nothing further to contribute to her true bliss.[167] Her liberation from the natural was completed. Her hopes were at last free from every vestige of whatever was immediately natural and concentrated instead on nature — not in its separation from God — but as it was renewed spiritually, remade, and restored in him through Christ. In short, her whole care was on the resurrection. The final words which Augustine reports of his mother say it all: " 'Nothing,' she said, 'is far from God nor is it to be feared that he will not know where to find me at the end of the world to raise me up' " (IX,xi,28).[168] Monica was ready to die.

This however must not be understood one-sidedly as if she was ready to flee from an evil and contemptible world. The contrary is the case. Monica was ready to die only because her work in the world was done. No one who understands how much she had worked and suffered in her worldly life as a pious Christian, for whom such temporal concerns had also an absolute significance, can say that she merely ignored or despised her temporal duties. If her son were not converted in this world then he would not be converted anywhere and yet, for the same reason, her role in the world was limited and, with Augustine now a Christian, her limits had been reached. Like the true mother she was, she had laboured to bear and raise him both in the flesh and also in the spirit. There was nothing more a mother could do. Monica deserved to die because her work was done. God's grace was not long delayed and, as Augustine says, "in the fifty-sixth year of her life and in my thirty-third that pious and religious soul was released from her body" (IX,xi,28).[169]

IX,xii,29-33. Augustine and Monica's death

Augustine completes the description of the death of a Christian by an account of his own reaction to her death and thus, at the end, brings his confession back to himself.

> I closed her eyes and there flowed into my breast a huge sadness which ran over into tears. At the same time, on a violent order of my soul, my eyes pushed back the tears into their spring so they remained dry, and in such a struggle things went very badly for me. (IX,xii,29)[170]

The reason Augustine made the effort was that:

We [Christians] did not think it proper to mourn such a death with lamentations, tears and howlings because in such tears what is deplored most often is a presumed misery in the dead person or else it is as if she were altogether annihilated. But for my mother in death she was neither miserable nor had she altogether died. We hold this both on the witness of her character and her *unfeigned faith* (1 Tim. 1:15) and for sure reasons. (IX,xi,29)[171]

Augustine strove mightily to see things in this way and did manage to keep himself in check until Monica was buried[172] but all the while his heart felt differently and a great grief pressed down on him, doubly awful because the thought he should not have such worldly attachments.[173] He prayed for relief but none came. "I believe this was because you were impressing on my memory, if only by this one example, how all habit is a chain even to a mind which is not fed by any false word" (IX,xii,32).[174]

What Monica had finally achieved in her last illness was not yet completed in Augustine but this was not his last word. He went to the baths and came back feeling no better[175] and finally went to sleep and awoke somewhat refreshed from his sorrow. Then at last, alone in his room, the words of Ambrose's hymn *Deus, creator omnium* came to mind and with them the truth they contained.[176] The point he took was that God provides temporal means for temporal needs and with this he was at last able to cry out his heart for his mother, "and it was a comfort to weep in your *sight* (Ps. 18:15) about her and for her, about me and for me" (IX,xii,33).[177] Like Monica, he too realized the place of the temporal in the Christian economy of salvation and was free to grieve for his mother who had meant so much to him in her time, and also for himself who had so much time ahead in which he would have to struggle with the world as she had had to do until her work was done. Monica, whose works was accomplished, had found her solace in seeing things in their heavenly significance where Augustine could find none. Augustine, whose work was not done, found his solace in the tears he shed for his earthly mother who had not shed tears for him on her death. Yet both were doing the same thing in spite of these differences because in Christ the temporal and eternal were united. Augustine shows this with wonderful clarity in the final sentences of this chapter where he allows that both positions were true. He confesses that his tears, though wept for only a "fraction of an hour" (IX,xii,33)[178] and in private, could be justly condemned by one who had his eyes on heaven. Yet he begs such a one not to mock him since just such tears, shed in time by Monica, had brought him to the church in the first place.[179]

IX,xiii,34-37. Conclusion

In the final chapter Augustine moves beyond his own immediate and natural reaction to the death of his mother to show and solicit the church's spiritual response to the death of a faithful Christian. This chapter is explicitly written from the standpoint of Augustine the bishop who was writing the *Confessions.* He was no longer looking back over his past but had brought the past up to the present by asking, at the time of writing, for the prayers of his readers for the rest of the souls of Monica and Patricius. In this way the final chapter was also a bridge between the account of his past life in the first nine books and the new confession he would begin in Book X — which is about the inner life of a Christian in the present.

Here he "sets aside" (IX,xii,35)[180] the praise of Monica's good works — those that had an objective visible character such as he had spoken of and which are, in any event, nothing but a reflection of God's good works through her[181] — and turns instead to petition Christ who is the true "medicine for our wound" (IX,xiii,35 — i.e., of original sin)[182] — to cover and remit any action which she may have done since her baptism which stemmed simply from her nature in its natural separation from God:

> for I do not dare to say that from the moment she was regenerated through baptism no word ever left her mouth which went against your precept. For it is said by the truth, your Son: "*If anyone says to his brother, 'you fool,' he will be answerable in the fires of hell* (Mt. 5:22)." (IX,xiii,34)[183]

This is the standard of God's holiness as revealed by Christ. When measured against the standard, what man or woman can stand secure in the consideration of his or her own natural virtue? The answer clearly and certainly is, no one. It is a standard which goes far beyond any objective embodiment in good works or any participation in the rites and sacraments of the church. Even when this side of things was fulfilled as well as it had been by Monica, Augustine could still not be certain that she had perfectly done the law nor that she was a complete Christian. The tenth commandment — "Thou shall not *covet* thy neighbour's house, nor his wife, nor his ox, nor his ass, nor anything that is his" (Ex. 20:17) — can have no objective embodiment. Christ not only echoed this commandment — which requires the same freedom from contradiction inwardly as the others demand outwardly — but insisted upon it as, for example, where he says that a man who merely looks at a woman lustfully has already committed adultery with her in his heart (Mt. 5:28). This last commandment which, alone, was of no concern to the ordering of human society because it had no objective embodiment was, so to speak, the main concern of the new society of Christians for whom, as in Augustine and Monica's case, objective compliance with the law was given in their baptism. He could not speak for Monica in these matters. Indeed no one can answer for another since we cannot see into the heart of anyone else.[184] All he could do was to offer up his prayers on her behalf and invite those of his readers in accordance with her last request, and in the faith that the same Christ who set this standard was also the one who had promised to redeem us from such failings.[185] But about himself he *could* speak and the necessity for his second confession, about how he stood inwardly in relation to these subjective demands, arises in this way out of the conclusion of the first.[186]

Through his own life and Monica's, Augustine has now shown all the necessary considerations in the complete movement of the human soul from its birth in nature, through rebirth in grace, to its eternal life in the heavenly *patria* such as they had seen at Ostia. The argument of the first part of his *Confessions* was complete.

NOTES

1 The title of the work is plural because Augustine makes three separate confessions about three separate aspects of his life. His first confession is in Books I-IX, the second in Book X, the third in Books XI-XIII. On this general tripartite structure see above, Preface, n. 1.

2 *O/sum* (179/19-180/1).

3 *Iam/libidinum* (180/18-21). On this *libido*, see Solignac (*BA*, Vol. 14, pp. 537-42). The three words *ambiendi*, *adquirendi*, and *volutandi* belong to the same trinitarian train of thought which Augustine had used to classify all sins under the headings of *principandi*, *spectandi*, and *sentiendi* in III,viii,16.

4 *ante oculos omnium sita* (181/26).

5 See IX,ii,2 *Et/suo* (180/23-181/2).

6 See IX,ii,3 *Verum/videri* (181/21-182/1).

7 See IX,ii,4.

8 *in cathedra mendacii* (182/24-25).

9 *servorum/meorum* (182/22-23).

10 *At/contendo* (182/25). This decision not to leave the world suddenly and announce his conversion with a big hullabaloo contrasts with Victorinus' splendid public profession of his new faith at his baptism (VIII,ii,5) but Augustine was not using a double standard: his reserve was recommended by his status — outwardly he was still a catechumen and would remain so until his baptism. The time for the public proof of his faith would come but he judged that it was not right to draw everyone's attention to his Christianity when he was not yet a member of the church.

11 *Sed/mihi?* (182/25-28).

12 See IX,ii,4 *Plenus/succederet* (182/16-21). When Augustine says that the ambition to make money had enabled him to bear the burden of teaching he is not contradicting what he earlier said (in VIII,i,2) that neither the hope of money nor glory was any longer a spur to his ambition and that he was only tied to the world by the love of women. What he means here is that the only reason he taught was for the sake of his salary, as a means of livelihood, and that now even this form of looking after his worldly interests had vanished.

13 *Consilium/effunderetur* (181/5-8).

14 *cor/nostrum* (181/14).

15 *gestabamus* (181/14-15).

16 *cogitationis nostrae* (181/17).

17 *accendebant nos* (181/19).

18 For Verecundus, see IX,iii,5 *Macerabatur/poterat* (182/29-183/4). For Nebridius, see IX,iii,6 *Nebridium/tandem* (184/17-20).

19 Augustine has several times mentioned the Christians' relations to non-Christians as for example in his mother's relation to himself and in his comments on the students in Rome in V,xii,22 — i.e., hate the sin, love the man.

20 *cruciaremur* (183/13), literally = "crucified."

21 *humanitatem* (183/23), literally = "humanity" = i.e., the natural "kindness" of one human to his or her fellows.

22 See IX,iii,5.

23 See VIII,vi,13 *Nebridius/nimis* (164/1-5). On the position of the *grammaticus* see Solignac (*BA*, Vol. 13, pp. 659-61).

24 The location of Cassiciacum is not exactly known. Perhaps it was at the modern Cassago di Brianza, 33 km from Milan near Lake Como in the foothills of the Italian Alps and from which Monte Rosa is visible. See Solignac (*BA*, Vol. 14, p. 79, n. 3) on the play *Cassiciaco ... incaseato* (IX,iii,5) "which ought to be an allusion to the mountainous site of Cassiciacum." On the use of this *in monte incaseato* (183/19) see also Gibb (*Confessions*, p. 637). The point is that as Verecundus brought Augustine to his natural mountainous paradise at Cassiciacum, God eventually repaid this kindness (IX,iii,5 *reddis* — 183/15) by bringing Verecundus to the heavenly paradise in the mountain of God. Courcelle refers to the literature on the location of Cassiciacum in *Recherches*, p. 203, n. 4.

25 This is because it was only in the church, whose members were on the way to eternal life in the *patria*, that friendship would be able to flourish forever rather than being cut off by natural limitations — i.e., death.

26 See IX,iii,5 — text quoted in n. 18. Augustine does not make it clear if Verecundus was "held back" by his wife because he wanted her, or she him. In either case, given the advice Augustine gave him (see n. 27), the attachment was not made solely for gratifying lust on either side. Verecundus became sick, was baptized, and died during Augustine's second stay in Rome (which extended from late summer 387 to 388 — after he had buried Monica at Ostia): see IX,iii,5 *Quamvis/emigravit* (183/7-10).

27 See IX,iii,6 *Sic/coniugalis* (184/14-17). Marriage here is called a *gradus* (184/16) = a "state," "condition," "dignity," "rank."

28 *fidem gradus sui* (184/16).

29 *inquisitor ardentissimus veritatis* (183/25-26). See Chapter Seven, n. 42 on the sense of this characterization of Nebridius.

30 See IX,iv,7 where Augustine says Nebridius stayed behind in Milan (when he went to Cassiciacum) and they communicated by letter, *quae/epistulae* (185/5). In the Benedictine edition of Augustine's works, *Letters* iii-xiv are to or from Nebridius and, of these, iii and iv were written by Augustine at Cassiciacum. They are found in English translation in *NPNF*.

31 See IX,iii,6 *Quod/tandem* (184/18-20). See also *ibid.*, *Nebridius/sacramentis* (184/20-25). Gibb (*Confessions*, p. 238) says of this *nondum ... sacramentis*, "i.e., he had not even entered the catechumenate. For the use of 'sacramenta' with reference to the rites of initiation, see VIII,ii,4 — [referring to *primis instructionis sacramentis* — 156/20-21]."

32 *conlaetabatur* (183/20-21).

33 This is the opposite of Verecundus who was "chewed up with worry" (IX,iii,5 *macerabatur anxitudine* — 182/29) that the conversion of Augustine and Alypius would deprive him of their company — notwithstanding which he offered them his house at Cassiciacum. That Nebridius did not insist on being with Augustine although he had come to Italy, leaving his family's rich estate and his mother behind, for no other purpose than to be with Augustine in a search for truth and wisdom (VI,x,17) is probably an indication that he had already come to the same point as Augustine or Victorinus in the moment before they went into the church — i.e., he knew the truth of Christianity so there was no need for further inquiry, but his will was still divided.

34 See IX,iii,6 *Quem/soluisti* (183/26-184/4).

35 *vivit/Abraham* (184/4). On Augustine's understanding of this phrase, see Solignac (*BA*, Vol. 14, pp. 549-50).

36 *cum/memor* (184/13-14).

37 For the list of these characters, see *DBV*, I,6 and *DO*, I,7.

38 On the first date, determined by the start of the holidays, see above, Chapter Eight, n. 86. The latter is determined by the time of Augustine's enrolment in the catechumenate in Milan — at the beginning of Lent which was on 10 March 387: see Solignac, *BA*, Vol. 14, p. 95, n. 1.

39 *Christianae vitae otium* (*Retr.*, I,i,1). See also IX,iii,5 *Cassiciaco/te* (183/16-17).

40 See above, n. 24 for the connection between the mountainous prospect of Cassiciacum and the mountain of God.

41 *Et/tempore* (185/6-8).

42 *Ibi/epistulae* (185/1-6). *Concerning the Good Life, On order*, and *Against the Academics* are the discussions Augustine had "with those present" (*cum praesentibus* — 185/4). They were taken down by a shorthand writer (*CA*, I,i,4). De Labriolle (*BA*, Vol. 5, p. 9) notes that the transcriptions were "revised and retouched by Augustine who adapted them to the Ciceronian manner." The discussion Augustine had "with myself alone before you" (*cum/te* — 185/4-5) refers to the fourth book he wrote at Cassiciacum, the *Soliloquies*. On the letters to Nebridius, see above, n. 30.

43 In the *Retractations* (I,ii) Augustine says that *Concerning the Blessed Life* was written at the same time as *Against the Academics* and was begun on his birthday (13 November 387): and (in I,iii) he says that *On Order* was written at the same time as *Against the Academics*. On

the date of the *Soliloquies*, see Bardy (*BA*, Vol. 12, p. 565). The discussion of the *DBV* was accomplished in three days — *Retr.*, I,ii: see also *DBV*, I,6.

44 On these points I refer the reader to the Appendix.

45 There is a serious logical problem in the position of the critics for if, as they maintain, the *Dialogues* are clearly Neo-Platonic with only a veneer of Christianity and the *Confessions* is a doctored account which falsely show Augustine converted to Christianity before he actually was, then they must explain why Augustine mentions them in the *Confessions* as serving God in a Christian way. If they really are not, and could not be seen as such by his contemporaries, then this would mean that he simply told a lie in the hopes that he would not be caught. I find this incredible since he did not have to mention the *Dialogues* in the *Confessions* at all.

46 Courcelle (*Recherches*, pp. 179-81) understands Augustine's conversion in Book VIII simply as the decision to give up women and live a life of celibacy on the model of "Plotinus and his friends [who], a little after 253, intended to found a Platonopolis in the countryside" (p. 179). This plan is mentioned in Porphyry's *Life of Plotinus*, 12. Courcelle understands the retreat to Cassiciacum as Augustine's first concrete realization of the idea of such a philosophical community — which he had entertained from the time of his sceptical period (see VI,xiv,24) — and a stepping-stone to the monastic community he finally managed to found in Thagaste (*Recherches*, p. 181, n. 1).

47 The word *otium* or "rest" in the phrase from the *Retractations* need not compel us to conclude that this was simply the "philosophical *otium*" (Courcelle, *Recherches*, pp. 156, 180) such as Manlius Theodorus had sought (though married) when, in 383, he left public life, retreated to his country estate, and wrote works of philosophy. Though Theodorus was a Christian, Courcelle sees him chiefly as a Neo-Platonist, and his retreat as the model of Augustine's at Cassiciacum: see *Recherches*, pp. 153-56, 179-81, 281-84, and *Les Lettres grecques*, pp. 122-28. Courcelle supposes that Theodorus was the "excessively puffed-up man" (VII,ix,13 *hominem/turgidum* — 137/12-13) from whom Augustine got the books of the Platonists in the first place and he supposes further that the reason Augustine did not mention his name and censured him so when he wrote the *Confessions* was that at just about the same time Theodorus had left his "philosophical retreat" and re-entered public life to the "joy of the heads of the pagan party" (*Recherches*, p. 284). Courcelle supposed that when he wrote the *Confessions* Augustine would have seen this return to the world as "semi-apostasy" (*Recherches*, p. 284, n. 1). The argument has shown that this would only be true if Theodorus' retreat from the affairs of the world had been motivated by Christian rather than merely philosophical ends and there are no grounds to think that this was so. There is no doubt that Augustine learned much about Platonism from Theodorus and even about the points of contact between Platonism and Christianity — the *DBV*, for example, is dedicated to Theodorus (Courcelle has much to say about this, *Recherches*, pp. 202-10). Nevertheless, Augustine's final word, in the *Retractations* (I,ii) is that in the *DBV* he overpraised Theodorus although he was "learned [in Platonism} and a Christian." I understand this to mean that while, as a new convert, Augustine had been impressed by Theodorus as a kind of second Victorinus — both a philosopher and a Christian — in his subsequent dealings with the man he had reason to suspect, from his actions, that however much he called himself a Christian, he acted as one who thought Christianity was simply identical with Platonism — although, of course, since Augustine could not see into his soul he could not say for certain if this were really the case as long as Theodorus did not break openly with the church.

48 But see IX,v,13 where Augustine tells that when he wrote Ambrose asking what he should read to prepare himself for baptism and the bishop replied, Isaiah; Augustine found he could not even understanding the beginning of the book (i.e., in a Christian sense) and so laid it aside.

49 Augustine specifies clearly that even the learned Victorinus — who had studied Holy Scripture and all the Christian books "most thoroughly" (VIII,ii,4 *studiosissime* — 155/23) could not be baptized until he had been formally and authoritatively "instructed in the first ele-

ments of the sacraments'' (VIII,ii,4 *imbutus est primis instructionis sacramentis* — 156/20-
21). On this last phrase, see above, n. 31. The point is that the doctrine of the church — those
things it holds which cannot be known by reason — have to be formally received as from the
authority of the church just because they cannot be known by reason alone, and to insure that
one receives the orthodox doctrine approved by the church rather than some other thing.
50 See IX,iv,7 *Ibi/tibi* (185/1-2).
51 See IX,iv,7 *quoque/nostris* (185/13-17).
52 *Magis/serpentibus* (185/17-20).
53 See for example, *CA*, III,xx,43. In the Prologue (3) to the *Rectractations*, Augustine himself
observes the unique status of his Cassiciacum books which he relates to his position as a catechumen. He says, ''I won't leave out of consideration the works which I wrote when I was
still a catechumen, when I had abandoned the hope of worldly things by which I had been
held, but [bear in mind] that when I wrote them I was still inflated with the literary conven-
tions of the world.''
54 I first presented this argument in a paper read to a conference commemorating the sedecen-
tennial of the conversion of St. Augustine held at Trinity College, Toronto, May 1987. The
paper, ''Augustine's Conversion and the Ninth Book of the *Confessions*'' is to appear in the
Acts of the congress.
55 *cantica spiritum* (185/22-23).
56 *Quas/humani!* (185/27-186/2). Along with the earlier discussion of the Christian's relation
with near non-Christians (in IX,iii,5-6) Augustine shows here his relation to those who were
not nearly Christian (i.e., the Manichees) which may be summed up as loving the men but
loathing their sin (see V,xiii,22 *Et/castissimam* — 95/9-13). And here, as before, the most he
could do was to pray for their conversion.
57 *illa sacraments, illa medicamenta* (186/5-6).
58 See IX,vi,9. The fear stems from the fact that his past sins had not yet been forgiven in baptism; see the text cited below, n. 62.
59 *expavi* (189/22).
60 *Sed/fugit?* (189/21-22).
61 *deum salutis omnimodae* (189/19).
62 *Et/erant* (189/24-190/2).
63 *credo/apertior* (190/12-13).
64 *exercitatior/eloquio* (190/15-16). The political imagery of Isaiah and its emphasis on Israel's
cultic life must have seemed a strange world to Augustine who had little or no contact with
this aspect of the Judaeo-Christian tradition. To the time of his baptism Augustine's
acquaintance with the Old Testament was probably limited to the Manichaean criticism of
parts of the Pentateuch, the Psalms, and to the Pauline account of the Jews.
65 *nomen dare* (190/17).
66 See IX,vi,14 *Inde/remeavimus* (190/17-18). On the date of Augustine's return to Milan and
the method of enrolling for baptism, see Solignac (*BA*, Vol. 14, p. 95, n. 1).
67 On the African baptismal rites, see the texts cited by Solignac (*BA*, Vol. 14, p. 95, n. 1).
68 For the last time in the *Confessions*, Augustine mentions Alypius whose career from nature
to grace paralleled Augustine's. Once again Augustine stresses the difference in their character by mentioning the latter's great practical virtue, witnessed by his ability to control and
subdue the body. To this end Alypius went so far as to walk barefoot on the frozen soil of
Italy (IX,vi,14) while they were at Cassiciacum. In addition to Augustine's description of
Adeodatus, given here, one should also consult the conversation of the *DM*. Augustine's
chief interest in his son, as Monica's in him, concerned the salvation of his soul although he
was also clearly ''astonished'' by his great intelligence (IX,vi,14 *horrori mihi erat illud
ingenium* — 191/7). Adeodatus and Nebridius both died c. 390: see Brown, *Augustine*, p. 74.
69 *educandum in disciplina tua* (191/12). ''God's disciplines'' — the rudiments of Christian
doctrine — are distinguished from the ''disciplines of this world'' — i.e., the liberal sciences.
Augustine's *Enchiridion* (421) is his own brief statement of the essential elements of the
Christian position organized in terms of the three ''theological'' virtues of faith (discussed

in relation to the Apostles' creed), hope (the Lord's prayer), and charity (the Ten Command-ments).

70 For an account of the catechism and baptismal practice, see Courcelle, *Recherches*, pp. 211-26 and Brown, *Augustine*, pp. 124-25. The baptistry itself is described in R. M. Mira bella, "Il Battistero di Saint' Ambrogio a Milano," *Recherches Augustiniennes*, 4 (1966), 3-10.

71 *et/praeteritae* (191/12-13).

72 *Nec/eis* (191/13-20).

73 See Gibb (*Confessions*, p. 248). "The legend which represents Ambrose and Augustine as improvising the 'Te Deum' in alternate strophes at the baptism of the latter occurs in the *Chronicon* ascribed to bishop Datius of Milan (d. 552) but now admitted to be the work of Landulphus Senior in the 11th century. . . . Apart from this, the earliest mention of it is in the Psalter presented by Charlemagne to Pope Hadrian in 722 (the Golden Psalter, Vienn. Cod. 1861) '*hymnus quem S. Ambrosius et S. Augustinus invicem composuerunt*'."

74 *Gratias/praeterieram?* (193/1-3).

75 See IX,vii,15 *Tunc/imitantibus* (192/3-7). On the Ambrosian hymns see Gibb, *Confessions*, p. 250.

76 *haeresis sua causa* (191/28).

77 The siege of the basilica is told in IX,vii,15. For an account and chronology of these events see Courcelle, *Recherches*, pp. 139-53. Ambrose states the demand of Justina, and his reply, in *Letter*, XX,19. See also the other references in *BA*, Vol. 14, p. 98. Gibbon gives his vivid and anti-Catholic account in *The Decline and Fall of the Roman Empire*, XXVII.

78 See IX,vii,15 *Ibi/vivebat* (191/28-192/1).

79 *Nos/tui* (192/1-2).

80 See IX,vii,15 *excitabamur/turbata* (192/2-3).

81 *incorrupta* (192/10).

82 The discovery of the remains of Gervasius and Protasius is told in IX,vii,16. On the differing evidence about the condition of the "uncorrupted" remains, see Courcelle, *Recherches*, p. 148. The precise dates are 17 June 386 for the discovery of the remains, and 19 June for their transport to Ambrose's basilica. Courcelle gives a thorough treatment of the episode and of Augustine's recollections and judgements on relics and miracles through the course of his life in *Recherches*, pp. 139-53, 265. Other ancient references to the affair of Gervasius and Protasius are found in *BA*, Vol. 14, p. 98 in the critical apparatus. See also J. Doignon, "Perspectives ambrosiennes: SS. Gervasius et Protais, génies de Milan,"*Revue des études augustiniennes*, 2 (1956), 313-34.

83 Courcelle, *Recherches*, p. 152.

84 *non currebamus* (193/5). Courcelle (*Recherches*, p. 150) says of these words, "Mindful of the Song of Songs (1:24) this phrase should be understood here in its literal sense: Augus-tine did not *run* like the faithful or the idlers to these spectacular ceremonies: far from giving credence to miracles and being led by them to Catholicism, he wasn't even interested." This is true of Augustine only before his conversion — the whole point of his including the account in the *Confessions* was to show how much he was inspired by these events after his conversion.

85 See IV,vi,14, text quoted above, n. 72. Much the same thing is expressed by Augustine in his exposition of Psalm 4 in IX,iv,7-12.

86 Augustine ascribes the thought to God in IX,vii,16, text quoted above, n. 74.

87 I agree with Courcelle's opinion that Augustine did not actually witness the translation of Gervasius and Protasius: see *Recherches*, pp. 148-51.

88 I use the word "invention" in the technical sense. See Courcelle (*Recherches*, p. 145): "The very fact of the 'invention,' which consists in discovering an unknown martyr and offering him a cult although he lacked the consecration of an uninterrupted tradition, was a new the-ory in the West."

89 Text quoted above, n. 79.

90 *quantum/faenea* (193/7-8). This heavenly "air" is opposed to the "breath" of pride of IX,iv,7.

91 See, for example, Augustine's praise of Psalm 4 in IX,iv,8-11 where he makes the same contrast between the things he now found nourishing and good which he had formerly spurned. He ends (in IX,iv,11) "Like a cur I had snarled bitterly against the Scriptures which are sweet with the honey of heaven and radiant with your light" (trans. Pine-Coffin, Penguin) – *pestis/luminosas* (189/9-11).

92 Courcelle argues that Augustine had heard Ambrose use this text in his sermon *De Isaac* at about the time of the "invention": (*Recherches*, p. 150, n. 4 and p. 152). On this sermon itself see *ibid.*, pp. 106-38.

93 *Et/faenea* (193/3-8).

94 *Tunc/possem* (146/17-22).

95 *comedere*, literally = "to eat."

96 Courcelle, *Recherches*, pp. 151 and 153.

97 The quoted words are from Courcelle, *Recherches*, pp. 150-53.

98 I say "limited" in the sense that Augustine himself had been a Christian for only about 15 years at the time he wrote the *Confessions* – and had not yet died as a Christian.

99 *parentibus carnis meae* (5/19).

100 *Sed/nascerer* (193/19-22). Compare I,xi,17 *Et/essem* (14/2-7).

101 *Et/tuae* (193/26-194/2). Compare Augustine's situation in I,xi,17-18, II,ii,2-II,iii,8.

102 See IX,viii,18 *sicut/narrabat* (194/22-23).

103 *sancta severitate* (194/10).

104 See IX,viii,17.

105 *superfluentibus/motibus* (195/2-3).

106 *Quo/exuit* (195/21-23).

107 *Numquid/nos?* (195/9-11).

108 *pudet/inpudentem* (36/13).

109 *Ubi/viro* (196/10-14).

110 See IX,ix,19 *Ita/iniurias* (196/14-15).

111 See IX,ix,19 *ira fervidus* (196/19).

112 See IX,ix,20.

113 See IX,ix,19 *Denique/opportere* (196/23-197/5). See Solignac (*BA*, Vol. 14, p. 552) on these *tabulae matrimoniales* and the condition of women in marriage generally in Augustine's day.

114 See IX,ix,21.

115 *horrenda/pervagante* (198/7-8).

116 On the date of Patricius' death, see Solignac, *BA*, Vol. 14, p. 201.

117 *Fuerat/cernebat* (198/21-26). This passage is not put in poetic form in the *BA* edition. P. Henry (*La Vision d'Ostie, sa place dans la vie et l'oeuvre de saint Augustin*, Paris, Vrin, 1938) provides a convenient summary of the effect of Monica on Augustine, from the evidence of the *Confessions* (pp. 49-52), and from the evidence of the Cassiciacum *Dialogues* (pp. 52-58).

118 *serva servorum tuorum* (198/18). See IX,i,1 where Augustine describes his new position as "God's servant" (*servus tuus* – 179/19-20) and his fellow Christians as "your servants, my brothers" (*servorum/meorum* – 182/22-23).

119 See IX,ix,22 *ita/fuisset* (199/1-2).

120 Augustine say in IX,xi,28 that Monica died in her 56th year, in his 33rd year, and thus, before his 34th birthday on 13 November 387.

121 Navigius was at his mother's bedside in Ostia: see IX,xi,27 *adstantes/meum* (210/27).

122 Adeodatus is mentioned at Ostia in IX,xii,29 and 30.

123 Evodius is first mentioned at Milan in IX,vii,17 and at Ostia in IX,xii,31.

124 *utilius/tibi* (193/15).

125 *simul/sancto* (193/13-14). This is also the sense of the opening line of this chapter with its quotation from Psalm 67.

126 See Brown, *Augustine*, p. 128.

127 *incumbentes/navigationi* (199/6-10).

128 For a full bibliography on the vision at Ostia, see the references in Courcelle, *Recherches*, p. 222, n. 3 (to 1949): his own treatment is on pp. 222-26. See also Solignac's references in *BA*, Vol. 13, p. 186, n. 2; p. 191, n. 1; and pp. 262-63 (to 1959).

129 Solignac, *BA*, Vol. 13, p. 191.

130 *Ibid.*

131 Courcelle, *Recherches*, p. 222. The two treatises of Plotinus are, respectively, *Enneads* I,vi and V,i.

132 Throughout his life Augustine always took the "Platonists" as the representatives of those who had come to the true knowledge of God through the consideration of nature — though they were not the only philosophers to have done so: see *DCD*, VIII,5-11.

133 Henry, *Vision*, p. 116. Henry devotes the whole of his Chapter 8 to proving this point and cites a number of other passages from the *City of God*: see esp. *Vision*, pp. 115-20. We have seen that the same point was already made by Augustine in Book VII of the *Confessions* where he maintained that the God he had seen in the Platonist vision was the goal of the human soul (VII,x,16).

134 *DCD*, X,16 (trans. Bettenson, Penguin), p. 394.

135 *Plotinus, Enneads* I,vi,7 (trans. Armstrong, *Loeb*).

136 Mandouze, ' "L'extase d'Ostie," possibilités et limites de la méthode des parallèles textuels," *Augustinus Magister*, 1, Paris, Études Augustiniennes, 1954. In his first note he cites the works of Henry, Courcelle, and Pepin with which he is concerned and adds that without much effort it would be possible to increase this list considerably. Of the nine conclusions which he gives about the limits of textual parallels, the following ought perhaps to be written over the study of any who seek to approach Augustine solely with the tools of philology. "[T]he careful author of the *Confessions* was surely concerned with something other than composing a learned puzzle in the sight of God" (p. 83). It is almost inevitable that philologists see the texts on which they are working as a puzzle whose meaning can only be unlocked if one knows which bits relate to what sources — with the unfortunate implication that the *Confessions* has had to wait for over 1,500 years for its meaning to be "unlocked" by the keys of philology.

137 Mandouze, "L'extase d'Ostie," p. 81.

138 Solignac (*BA*, Vol. 14, pp. 550-52) makes a study of this phrase and quotes Augustine's own clear explanation of it from *EP*, CXXI,3, quoted below, n. 154. He concludes: "As we see, this is the technical term which is equivalent to the 'I am who I am' and to the 'who is' of Exodus, the term which, taken in a metaphysical sense, defines God as he defines himself: being in the full sense of the word, immutable being, eternal being." This is certainly true as far as it goes and it correctly ties the object of the vision at Ostia to the object of the vision at Milan where God was described in the Biblical epithet (in VII,x,16) as "*I am he who is* (Ex. 3:14)" — *Ego/sum* (141/17). Henry (*Vision*, pp. 40-41) also shows that this *in id ipsum* was the key phrase of Psalm 4 which Augustine discussed at length in the description of his life at Cassiciacum.

139 These nine points are reproduced from the argument of my "Augustine's Conversion and the Ninth Book of the *Confessions*."

140 *instaurabamus* (199/9-10). *ALD* gives all the quoted words as meanings of the verb. I cannot help but think of this as a precursor of the inner garden laid out by design in the centre of Benedictine monasteries all over Europe as a kind of earthly paradise in the wilderness of the world. On the place of the garden as a paradise in Christian thought see G. H. Williams, *Wilderness and Paradise in Christian Thought*, New York, Harper and Brothers, 1962. Recall also that Augustine specified that the conversion of the two friends of Ponticianus occurred in a garden (VIII,vi,15 *hortos* — 165/20) as did his own (see VIII,viii,19-169/17).

141 *Enneads* VI,ix,11.

142 See VII,viii,12, VII,ix,13-15, and VII,xx,26.

143 *Conloquebamur/dulciter* (199/10-11). The Watts translation is found in *Loeb*.

144 *Impendente/nobis* (199/3-4).

145 See IX,x,24. Throughout the whole description of the vision from the time Augustine says "I believe" (*credo* — 199/5) that God procured this for us etc., in IX,x,23, to the first word of IX,x,25, "I said" (*dicebam* — 200/14) — where he turns to Monica's resignation to her death — the whole account is put in the first person plural.

146 Monica's presence at Ostia has been much remarked on as one of the differences between the two visions but this has not been understood very deeply. Henry, for example, writes "The active and principal part which Monica takes in the ecstasy gives it an authentic and specifically Christian character. Her presence is a fact, a fact one cannot eliminate, a brutal and clarifying fact" (*Vision*, p. 45). As the rest of his discussion shows, the enlightenment consists in this: Monica was definitely a Christian so any vision she has would be Christian and since Augustine had the same vision his too was Christian. Courcelle, on the other hand, sees Monica's presence as tearing Augustine away "from the feeling of solitude that followed the experiences of Milan" (*Recherches*, p. 224). There is much more here.

147 The thought occurs in many places in the *Enneads*: i.e., I,vi,7, "passing in the ascent all that is alien to the God, one sees with one's self alone that alone, simple, single and pure" (trans. Armstrong, *Loeb*).

148 See IX,x,23 *quaerebamus/sanctorum* (199/12-14).

149 See, for example, the outrage of Plotinus at such a suggestion in *Enneads* I,ix,46-60. Plotinus' argument is directed against the Gnostics but on this point it could just as well be aimed against the Christians.

150 See IX,x,24, "We were raising ourselves up with a more ardent affection to the *in id ipsum*" — *erigentes/ipsum* (199/24).

151 See Henry (*Vision*, p. 114). "But the formal characteristics of this vision — to know its object, God himself, in his own proper fashion, God seen in himself and through himself, without any intermediary — are identically those of the highest Plotinian contemplation: the object contemplated is equally the One, the absolute of Plotinus, and between the soul and it no created thing is interposed" and "this intellectual soul then recognizes no nature superior to it except that of God — note it, the absence of any intermediary in the vision — the creator of the world and of the soul" (p. 118).

152 *et/possem* (146/21-22).

153 *attingeremus/pabulo* (199/29-200-1).

154 The text of *EP*, CXXI,5 is worth quoting at length. In it Augustine answers the question, "What is the *id ipsum*?" He says: "You cannot conceive of it. It is too great to understand, too great to grasp. Hold on therefore to what he became for you, he who you can never conceive. Hold on to the flesh of Christ: it is towards the flesh of Christ that you were raised up like a sick man, like a man left half dead after an attack of thieves, to be led to the inn and cured there [allusion to the good Samaritan of Lk. 10:30-34]. Let us run therefore to the house of the Lord, to the city where our feet can rest: this city which *is built like a city that participates in the id ipsum* (Ps. 121:3). To what ought you therefore to hold? To that which Christ made himself for you, because it [the flesh of Christ] is Christ himself and to Christ himself one legitimately applies the *I am who I am* (Ex. 3:14). He is in this way in the form of God. There where it is no falsehood to be equal to God, there is the *id ipsum*. And in order that you could participate the *id ipsum* he first made himself participate in you and *the Word was made flesh* (Jn. 1:14) so that flesh could participate in the Word." Augustine's point is clear. The *id ipsum* towards which he and Monica arose at Ostia was not simply the eternal Word of God in whom all things were made (which was the object of the Platonist vision in Book VII) but the same Word, made flesh. But this is to say that the vision at Ostia was the vision of the true church, the heavenly Jerusalem, the community of saints who can see God face to face because they see him in Christ who is fully God and fully man and who, by becoming flesh himself, has raised our flesh to the possibility of seeing and being with God in a manner that we do not posses by nature — i.e., where mutable and corporeal distinctions are not obliterated in the One.

155 See esp. IX,x,25 read in this light.

156 *spiravimus/spiritu* (200/9-10). The heavenly city was the goal. There they "left attached" (*religatas* — 200/9 — from the same root as "religion" in Augustine's etymology: see *Retr.* I,xiii,9), the first fruits of the Spirit as the end to which they aimed and "we returned to the sounds of our mouths where the word both begins and ends" (IX,x,24 — *remeavimus/finitur* — 200/10-11).

157 Courcelle sees in the phrase *primitias spiritus*, "nothing but a transcription of Plotinus into Biblical style [signifying] that Augustine remains attached, by the best in himself, to the Intelligence glimpsed fleetingly" (*Recherches*, p. 224 — following Henry, *Vision*, p. 39). It is not clear what sense is attached to this teaching. Do they mean that Augustine's soul is divided after Ostia with the best part in heaven and the rest down on earth, or that he is simply repeating Plotinus' teaching about the undescended soul (*Enneads* IV,viii,8)? Nothing much is said beyond the comparison of texts and none of the supporters of this interpretation maintain that *primitias spiritus* is in any sense a literal translation of something from Plotinus — which it most certainly is not. If it is not a translation but only a "transcription," then we are operating in the realm of subjective judgement — some will see it as such and others will not and there is no way of settling the question. With this the Plotinian interpretation becomes unfounded and we are left with the explicit Pauline quotation which is all Augustine actually put before us. The text of Plotinus which Courcelle maintains Augustine "transcribed" is *Enneads* V,i,3. A review of this question is found in J. Pepin, "*Primitiae spiritus*. Remarques sur un citation paulinienne des *Confessions* de saint Augustin," *Revue de l'histoire des religions*, 140 (1951), 155-201. See also Mandouze, "L'extase d'Ostie," and Solignac's note in *BA*, Vol. 14, pp. 552-55.

158 *Et/resurgimus* (201/8-9).

159 *consuetudo carnalis* (145/16).

160 On the opposition between this *regio ubertatis indificientibus* (199/29-200/1) and the *regio egestatis* (36/23) of II,x,18 or the *regio dissimilitudinis* (141/8) of VII,x,16, see Chapter Two, n. 89.

161 Courcelle is wrong to suggest that Plotinus teaches that we can enjoy the vision of God "indefinitely prolonged" (*Recherches*, p. 224). He implies that Plotinus does so in a text which he quotes from *Enneads* I,vi,7 (*Recherches*, p. 224, n. 6) but this is to read far too much into the word μέυου. As long as Neo-Platonism stays simply and exclusively with its own logic, and is not converted to Christianity, such a union of God and the world is impossible. This was well recognized by Plotinus — see for example the passage from *Enneads* I,ix,46-60.

162 *non/habitandam* (149/26-27).

163 *ait/facio?* (201/13-21).

164 See IX,xi,27.

165 *die/suae* (203/6).

166 *inanitas* (202/23).

167 Augustine says that he did not know when Monica gave up her longstanding desire to be buried beside Patricius but suggests that it was most likely after the vision at Ostia when she asked what was left for her to do in this world: see IX,xi,28.

168 "*nihil/resuscitet*" (203/4-5).

169 *quinquagesimo/est* (203/6-8).

170 *Premebam/erat* (203/9-13).

171 *Neque/tenebamus* (203/17-23).

172 A stone with the epitaph of Monica was found in 1945 at Ostia by some boys erecting a basketball hoop. See Solignac (*BA*, Vol. 14, pp. 555-56) and Courcelle (*Recherches*, p. 222, n. 2).

173 See IX,xii,31.

174 *Credo/pascitur* (205/8-11).

175 On Augustine's etymological explanation about why he went to the baths (IX,xii,32), see Solignac (*BA*, Vol. 14, p. 131, n. 1).

176 See IX,xii,32.

177 *et/me* (206/6-7). Augustine goes on to say what it was about Monica that he wept for. It was
     not Monica as his natural mother but as God's servant – but see IX,xii,33 where, in hind-
     sight, he reckons that much of his grief had its root in a simple worldly attachment to his
     mother.
178 *partae horae* (206/14).
179 See IX,xii,33 *Legat/tui* (206/12-18).
180 *sepositis* (207/9).
181 See IX,xiii,34 *Quamquam/eius* (206/24-26).
182 *medicinam vulnerum nostrorum* (207/11-12).
183 *non/ignis* (206/26-207/1).
184 See the text from X,iii,3 quoted above, Chapter Eight, n. 43. For such inward, unseen, and
     unseeable sins none of us can stand secure in the consideration of our own virtue. But, as
     Augustine points out in IX,xiii,36, he who sets the standard is also the one who has promised
     that he will redeem us and cover our faults.
185 See IX,xii,27 *"Ponite/fueritis"* (202/6-9). Compare IX,xiii,37.
186 Book X is a systematic consideration of the struggles and trials in the inner life of the Chris-
     tian who lives and works in and with an unreformed nature. With this in mind we can see
     how the second part of the *Confessions* is generated out of the conclusion of the first. Much
     more than an afterthought or an interpolation, the content of Book X is a logical continuation
     of the argument in the first part. Solignac gives a succinct account of the many connections
     that have been suggested between Books I-IX and Book X: see *BA*, Vol. 13, pp. 19-23. Dif-
     fering from all of these, I say that in Book IX, Augustine has shown the external and, one
     might say, objectively visible life of the convert in the world, yet it is clear from these last
     chapters that the demands on the Christian are not fulfilled at this level alone – by comply-
     ing with the objective requirements of the divine law and participating in the rites and sacra-
     ments of the church. Between baptism and death there is a whole inner and subjective aspect
     to the Christian's life that cannot be adequately treated in terms of what appears objectively
     or externally inasmuch as Christ demands the same freedom from contradiction inwardly as
     in our outward and publicly seen actions. The discussion of this aspect of Christianity
     required a new method – and a new confession to a new audience – which Augustine gives
     us in Book X. Logically therefore it forms the second of Augustine's complete *Confessions*.
     For a brief account of my understanding of the place and purpose of the tenth book of the
     Confessions, see my article on "The place and purpose of the tenth book of the *Confes-
     sions*."
          In terms of the argument of the *Confessions* as a whole this book covers only the first
     third. Of the five verbs Augustine listed in III,iv,8 – describing the task that lay ahead of him
     from the moment that he first came to the idea of God after reading the *Hortensius* – these
     nine books have dealt with the first three only: "to love," "to seek," and "to follow." Of
     the other two, "to hold" – or how the inner man holds himself on the way of Christ in this
     life – is the matter of his second confession in Book X; the last, "to love and honour" –
     which treats of how we honour and love God for his own sake – is the content of the final
     confession in Books XI-XIII where Augustine explains how far he understands the relation
     of the trinity to the world through his exegesis of the opening verses of Genesis. I have
     attempted to show how this final confession arises out of the other two and completes them
     in my paper on "The unity of the *Confessions*." Only when the inner logic and connection
     of all three parts have been fully brought to light will it be possible to support the claim,
     which I have made perhaps too often, that the whole of the *Confessions* is organized and
     informed by a thoroughgoing trinitarian structure and understanding. The proof of this point
     lies beyond the scope of this volume. In time perhaps I, or some other, will turn to this task.

Appendix
AN ESSAY ON THE HISTORICITY DEBATE

In the scholarly community a great controversy concerning the first nine books of the *Confessions* has gone on now for a hundred years.[1] It has turned, ostensibly, on the question of the historical value of the *Confessions*. Are they a true historical account of Augustine's conversion, or a version in which the facts have been altered to suit some ulterior purpose? There is a distinct difference in tone between the *Confessions*, written some ten years after Augustine's conversion, and his first works, known as the *Dialogues*, written right after the event.[2] The *Confessions* show Augustine suddenly and completely converted to Christianity and thereafter moved by a thoroughly Christian spirit, grieving over his sins or rejoicing with thankfulness for the grace he had received — while the *Dialogues*, though written right after the time he says he was converted, show almost no evidence of this. In them Augustine appears to be still simply and contentedly immersed in the culture of late pagan antiquity and concerned only with philosophical questions.

In 1888 Adolf Harnack, noting this discrepancy, proposed that the account in the *Confessions* was not strictly historical but was organized rather on a theological principle.[3] This, he said, made it convenient for Augustine to doctor the facts and to present his conversion as a sudden break, when it must actually have been a slow, cumulative process stretching years beyond the time when he wrote the *Dialogues*. This apparent contradiction was also noted in an article by Gaston Boissier that appeared in the same year as Harnack's.[4] Both papers called into serious question the historical truth of Augustine's account. Indeed for the ensuing century, scholarly studies of the first part of the *Confessions* have been dominated by this question. This fact itself is remarkable and requires an explanation. Calling into question the "historicity" of Augustine's account involves much more than simply determining whether Augustine was really and suddenly converted in 386 A.D. after the events in the garden in Milan, as he tells us in the *Confessions*, or more slowly and at some other date, as the evidence of the *Dialogues* seems to indicate. Because the *Confessions* propose to explain precisely how and why Augustine came to the church, questions about the time and manner of his conversion are not simply clarifications of detail. The issue, from the beginning, has been about the content of the *Confessions* and the nature of Augustine's Christianity. And here historical and theological judgements are inextricably interwoven.

On the one hand, critics like Harnack deny the historical veracity of the *Confessions* and find it to be essentially theology. On the other side are the *Confessions'* defenders who, looking chiefly to its theological content, find that the work is his-

---

torically sound. During the first half of this long debate the critics had the upper hand, while in the second half the position of the defenders has been accepted. But this does not mean that there is yet a satisfactory reading of the *Confessions*. Many scholars, who intend all the while to maintain the historical accuracy of the text,[5] have criticized the defenders' methods and conclusions. The historicity of the text is generally accepted without there being an equal acceptance of the arguments by which it has been established. I propose that we take a fresh look at the entire controversy. If we can discover how this state of affairs came to pass, we may hope also to find some way of resolving the problems. To this end I will characterize the controversy as being between an historical and a theological approach. Although my sketch does not represent the nuances of any particular effort on either side, it is intended to state the essential character of each.[6] I have adopted a detached point of view having no brief for one position over the other — which is now possible because both sides have been fully developed so that we can reflect in this way on their mutual relationship.

Critics of the historical value of the *Confessions* prefer the evidence of the *Dialogues* in which the recently converted Augustine seems largely untouched by Christian concerns. These critics make the reasonable historical judgement that, as the *Dialogues* are closer to the event, they give better evidence of Augustine's state after his conversion in the garden at Milan than do the *Confessions*. However, because none who hold this position have doubted that Augustine did finally and truly become a Christian, all are faced with the task of explaining to what he was in fact converted in 389 A.D., and of determining when he was really converted to Christianity. The answer invariably given to the first question is, to Neo-Platonic philosophy and morals, and to the second: years later, either in the monastery he founded in North Africa, or when he was ordained.

But once the critics had destroyed any claims for the direct historical value of the account in the *Confessions*, the work itself remained to be explained. This was done either by trying to save its historical credibility by reinterpreting everything which Augustine says about his conversion to Christianity as being about a conversion to Neo-Platonic philosophy, or, by abandoning it as history because it is a doctored text in which the facts have been altered, treating it as a work which has merely a theological value. This critical position is certainly important and the important critics are all men of an historical spirit: they are inclined to look for the truth, and to find it, in history. They have examined Augustine's account of his conversion in the light of the more reliable evidence, as determined by the canons of historical inquiry, and have found it wanting in truth. The *Confessions*, they say, may be true in a philosophical or theological sense, as an idealized account of the move from nature to grace, and as such it may well have religious and catechetical value. But history it is not.

This challenge to the historical value of the *Confessions* was serious indeed but it led these scholars into strange paths, for they have ended up shunning as history the document which purports to be historical (the *Confessions*) and defending as history those which make no such claim but are evidently philosophical (the *Dialogues*). Thus, in *L'évolution intellectuelle de saint Augustin* (1918), the most sustained and complete of the critical works, which represents the high-water mark of the position, Prosper Alfaric states:

In reality, nowhere does he [Augustine] show himself so frankly and naturally as in the course of these first works [the *Dialogues*]. Which is to say that in order to know the state of his soul when he wrote them we ought to look to them much more than to the *Confessions*.

The evidence of the *Confessions* is rejected in favour of the *Dialogues* because they were written right after his "conversion." Here the historian is simply using the tools and methods of his science — but it becomes problematic when we look to the conclusion. Alfaric immediately goes on to say:

Thus we are driven to consider him much less as a catechumen almost uniquely occupied with the Christian ideal, than as a disciple of Plotinus desirous above all to bring his life into conformity with the teaching of the Master. Morally, as intellectually, he was converted to Neo-Platonism rather than to the Gospel.[7]

Allowing that the *Dialogues* do give better evidence of the "state of Augustine's soul" right after his conversion, because of their contemporaneity, is it true that they could not have been written by a Christian? This is a theological judgement and one that is very difficult to make.[8] But questions of this sort are not raised by the historians. For them the argument is clear. The *Dialogues* are the better historical documents for the period of Augustine's conversion (a reasonable historical judgement); the *Dialogues* are pagan (a theological judgement on the strength of the *prima facie* evidence); therefore, Augustine was not converted to Christianity when he says he was and the *Confessions* are not a reliable historical document. Whether or not this is a reasonable conclusion depends entirely on the middle term which clearly involves a theological opinion about the nature of the difference between paganism and Christianity. No doubt there is a distinction — but is it the one on which the historians insist?

Here we must suspect that the historical spirit reveals its limitation and its prejudices. It can certainly appear that it is limited, by its insistence on facts, to judging the theological content of the *Dialogues* by their immediate appearance. That is not Christian which does not talk of Christ, grace, and sin, etc., and that is, which does. More seriously it seems that certain modern theological prejudices have crept into the argument to the detriment of the historian's scientific objectivity. For example, the distinction between Christianity and paganism, on which the historian's argument depends, appears to derive from that nineteenth-century liberal Protestant theological opinion which holds that Christianity is essentially a matter of history and faith — of one's particular relation to the historical facts recorded in the Gospel — and, as a result, is to be thoroughly and absolutely distinguished from pagan philosophy.[9] The introduction of this theological perspective into the core of the critic's argument makes it possible to take exception to his conclusions. Insofar as they depend on this latent theological assumption it can seem that they are, from a purely historical point of view, unfounded and subjective.

The Catholic defenders of the historical value of the *Confessions*,[10] spurred by the critics to explain the apparent contradiction between the *Dialogues* and the *Confessions*, have gone to the heart of the problem as they see it and have shown how, on theological considerations, the *Dialogues* are really Christian. From the first they have attacked the critics at their weakest point, namely in the assumption that Christianity and Neo-Platonism are poles apart. The defenders insist, on sound theological grounds, that more joins these two than separates them. Already in 1903, Eugène Portalié had argued in his article on Augustine in the *Diction-naire de Théologie Catholique*, that what seems in the *Dialogues* to be Neo-Platonism is simply the philosophical expression of a truth which derives from Scripture. He concluded that "it is not a Platonist who speaks in these dialogues but a Christian; or, to be more exact, a man who is both."[11]

This position lies behind all subsequent arguments for the historical value of the *Confessions*. The line of defence is clear. By showing that Christianity and Neo-Platonism are not two different things, as supposed by the historians, the apparent contradiction between the evidence of the *Dialogues* and the *Confessions* dissolves and the historical value of the latter is re-established.[12] However, the argument of the defenders led immediately to certain historical considerations, just as the argument of the critics involved them in theological judgements.

In 1919, in a long review of Alfaric's book, Etienne Gilson said:

> But the truth, which the texts cited by Alfaric himself suggest, seems to be that on leaving scepticism behind, he [Augustine] became a Catholic at once because he believed that Neo-Platonism was Catholicism and Catholicism was Neo-Platonism, indivisibly. It is true that this Neo-Platonism passed away and that the Catholicism remained, but one cannot conclude that he was first a Neo-Platonist and then a Catholic. Alfaric perhaps failed to see at what point the changes imposed on Augustine's Neo-Platonism by his Catholicism were essential and while he faithfully noted them he has not exactly thought them. The mere fact that Augustine admitted, from the first, the doctrine of creation and the equality of the divine persons suffices to establish that he became a Catholic and not a Neo-Platonist. In the exchange of these two doctrines [for what Neo-Platonism teaches in their stead], Catholicism imposed much more of its form than did what he took from Neo-Platonism.[13]

Similarly, in the following year, Charles Boyer argued,

> It is true that he [Augustine] became a Christian because he was a Neo-Platonist. It would be truer to say that he became a Neo-Platonist because he was a Christian. But these formulas are simplistic. The truth is that the son of Monica became a Christian because certain evidences, grouped around the fact of the church, imposed themselves on his spirit and that he then accepted many Neo-Platonic ideas because these ideas appeared to him both true and enlightened in themselves and, in their consequences, in accord with his faith.[14]

As both of these statements make clear, the problem for the defenders of the historical accuracy of the *Confessions* was that having once brought Neo-Platonism and Christianity together on sound theological grounds, they were immediately faced with the task of showing how, historically, the Christian element outweighed and preceded the Neo-Platonic. Otherwise the critics who could well reply, "You argue against us that Christianity and Neo-Platonism were one and the same to Augustine. But that's just our point — and the *Dialogues* show that the Neo-Platonic elements were, at first, far more important to him than the Christian and that it was in reality to Neo-Platonism that he was first converted."

By this logic the theologians were forced to become historians, and none have done this more thoroughly than the philologian, Pierre Courcelle, in his important work, *Recherches sur les Confessions de saint Augustin*, which appeared in 1950. He saw that until questions of meaning and chronology could be settled on firm historical grounds, the dispute over whether one was to see in Augustine "not so much a Neo-Platonism tinted with Christianity as, on the contrary, a Christianity tinted with Neo-Platonism,"[15] could only result in a situation where, as he says, "Each scholar proposes the dose that suits him, with heaps of references capable of being cited in each sense."[16]

Courcelle showed, not on the basis of any *a priori* theological position but on what he saw as sure historical grounds — founded on the comparison of parallel texts from Neo-Platonic philosophers, from Ambrose and from Augustine — that Augustine certainly could have, and very probably did, discover Platonism through the sermons of Ambrose.[17] If the celebrated and indisputably Christian Ambrose, the bishop of Milan, taught Neo-Platonic doctrines from the pulpit then none could doubt that "Neo-Platonism and Christianity were intimately connected for the thinking men of the church in Milan."[18] Thus, as Courcelle concludes, "the controversy about the conversion loses its sense from the instant [we see] that Ambrose, bishop for twelve years and not a Christian of recent date, did not hesitate to recommend to his charges Neo-Platonic theses assimilated to Christian doctrine."[19]

This settled, Courcelle was able to adopt a chronology of Augustine's conversion more in accord with the testimony of the *Confessions* than were those of the earlier defenders of its historicity.[20] Gilson, and especially Boyer, felt compelled to insist that Augustine came to Christianity *before* he discovered Neo-Platonism and consequently "read the *Enneads* [of Plotinus] as a Christian."[21] Courcelle agrees that Augustine did read Plotinus' work as a Christian, but he can also show that he did not do so because he was first a Christian who only later discovered in Neo-Platonism a suitable handmaid for theology.[22] To Courcelle, no such strained interpretation of the chronology of the *Confessions* is necessary, because he shows that Augustine's intellectual conversion was to an already Platonized faith (the events of Book VII), followed some months later, as the *Confessions* indicate, by the conversion of his morals under the particular guidance of the priest Simplicianus (the events of Book VIII). "Everything," says Courcelle, "becomes clear from the moment that we recognize that Augustine was initiated to Neo-Platonism within the church at Milan itself."[23]

Courcelle's work re-established the traditional view of the historical validity of the *Confessions*, yet there are serious problems with his defence and these have become even more marked in subsequent works which draw on his conclusions.[24] The greatest strength of this position is also its greatest weakness. For, having once brought Neo-Platonism and Christianity together on sound historical grounds, the defenders seem incapable of making any credible theological distinction between them. The substantial historical validity of the text is confirmed, but at the cost of a theological interpretation which does not appear to be adequate to the theology of the *Confessions* itself.

The defenders very properly maintain that Christianity is not antithetically opposed to philosophy. They know and show that thought and reason did have a vital place in the early church and that it lived, in large part, through the assimilation of pagan philosophy. What is not understood is the manner in which Christianity and philosophy are radically different. If, as this position would have it, Augustine saw no essential difference between Neo-Platonism and Christianity, then he was converted to Christianity through his spiritual awakening to the truths of Neo-Platonic philosophy. When asked to explain what happened in the famous conversion scene in the garden, this argument is forced to distinguish between an "intellectual" conversion which occurred first, assisted by Neo-Platonic philosophy, and a "moral" conversion which followed, in which he decided to "reform his conduct."[25]

But this is simply the old problem in a new form. For which is the true conversion to Christianity: the intellectual or the moral? The defenders have no doubts, it is the former. Of course these scholars insist that there is a difference between Christianity and philosophy, and they allow that, once converted intellectually, Augustine himself became ever more aware of the distinctions through his practical involvement in the life of the church.[26] But the differences, which centre on practical matters such as the reform of his conduct and the acceptance of uniquely Christian doctrines and rites, seem peripheral. If the logic of Augustine's move from his "intellectual" into his "moral" conversion does not much interest them, it is because they take it as self-evident. Once intellectually converted to a Neo-Platonized Christianity, these practical differences having to do with an historical and institutional church are assumed to follow as a matter of course.[27]

But is it so? There is much that is suspect here on both historical and, more importantly, theological grounds. As a defence of the historical accuracy of the *Confessions*, this argument ends up in the curious position of denying the truth of Augustine's own account. He places his conversion to the church at the time of the scene in the garden in Milan, and yet the proponents of this position say that he was really converted before — when he discovered the intellectual agreement of Christianity and Neo-Platonism. This treatment which forces the text is objectionable in itself, but it is supported by a theological judgement of the most far-reaching consequences.

What is at stake is whether Augustine teaches that conversion to Christianity is essentially an intellectual matter or something of another kind. The defenders are certain that it is the former. After all, in Book VII where he describes his discovery of the true God through reading certain "books of the Platonists," he not only says that what he found there he also found in the New Testament, but more, he gives, as a fully adequate summary of what the Platonists taught, the precise words of the prologue to the Gospel of John: "In the beginning was the Word, and the Word was with God, and the Word was God," etc.[28]

To this point the theologians have Augustine on their side. From here on things are much less clear. For Augustine goes on, still in the words of John, to make an absolute distinction between Platonism and Christianity — between those who only *know* of the Word with God, and those who also *believe* in the Word made flesh: between those who see the goal but do not know how to get to it, and those who know both the goal and the Way. The former, Augustine says, are arrogant, presumptuous men wholly in the power of the Devil; the latter, humble God-serving spirits on the way to heaven. It is worth quoting Augustine to show just how strongly he distinguishes the one from the other — the Platonist from the Christian. He says:

It is one thing to see, from a wooded height, the homeland of peace but not to find the way to it and in vain to try through impassible ways, surrounded by fugitive deserters, besieging and lying in wait with their chief who is lion and dragon [see Ps. 90:13]. It is another thing to hold to the way there which is protected by the care of the heavenly general, where there is no practice of robbery by those who have deserted the heavenly army for they avoid this way as if it were punishment.

He adds:

These things [i.e., the *differences* between Platonism and Christianity] were gotten into my innermost being in a wonderful way when I read the least of your apostles [Paul]. And I considered your works and dreaded exceedingly. (VII,xxi,27)[29]

If Platonism, which admittedly teaches truths that Christianity also teaches, is nevertheless as different from Christianity as heaven from hell, can it be that Augustine thought or taught that he was really converted to Christianity with his "intellectual" awakening to the truths of Neo-Platonism and the discovery of a similar teaching in the New Testament?

Clearly this can only be the case if Christianity is taken to be essentially an intellectual matter and the differences between it and Platonism ignored, or regarded as belonging to a world of secondary importance — the practical corollaries of such a conversion.[30] But are they, and is it so? Certainly Augustine knew of many Platonists who knew of the church and yet refused to join it — that is, men for whom their conversion to Platonism did *not* automatically entail a conversion to Christianity.[31] There is considerable evidence to make us suspect that the defenders have introduced just such a prejudice to the detriment of their interpretation of Augustine.

* * * * *

Viewed from our detached viewpoint, favouring neither camp, it now becomes clear that there is a strange symmetry and complementarity between the two sides of this debate. One side holds that Christianity is essentially historical: the other, that it is essentially rational. One side says that the *Confessions* are essentially theology: the other, that they are basically historical. The critics insist that Christianity and Neo-Platonism are two different things. The defenders insist that they are one and the same. The historians find that Augustine was converted after he says he was: the theologians, that he was converted before. The historians' argument ends up in theology. The theological argument becomes history. What began with the critics as a question about the historical value of a particular texts ends as a general problem about the nature of Christianity and of its differences from pagan philosophy. What begins, with the defenders, in the theology of the early church ends in the most extensive researches into historical detail. Each position strives after its fashion to provide a total view and each seems to have considerable truth on its side. Yet in both there is much that is partial and questionable.

Because the defenders have been able to show that Christianity was not simply opposed to pagan philosophy, no one has seriously attempted to revive the criticism of the historicity of the *Confessions*. The question could therefore be regarded as a dead issue, were it not that there are considerable difficulties in the position of the defenders. On their side, and especially in the work of Courcelle, these problems can be identified as a direct consequence of his *external* way of approaching the text through the exclusive use of the tools and methods of modern historical and philological science. His scholarship is immense – indeed, almost too immense. Where he assumes that the most reliable check on the historical accuracy of Augustine's account is to be found outside the text itself – in the various parallels, reminiscences and sources that the philologian is able to uncover – it is impossible to avoid the consequence that whenever we are unable to find any external corroboration we cannot know what really happened[32] and, where we can, that it will mean the same thing as the source means. The more erudite the scholar, the more texts he can bring to bear, the more inevitable this will be. And, since the meaning of the *Confessions* is not assumed to be accessible to us from the text itself, this position has the unfortunate implication that its real meaning has been unavailable until finally brought to light by modern research.[33] Thus Augustine appears to have done nothing more than to have composed a literary puzzle, which remained unsolved until 1950.[34] This, of course, bears no relation to the actual history of the reception of the text. It is wrong to suppose that Augustine wrote for an audience who knew just what Courcelle knew, or that no one who did not can have understood the work in almost 1,600 years.

The only way around this difficulty can lie in the discovery of some adequate check on the presuppositions of its interpreters and on the applicability *to the text* of the discoveries which the philologian is able to bring to bear. And the only check on the validity of such external considerations must lie in the text itself – that is, if it can be shown that the *entire text has an inner integrity*, that it is a connected whole in terms of its own inner logic. This is what in this book I have attempted to show for the first part of the *Confessions* and, to the degree that there is such an inner logic, it can be used to judge how far and in what sense the various parallels and sources are applicable.

Our argument has shown that there is such a logic running through every word and that, in its light, we can see that the critics were right to insist that Augustine understood Christianity to be radically different from any of the forms of antiquity. They were wrong in locating this difference in a modern position – chiefly deriving from Protestant spirituality – which assumes a distinction between human philosophy on the one hand and Christianity, conceived of as a purely voluntary assent to Christ, on the other hand. The conversion of Augustine's soul was, and had to be, voluntary but in this his will was not opposed to reason as the critics supposed. Rather, he was driven to the church by the dictates of reason itself – when these were followed in the strictest and truest sense. It is not right then to suggest that Augustine's will for Christ was opposed by human reason as such – as if, for him, Christianity was opposed to philosophy. It was opposed only by the illogical choice of demon worship or self-aggrandizement. To put this in its bluntest form, Augustine has shown that ancient philosophy failed in the face of Christianity not because it was drawn from human reason, but because it was not sufficiently faithful to the demands of reason insofar as the philosophers turned, at the crucial moment, from Wisdom to folly. By ignoring this aspect of Augustine's teaching the critics erred not so much by their insistence on the will, but by their failure to do so as thoroughly as did Augustine who certainly had to enter the church voluntarily — not because this route opposed human reason but because it was the only rational choice in which his will could find its integrity.

On the other hand the defenders are right when they insist that for Augustine, as for the whole of the patristic period, there was no radical difference between Christianity and pagan philosophy — at least not from the side of the Christians. They err however in their unwillingness to see and treat rationally of anything in Augustine's teaching which goes beyond the true conclusions of natural reason. This standpoint derives mostly from the suppositions of a modern Catholic intellectualism which would have it that Christianity must be defended against anything that tends to weaken or destroy its rational core. But here, where the argument of the *Confessions* has shown the essential role of particular circumstances — Monica, the preaching of Christ as God incarnate, the *tolle lege*, etc. — and the absolute necessity of the conversion of the will, the defenders gloss over these things as being incapable of rational explanation. Augustine has provided a full and sufficient account of the necessity of these moments in the process of conversion, where Courcelle, for example, sees only insignificant details lost in the mists of history. Thus it turns out that the defenders of the rationality of Christianity err in the end, not by making it too rational, but by their failure to do so as completely as Augustine.

Each side in this debate has a possible interpretation because both sides are indeed found in the *Confessions*. The difficulty comes from the partiality of each view which is claimed to be an adequate interpretation of the whole. On this basis no ultimate reconciliation or resolution is possible. The division can only harden into a stalemate where neither side can incorporate what is correct in the other and the student is left between mutually exclusive positions, neither of which is entirely satisfactory.

If we would have a complete interpretation of the *Confessions* it seems that, like Dante at the start of the *Divine Comedy*, the only way to this goal is to take the long way around. This means that we must turn back to the *Confessions* to see whether the text itself — in which such startling and complete oppositions are found — does not also provide the principle in terms of which they may also be reconciled. This is what I have attempted and our argument has shown that neither the modern Protestant nor the Catholic interpretation has the true Augustine — who shows a Christianity more complete than either side possesses in its separation from the other. At the same time we see that both the Protestant and the Catholic views are firmly grounded in Augustine whose Christianity embraces both faith and intellect, nature and reason — in a moment before the two positions separated — and which does therefore truly comprehend both.

NOTES

1 For other accounts of the history of the debate see the brief and clear statement by Courcelle in the Introduction to his *Recherches*. For a fuller treatment which takes into account Courcelle's own contribution to the argument, see Solignac, *BA*, Vol. 13, pp. 55-84. Both Courcelle and Solignac provide useful bibliographies to the history of the controversy. The latter gives a select bibliography of the histories of the debate (*ibid.*, p. 55, n. 1) to which add J. J. O'Meara's review in "Augustine and Neo-Platonism" where he also discusses the secon-

dary question as to whether the Neo-Platonism which most influenced Augustine was that of Plotinus or Porphyry.

2 The works in question, grouped under the title of the *Dialogues*, are the first which Augustine wrote with the exception of *On the Beautiful and the Fitting*, composed in his Manichaean days (*c.* 380-81; see IV,xv,27) and lost already in his own lifetime. The individual works included in the *Dialogues* are those he wrote at Cassiciacum between his conversion in August 386 and his baptism at Easter in 387: *Against the Academics, Concerning the Blessed Life, On Order*, and the *Soliloquies*.

3 A. Harnack, "Die hohepunkte in Augustins Konfessionen."

4 G. Boissier, "La conversion de saint Augustin," *Revue des Deux Mondes*, 85 (1888), 43-69: reprinted in *La fin du paganisme*, Paris, Hachette, 1891, Vol. 1, pp. 339-79. Until the complete secularization of the Christian tradition around the end of the last century there was very little criticism of Augustine's account of his conversion. O'Meara, "Augustine and Neo-Platonism," (p. 91, n. 2) cites only two critical works before 1888, by Johannes Clericus (1657-1736), who argues against the account of the *Confessions* on internal grounds and the other by Naville (1872), which anticipated Harnack and Boissier.

5 See for example, A. Mandouze's article (which appeared soon after the first ed. of the *Recherches*), "L'extase d'Ostie." See also the more recent articles of G. Madec which are sensitive to Courcelle's overemphasis on the identification of Neo-Platonism and Christianity, "Connaissance de Dieu et l'action de grâces"; "Christus, scientia et sapientia nostra"; and "Une lecture de *Confessions* VII,ix,13-xxxi,27: Notes critiques à propos d'une thèse de R. J. O'Connell," *Revue des études augustiniennes*, 16 (1970), 79-137.

There are by now a great many articles on a number of questions related to Books I-IX of the *Confessions* which take exception to the conclusions of the purely philological approach of which, in this book, I take Courcelle to be the chief spokesman. Some, like R. D. di Lorenzo, "*Non Pie Quaerunt*: Rhetoric, Dialectic, and the Discovery of the True in Augustine's *Confessions*," *Augustinian Studies*, 14 (1983), 117-28, insist on the differences which Augustine draws between Christianity and Neo-Platonism. Others, like the many articles of L. C. Ferrari (mainly in *Recherches Augustiniennes* and *Augustinian Studies*), for the most part treat of Augustine without reference to Neo-Platonism, and others, like those of Mandouze and Madec (cited above), or J. J. O'Donnell (see for example "Augustine's Classical Reading"), are wary of the dangers in a purely philological approach. This list can be considerably enlarged but what is still lacking — as against the criticism of this or that part of Courcelle's coherent position — is an equally total and unified account of the *Confessions* which is not so one-sidedly Neo-Platonic as that which Courcelle and his followers developed in the 1950s and 1960s. This is what I have aimed to provide.

6 In addition to the essays of Harnack and Boissier cited above, I have had the following in mind as the most important works in the controversy — ranged here in chronological order on either side of the question.

The critics: F. Loofs, art. "Augustinus," *Realencyclopädie für Protestantische Theologie und Kirche*, 2, 1897, pp. 257-85. L. Gourdon, *Essai sur la conversion de saint Augustin*, thesis for the Faculty of Protestant Theology at Paris (Paris, A. Couselant, 1900). O. Scheel, *Die Anschauung Augustins über Christi Person und Werk*, Tübingen, 1901. H. Becker, *Augustin, Studien zu seiner geistigen Entwicklung*, Leipzig, Hinrich, 1908. W. Thimme, "Grundlinen des geistigen Entwicklung Augustinus," *Zeitschrift für Kirchengeschichte*, 31 (1910), 172-213: this is the author's own abbreviation of his dense thesis in *Augustins geistige Entwicklung in den ersten Jahren nach seiner Bekehrung (386-391)*, Neue Studien zur Geschichte der Theologie und Kirche, Vol. 3, Berlin, Trowitzch, 1908. P. Alfaric, *L'évolution intellectuelle de saint Augustin*, Vol. 1, *Du Manecheisme au Neoplatonisme*, 1918: the title of the second volume is *Les Écritures manichéennes, leur constitution, leur histoire*; two other volumes appear to have been proposed (see the preface in Vol. 1, pp. viii-ix) but never appeared. M. Wundt, "Ein Wendepunkt in Augustins Entwicklung," *Zeitschrift für die neutestamentliche Wissenschaft*, 21 (1922), 53-64, and "Augustins 'Konfessionen,'" *ibid.*, 22 (1923), 161-206. M. Zepf, *Augustins Confessiones*, Tübingen, J. C. B. Mohr, 1926.

The defenders: E. Portalié, art. "Augustin," *Dictionnaire de Théologie Catholique*, Vol. 1: trans. R. Bastian (the text cited here), *A Guide to the Thought of Saint Augustine*, Chicago, Henry Regnery Co., 1960, pp. 15-19. E. Gilson, review of Alfaric's *L'évolution, Revue Philosophique*, 88 (1919), 501-505. C. Boyer, *Christianisme et néo-platonisme dans la formation de saint Augustin*, Rome, Officium libri catholici, 2nd ed., 1953: this is the edition cited; the first appeared (Paris, Beauchesne) in 1920. Courcelle, *Recherches*, and *Les Confessions*. Solignac's essay "Historicité des Confessions," *BA*, Vol. 13, pp. 64-84. J. J. O'Meara, *The Young Augustine*. O'Connell, *Odyssey*.
7 See Alfaric, *L'évolution*, Vol. 1, pp. v-vi.
8 *Ibid.*, p. 379. For my explanation of why the *Dialogues* have very few explicitly Christian references though written by the converted Augustine, see above, Chapter Nine, and "Augustine's Conversion and the Ninth Book of the *Confessions*."
9 Others too have recognized that the position of the critics has a very close connection with the theology of nineteenth-century liberal Protestantism. See Solignac, *BA*, Vol. 13, p. 57, and Portalié, *Guide*, pp. 15-17. Certainly all the important critics from Harnack to Zepf have stood in this Protestant tradition — with the exception of Alfaric who, however, is rightly described by Solignac as "a priest gone over to 'modernism' " (*BA*, Vol. 13, p. 58), which he equates with "liberal-protestant ideas" (*ibid.*, p. 57).
10 All the important defenders in note 6 are in communion with Rome.
11 Portalié, *Guide*, p. 16.
12 Put in the form of a question at the end of the Introduction to his *Recherches*, Courcelle has expressed this fundamental argument very nicely: "But the opposition between Hellenism and Christianity [assumed by liberal Protestants like Harnack], isn't it above all a view of moderns? But if one supposed that, in the milieu Augustine was in at the time, this opposition was not felt, wouldn't the very discussion become groundless?" (p. 12).
13 Gilson, review of Alfaric, p. 503.
14 Boyer, *Christianisme*, p. 107. Of Boyer's book, O'Meara ("Augustine and Neo-Platonism," p. 94) rightly says, "Certain it is that it put an end to the notion [of the critics] that Augustine's conversion to Christianity in 386 was not fully sincere." The problem, which O'Meara recognizes, is that this did not put an end to the debate even if it successfully countered Alfaric's thesis.
15 Gilson, review of Alfaric, p. 505, quoted in Courcelle, *Recherches*, p. 11.
16 Courcelle, *Recherches*, p. 11, n. 3.
17 See Courcelle on the method of his *Recherches*, at the beginning of his work (pp. 7-47). "Cross-checking with the aid of texts offers fewer chances of error than the subjective reconstruction of the intellectual evolution as has been attempted, for example, without any agreement between them, by Mr. Alfaric and Father Boyer" (p. 47). On Courcelle's view of the value of his conclusions, see what he says at the end, "Now we have, on the contrary, in the course of the present work, acquired *a certainty* founded on textual parallels" (p. 251, italics mine).
18 *Ibid.*, p. 252.
19 *Ibid.*
20 Boyer, in the second edition of his *Christianisme*, published after the appearance of Courcelle's *Recherches*, continued to maintain that Augustine became a Christian *before* he discovered the Neo-Platonic writings: see p. 107-13.
21 Gilson, review of Alfaric, p. 505: see also above, n. 20.
22 See Courcelle, *Recherches, passim*, and especially pp. 139-53 where he argues against the significance to Augustine's conversion of certain wonders in the Christian environment on which Boyer's defence of the historical value of the *Confessions* particularly depends. Courcelle is opposed to Boyer's method and conclusions as much as he is to Alfaric's, though Boyer, like Courcelle, aims to defend the historicity of the *Confessions*.
23 *Ibid.*, p. 257.
24 Here I have in mind especially O'Connell (*Odyssey*), who has attempted a thoroughgoing reconstruction of Augustine's history on the assumption of the identity of Neo-Platonism and

Christianity. Moved as it were by the success of Courcelle's defence, O'Connell has taken the instrument Courcelle used for this end (i.e., the identity of Neo-Platonism and Christianity) as an end and reads this everywhere into the *Confessions* in places where Courcelle and his predecessors never ventured. O'Connell's reading has not been accepted by the scholarly community but he would have good reason to wonder why this is so since he has only made explicit what is latent in Courcelle's position. It is his work, more than that of any other, which has brought to light the real difficulties in the argument which re-established the historicity of the *Confessions*.

25 See Courcelle (*Recherches*, p. 253): "Simplicianus hastened his moral conversion, proposed Victorinus to him as a model, incited him to an act of adhesion to the church and, by his ascetic holiness, put him on the road to the decision to reform his conduct." The point for Courcelle is that this act of adhesion to the church and the reform of conduct are understood as secondary consequences of the real, intellectual, conversion to those Neo-Platonic ideas that Christianity shared with that philosophy.

26 So for example, O'Meara (*The Young Augustine*, p. 153): "Augustine was convinced at the time that Neo-Platonism and Christianity were two approaches to the same truth. In this he was deceived; but the realization of this came later." Such talk about Augustine's "mistaking" or "confusion" in this matter is common to the position of the Neo-Platonizing defenders. See for example, Gilson's review of Alfaric, p. 505: "We hold therefore that for some time Augustine believed himself to have found one and the same truth in Plotinianism and Christianity, but this fertile confusion was only possible because, from the beginning he reads the *Enneads* as a Christian." See also Courcelle (*Recherches*, p. 157, n. 2): "All that is true is that Augustine, as Ambrose, took Plotinianism to be much closer to Christianity than it was in reality." The problem lies in the explanation — or want of it — about the precise nature of this confusion between Christianity and Neo-Platonism which these men say Augustine committed. If he really was mistaken, then how could he have been converted to Christianity by his conversion to Neo-Platonic philosophy: if he was not mistaken, then whence this talk of his confusion?

27 The position is well expressed by Solignac in his essay, "Historicité des *Confessions*," BA, Vol. 13, pp. 55-84. Here, speaking of the time after Augustine's "intellectual" conversion, he says: "Meanwhile, Augustine progresses but does not change: without doubt his reflection deepened, enlarged and became more precise in contact with the Scriptures and under the guidance of the ecclesiastical tradition, while the exercise of priestly and episcopal functions brought him more under the actuating force of the Holy Spirit; but he remained the same man" (pp. 73-74).

28 VII,ix,13-15 *in/verbum* (137/16-18).

29 VII,xxi,27 *Et/expaveram* (151/27-152/8). See also VII,ix, xviii-xxi, and VIII,i.

30 See for example, Solignac, in his "Nouvel examen du problème," BA, Vol. 13, pp. 64-84. While he gives a most judicious and useful account, it is nevertheless striking that he is able to discuss Augustine's conversion with only the most incidental references to Book VIII. Later in his "Introduction," Solignac reconsiders the question of Augustine's conversion from a "different point of view" (BA, Vol. 13, p. 158) in the chapter "Les étapes de la conversion à la foi catholique" (pp. 138-63). Here, in close dependence on the text, he finds that Augustine's conversion is not completed until the conversion of his "will and flesh" described in Book VIII of the *Confessions*. No doubt because he is not arguing a thesis as does Courcelle, Solignac seems to sense the radical difference Augustine draws between his "intellectual" and his "moral" conversion, and that the latter only is the conversion to Christianity. But if Solignac's fidelity to the text makes him insist on the point in this second look at the question, the reason behind this difference remains obscure and the "moral" conversion ends up, with Courcelle, as a necessary and inevitable corollary of the intellectual conversion rather than something of a different order altogether.

31 So, for example, Victorinus, during the period when he privately began to want to call himself a Christian because he had discovered the co-incidence of the Christian and Neo-Platonic ideas of God and before the day that he told Simplicianus he wanted to be baptized — i.e., join

the church: see VIII,ii,3-5. Augustine knew of many famous Platonists, such as Apuleius and Porphyry, who knew of the church yet refused to join it. For such people baptism and the reform of conduct along Christian lines were certainly not inevitable corollaries to their philosophical position and Augustine's constant position is that no one can become a Christian until his will has submitted to Christ — which we have seen is the whole point of the argument in Book VIII.

32 Thus, for example, Courcelle concludes, after the most exhaustive survey about the "walls of a church" which turned up nothing to support the view that one must be within the walls to be a Christian, that "*Without a doubt* [italics mine] we shall never know why Simplicianus raised the objection [that he would not count Victorinus a Christian until he was within the walls of a church] or why Victorinus was suddenly moved to inscribe himself for baptism" (*Recherches*, p. 391). The *argument* of the text however has shown that Augustine has given a full and complete explanation of this. For my discussion of the matter, see above, Chapter Eight, at the commentary on VIII,ii,3-5. In the same vein Courcelle concludes, since he can find no reference to a child's game in antiquity using the refrain *tolle, lege*, that this was not the voice of an actual child: see my discussion and the references in Chapter Eight, at VIII,xii,29.

33 The general problem in the unchecked use of philology is that so long as the text itself is not supposed to have any inner integrity that is accessible to us, it becomes impossible to prevent its meaning from being forced to accord with the meaning of the external sources and parallels that are supposed to explain it. This is what has required Courcelle in case after case to *alter* Augustine's record to make it conform to the meaning of the source. For the most part Courcelle was far too good a scholar to present his speculations as anything other than that, but it is quite remarkable how much of his position in the *Recherches* and *Les Confessions* depend on a speculative interpretation which has no other ground than in his own presuppositions and which require changes in what Augustine actually says. Thus, to mention but a few, Courcelle was forced to maintain that Augustine did not state accurately the length of time he was a Manichee, that he could not have liked Ambrose from the start as he says he did, that he went to Simplicianus not, as he tells us, for help with his practical life but to regain the ecstatic philosophical vision of God — and then there are all the many changes he wants to make to the conversion scene in the garden in Book VIII. In general it can be said that although Courcelle has defended the historical accuracy of the text against the points raised by the critics, he has only been able to do so at the cost of altering Augustine's record in so many other ways that the resulting position is no longer Augustine's. If all copies of the *Confessions* were suddenly destroyed and we had to reconstruct it on the basis of Courcelle's position in the *Recherches* we would end up with a very different text.

34 Mandouze raised this point as early as 1954 in his "L'extase d'Ostie." If his warning was largely ignored at the time this was because Courcelle's method was so successful in countering the critics that at first such difficulties seemed unimportant. This has changed with time as the challenge of the critics has faded and scholars generally are now much more conscious of the problems Mandouze correctly identified from the start.

BIBLIOGRAPHY

The following is a list of works cited. Unless otherwise indicated — by their inclusion in this bibliography — the ancient authors may be conveniently located in the Loeb Classical Library. Whenever Augustine is quoted in Latin or in translation I have given the edition used in the notes (*BA*, *NPNF*, etc.); in other cases the text can easily be located in one of the many editions of his works.

See also list of abbreviations, pages ix-x.

Alfaric, P. *L'évolution intellectuelle de saint Augustine.* Vol. 1: *Du Manichéisme au Néoplatonisme.* Vol. 2: *Les Écritures manichéennes.* Paris: Nourry, 1918.

Ambrose. *De Isaac vel anima.* Ed. C. Schenkl. C.S.E.L. XXXII, 1.

Anonymous. *The Song of Roland.* Trans. D. Syers. Harmondsworth: Penguin, 1937.

Apuleius. *De deo Socratis*, in *Opuscules philosophiques*. Ed. and trans. J. Beaujeu. Paris: Les Belles Lettres, 1973.

Armstrong, A. H., ed. *The Cambridge History of Late Greek and Early Medieval Philosophy.* Cambridge: Cambridge University Press, 1967.

Becker, H. *Augustin, Studien zu seiner geistigen Entwicklung.* Leipzig: Hinrich, 1908.

Bettenson, H., trans. *Augustine: Concerning the City of God against the Pagans.* Ed. D. Knowles. Harmondsworth: Penguin, 1972.

Beyenka, B. "The Names of St. Ambrose in the Works of St. Augustine." *Augustinian Studies*, 5 (1974).

Boissier, G. "La conversion de Saint Augustin." *Revue des Deux Mondes*, 85 (1888). Repr. in *La fin du paganisme*, Vol. 1. Paris: Hachette, 1891.

Bouillet, M.-N. *Les Enneades de Plotin.* 3 vols. Paris: 1857-61. Repr., Frankfurt: Minerva, 1968.

Boyer, C. *Christianisme et néo-Platonisme dans la formation de Saint Augustin.* 2nd ed. Rome: Officium libri catholici, 1953. 1st ed. Paris: Beauchesne, 1920.

Brown, P. *Augustine of Hippo: A Biography.* Berkeley and Los Angeles: University of California Press, 1967.

_____. "The Diffusion of Manichaeism in the Roman Empire. *Journal of Religious Studies*, 59 (1969). Repr. in P. Brown, *Religion and Society in the Age of Saint Augustine.* New York: Harper & Row, 1972.

Chatillon, F. "Références et remarques complementaires sur le symbolisme de la mer chez saint Augustin." *Revue du moyen âge Latin*, 10 (1954).

Clark, E. A. "Adam's Only Companion: Augustine and the Early Christian Debate on Marriage." *Recherches Augustiniennes*, 31 (1986).

_____. *Jerome, Chrysostom, and Friends: Essays and Translations.* Studies in Women and Religion, Vol. 2. New York and Toronto: Edwin Mellen Press, 1979.

Courcelle, P. *Les "Confessions" de Saint Augustin dans la tradition littéraire, antécédents et posterité.* Paris: Études Augustiniennes, 1963.

—————. *Lettres grecques en Occident, de Macrobe à Cassiodore.* 2nd ed. Paris: E. de Boccard, 1948.

—————. "Litiges sur la lecture des *'Libri Platonicorum'* par s. Augustin." *Augustiniana*, 4 (1954).

—————. *Recherches sur les Confessions de saint Augustin.* 2nd ed. Paris: E. de Boccard, 1968. The first edition appeared in 1950.

—————. "Saint Augustin 'photinien' a Milan." *Ricerche di storia religiosa*, 1 (1954).

Dante Alighieri. *The Divine Comedy.* 3 vols. Trans. D. Sayers and B. Reynolds. Harmondsworth: Penguin, 1978.

de Labriolle, P. *La réaction paienne. Étude sur la polémique antichrétienne du premier siècle au sixième siècle.* Paris: L'Artisan du Livre, 1934.

—————, ed. and trans. *Saint Augustin. Confessions.* Collection Guillaume Budé. 2 vols. Paris: Les Belles Lettres, 1961.

Decret, F. *L'Afrique manichéene (IVe-Ve siècles). Étude historique et doctrinale.* 2 vols. Paris: Études Augustiniennes, 1978.

—————. *Aspects du Manichéisme dans l'Afrique romaine. Les controverses de Fortunatus, Faustus et Felix avec saint Augustin.* Paris: Études Augustiniennes, 1970.

Dill, S. *Roman Society in the Last Century of the Roman Empire.* 2nd ed. Repr. New York: Meridian, 1958.

di Lorenzo, R. D. "*Non Pie Quaerunt*: Rhetoric, Dialectic, and the Discovery of the Truth in Augustine's *Confessions.*" *Augustinian Studies*, 14 (1983).

Diogenes Laertius. *Lives of Eminent Philosophers.* 2 vols. Trans. R. D. Hicks. Cambridge, Mass.: Harvard University Press, London: William Heinemann, 1970.

Diognon, J. "Perspectives ambrosiennes: S. S. Gervais et Protais, génies de Milan." *Revue des études augustiniennes*, 2 (1956).

Doull, J. A. "Augustinian Trinitarianism and Existential Theology." *Dionysius*, 3 (1979).

du Beausobre, Isodore. *Histoire critique de Manichée et du Manichéisme.* 2 vols. Amsterdam: 1734, 1739.

Dulaey, M. *Le rêve dans la vie et pensée de saint Augustin.* Paris: Études Augustiniennes, 1973.

du Roy, O. *L'intelligence de la foi en la Trinité selon saint Augustin. Genèse de sa théologie trinitaire jusqu'en 391.* Paris: Études Augustiniennes, 1966.

Eusebius. *Vita Constantini. The Life of Constantine by Eusebius.* Trans. E. C. Richardson. NPNF, 2nd series, Vol. 1. Grand Rapids: Eerdmans, 1976.

Ferrari, L. C. "Monica on the Wooden Ruler." *Augustinian Studies*, 6 (1975).

—————. "Paul at the Conversion of Augustine." *Augustinian Studies*, 11 (1980).

—————. "Symbols of Sinfulness in Book II of Augustine's *Confessions.*" *Augustinian Studies*, 2 (1971).

—————. "The Theme of the Prodigal Son in Augustine's *Confessions.*" *Recherches Augustiniennes*, 12 (1977).

Fowler, H. W. *Modern English Usage.* Oxford: Clarendon Press, 1937.

Gibb, J. and W. Montgomery, eds. *The Confessions of Augustine.* Cambridge: Cambridge University Press, 1908. 2nd ed. 1927. Repr. New York and London: Garland, 1980.

Gibbon, E. *The History of the Decline and Fall of the Roman Empire.* 7 vols. Ed. with intro., notes, appendices and index J. B. Bury. London: Methuen, 1909-13.

Gilson, E. "Revue critique" of Alfaric's *L'évolution. Revue philosophique*, 88 (1919).

Gourdon, L. *Essai sur la conversion de Saint Augustin.* Thesis for the Faculty of Protestant Theology at Paris. Paris: A. Couselant, 1900.

Guardini, R. *Anfang. Eine Auslegung der ersten fünf Kapitel von Augustins Bekenntnissen*. Munich: Kosel, 1950.

Harnack, A. "Die Hohepunkte in Augustins Konfessionen" (1888). Repr. in A. Harnack, *Redens und Aufsatze*, Vol. 1, pt. 2. Giessen: Ricker, 1904.

Hadot, P. "Citations de Porphyry chez Augustin (à propos d'un livre récent)." *Revue des études augustiniennes*, 6 (1960).

──────────. *Marius Victorinus. Recherches sur sa vie et ses oeuvres*. Paris: Études Augustiniennes, 1971.

Hagendahl, H. *Augustine and the Latin Classics*. Studia Graeca et Latina Gothoburgensla, Vols. 21-22. Göteborg, 1958.

Henry, P. *La vision d'Ostie, sa place dans la vie et l'oeuvre de saint Augustin*. Paris: Vrin, 1938.

──────────. *Plotin et l'Occident*. Louvain: Spicilegium sacrum Lovaniense, 1934.

Herrmann, L. "Remarques philologiques: *Confessions*, I,16,25; VII,2,3; X,6,9 et 10." In *Augustinus Magister*. Vol. 1. Paris: Études Augustiniennes, 1954.

House, D. "A Note on Book III of St. Augustine's *Contra Academicos*." Available in Spanish trans. in *AVGVSTINVS*, 16 (1981).

Katô, T. "Melodia interior: sur le traité *De pulchro et apto*." *Revue des études augustiniennes*, 12 (1966).

Kelly, H. "Tragedy and the Performance of Tragedy in Late Roman Antiquity." *Traditio*, 35 (1979).

Knauer, G. N. "*Peregrinatio animae*. Zur Frage nach der Einheit der augustinschen Konfessionen." *Hermes*, 85 (1957).

──────────. *Psalmenzitate in Augustins Konfessionen*. Göttingen: Vandenhoeck und Ruprecht, 1955.

Knoll, P., ed. *Confessionum libri tredecim*. Leipzig: Teubner, 1898.

──────────, ed. *Sancti Avreli Avgvstini. Confessionvm libri tredecim*. C.S.E.L. Vol. 33, sect. 1, pt. 1. New York: Johnson Reprint, 1962.

Lactantius. *Divine Institutiones*. Ed. S. Brant. C.S.E.L. Vol. 19, pts. 1 and 2. New York: Johnson Reprint, 1965.

Leitzmann, H. *History of the Early Church*. Vol. 4: *The Era of the Church Fathers*. Trans. B. L. Woolf. Rev. ed. Cleveland and New York: Meridian Books, 1953.

Lewis, C. T. and C. Short. *A Latin Dictionary*. Oxford: Clarendon Press, 1969.

Lods, M. "La personne du Christ dans La 'conversion' de saint Augustin." *Recherches Augustiniennes*, 11 (1976).

Long, A. A. *Hellenistic Philosophy*. London: Duckworth, 1974.

Loofs, F. "Augustinus." In *Realencyclopädie für Protestantische Theologie und Kirche*. Vol. 2.

Madden, M. D. *The Pagan Divinities and Their Worship as Depicted in the Works of Saint Augustine Exclusive of the City of God*. Washington: Catholic University of America, 1930.

Madec, G. "Christus, scientia et sapientia nostra. Le principe de cohérence de la doctrine augustinienne." *Recherches Augustiniennes*, 10 (1975).

──────────. "Connaissance de Dieu et action de grâces. Essai sur les citations de *l'Ep. aux Romains*, 1:18-25 dans l'oeuvre d'Augustin." *Recherches Augustiniennes*, 2 (1962).

──────────. " 'Ex tue castitate' (*Confessions*, IV,ii,3), 'Adulesiens . . . valde castus' (*ibid.*, IV,iii,6)." *Revue des études augustiniennes*, 7 (1961).

──────────. "Une lecture de *Confessions* VII,ix,13-xxxi,27: Notes critiques à propos d'une thèse de R. J. O'Connell." *Revue des études augustiniennes*, 16 (1970).

Maher, J. P. "Saint Augustine and Manichaean Cosmogony." *Augustinian Studies*, 10 (1979).

Mallard, W. "The Incarnation in Augustine's Conversion." *Recherches Augustiniennes*, 15 (1980).

Mandouze, A. " 'L'extase d'Ostie,' possibilités et limites de la méthode des parallèles textuels." In *Augustinus Magister*. Vol. 1. Paris: Études Augustiniennes, 1954.

_____. "Saint Augustin et la religion romaine." *Recherches Augustiniennes*, 1 (1958).

Marrou, H. I. *L'histoire de l'éducation dans l'Antiquité*. Paris: Éditions du Seuil, 1948. Trans. G. Lamb, *A History of Education in Antiquity*. London: Sheed and Ward, 1956.

_____. *Saint Augustin et la fin de la culture antique. Retractatio*. Paris: E. de Boccard, 1949.

Martianus Capella. *The Marriage of Philology and Mercury*. Ed. and trans. W. H. Stahl, R. Johnson, and E. L. Bunge, *Martianus Capella and the Seven Liberal Arts*. 2 vols. New York: Columbia University Press, 1971-77.

May, H. G. and B. M. Metzger. *The Oxford Annotated Bible*. Rev. standard version. New York: Oxford University Press, 1962.

Mirabella, R. M. "Il Battistero di Sant' Ambrogio a Milano." *Recherches Augustiniennes*, 4 (1966).

Mourant, J. A. "Augustine and the Sceptics." *Recherches Augustiniennes*, 4 (1966).

O'Connell, R. J. *Saint Augustine's Confessions: The Odyssey of Soul*. Cambridge, Mass.: Harvard University Press, 1969.

_____. *St. Augustine's Early Theory of Man, A.D. 386-391*. Cambridge, Mass.: Harvard University Press, 1968.

O'Donnell, J. J. "Augustine's Classical Reading." *Recherches Augustiniennes*, 15 (1980).

_____. "The Demise of Paganism." *Traditio*, 35 (1979).

_____. "Salvian and Augustine." *Augustinian Studies*, 14 (1983).

O'Ferrall, M. M. "Monica, the Mother of Augustine: A Reconsideration." *Recherches Augustiniennes*, 10 (1975).

O'Meara, J. J. "Arripui, aperui et legi." In *Augustinus Magister*. Vol. 1. Paris: Études Augustiniennes, 1954.

_____. "Augustine and Neo-Platonism." *Recherches Augustiniennes*, 1 (1958).

_____. *Porphyry's "Philosophy from Oracles" in Augustine*. Paris: Études Augustiniennes, 1959.

_____. *The Young Augustine: The Growth of Augustine's Mind Up to His Conversion*. London: Longmans Green & Co., 1954.

Pellegrino, M. *Les Confessions de saint Augustin*. Paris: Éditions Alsatia, 1960.

Pepin, J. "*Primitae spiritus*. Remarques sur un citation paulinienne des *Confessions* de saint Augustin." *Revue de l'histoire des religions*, 140 (1951).

Pine-Coffin, R. S., trans. *Saint Augustine: Confessions*. Harmondsworth: Penguin, 1961.

Plotinus. *The Enneads*. Trans. S. MacKenna. London: Faber & Faber, 1969.

Porphyry. *Life of Plotinus*, in Vol. 1 of *Plotinus*. Trans. A. H. Armstrong. Loeb Classical Library. Cambridge, Mass.: Harvard University Press; London: William Heinemann, 1966.

Portalié, E. "Augustin." In *Dictionnaire de theologie catholique*. Trans. R. Bastian. *A Guide to the Thought of Saint Augustine*. Chicago: Henry Regnery Co., 1960.

Possidius. *Vita Augustini*. Ed M. Pellegrino. *Vita di s. Agostino*. Alba: Edizioni Paoline, 1955.

Puech, H.-Ch. *Le Manichéisme. Son Fondateur. Sa Doctrine*. Annales du Musée Guimet, Vol. 56. Paris: Civilizations du Sud, 1949.

Pusey, E. B., trans. *The Confessions of St. Augustine*. With a foreword by A. H. Armstrong. London: Everyman's Library, 1953.

Rondet, H. "Le symbolisme de la mer chez saint Augustin." In *Augustinus Magister*. Vol. 2. Paris: Études Augustiniennes, 1954.

Ruch, M. *L'Hortensius de Cicéron: histoire et reconstitution*. Paris: Les Belles Lettres, 1958.

Salvian. *De Gubernatione Dei*. In F. Pauly, ed., *Salviani Presbyteri Massiliensis Opera Omnia*. C.S.E.L. Vol. VIII. New York: Johnson Reprint, 1967. Trans. E. M. Sanford, *On the Government of God . . . by Salvian*. New York: Columbia University Press, 1930. Repr., New York: Octagon Books, 1966.

Scheel, O. *Die Auschauung Augustins über Christi Person und Werk*. Tübingen, 1901.

Schmidt-Dengler, W. "Der rhetorische Aufbau des achten Buches der *Konfessionen* des heiligen Augustin." *Revue des études augustiniennes*, 15 (1969).

Schmitt, E. *Le Mariage chrétien dans l'oeuvre de saint Augustin. Une théologie baptismale de la vie conjugale*. Paris: Études Augustiniennes, 1983.

Scullard, H. H. *From the Gracchi to Nero: A History of Rome from 133 B.C. to A.D. 68*. London and New York: Methuen, 1958.

Smith, D. "Augustine's Criticism of Manichaeism in Confessions III,vi-viii." Unpublished thesis.

Solignac, A. "Doxographies et manuels dans la formation philosophique de saint Augustin." *Recherches Augustiniennes*, 1 (1958).

_____. "Réminiscences plotiniennes et porphyriennes dans le début du *De Ordine* de s. Augustin." *Archives de Philosophie*, 20 (1957).

Starnes, C. "Augustine's Conversion and the Ninth Book of the *Confessions*." Forthcoming.

_____. "The Place and the Purpose of the Tenth Book of the *Confessions*." *Studia Ephemeridis "Augustinianum,"* 25 (1987).

_____. "The Unity of the *Confessions*." Forthcoming in *Studia Patristica*. Available in Spanish translation: "La unidad de las *Confessiones*." *AVGVSTINVS*, 31 (1986).

Studer, B. "Augustin et la foi de Nicée." *Recherches Augustiniennes*, 19 (1984).

Tescari, O. "Nota augustiniana (*Conf.* III,iv,7)." *Convivium*, 5 (1933).

Testard, M. *Saint Augustin et Cicéron*. Paris: Études Augustiniennes, 1958.

Theiler, W. *Porphyros und Augustin*. Halle: Niemeyer, 1933.

_____. "Review of Courcelle's *Recherches sur les Confessions de saint Augustin*." *Gnomon*, 25, 2 (1953).

Thimme, W. *Augustins geistige Entwicklung in den ersten Jahren nach seiner "Bekehrung" (386-391)*. Neue Studien zur Geschichte der Theologie und Kirche, Vol. 3. Berlin: Trowitzsch, 1908.

_____. "Gundlinen des geistigen Entwicklung Augustins." *Zeitschrift für Kirchengeschichte*, 31 (1910).

Verbecke, G. "Augustin et le stoicisme." *Recherches Augustiniennes*, 1 (1958).

von Arnim, J. *Stoicorum Veterum Fragmenta*. 2 vols. Stuttgart: Teubner, 1964.

Watts, W., trans. (1631). *The Confessions of St. Augustine*. Loeb Classical Library. 2 vols. Cambridge, Mass.: Harvard University Press; London: William Heinemann, 1968.

Wendt, M. "Augustins 'Konfessionen.'" *Zeitschrift für die neutestamentliche Wissenschaft*, 22 (1923).

——————. "Ein Wendepunkt in Augustins Entwicklung." *Zeitschrift für die neutestamentliche Wissenschaft*, 21 (1922).

Widengren, G. *Mani and Manichaeism*. New York: Holt, Rinehart and Winston, 1963.

Wijdeveld, G. "Sur quelques passages des *Confessions* de saint Augustin." *Vigiliae Christianae*, 10 (1956).

Williams, G. H. *Wilderness and Paradise in Christian Thought*. New York: Harper and Brothers, 1962.

Zeller, E. *Outlines of the History of Greek Philosophy*. 13th ed., rev. W. Nestle. Trans. L. R. Palmer. New York: Dover, 1980.

Zepf, M. *Augustins Confessions*. Tübingen: J. C. B. Mohr, 1926.

Index